Second Edition

EDUCATING STUDENTS
with Severe or Profound Handicaps

Edited by

Les Sternberg
Florida Atlantic University
Boca Raton, Florida

AN ASPEN PUBLICATION®
Aspen Publishers, Inc.
Rockville, Maryland
Royal Tunbridge Wells
1988

Library of Congress Cataloging-in-Publication Data

Educating students with severe or profound handicaps.

"An Aspen publication."
Rev. ed. of: Educating severely and profoundly handicapped students. 1982.
Includes bibliographies and index.
1. Handicapped children—Education—United
States. I. Sternberg, Les. II. Educating
severely and profoundly handicapped students.
LC4031.E387   1988   371.9   87-19596
ISBN: 0-87189-894-2

The first edition of this book was entitled *Educating Severely and Profoundly Handicapped Students.*

Editorial Services: Marsha Davies

Library of Congress Catalog Card Number: 87-19596
ISBN: 0-87189-894-2

Printed in the United States of America

1   2   3   4   5

To *Hy* and *Natalie,*
for allowing me the freedom to pursue my own goals

To *Bill, Karen, Katie,* and *Matthew,*
for their efforts at bringing me down to earth

And to *Jean,*
whose unwavering support and love will continue to provide all of
the motivation I need

Table of Contents

v

Contributors

Paul A. Alberto
Department of Special
  Education
Georgia State University
Atlanta, Georgia

Marilyn Mulligan Ault
Department of Special
  Education
University of Kansas
Lawrence, Kansas

William L. Geiger
Department of
  Rehabilitation and
  Special Education
University of Arkansas
Little Rock, Arkansas

Janet W. Hill
Office of Supported
  Employment
Department of Mental Health
  and Mental Retardation
Richmond, Virginia

Patricia L. McDonald
Dallas Independent School District
Dallas, Texas

Colleen D. McNerney
Special Education
SUNY-Geneseo
Geneseo, New York

Lawrence F. Molt
Department of Exceptional
  Student Education
Florida Atlantic University
Boca Raton, Florida

M.V. Morton
Rehabilitation Research and
  Training Center
Virginia Commonwealth University
Richmond, Virginia

Jeffrey Schilit
Department of Exceptional
  Student Education
Florida Atlantic University
Boca Raton, Florida

William Sharpton
Department of Special Education
University of New Orleans
New Orleans, Louisiana

Les Sternberg
Department of Exceptional
 Student Education
Florida Atlantic University
Boca Raton, Florida

Ronald L. Taylor
Department of Exceptional
 Student Education
Florida Atlantic University
Boca Raton, Florida

Ruth Turner
Dallas Independent School District
Dallas, Texas

Bonnie L. Utley
Special Education
University of Pittsburgh
Pittsburgh, Pennsylvania

Ruth Wilson
Dallas Independent School District
Dallas, Texas

Kay Younginger
Department of Exceptional
 Student Education
Florida Atlantic University
Boca Raton, Florida

Preface

The idea for this text was shaped by three rather simple if-then statements. First, *if* the field of education for students with severe or profound handicaps is still in its infancy, *then* we must expect to experience significant and ongoing changes of suggested practices. Second, *if* practitioners are to continue to provide quality services to this population, *then* these practitioners must be continually apprised of new advances, especially those related to best practice interventions. And third, *if* written works have provided some direction to practitioners, *then* updating these works should prove beneficial.

With these statements in mind, I set out to update an earlier (1982) text (*Educating Severely and Profoundly Handicapped Students*). My direction was toward a second edition. Very early on, however, I realized that the traditional type of update or second edition was not going to suffice. As a rule of thumb, a second edition reflects an approximate one-third content change in comparison with the earlier edition. Although the organizational format for the current text remained as it was in the earlier effort (for example, each methods chapter has problem statements, coverage of past practices, suggested methods, and a conclusion), there is a much greater content discrepancy than one might expect. This is due to the fact that, as expected, dramatic changes *have* occurred in the field. These changes are reflected not only in methods but in philosophy. Professionals are beginning to focus on the concept of options and alternatives rather than on a single philosophy or mode of delivery. Questions are being raised in terms of what we are doing, why we are doing it, and the ultimate relevance of it all. All of the questions being raised are indeed important and will continue to drive the field toward excellence. It is my hope that this text provides a necessary forum for these questions. It is also my hope that the answers provided are taken in the context of what we think is appropriate *now*; and that discussions concerning changes in philosophy and method must be constantly encouraged. It would be unwise for us to assume we have all the answers.

L.S.

Acknowledgments

It is certainly difficult to commit oneself to completing an endeavor of this nature without the help of others. Too often, however, we tend to forget the influence of those who helped shape our thinking and our professional behaviors. Therefore, I would like to pay a special debt of gratitude to Dr. John Cawley, who encouraged me to pursue a career in special education. By his example, he has established optimal performance standards that will continue to provide professional direction to me. And I would also like to thank Dr. Philo T. Pritzkau, whose guiding words "always put yourself into question" have certainly helped me to understand myself and those directives I espouse.

Part I

Introduction

An Overview of Educational Concerns for Students with Severe or Profound Handicaps

Les Sternberg

In society's quest to meet the educational needs of all students with disabilities, education of those with the most pronounced handicaps has been a rather recent phenomenon (Sternberg, 1982). This is probably due to two interrelated factors. First, in the past, society had judged the educability of individuals on the basis of preconceived notions of how the presence of a severe handicapping condition might affect one's ability to benefit from various types of interventions. This preconception was based on little, if any, substantive data pertaining to educability. Second, these preconceived notions led society to isolate these individuals far from the normal mainstream of life. Treatment, rather than education, became the callword of service provisions to this population. Interestingly, the isolation itself continued to perpetuate the concept of helplessness and noneducability.

With the advent of various laws, notably P.L. 94-142, this state of affairs drastically changed. Those concerned with education, from the standpoint of both policy and implementation, quickly began to realize that students formerly denied education because of the severity of their handicap were going to enter the public education arena. It became a question of not *if* but *how* education was going to be provided. Much that has happened between then and now continues to revolve around instructional factors that will most effectively address the *educational* needs of students with severe or profound handicaps.

PROVIDING A DEFINITION OF STUDENTS WITH SEVERE OR PROFOUND HANDICAPS

To provide educational services to a target population, some consensus concerning who that population is must occur among administrators, educators, and other individuals responsible for providing these services. In regard to severe and profound handicaps, this has not been an easy task, especially given the divergent viewpoints and professional backgrounds of the individuals responsible for such decision making. The fact is that definitions used by professionals typically reflect the type of classification scheme they support. In this case, many individuals prefer etiologic classifications (e.g., on the basis of chromosomal aberrations). Others tend toward psychometric descriptions (such as a measured intelligence quotient of 20) or educational classifications (e.g., trainable mentally retarded). More recently, behavioral descriptions (e.g., self-abuse) have received attention. The result is one of two extremes: either the categorical labeling of students, which precludes consideration of their individual needs (as typified by the use of etiologic, psychometric, or educational classifications), or the total individualization of students, which precludes consideration of shared characteristics with other students (as typified by the use of specific behavioral descriptors).

A number of conceptual foundations should be evident with any definition posited. First, the definition should reflect both the individual *and* group context of the student being considered. In this way, between-group differences (as, for example, between students with severe or profound handicaps and students with mild or moderate handicaps) and within-group similarities and differences can be delineated. Second, a definition should not be developed only to assist educators in making administrative decisions (such as where to place a student for service provision or in what category to place a student for purposes of state reimbursement). A definition ought to provide direction for both assessment and programming practices. Given the fact that assessment is typically the first step in determining instructional alternatives, a definition should assist in specifying three basic conditions: (1) the eligibility of the individual to qualify as a student with severe or profound handicaps; (2) the general performance level of the student; and (3) the competencies (specific strengths and weaknesses) of the student. A statement in regard to these conditions can be of invaluable assistance in determining the direction and content of an appropriate instructional program.

Specific problems have been inherent in a number of definitions drafted to describe students with *severe* handicaps. Justen (1976) summarized a number of such issues. First, some of the definitions tend to be based on an exclusion principle. That is, if one's handicapping condition were of such a nature that he or she would be excluded from any currently operating special education instructional unit, then that individual would be defined as having a severe handicap. A classic example of this type of definition is one adopted by the U.S. Office of Education (1974):

> Severely handicapped children are those who because of the intensity of their physical, mental, or emotional problems, need educational, social, psychological and medical services beyond those which are traditionally offered by regular and special education programs, in order to maximize participation in society and self-fulfillment (Sec. 121.2).

A second problem with most definitions is that if a category of handicapping condition is specified (such as deaf/blind), there is no distinction between a category for eligibility and a category for specific services. This can lead to instructional decisions based solely on the individual's label rather than the individual's needs. Third, some definitions describe students with severe handicaps in terms of specific behaviors but do not classify the behaviors within a developmental framework. Without including the developmental perspective, one may very well lose sight of expectations for the individual student. The behaviors observed may be developmentally appropriate and, in terms of the age of the student, may not constitute a severe disability. Fourth, very few definitions provide information that is of educational significance. If a definition is available to assist in making instructional program and placement decisions, some description of educational parameters should be an integral part of that definition.

It is also interesting to note that, if definitions are posited, they usually only refer to those with *severe* handicaps. One is left only with hypotheses as to why this is the case. If profound handicaps are subsumed under the severe handicaps category, various questions will naturally arise. What, if any, are the differences between one who has severe handicaps and one who has profound handicaps? If differences do exist, are they differences in degree, in types of behaviors or skills displayed, or in instructional needs? Unfortunately, conjectures do not necessarily lead to valid conclusions. It should not be concluded however that concern for students with profound handicaps has necessarily been lacking. Professionals have and will continue to confront issues and provide answers to questions concerning this group (Rainforth, 1982).

A consensus opinion has not emerged over the years even though most everyone continues to think that it is important to have an agreed-upon definition (Baker, 1979; Van Etten, Arkell, & Van Etten, 1980). In a survey of state education agencies, Justen and Brown (1977) found that 50% of the states that responded to the survey had a definition for students with severe handicaps. Six years later, the results of another survey indicated that this percentage had increased to 70% (Geiger & Justen, 1983). Yet even with this improvement in the percentage of states adopting definitions, extreme variance was noted in the types of definitions posited. On the one hand, some states used definitions that could be considered *categorical*. In these cases, students with severe handicaps would be considered such only if they fell within some type of identified category of handicap (e.g., deaf/blindness, severe mental retardation, autism, etc.). Other states used more *generic* types of definitions that specified specific types of behaviors (e.g., extreme self-stimulation, self-injurious behavior, etc.) and/or educational need (e.g., the need for self-contained instructional options, the need for instructional emphasis on daily living skills).

Aside from the obvious inconsistencies in definitions and the apparent lack of consensus, further problems become evident. One of these has to do with preparing instructional personnel for this population. As Geiger and Justen (1983) pointed out, even though some states have no definition of this population, it has not prevented institutions of higher learning in those states to train students and for those states to certify these individuals to teach students with severe or profound handicaps. Some states that have definitions do not have training or certification programs that conform to their definitions. Perhaps what is even more disturbing is the effect of this situation on communication among professionals. For example, people in one state using one definition of "severely handicapped" may be espousing a certain type of programming design or curricular approach with their students. It is highly likely that the applicability of that design or approach to students with severe handicaps in another state would be very limited if the term were defined in a considerably different way. This situation complicates research practices and their conclusions based on this population. Discussion and arguments continue to surface concerning whether, for example, "that researcher was *really* working with students with *profound* handicaps."

Given all of these criticisms, it is clear that a definition should have at a minimum the following components: (1) a statement that describes the behavioral domains that must be considered in making a diagnosis of a severe or profound handicapping condition; (2) a description of the functional level in those behavioral domains that takes into account developmental concerns; (3) a statement reflecting the educational needs of the individual; and (4) if a label specification is mandated (as is the case in certain states), a label designation that is used only for the purpose of determining eligibility for services. The following is tendered as an adequate and acceptable definition of students with severe handicaps and is based, in part, on one I drafted earlier (1982):

A student with severe handicaps is one who (1) is eligible to receive educational services under one or more legally defined categories of handicapping condition; (2) exhibits severe developmental discrepancies in at least three of the following behavioral/content areas: motor/mobility, activities of daily living (self-help skills), communication, cognition, and social/emotional development; and (3) requires an educational structure with continuous monitoring and observation.

A severe developmental discrepancy is defined as one in which the individual's current performance level is less than one-half but more than one-fourth of expectancy based on the individual's chronological age. However, a developmental age ceiling of six years per behavioral/content area is imposed (that is, if an individual is functioning at or above a six-year developmental level in an area, that individual would not be considered to have a severe developmental discrepancy in that area regardless of chronological age). Required educational structures are instructional units (classrooms, small groups, or one-to-one settings) in which educational needs of the individual are met by specially trained personnel. These structures may be found in the full range of environments, from segregated facilities such as state schools to fully integrated public schools to community-based facilities and programs.

In terms of students with profound handicaps, the following definition is tendered:

A student with profound handicaps is one who (1) is eligible to receive educational services under one or more legally defined categories of handicapping condition; (2) exhibits profound developmental discrepancies in all five of the following behavioral/content areas: motor/mobility, activities of daily living (self-help skills), communication, cognition, and social/emotional development; and (3) requires an educational structure with continuous monitoring and observation.

A profound developmental discrepancy is defined as one for which the individual's current performance level is no more than one-fourth of expectancy based on the individual's chronological age. However, a developmental age ceiling of two years per behavioral/content area is imposed (that is, if an individual is functioning at or above a two-year developmental level in an area, the individual would not be considered to have a profound developmental discrepancy in that area regardless of chronological age). Although the range of educational structures for this group may be the same as for students with severe handicaps, a higher probability exists for more restrictive structures for those students with the most pronounced handicaps.

The above-stated definitions and the preceding points of clarification are a compilation of ideas presented in other definitions and classification schemes (Haring, 1978; Justen, 1976; Sternberg, 1982). For an individual to be considered to have a severe or profound handicap, that individual would have to meet all three criteria specified in the corresponding definition.

The two definitions are not intended to provide the kind of fragmentation that has occurred as the result of the use of categorical types of definitions. Students with profound handicaps do have more severe degrees of handicap than do those with severe handicaps, and the degree of involvement (in terms of number of areas of functioning affected) is higher. However, the key differences between students with profound handicaps and those with severe handicaps have more to do with their *instructional needs* than with the types and degree of impairment. Although overall similar models of best practice curriculum and management provision *may* be used with both groups, various adaptations or modifications will certainly be necessary for those with more pronounced handicaps.

CRITICAL EDUCATIONAL CONCERNS

Compared with the educational situation for students with mild or moderate handicaps, provision of educational services for students with severe or profound handicaps is a relatively recent endeavor. Interestingly, the historical development of educational practices for students with severe or profound handicaps seems very similar to that for students with mild or moderate handicaps. Early educational interventions for the latter group were often characterized as being "piecemeal," with instruction geared toward meeting very specific and separate needs (such as academic and behavioral control concerns). Actual interventions to meet these needs were accomplished under an isolated training model. If the student had a reading problem and an out-of-seat problem, for example, the two were treated as separate entities. Techniques that emphasized the isolated qualities of these problems were used. This ensured the continuation of an instructional practice that did not allow for the integration of strategies based on the integrated quality of student needs. As the years progressed and research data began to prove the worth of the integrated instructional model, dramatic and beneficial changes were wrought in the area of education of students with mild or moderate handicaps.

Although it is generally accepted that the educational needs of students with severe or profound handicaps are considerably different from those with mild or moderate handicaps, most agree that students with handicaps are students first. It should then stand to reason that what we have learned as general best practice approaches in relation to students with mild or moderate handicaps *may* be applied in some fashion to those with more severe handicaps. Unfortunately, most current best practice approaches with students with severe or profound handicaps are only *now* beginning to mirror some of the *components* of validated best practice approaches used with students with mild or moderate handicaps. One of the most important of these involves the final realization that needs of students with severe or profound handicaps can be looked upon from an integrated point of view. Integration is now judged not just in terms of how the student can more effectively become a part of "normal" society but how his or her targeted instructional needs can best be integrated into more cohesive and meaningful behaviors. Obviously, in order to proceed into this integrated model of education, it is paramount that personnel responsible for providing education for students with severe or profound handicaps look at the complete picture. The entire ecology of this population must be analyzed and addressed.

THE UMBRELLA MODEL OF EDUCATION

A number of interacting components, when combined, will constitute the educational arena for students with severe or profound handicaps. These components can be placed in a structure that describes them in terms of their level of consideration. This structure is termed the *vertical umbrella model* (Sedlak & Sternberg, 1978; Sternberg, 1982; see Figure 1-1). Within multiple "umbrellas," specific components and areas are addressed in a supraordinate to subordinate fashion. The overriding umbrella is the individual's environment and is represented by the individual's school, home, and community setting and by the people who provide services in those situations (administrators, parents, teachers, etc.). Below this umbrella, one would find another dealing with assessment procedures that should be used with the student. The placement of this umbrella below the environmental umbrella indicates that assessment must take into account the environmental constraints imposed upon the student. The third umbrella is devoted to management or behavior control. Its position dictates that direction in management techniques should stem from assessment data and that behavior control must be considered in the context of the individual's environment. The last umbrella deals with curriculum designs and skill development. Inherent in its placement are consideration of skill instruction in the context of the behavioral needs of the individual, education that is based on assessment information, and instruction that relates to the total environment in which the individual finds himself or herself.

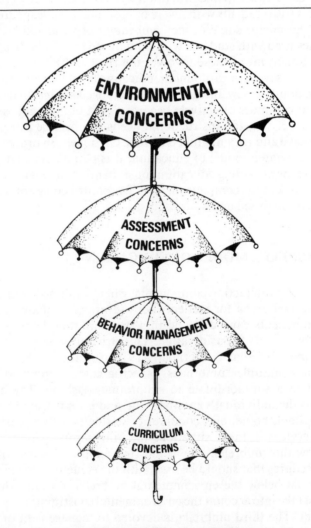

Figure 1-1 The Vertical Umbrella Model of Educational Concerns.

The order of these umbrellas does not dictate an order of importance. What we have is a model for viewing the education of students with severe or profound handicaps from an integrated point of view rather than in a piecemeal fashion. The umbrella model also provides an organizational framework in which topics addressing the educational needs of these students can be presented and discussed.

Various components related to educational practices may be described in each of the pragmatic umbrellas. Material presented in this text is arranged so that each umbrella area of concern is addressed comprehensively. Chapter 2 discusses variables directly affecting the type of appropriate educational environment that should be established for students with severe or profound handicaps. Emphasis is placed on the interaction between actual placements and people. Chapter 3 presents information related to a more narrow aspect concerned with the educational environment; that being the scope and role of classroom-based medical interventions for support of the student in his or her educational environment.

Concerns related to the assessment of students with severe or profound handicaps are presented in Chapters 4 and 5. In the first of these chapters, an explanation is given of effective policy and procedures to use in assessing these students. In the second chapter, various assessment instruments are described and analyzed. Since one major purpose of assessment is the generation of educational goals and objectives, a pragmatic approach is presented for determining which procedures or instruments to select in the assessment process.

Chapter 6 presents material related to the behavior management umbrella in the framework of four interrelated components: decision-making systems for designing behavioral programs for increasing social skills and aberrant behavior control; general techniques for changing behaviors; experimental behavior change programs; and concerns related to validation.

The curriculum umbrella is represented by Chapters 7 through 13. In Chapter 7, crucial components regarding curriculum delivery are presented and analyzed. In Chapter 8, curriculum development is discussed. Suggested development reflects the best practice components outlined in the prior chapter. Chapter 9 discusses motor aspects of severe or profound handicapping conditions. Emphasis is placed on relating motor adaptations (such as different handling techniques) not only to motor skill development but also other curricular areas (e.g., different positioning strategies for developing attending behavior). In Chapters 10 and 11, communication skill development is considered. Chapter 10 focuses on prelanguage communication, and Chapter 11 discusses language skills training. Transition programming is emphasized in Chapters 12 and 13, with the first of the chapters emphasizing the development of independent living skills and the second, the development of vocational skills. A step-by-step procedure for implementing various types of vocational programs for students with severe handicaps draws the discussion of curriculum concerns to a close.

Chapter 14 provides an overview of future concerns related to educating students with severe or profound handicaps. Taking as a premise that future directions will be based on how we address crucial questions of today, attempts are made to answer those questions so that a proper and viable foundation for future progress is established.

CONCLUSION

The population of students with severe or profound handicaps is a rather small percentage of all those considered to have handicaps. This low incidence has led some to believe that provision of educational services to this population may not be worthwhile or cost effective. However, the real issue should not be whether we should provide services but rather how the services can be made more worthwhile and more cost-effective. Historically, this question has permeated all of special education, and to draw the line now in terms of students with severe or profound handicaps would be ludicrous.

We are now left with consideration of what *are* best practice educational approaches to use with students with severe or profound handicaps. It is important, however, to always look at best practices in terms of evolution. One must be cautioned against expecting that the best practice of today will invariably be the best practice of tomorrow. As Guess (1983) succinctly stated in comments made to members of the Association for Persons with Severe Handicaps:

> It would be an error to assume that the profession already has the available technology to meet the task of appropriately educating students who are severely handicapped. Nor can we assume that any one theoretical orientation has a justifiable monopoly on either knowledge or wisdom. To think the profession knows all the answers is to fail to ask the right questions. As best-practices tend to become conventional wisdom or dogma, the opportunity to advance science is reduced (p. 82).

REFERENCES

Baker, D.B. (1979). Severely handicapped: Toward an inclusive definition. *AAESPH Review,* 4(1), 52-65.

Geiger, W.L., & Justen, J.E. (1983). Definitions of *severely handicapped* and requirements for teacher certification: A survey of state departments of education. *Journal of the Association for Persons with Severe Handicaps,* 8(1), 25-29.

Guess, D. (1983). Some parting thoughts and reflections from the editor. *Journal of the Association for Persons with Severe Handicaps,* 8(4), 82-83.

Haring, N.G. (1978). The severely handicapped. In N.G. Haring (Ed.), *Behavior of exceptional children* (2nd ed.) (pp. 195-229). Columbus, OH: Charles E. Merrill.

Justen, J.E. (1976). Who are the severely handicapped?: A problem in definition. *AAESPH Review,* 1(5), 1-12.

Justen, J.E., & Brown, G.E. (1977). Definitions of severely handicapped: A survey of state departments of education. *AAESPH Review,* 2(1), 8-14.

Rainforth, B. (1982). Biobehavioral state and orienting: Implications for educating profoundly retarded students. *Journal of the Association for the Severely Handicapped,* 6(4), 33-37.

Sedlak, R., & Sternberg, L. (1978). A teacher training program for the severely/profoundly retarded. *Journal for Special Educators of the Mentally Retarded,* 14(3), 193-196.

Sternberg, L. (1982). Perspectives on educating severely and profoundly handicapped students. In L. Sternberg & G.L. Adams (Eds.), *Educating severely and profoundly handicapped students* (pp. 3-9). Rockville, MD: Aspen.

United States Office of Education (1974). Definition of severely handicapped children. *Code of federal regulations,* Title 45, Section 121.2. Washington, DC: Bureau of Education for the Handicapped.

Van Etten, G., Arkell, C., & Van Etten, C. (1980). *The severely and profoundly handicapped.* St. Louis: C.V. Mosby.

Part II

Environmental Concerns

Chapter 2

Providing Appropriate Educational Environments

William L. Geiger and Jeffrey Schilit

PROBLEM AND PAST PRACTICES

One of the most important issues pertaining to education of students with severe or profound handicaps has to do with the principle of *least restrictive environment* (LRE). Although definitions have been drafted and modified, the concept has typically been envisioned as one that establishes a definite preference for providing education for students with handicaps with those students who have no handicaps. For example, P.L. 94-142 (Education of All Handicapped Children Act, 1975) requires that states establish

> procedures to assure that, to the maximum extent appropriate, handicapped children, including children in public or private institutions or other care facilities, are educated with children who are not handicapped, and . . . that special classes, separate schooling, or removal of handicapped children from the regular education environment occurs only when the nature or severity of the handicap is such that education in regular classes with the use of supplementary aids and services cannot be achieved satisfactorily (20 U.S. Code, sect. 1412 [5] [B], p. 42497).

Historically, the concept has generated considerable debate, especially regarding LRE for students with severe or profound handicaps. Although LRE is to be determined on an individual basis, and although there seems to be a legal mandate for public school services for students with severe or profound handicaps (Sailor & Guess, 1983), there still seems to be continued debate as to how the concept should be applied to this group. For example, in many instances past and current practices have given "modified" support to the LRE concept by implying that students with

17

severe or profound handicaps could not survive in a regular educational environment. Therefore, the LRE for this group has usually been more restricted and more often segregated. In essence, then, there seems to have been more attention paid to the latter section of the definition of LRE than to the initial part.

Students with severe or profound handicaps have been educated, generally, in settings that are among the most restrictive and/or segregated. Residential schools and institutions and special day schools have been common placements for these students. Kenowitz, Zweibel, and Edgar (1978) reported that 70% of the children diagnosed as "trainable mentally retarded" and 69% of those identified as "severely/profoundly handicapped" were served in special education "centers." The results of this nationwide study illustrate the reliance of school systems on restrictive placements for the education of students with severe or profound handicaps.

In the early and mid 1970s, Congress addressed the longstanding practices of exclusion and segregation that had been employed by schools relative to the education of students with severe or profound handicaps. It did so by advancing policies that promoted normal, integrated styles of life (Gilhool & Stutman, 1978). Among the potential benefits of the policies endorsed by Congress were:

- improved learning by students with severe or profound handicaps of skills needed for participation in community life (Biklen, 1981; Brinker & Thorpe, 1984);
- the availability of modeling by peers without handicaps as a method of teaching students with handicapping conditions (Gilhool & Stutman, 1978);
- the creation of opportunities for individuals to get to know one another, thereby fostering more positive attitudes toward persons with severe handicaps and challenging existing stereotypes and prejudices (Wolfensberger, 1972; Biklen, 1981; Gilhool & Stutman, 1978); and
- the provision of an object lesson in democracy by ensuring that all citizens (including those with handicapping conditions) were given equal opportunities to participate in community life and to develop their potentials to the maximum (Biklen, 1981; Gilhool & Stutman, 1978).

This shift in social policy with regard to treatment of persons with severe or profound handicaps, if it continues, will require obvious adjustments of major social systems. Systems that were designed to support the management of these persons through practices of exclusion, isolation, or confinement must be dismantled in a manner that will not be destructive to individuals, and new models that reflect the positive valuation of these persons must be designed, supported, and implemented.

SUGGESTED METHODS

For a successful transition in social policies to occur, attention should be given to both the *interactive* and *interpretive* dimensions of the change process (Wolfensberger, 1972). In the interactive dimension, attention is focused on actions that have an impact on persons with handicapping conditions and on systems designed to assist them. Through the interactive dimension, systems are developed that enable persons with severe or profound handicaps to participate, to the maximum extent possible, in the full range of community life. These systems should support residential, educational, vocational, and recreational aspects of integrated life in communities (Lehr & Brown, 1984). The interpretive dimension of the change process focuses on the presentation of persons with handicapping conditions to the general public. It is concerned with the development of tolerance and positive attitudes toward individuals who, historically, have been perceived unfavorably and treated in unpleasant ways. Unless attention is given, through the interpretive dimension, to the modification of fears and negative attitudes that many citizens possess, public support will be lacking for the development and implementation of services needed to integrate persons with severe handicapping conditions into our communities. The absence of tolerance of personal differences and accepting attitudes will frustrate the ultimate goal of integration, i.e., the development of positive social interactions among all the citizens of our nation. The interdependence that exists between the interactive and the interpretive aspects of the process of change make it essential that actions will be taken in both dimensions to ensure the success of a policy of integration.

The remainder of this chapter addresses methods that are helpful in advancing a social policy of integration for persons with severe handicapping conditions. They relate principally to the interactive dimension of the change process and focus primarily on the educational system as it is represented through local school districts. This emphasis is not intended to minimize the critical importance of other systems in the interactive dimension or of the interpretive actions that will alter public perceptions and attitudes toward persons with severe or profound handicaps. Rather, it is in keeping with the general theme of this text, which addresses the education of students with severe or profound handicaps.

For the benefits of a policy of integration to be realized, educational and other social systems must be successful in designing programs and implementing practices consistent with that policy. The revision of educational programs and practices is a significant challenge that must be given immediate and sustained attention. An initial step is the examination of critical factors in education, such as curriculum, service provision, personnel preparation, and support systems, in light of the standard of integration.

Integration and Curriculum

The concept of integration gives direction for establishing a goal for the education of children with severe or profound handicaps and, thereby, guides educators in their efforts to design appropriate curricula for this population of students. Bates and Pancsofar (1981) suggested that education for these persons should provide "the opportunity and training necessary to enable them to live, recreate and work to the fullest possible extent in the community." This goal is compatible with a policy of integration, and curricula derived from it will, through appropriate instruction, prepare students to participate in an integrated world by acquiring skills that are both *functional* and *appropriate to their chronological ages.*

Functional Curriculum

A curriculum compatible with the goal of education for students with severe or profound handicaps is functional in that it contributes directly to their abilities to live, work, and recreate in their communities. The use of the goal of education to guide the development of curricula for these students has been called a "top-down" approach (Brown, Branston, Hamre-Nietupski, Pumpian, Certo, & Gruenewald, 1979). When developing curriculum through this approach, educators begin with the goal and, through a series of analyses, identify skills consistent with it. Brown et al. (1979) use the top-down approach to develop functional curricula. They begin with the identification of major domains of living (e.g., domestic, recreation and leisure, vocational, and community living). Each domain is analyzed into related environments, which, in turn, are divided into subenvironments. The activities in each subenvironment are then identified, and the skills needed to perform the activities are listed. The process is concluded with the design and implementation of instructional programs that ensure the acquisition of the skills identified. As an example of this process, a house is one environment associated with the domestic domain, and a kitchen is one subenvironment of a house. Cooking soup is an activity that occurs in the kitchen, and it can be reduced to the following skills: retrieving a pan and a can of soup, opening the can, pouring the soup into the pan, adding water, placing the pan on a burner, turning on the burner, stirring the contents of the pan, and removing the pan from the burner when the soup has been adequately heated. By performing all of the required skills, the student completes the activity of preparing soup and participates more independently in his or her home environment.

The goal of education can be used not only as a starting point for the design of curricula but also as a standard or criterion for assessing the *functional values* of specific skills that might be taught (Brown, Nietupski, & Hamre-Nietupski, 1976). Skills that are strongly related to the goal of education may be considered highly functional; skills with less obvious relations to the goal are viewed as less functional. Judgments regarding the functional value of skills are generally not either-or propositions. Brown et al. (1979) offered guidelines that can assist in establishing the relative functional values of skills for individual students. One guideline is the frequency with which a skill will be used. Skills used more frequently are more likely to have greater functional value for students. Similarly, skills that will greatly enhance the independence of students are considered to have substantial functional values. In addition to the factors of how often a skill will be used and its impact on independence, Brown et al. (1976) identified six questions that can be used when making decisions about the functional values of educational objectives or activities:

1. Why should we engage in this activity?
2. Is this activity necessary to prepare students to ultimately function in complex, heterogeneous community settings?
3. Could students function as adults if they did not acquire the skill?
4. Is there a different activity that will allow students to approximate realization of the criterion of ultimate functioning more quickly or more efficiently?
5. Will the proposed activity impede, restrict, or reduce the probability that students will ultimately function in community settings?
6. Are the skills, materials, tasks, and criteria of concern similar to those encountered in adult life? (p. 9).

The preceding guidelines and questions are helpful in evaluating, in a general sense, the functional value of skills. However, educators must recognize that the functional value of a skill must be determined for each student on an individual basis. A skill that may have a high functional value for one student may not have a similar value for another student who lives in a different environment. Also, the concept of functionality may have to be re-examined or retooled in relation to certain individuals with extremely debilitating types of handicaps. Brown, Sweet, Shiraga, York, Zanella, and Rogan (1984) indicated that a necessary skill may not be one that is performed by the individual student. It may be that, due to the severity of the handicapping condition, someone else may have to perform the skill for the student. In this case, the skill would still be considered functional if it met the criteria of frequent use and increased independence. Sternberg (in press) raised the issue that the concept of functionality for these students may have to reflect more clearly the individual to whom the concept is being applied. In essence, the question should not be only whether the skill is functional but also for whom it is functional.

Chronologically Age-Appropriate Curriculum

A curriculum that will prepare students with severe or profound handicaps to live in integrated environments should incorporate skills and information that are appropriate to their chronological ages and will enable them to exhibit skills that are similar to those of their peers. The acquisition of skills that are appropriate for one's age can reduce stigma and negative perceptions, which often result from differences in abilities, and can, thereby, enhance the likelihood of greater acceptance and social integration.

A chronologically age-appropriate curriculum for young students should emphasize skills they will be called upon to exhibit in the environments in which they often participate: the school, home, and neighborhood. An age-appropriate curriculum for adolescents should include skills needed presently in their home and community environments and also skills that will be needed in the integrated community environments in which they will likely participate after leaving school (Brown et al., 1979; Brown, Ford, Nisbet, Sweet, Donnellan, & Gruenewald, 1983).

Instruction in "Natural" Environments

If students with severe or profound handicaps are to acquire the functional and age-appropriate skills they need to participate in communities with peers without handicaps, instruction should be provided in the "natural" environments in which the skills are required. This practice is consistent with both the goal of education and the educational characteristics of these students. One of the greatest difficulties for this population is transferring and generalizing skills and problems with skill synthesis (Brown, Nisbet, Ford, Sweet, Shiraga, York, & Loomis, 1983). Instruction in natural environments can reduce problems associated with the transfer and generalization of skills and enhance the likelihood that students will be able to perform skills in the environments in which they are needed.

Recognition of the value of instruction in natural environments has led many persons to advocate the extensive use of "community-based instruction" in educational programs for students with severe handicapping conditions (Falvey, 1986; Wehman, Renzaglia, & Bates, 1985; Freagon, Wheeler, Brankin, McDaniel, Costello, & Peters, 1983; Wershing, Gaylord-Ross, & Gaylord-Ross, 1986). Proponents of "community-based instruction" argue that the use of artificial materials, tasks, and settings seldom provides these students the information needed to solve problems in the environments in which they usually occur (Brown et al., 1976; Brown, Nisbet, Ford, Sweet, Shiraga, York, & Loomis, 1983). To be effective, instruction should incorporate materials, tasks, consequences, objectives, and criteria students will encounter in natural environments outside the classroom. Hence, community environments should become *instructional sites* wherein students are taught the skills they need to participate in these environments. Community environments in which a student is likely to be engaged should also be used as *sources* for identifying the knowledge and skills students need to acquire and the standards of performance they will need to meet to participate independently in these environments.

Integration and the Provision of Special Education Services

The educational placement of students with severe or profound handicapping conditions is a major issue that must be addressed in attempting to implement a social policy of integration. The educational placement of such a child is a primary concern from the perspective of a policy of integration. Decisions regarding educational placements should be made jointly by parents and professionals and arrived at by translating the policy of integration through the circumstances that pertain in individual cases (Lehr & Haubrich, 1986; National Information Center for Handicapped Children and Youth (NICHCY), 1986a; Kenowitz et al., 1978). The ten guidelines that follow should assist parents and professionals to make placement decisions that will maximize students' opportunities to benefit from education in accordance with a policy of integration.

1. Children should be taught in environments that facilitate the acquisition of needed knowledge and skills.
2. Children should be taught in the same schools they would attend if they were not disabled (Education for All Handicapped Children Act, 1975; NICHCY, 1986a).
3. To the maximum extent appropriate, children with disabilities should be taught in regular classes with nondisabled peers (Education for All Handicapped Children Act, 1975; NICHCY, 1986a).
4. Children who cannot be fully integrated into regular classes should be integrated into regular schools and the general education program to the maximum extent they will benefit (Education for All Handicapped Children Act, 1975; NICHCY, 1986a).
5. Special services should be provided in regular schools, and their lack of availability should not be used as a basis for denying education in those facilities (Brown, Wilcox, Sontag, Vincent, Dodd & Gruenewald, 1977; Taylor, 1982).
6. There should be a reasonable ratio between students with severe handicapping conditions and their peers without handicaps (Brown et al., 1977).
7. Educational environments should be appropriate for the chronological ages of the students (Brown et al., 1977; Taylor, 1982).
8. Students should be provided access to all facilities and resources of the school (Brown et al., 1977).
9. The school environment should be accessible to all students (Brown et al., 1977).
10. Staff in integrated settings should display positive attitudes and actively promote social integration (Brown et al., 1977; NICHCY, 1986a).

Placement in integrated educational settings complements the goal of education for students with severe or profound handicaps and should be helpful in ensuring that it is attained. In other words, instruction in integrated settings should prepare students to participate to the maximum extent possible in community environments. The provision of educational services in more restricted or segregated environments than are needed is counterproductive to the purpose of education and may interfere with students' mastery of skills that are needed in more complex, integrated community settings.

Placement Options

School districts must ensure the availability of a continuum of alternative educational placements to meet the special needs of students with handicapping conditions. The traditional continuum of placement options has included those presented in Table 2-1.

Proponents of segregated or restrictive approaches (e.g., institutions and special day schools) offer a wide range of arguments in support of these options. Examples include: clustering large numbers of students with severe handicaps allows for homogeneous grouping, thereby fostering program efficiency; costs of programs can be reduced by concentrating ancillary and related services at a single site and by modifying and making accessible only one facility instead of a wide range of school buildings; many parents prefer their children to be educated in environments in which everyone is knowledgeable about and sympathetic to their handicaps rather than in less protected, integrated settings where there may be less understanding and tolerance of differences by other students and professionals; and segregated centers may help build morale among professionals by providing opportunities for collaborative problem solving and communication among individuals who share a common

Table 2-1 A Continuum of Alternative Placement Options

Placement	Options
Less restrictive/ more integrated	1. Regular class placement with special instructional materials and equipment provided to classroom teachers
	2. Consultant services provided by special education teachers to regular teachers
	3. Itinerant or tutorial assistance provided to students by special education teachers
	4. Special education provided in resource rooms
	5. Part-time instruction provided in self-contained special education classes
	6. Full-time instruction provided in self-contained special education classes
	7. Instruction provided in special day schools (segregated schools exclusively for students with handicapping conditions)
	8. Instruction provided in residential or boarding school facilities
More restrictive/ less integrated	9. Instruction provided in hospitals
	10. Home-based instruction

interest in the education of students with severe handicaps (Thomason & Arkell, 1980).

Persons who favor providing educational services to students with severe or profound handicapping conditions in regular school buildings base their preference on the benefits of a policy of integration. They argue that services can be efficiently managed in regular school settings and that education in integrated settings better equips students to meet the demands of the "real" world. Among the benefits of integrated programs in regular schools are opportunities to learn socially normative, age-appropriate behaviors through exposure to peers who do not have handicapping conditions; opportunities to participate in a variety of experiences that are part of the regular educational programs provided to all students; and the promotion of an understanding of individuals with severe or profound handicaps by their peers without handicaps. These arguments have been persuasive and, when combined with legislative mandates, have resulted in reconsideration of restrictive placement practices by many educational agencies.

Several school districts have developed models for providing special education services that incorporate the strengths of both segregated and integrated approaches to educating students with severe or profound handicaps (Taylor, 1982). One such model is the side-by-side approach adopted by the Albuquerque, New Mexico school system (Thomason & Arkell, 1980). A primary characteristic of this approach is the dispersal and integration of several classes for students with severe handicaps through individual schools in the district. Between 60 and 80 students with severe handicaps are integrated among a minimum of 300 students enrolled in each of the selected schools. Advocates of this model consider that number of students with severe handicaps in any one school to be sufficient to ensure their visibility but not so large that it creates an imbalance in the composition of the student body. The presence of relatively large numbers of students with severe handicaps in selected schools in the district enables it to assign full-time special education administrators and related service personnel to these schools to provide needed services and support for integrated programming.

Other school districts have developed different models for achieving integration. Some districts employ the rule of "natural proportions" (Brown, Nisbet, Ford, Sweet, Shiraga, York & Loomis, 1983); that is, the proportion of students with severe handicaps in a school should approximate their proportion in the general school population. The school districts of Madison, Wisconsin and Birmingham, Alabama are examples of those that restrict the number of students with severe handicaps in any one school to well below the minimum recommended by the side-by-side approach.

Planning for Integration

Regardless of the model adopted for integration, planning and organizational support for the provision of special education and related services in regular public schools are essential (Stetson, 1984). Taylor (1982) recommended that a district that is interested in providing integrated educational services begin by designating an individual as responsible for coordinating the activities needed to develop a plan for integration. Effective plans must attend to several factors that are critical to the success of integrated education for students with severe or profound handicapping conditions. Among these are (1) identification of a model for the provision of services; (2) assignment of personnel to provide administrative assistance and leadership to those involved in the education of students with severe handicaps (Thomason & Arkell, 1980; Stetson, 1984); (3) a staff development program that will prepare personnel to implement integrated educational services (Thomason & Arkell, 1980; Stetson, 1984); (4) selection of school sites that are staffed by principals and teachers with positive attitudes toward integration (Taylor, 1982; Stetson, 1984); (5) activities to promote community acceptance of integrated programming for students with severe handicaps (Thomason & Arkell, 1980; Stetson, 1984); and (6) practices that will assist parents of children with severe or profound handicapping conditions to accept the concept of integrated education for their children (Thomason & Arkell, 1980; Stetson, 1984). These factors seem to be obvious prerequisites for any successful program. Often, however, they are not consciously addressed by well-intentioned administrators. This oversight can lead to numerous problems in the process of integration and, in some cases, result in failure to attain the desired goal.

Physical integration provides an occasion for persons with severe or profound handicaps to become involved in the social lives of their communities. Physical proximity alone, however, is not sufficient to cause the interactions and acceptance that are characteristic of social integration (Wolfensberger, 1972; Brady, McEvoy, Gunter, Shores, & Fox, 1984; Birenbaum, 1986; Kregel, Wehman, Seyfarth, & Marshall, 1986; Crapps, Langone, & Swaim, 1985; Stainback & Stainback, 1985). To help ensure the goal of social integration is attained, time and attention must be devoted to the preparation of the variety of individuals—students, teachers, administrators, and parents—who will be involved in the process (Thomason & Arkell, 1980).

Positive social interactions among all students in a school is a major goal of integrated education. To achieve these interactions, both students with severe or profound handicapping conditions and their peers without handicaps must be prepared. By providing instruction that will reduce discrepancies in skill repertoires and that will increase tolerance of individual differences, teachers can facilitate successful social interactions among students. Teachers of students with severe or profound handicaps should identify the skills they will need to gain acceptance and to perform more successfully in regular school environments. These students must, then, be provided instruction that will lead to the acquisition of those skills. Similarly, teachers of students who are not handicapped should prepare them to understand factors that can cause severe or profound disabilities and the limitations that such disabilities impose. These students will also need instruction on commonalities among all children and on how to interact with children who have severe or profound handicapping conditions. These types of instructional preparation should facilitate social interactions and acceptance among all students in a school (Thomason & Arkell, 1980).

If integration is to be successful, teachers (both general educators and special educators) in a school must be supportive. Opportunities to discuss the relation between special education and general education programs and the contributions each makes to the school may help generate the required support. Such discussions enable teachers to appreciate their roles and responsibilities for providing all students in a school with optimal educational experiences. Once the faculty of a school has affirmed its commitment to providing the array of educational services needed by the total population of students it serves, cooperation on specific activities that will foster integration among students should follow.

One way that teachers can contribute to the success of integration is by designing opportunities for interactions between students with severe or profound handicaps and their peers without handicaps (Stainback & Stainback, 1985; Hamre-Nietupski & Nietupski, 1981). Brown, Ford, Nisbet, Sweet, Donnellan, and Gruenewald (1983) identified four types of interactions that are beneficial to students with severe handicaps and that can facilitate social integration. *Proximal interactions* are those in which there is sensory contact among students; in other words, the students are physically present in the same environment. Through such associations, students with severe or profound handicaps are exposed to the variety of behaviors that are exhibited by their peers without handicaps. In *helping interactions,* students without handicaps provide direct assistance or instruction, which affords opportunities for students with severe or profound handicaps to generalize across persons and cues, to learn to indicate acceptance or rejection of offers of assistance, and to establish effective relationships. Through *service interactions,* students with severe or profound handicaps learn to relate appropriately to the variety of individuals employed by school districts (e.g., school bus drivers, cafeteria personnel, and others). *Reciprocal interactions* represent meaningful social integration in which the involved students receive personal benefits from their relationships.

Opportunities for proximal interactions may be facilitated by scheduling the use of specific school facilities (e.g., playgrounds, cafeteria, and libraries) by both groups of students at common times. Also, placing students in "regular" education activities, such as participation in art, music, and other classes, involvement in extracurricular activities, and the performance of school jobs, will provide opportunities for proximal and other types of relationships to develop. Tutorial or "buddy" systems and opportunities for both groups of students to visit each other's classrooms have been instrumental in promoting helping and/or reciprocal relationships. These and other teacher-designed activities should assist students to learn to interact in a positive and accepting manner.

Administrators are keys to the success of integrated programs. As instructional leaders, they provide direction to their faculties relative to attitudes and to the priority that will be given to integration. Principals of schools that will be integrated should possess positive attitudes toward the enterprise and must be actively involved, from the onset, in planning for the integration of programs in their buildings. Visits to ongoing programs and the review of written descriptions of programs that have been integrated successfully should provide valuable preliminary information that administrators will need for meaningful participation in the planning process.

Parents of both students with severe or profound handicaps and those in general education programs should be involved in planning and implementing integrated education. Both groups of parents will frequently have concerns and fears about integration. Parents of students with severe or profound handicaps may be apprehensive about their child's safety, the curriculum, and the availability of related services. The preparation of a manual on policies relative to the quality of the program and to practices that will help ensure safety may help allay their fears. A "buddy" system between parents whose children have been in the program and parents of children who are new to the program can also generate support. Parents of students in general education may be apprehensive that integrated programming will have deleterious effects on the education of their children. The distribution of information that underscores the fact that general education and special education are elements of a comprehensive system designed to serve a population of students with a variety of educational needs should help reduce anxiety and foster acceptance of integration. If integrated programming is presented in a manner that emphasizes its benefits for all students, parents are likely to support the concept and to contribute to the preparation of a plan for integration and its successful implementation.

Integration and the Provision of Related Services

Students with severe or profound handicaps frequently need *related services* to meet the goals and objectives that are part of their educational programs. The regulations for the Education for All Handicapped Children Act (1975) define "related services" as "transportation and such developmental, corrective, and other supportive services as are required to assist a handicapped child to benefit from special education."

Among the related services often needed are speech, occupation, and physical therapy. Speech therapy services include the identification, diagnosis, and appraisal of specific speech or language disorders, the provision of services designed to habilitate or prevent communication disorders, and the provision of counseling and guidance related to the disorders (Education of All Handicapped Children Act, 1975). Occupational therapy is a health profession concerned with improving, developing, restoring, or preventing the loss of abilities needed to perform daily living activities as independently as possible (Education for All Handicapped Children Act, 1975). Physical therapy is concerned with the evaluation of physical capacities and limitations, and with administering treatments that will prevent or minimize disability, alleviate pain, correct or minimize deformity, and develop and improve strength and motor functions (Goldenson, 1978).

Speech, occupational, and physical therapy have traditionally been provided through procedures evolved from a medical model of service provision. This model has been characterized as emphasizing services that are direct, isolated, and centralized (Giangreco, 1986). Hence, the model lends itself to the practice of clustering large numbers of students with severe or profound handicaps in segregated facilities and may not be compatible with the educational goal of preparing these students to function as independently as possible in community environments. The traditional model of providing therapeutic services to these students should be re-evaluated against the criterion of integration, and alternatives that conform to this standard should be encouraged.

One model that has been proposed as being compatible with this policy is "integrated therapy" (Campbell, 1987; Wehman et al., 1985; Giangreco, 1986). In this model, therapists assume, to a significant degree, the roles of consultants to teachers and others who have frequent interactions with students. The therapists provide these individuals with information on ways to integrate therapeutic techniques into the schedule of activities and natural environments in which the student normally engages. This practice emphasizes the functional value of therapeutic services and their ancillary character in helping students attain educational goals and objectives. Direct therapeutic services with this model are frequently provided in classrooms or in other environments rather than in isolation. This practice provides teachers and other instructional personnel with opportunities to become familiar with therapeutic techniques. The adoption of "integrated therapy" or a similar model is necessary if related services are to be provided in a manner that conforms to integrated education for students with severe or profound handicaps.

Integration and the Coordination of Services

The coordination of professionals who deliver special education and related services should be reviewed from the perspective of a social policy of integration. Educational and related services have generally been provided through three approaches: multidisciplinary, interdisciplinary, and transdisciplinary. The first two are characterized by the autonomy of the involved professionals. In the multidisciplinary approach, specialists independently conduct evaluations, prepare reports, and evaluate the services they provide. This model does not emphasize collaboration or communication among the service providers nor is group decision making or teamwork fostered. The interdisciplinary model is intended to reduce some of this fragmentation. Although professionals continue to exercise independence in evaluating students and in providing needed services in the interdisciplinary approach, this model requires that they convene periodically to make group decisions on behalf of students.

The transdisciplinary approach is characterized by mutual dependence and shared responsibilities among professionals and has been found to be compatible with the provision of therapeutic services in integrated settings (Campbell, 1987; Giangreco, 1986). In this model, individuals function as a team that assesses a student and then designs, implements, and monitors the effectiveness of a comprehensive program for that student. Although specific components of the service program are primary responsibilities of specialists in the respective areas, these individuals work cooperatively with the other members of the team. Each member of the transdisciplinary team provides the others with consultative assistance and contributes his or her perspective and expertise to the solution of problems. The willingness of professionals to share their own expertise and to acquire that of others is a key to the success of this model. When mutual consultation is achieved, the model can be successful in providing coordinated services based on a comprehensive view of the student (Sears, 1981).

Bricker (1976) proposed an alternative to the transdisciplinary model. She suggested that teachers function as "educational synthesizers" of the information and techniques required to meet the varied educational needs of students with severe or profound handicaps. The fact that teachers have more contact with the students than do other professionals and, as a result, may be in a better position to coordinate the array of services needed is cited as support for this model. To perform successfully as educational synthesizers, teachers must:

- be able to determine a student's specific needs or problems;
- pursue, from professionals in a variety of disciplines, appropriate information or techniques relative to a student's needs;
- develop effective intervention strategies using the information obtained from other professionals;
- implement these strategies to remedy problems or facilitate the acquisition of new skills; and
- evaluate the effectiveness of the strategies employed.

The role of the teacher as an educational synthesizer seems compatible with a policy of integration in that it allows students to be served in schools or school districts that do not employ a staff of related service professionals. This model also implies that therapists should be used as consultants who assist teachers to infuse therapeutic services into the daily programs of students and to ensure that therapeutic techniques are used to support the acquisition of skills that will enhance a student's ability to participate in present and future community environments.

Integration and the Preparation of Personnel

The learning characteristics of students with severe or profound handicaps necessitate that they receive instruction and related services through staffing patterns that are highly intensive. Ratios of one staff person to 2 or

3 students with severe handicaps are common (Geiger, 1984). Such intensive instructor-student ratios can contribute to providing students with more instructional time and are conducive to optimal instruction (Fredericks, Anderson, & Baldwin, 1979; Snart & Hillyard, 1985). Consequently, the availability of adequate numbers of appropriately prepared personnel is crucial to the education of these students and presents a challenge that must be addressed in the process of successfully implementing a social policy of integration.

Teachers

Many regions of the country experience significant shortages of qualified teachers for students with severe or profound handicaps (Smith-Davis, Burke, & Noel, 1984) that adversely affects the abilities of school districts to provide appropriate educational services. Contributing to these shortages are the facts that many individuals are not attracted to teaching students with severe or profound handicaps, and as many as 30% of those who choose to teach this population of students change jobs every three years (Smith-Davis et al., 1984). To alleviate shortages of qualified instructors, many educational agencies employ teachers who are not adequately prepared or appropriately certified. This practice can have an adverse impact on the education of these students, reducing their opportunities to acquire the skills needed to function as independently as possible in community environments.

To teach students with severe or profound handicaps in an appropriate manner, individuals must be able to create or arrange environments so that specified changes occur in the behavioral repertoires of students (Brown & York, 1974). Teaching requires that individuals be able to (1) describe, in objective terms, the behaviors that students will exhibit as a consequence of instruction; (2) identify the instructional strategies and activities that will be employed to enhance the behavioral repertoires of students; and (3) verify that the preselected behavioral changes have or have not occurred. This conceptualization of instruction serves as a basis for the identification of clusters of competencies that teachers of students with severe or profound handicaps should possess.

Horner (1977) suggested that a curriculum to prepare teachers for students with severe or profound handicaps should incorporate at least three clusters, or "blocks," of competencies. The primary block focuses *directly* on altering the behaviors of students and is the nucleus of a well-designed teacher preparation program. Specific strategies for teaching students to acquire new skills, to maintain or generalize behaviors, or to decrease behaviors considered dangerous or inappropriate are included in this block. The second cluster suggests that teachers of students with severe or profound handicaps should also demonstrate proficiency in skills that relate *indirectly* to changing behaviors. Included among these are the abilities to (1) develop individual education programs; (2) perform task analyses; (3) schedule instructional activities; and (4) identify potential reinforcers. The third cluster includes knowledge that has no known relation to changing behaviors but that seems to be related to professional performance. Included in this category is information on the legal rights of students, a philosophy of service provision, and knowledge of medical aspects of syndromes. Each of these blocks contains both knowledge and performance competencies that, when acquired, should equip teachers to enhance the behavioral repertoires of students with severe or profound handicaps successfully.

Clusters of competencies, such as those recommended by Horner, can be reduced to subsets that more clearly describe the curricula of teacher preparation programs. Burke and Cohen (1977) reported nineteen major subsets of competencies (Exhibit 2-1) based on their reviews of selected personnel preparation projects funded by the Bureau of Education for the Handicapped, U.S. Department of Education.

Exhibit 2-1 Recommended Clusters of Teaching Competencies

Administrative skills
Applied behavioral analysis
Assessment
Classroom organization
Curriculum development
Curriculum units
Development of community-based services
Exceptional child development
Handling health problems
History
Interdisciplinary communication
Medical basics
Normal child development
Parents
Prosthetic strategies
Public speaking and writing
Right to education
Training
Use of local, state, and national resources

These nineteen categories, while masking an extensive array of specific competencies that should be acquired by teachers of students with severe or profound handicaps, provide a broad outline for a teacher preparation curriculum and establish parameters of expertise that should be expected of such teachers.

Despite efforts to identify common competencies needed by all teachers of these students, diversity exists among programs that prepare such teachers. Differences in curricula, which can be at least partially attributed to variations among the certification requirements adopted by states and to differences in the theoretical orientations of programs, can have a bearing on how adequately teachers are prepared to design curricula that are functional and age-appropriate and to provide instruction in settings that are consistent with a goal of integration. To ensure that students with severe or profound handicaps are provided the instruction they will need to function as independently as possible in their communities, teacher preparation programs will need to adopt curricula that will equip teachers with the knowledge and skills they need to provide instruction that conforms to a social policy of integration.

Therapeutic Personnel

The supply of therapists prepared to work in public schools with students who have severe or profound handicaps falls far below the number required to adequately provide the services needed. The initial shortfall of qualified therapists is exacerbated by the fact that public schools generally pay substantially less than do other agencies that provide therapeutic services (e.g., clinics and hospitals). It is, therefore, not surprising that many therapists who accept positions with public schools transfer to more lucrative positions when they become available.

The characteristics of programs that prepare therapists may need to be examined if these professionals are to perform comfortably in integrated educational settings. Therapists are generally educated in a medical model of treatment and frequently receive clinical experiences in environments that emphasize the direct provision of therapeutic services and consultation with professionals who have a similar medical orientation. In many cases, the professional curricula for the preparation of therapists place relatively little emphasis on educational or behavioral treatment strategies, do not require clinical experiences with children who have severe or profound handicaps, and provide little exposure to public school environments. As a consequence, many therapists who work in schools attempt to implement the medical model of service provision in educational environments with which they are unfamiliar. This lack of preparedness necessitates that therapists make significant adjustments to provide related services in a manner that will contribute to attaining the goal of education for students with severe or profound handicaps.

It is likely that in-service education will be needed for many therapists to adjust to a service provision model that emphasizes integration and to acquire the skills needed to work successfully with educationally oriented professionals. However, in-service education alone will not be sufficient to orient therapists to public school programs that strive to prepare students to function as independently as possible in community environments (Geiger, Bradley, Rock & Croce, 1986). University programs will need to adjust their curricula to assure that their graduates are adequately prepared to work as team members with persons who espouse educational and behavioral intervention strategies; consult effectively with others; and design, implement, and evaluate therapy in integrated environments. This adjustment will not occur rapidly but must be done if related services are to be provided in a manner consistent with a policy of integration.

The need for a review of how related services are provided to students with severe or profound handicaps has been recognized by the Office of Special Education Programs, U.S. Department of Education, which, in 1985, sponsored a symposium titled "Children and Youth with Severe Handicaps: Effective Communication." The participants in this symposium, most of whom had backgrounds in communication disorders, recognized the importance of integration as a goal for the education of these students. The impact of this goal on services was acknowledged by the adoption of the following assumptions:

— educational services for severely handicapped children and youth shall be provided in the least restrictive environments
— communication programs for children and youth who are severely handicapped shall be provided within and functionally oriented in terms of the home, school, social, recreational, leisure, and vocational environments. These programs and the communication skills of severely handicapped children and youth shall be evaluated within each of these environments (p. III 4).

This group also recognized the need to prepare professionals in speech and language adequately to serve students with severe handicaps in integrated environments. To that end it recommended that:

— preservice preparation programs for speech-language pathologists should include information about and experiences with children and youth who have severe handicaps, and

— processes must be developed to achieve positive change in knowledge and attitudes toward the delivery of services for communication skills through team models in functional environments as differentiated from isolated therapy for children and youth who are severely handicapped (pp. III 7-8).

The implementation of these and similar recommendations should enhance the likelihood that speech-language pathologists will be better prepared to serve students with severe or profound handicapping conditions in a manner consistent with the goal of those students' education. If other related service professionals adopt similar recommendations, it is likely that teams of professionals will be able to work together toward a common educational goal, using procedures compatible with the desired outcome of their efforts.

Parents

Sternberg and Caldwell (1982) recognized that "parent involvement in the education of handicapped students has become not only a quasi-legal requirement . . . but also a necessity if one is to expect generalization of skills between the home and school environment" (p. 27). As noted previously in this chapter, an appropriate curriculum for students with severe or profound handicaps should address skills that are functional in the home and other community environments (Brown et al., 1979; Wehman et al., 1985). Instruction in these skills should be provided in the environments in which they are expected to occur. By virtue of the facts that they spend extensive amounts of time in "natural" environments with their sons and daughters and that they usually have reinforcing value to their children, parents are excellent persons to intensify the instruction in functional skills provided by school personnel (Turnbull, 1978).

Although the benefits of parental involvement in the education of their sons and daughters should be obvious, there are variables that affect the likelihood and success of participation by parents. One such variable is the quality of the relationships between parents and school personnel. Parents and school personnel often adopt attitudes that communicate an unwillingness to cooperate in the planning and implementation of instructional programs. The barriers that can be erected through one-way communication and negative interactions must be avoided if there is to be any possibility of establishing viable parental involvement in educational programs (Turnbull, 1978; Sternberg, Taylor & Schilit, 1986). A second variable is the availability of programs that will prepare them to provide instruction in home and community settings. Such programs will need to be in place if there is to be continuity between school- and home-based instruction and if students with severe or profound handicapping conditions are to be provided a maximum number of opportunities to practice skills in the multiplicity of settings that are part of their daily lives.

School systems and/or other agencies need to face the challenge of assisting parents to help their sons and daughters acquire functional skills if the benefits of a social policy of integration are to be fully realized. A variety of models for involving parents in educational programs have been designed. Some emphasize preparation in home environments; others use school environments or a combination of the two. Several models employ school personnel to assist parents, while others rely on parents as instructors. Jenkins, Stephens, and Sternberg (1980) reviewed several approaches to involving parents in the education of their children. Among these are the *individualized home intervention model,* which uses a home trainer to assist the parents, siblings, and student with a disability at home. The *continuous group training model* (Bricker & Bricker, 1976; 1977; Turnbull, Strickland, & Goldstein, 1978) features ongoing training sessions conducted in the school. The content of the training usually involves educational or behavioral aspects common to all students with handicaps in a group. The *restrictive group training model* (Baker & Heifetz, 1976; Huber & Lynch, 1978) is a variation of the preceding model, but a limited number of sessions are conducted (usually in school) to address the specific needs of each student. The *classroom involvement model* (Hayden & Haring, 1976; Wiegerink & Parrish, 1976) features parents assisting teachers in classrooms. A strong aspect of this model is the fact that parents are able to see, first hand, the educational emphases (including strategies and techniques) being used in the school. In the *telecommunication training model* (Tawney, 1977; Tawney, Aeschleman, Deaton, & Donaldson, 1979), parents receive mediated instructional packages that explain how best to teach their child at home. Also, a telecommunication system between a teacher and the family is established. The presence of this system enables the teacher to address the day-to-day variances parents may find in the learning or behavioral repertoire of their child. The *center-based training model* (Watson & Bassinger, 1974; Fredericks, Baldwin, & Grove, 1976) features parental involvement and assistance in both home and school. Through this model, parents receive assistance in both home and school settings and are exposed to the requirements of the classroom in which their child will subsequently be placed.

Although the previously described models used professionals to assist and prepare parents, there are benefits to the use of parents as instructors for other parents (Bruder, 1987). Sensitivity and communication are among the reasons frequently cited for recruiting parents of children with handicaps as instructors for other parents. It may be argued that an individual who has not personally experienced the frustrations and hardships of dealing with a child who has a severe or profound handicap in the family context can never truly comprehend the feelings and attitudes that develop among family members. The parent of such a child is more likely than a teacher to understand what another parent is experiencing and to be more sensitive in the recommendations that he or she offers. Similarly, the commonality of being the mother or father of a child with a severe or profound handicap enhances the likelihood of communication between the parents. These factors and others elevate the probability that parents can effectively prepare other parents to be of assistance in their child's education.

Jenkins et al. (1980) supported the use of parents as trainers and surmised that, at least, four components are critical to the success of such programs.

1. Training should be provided in the home so that parents and other family members can begin to use techniques to foster educational and behavioral changes under the control of at-home environmental stimuli.
2. Training should be provided, at certain times, in a group format that emphasizes common educational and behavioral concerns of all parents and family members.
3. There should be mandatory in-school attendance for students with severe or profound handicapping conditions so that respite is afforded to parents.
4. There should be coordination of the school- and home-based educational and behavioral programs so that consistency and continuity of instructional emphases are ensured.

These recommendations should assist educational agencies to design programs that will assist parents in collaborating with schools to meet the instructional needs of students with severe or profound handicaps. The establishment of such programs is a challenge that will need to be addressed in the process of educating students in least restrictive environments. One must not lose sight of the individual needs of each parent, however, for it is how these needs are addressed that will dictate the ultimate success of any parent involvement program (Turnbull, 1983; Allen & Hudd, 1987).

Paraprofessionals

The intense staffing needs of public school programs for students with severe or profound handicapping conditions may be reduced through the use of paid and/or unpaid paraprofessionals to assist teachers and other professionals. If this solution to shortages of professionals is adopted by educational agencies, it is imperative that programs of training be developed for all paraprofessional personnel. Supplementing professional staff with untrained personnel is not an acceptable solution to the staffing needed, and this practice could have serious detrimental effects on programs and students. Regardless of whether or not an agency employs teacher aides, unpaid volunteers, or peer-tutors to assist in educational programming for students with severe or profound handicaps, it is essential that these persons be adequately prepared to perform the tasks they are assigned.

Teacher aides and teacher assistants are paid employees who work under the supervision of teachers to implement programs of instruction and perform other duties. The specific responsibilities of teacher aides are likely to vary depending on the district, school, or teacher to whom they are assigned. Many programs for students with severe or profound handicaps use teacher aides to perform instructional tasks. To work effectively with teachers and other members of instructional teams, teacher aides must acquire informational and performance competencies that are directly related to instruction, in other words, changing the behaviors of students with severe or profound handicaps (Tucker & Horner, 1977). Among the necessary competencies that have been identified for paraprofessionals are knowledge of the characteristics of persons with severe or profound handicaps; child management skills; methods for teaching self-care, social, and other functional skills; and strategies for modifying maladaptive behaviors (Reid and Johnston, 1978).

When employing teacher aides, attention should be given to matching teachers and paraprofessionals into teams. McKenzie and Houk (1986) identified the match between paraprofessional skills and the staffing needs of teachers as a critical factor to be considered when establishing educational teams; they suggested a process for "matching" paraprofessionals with teachers. At the beginning of the process, teachers are asked to complete two inventories, one related to areas in which they need assistance in their classrooms and the other on supervisory style. Prospective teacher aides are also asked to complete inventories, one related to the skills they possess and another on work styles. The completed inventories are subsequently compared to determine if satisfactory correspondence exists between the skills possessed by the paraprofessional and needs of the teacher, and between the work style of the prospective aide and the supervisory style of the teacher. The comparison of completed inventories provides a basis for the discussion and resolution of any differences. After a match has been made, the process is concluded with the development of a job description for the paraprofessional.

Any responsibilities assigned to a teacher aide should be consistent with his or her skills. Assignments that build on the strengths of aides will enable them to make maximum contributions to the education of students and should reduce the need for intense, time-consuming supervision. In situations in which paraprofessionals need additional preparation to enhance existing skills or to meet requirements of their job descriptions adequately, a planned program of training should be designed and provided.

Unpaid volunteers can also be used as paraprofessionals, thereby increasing the amount of instructional time provided to students with severe or profound handicaps (Fredericks et al., 1979). Parents, members of civic or religious clubs and organizations, persons who are retired, and students have all been used as volunteers. School districts that decide to use volunteers should develop programs for recruiting reliable persons and provide them with systematic programs of orientation. An appropriate orientation program might begin by assigning volunteers to engage in structured observations, concurrent with or followed by participation in workshops designed to develop needed instructional skills. Only at the conclusion of the training program should volunteers be introduced to working with students. This introduction should be provided in a systematic gradual fashion that affords the volunteer the supervision needed to ensure that he or she effectively contributes to the education of students.

Volunteer services should be formalized through agreements between the volunteers and school personnel. Schedules should be developed cooperatively, and attendance should be monitored. Agreements for volunteer services should establish procedures for reporting absences and tardiness and should include provisions for terminating services in the event that either becomes excessive. The existence of formal guidelines for volunteer services provides an opportunity for the discussion of expectations related to such services and may prevent volunteers from behaving in ways that have disruptive effects on instruction.

Student-peers have been used effectively as volunteers and paraprofessionals. After receiving suitable instruction, peers have succeeded in teaching students with educational handicaps. Donder and Nietupski (1981) reported that junior high students were successful in teaching age-appropriate playground skills to students with mild or moderate degrees of mental retardation. Similar success was reported by Fenrick and McDonnell (1980) who found that four junior high students were able to use behavioral principles to teach students who had severe mental retardation. Peer-tutoring has also been performed by classmates of students with severe handicapping conditions. Wacker and Berg (1985) found that students with moderate and severe handicaps were successful in providing instruction and monitoring the performance of peers with severe handicaps. The apparent success of peer-tutoring is encouraging in that it fosters constructive helping interactions between students, thus enhancing social integration. It also provides a source of personnel that may be of assistance in increasing the amount of instructional time provided to students with severe or profound handicaps.

Support for Integrated Services

Administrative Support

For students with severe or profound handicapping conditions to be integrated successfully in public schools, policies that support integrated programming must be in place. These policies should address funding; staffing; nontraditional educational supplies, materials, and equipment; transportation; scheduling; off-campus instruction; and liability for students in out-of-school settings. The existence of supportive policies will facilitate provision of instruction and services that are atypical of those provided to most students, but essential for students with severe or profound handicapping conditions.

The assignment of personnel who are responsible for administering or coordinating integrated programs will also contribute to the success of these programs. Among the support services that can be provided by school-based administrators or coordinators are the development and implementation of strategies that will facilitate social integration in the schools, case management, technical assistance, in-service training for staff, resource management, and coordination of scheduling and curriculum.

Administrative support services have been provided through a variety of models. In Albuquerque, New Mexico, special education administrators have been assigned to schools to coordinate services to students with severe handicaps. Their responsibilities include identifying needed technical assistance, coordinating this assistance with other in-service activities, evaluating staff, monitoring programs, consulting on curriculum, coordinating the development and implementation of individualized education programs (IEPs), planning schedules, serving as liaisons with parents, and conducting team meetings (Thomason & Arkell, 1980; Taylor, 1982). In Madison, Wisconsin, program support teachers consult with special education teachers, provide in-service training to regular teachers, and serve as liaisons with parents and community agencies.

Statewide support systems have also been designed to assist teachers of students with severe handicaps who are dispersed geographically. Vermont uses an I-Team (Interdisciplinary Team) model with the following characteristics:

- *Interdisciplinary.* Professionals from several disciplines work together when needed to meet the complex educational needs of learners with severe handicaps.
- *Educational.* Guidelines are established to describe "what" and "how" to teach students with severe handicaps.
- *In-service training.* Interdisciplinary in-service training is provided to develop the skills needed to implement the educational model.
- *Community-based interdisciplinary service.* Interdisciplinary technical assistance and training are provided to assure appropriate placement, assessment, and instructional program design, implementation, and evaluation (Williams, Fox, Christie, Thousand, Conn-Powers, Carmichael, Vogelsberg, & Hull, 1986).

When the I-Team model was initiated, specialized services were virtually nonexistent in rural Vermont. Through the support services provided by the team, the competencies needed to develop and/or remediate local services were disseminated across the state.

Family Support Services

By itself, integration in schools can never be a sufficient means of attaining integration in the community. Comprehensive integration requires a broader array of services than those available through the educational system. When families with children who have severe or profound handicaps are provided assistance, they are more apt to maintain their children in their homes and communities (Castellani, Downey, Tausig, & Bird, 1986).

NICHCY (1986b) identified an array of family support services that can assist persons with severe or profound handicaps and their families.

Respite care is one such service that provides families periodic relief from the constant physical and emotional demands of caring for children with severe or profound handicaps. *Parent involvement or assistance* programs (discussed previously in this chapter) are beneficial means of supplementing educational and therapeutic services provided by schools and other agencies. *Case management* services help persons with severe or profound handicapping conditions or their families to identify needs and to find services. The case manager coordinates the provision of services from multiple sources, maintains records, and monitors the services provided to ensure they are meeting the needs of the individual or the family. Many adults with severe or profound handicaps need *habilitative services* (training in self-care and independent living skills). *Homemaker services* are also useful for both parents and adults with handicapping conditions and consist of household care (meal preparation, cleaning, and laundry) and home management skills. *Nursing care* and *home health aides* are valuable for persons who have health problems or motor disabilities.

In addition to family support services, a variety of post school services that address domestic, vocational, recreational, and other dimensions of independent community living by adults must be provided if persons with severe or profound handicapping conditions are to be integrated successfully into community life. Without such services, adults with handicaps will be unable to participate extensively in their communities, and the benefits of a functional integrated education will be lessened.

Availability and adequacy of adult services and family support services are crucial ecologic factors that affect the success of a social policy of integration. The availability of selected family support services differs substantially from one geographic region to another. For example, Castellani et al. (1986) found that although information and referral, diagnosis and evaluation, and transportation were available in more than 70% of the agencies providing services in selected counties in New York, home habilitation and respite care services were provided by 30% or fewer of the agencies. The adequacy of services also varies. Slater and Black (1986), in a study of services in selected counties in Wisconsin, found that training services designed to increase the skills of individuals with disabilities were judged to be inadequate by 30% of the primary caretakers. A minimum of 10% of the caretakers also identified medical and dental, sheltered employment, recreation, transportation, and diagnostic services as being inadequate. The lack of available and adequate support services for persons with severe or profound handicaps and their families jeopardizes the abilities of families to maintain relatives in the community, and endangers the development of integrated educational services.

For a policy of integration in schools and communities to be effective, advocates will need to engage in activities that will bring about positive changes in the quantity and quality of educational and social support services. Budde and Bachelder (1986) suggested three methods that may improve the availability and quality of needed services. They recommended that a variety of public awareness activities including media campaigns, public presentations, and organized activities be initiated to alert citizens to the need for and benefits of community-based programs for persons with disabilities. Technical assistance should also be employed as a means of sharing expertise that can improve existing services or lead to the development of new ones. Finally, direct advocacy by or on behalf of individuals or groups can assist in devising solutions that will advance the quantity and quality of services to persons with disabilities. Unless these or similar actions are taken, support services are likely to remain inadequate.

Financial Support

Services follow funds. Adequate appropriations are essential for the development and maintenance of the educational and social support services needed for a policy of integration to be successful. Braddock (1986) noted that federal funding of services to persons with developmental disabilities increased every year from 1954 to 1980. However, in 1981 spending for these services slowed considerably, and since that time it seems to have reached a plateau. Braddock's analysis also revealed a possible "institutional bias" in federal programs that provide services to persons with developmental disabilities. This bias is reflected in the fact that in fiscal year 1984, 41% of the federal funds spent on persons with developmental disabilities supported approximately 100,000 individuals who resided in segregated institutional facilities; the remaining 59% supported services to the tens of hundreds of thousands of persons who resided in communities. This distribution of federal monies seems to perpetuate segregated services and to hinder the development of community services and the implementation of a policy of integration (Braddock, 1986; Fernald, 1986).

During the time period in which federal funding has slowed, the number of community-based residential facilities has increased (Hill, Lakin & Bruininks, 1984) and the number of persons living in institutions has decreased (Scheerenberger, 1982). These trends provide evidence that a shift from segregation to integration has occurred in both social policy and the provision of services. To maintain the momentum behind community-based services, The Association for Retarded Citizens, The Association for Persons with Severe Handicaps, and other organizations and individuals have supported legislation (e.g., The Community and Family Living Amendments of 1985) and other actions that would alter funding patterns that contribute to segregated services in favor of those that will increase and improve services in community settings. Advocates will need to be successful in their attempts to increase and to realign funding for community services if the transition from a segregated to an integrated model of services delivery for persons with severe or profound handicaps is to be accomplished.

CONCLUSION

The history of education and other services to persons with severe or profound handicaps in the United States has been largely characterized by practices of neglect, isolation, and segregation. In the 1960s, a modern era of federal concern for persons with severe or profound handicaps was initiated, reflecting an examination and alteration of past social policies. Since that time, litigation and legislation at both the state and federal levels have established and clarified rights of citizens with severe or profound disabilities, and programs have been funded to provide education and other needed services.

The transition from a policy that emphasized exclusion and segregation to one that stresses the value of integrating all citizens into the lives of their communities poses significant challenges for education and other social systems. If integration is to be successful and provide all of the benefits envisioned by advocates, educators and others must realign service systems to conform to this goal. For local education agencies, a policy of integration requires, at a minimum, that curricula used to educate students with severe or profound handicaps focus on the *goal* of enabling them to participate in integrated community environments to the maximum extent they are able, and education and related services be provided in the least restrictive settings consistent with the goal of education for individual students. Institutions of higher education must also become involved in the reformation process by examining their personnel preparation programs to ensure that graduates can provide education and related services in a manner consistent with a policy of integration and will contribute to the abilities of students with severe or profound handicaps to participate in their communities.

A comprehensive program of integration necessitates that an array of community-based services be available for citizens with severe or profound handicaps, that systems to support services in integrated settings be established, and that adequate funding for needed services systems be appropriated. If these key elements are not given proper attention, community-based services will not be adequate to meet the needs of citizens with severe or profound handicaps, and a clamor may arise urging a return to models of the past.

REFERENCES

Allen, D.A., & Hudd, S.S. (1987). Are we professionalizing parents? Weighing the benefits and pitfalls. *Mental Retardation, 25*(3), 133-139.

Baker, B.L., & Heifetz, L.J. (1976). The read project: Teaching manuals for parents of retarded children. In T.D. Tjossem (Ed.), *Intervention strategies for high risk infants and young children.* (pp. 351-369). Baltimore: University Park Press.

Bates, P., & Pancsofar, E. (1981, May). Exploring appropriate instructional programs for severely/profoundly handicapped. Title XX workshop conducted in Hope, Arkansas.

Biklen, D. (1981). *Public education for children with severe, profound, and multiple disabilities: The least restrictive environment.* Syracuse, NY: Syracuse University, Special Education Resource Center.

Birenbaum, A. (1986). Symposium overview: Community programs for people with mental retardation. *Mental Retardation, 24*(3), 145-146.

Braddock, D. (1986). From Roosevelt to Reagan: Federal spending analysis for mental retardation and developmental disabilities. *American Journal of Mental Deficiency, 90*(5), 479-489.

Brady, M.P., McEvoy, M.A., Gunter, P., Shores, R.E., & Fox, J.J. (1984). Considerations for socially integrated school environments for severely handicapped students. *Education and Training of the Mentally Retarded, 19*(4), 246-253.

Bricker, D. (1976). Educational synthesizer. In M. Thomas (Ed.), *Hey, don't forget about me!* (pp. 84-97). Reston, VA: The Council for Exceptional Children.

Bricker, W.A., & Bricker, D.D. (1976): The infant, toddler, and preschool research intervention project. In T.D. Tjossem (Ed.), *Intervention strategies for high risk infants and young children.* (pp. 545-572). Baltimore: University Park Press.

Bricker, W.A., & Bricker, D.D. (1977). A developmentally integrated approach to early intervention. *Education and Training of the Mentally Retarded, 12,* 100-108.

Brinker, R.P., & Thorpe, M.E. (1984). Integration of severely handicapped students and the proportion of IEP objectives achieved. *Exceptional Children, 51*(2), 168-175.

Brown, L., Branston, M.B., Hamre-Nietupski, S., Pumpian, I., Certo, N., & Gruenewald, L. (1979). A strategy for developing chronological age appropriate and functional curricular content for severely handicapped adolescents and young adults. *Journal of Special Education, 13*(1), 81-90.

Brown, L., Ford, A., Nisbet, J., Sweet, M., Donnellan, A., & Gruenewald, L. (1983). Opportunities available when severely handicapped students attend chronological-age appropriate regular schools. *The Journal of the Association for the Severely Handicapped, 8*(1), 16-24.

Brown, L., Nietupski, J., & Hamre-Nietupski, S. (1976). Criterion of ultimate functioning. In M.A. Thomas (Ed.), *Hey, don't forget about me!* (pp. 2-15). Reston, VA: The Council for Exceptional Children.

Brown, L., Nisbet, J., Ford, A., Sweet, M., Shiraga, B., York, J., & Loomis, R. (1983). The critical need for nonschool instruction in educational programs for severely handicapped students. *The Journal of the Association for the Severely Handicapped, 8*(3), 71-75.

Brown, L., Sweet, M., Shiraga, B., York, J., Zanella, K., & Rogan, P. (1984). *Functional skills in programs for students with severe handicaps.* Madison, WI: University of Wisconsin and Madison Metropolitan School District.

Brown, L., Wilcox, B., Sontag, E., Vincent, B., Dodd, N., & Gruenewald, L. (1977). Toward the realization of the least restrictive educational environments for severely handicapped students. *AAESPH Review, 2*(4), 195-201.

Brown, L., & York, R. (1974). Developing programs for severely handicapped students: Teacher training and classroom instruction. *Focus on Exceptional Children, 6*(2), 1-11.

Bruder, M.B. (1987). Parent-to-parent teaching. *American Journal of Mental Deficiency, 91*(4), 435-438.

Budde, J.F., & Bachelder, J.L. (1986). Independent living: The concept, model, and methodology. *The Journal of the Association for Persons with Severe Handicaps, 11*(4), 240-245.

Burke, P.J., & Cohen, M. (1977). The quest for competence in serving the severely/profoundly handicapped: A critical analysis of personnel preparation programs. In E. Sontag, J. Smith, & N. Certo (Eds.), *Educational programming for the severely and profoundly handicapped.* (pp. 445-465). Reston, VA: The Council for Exceptional Children.

Campbell, P.H. (1987). The integrated programming team: An approach for coordinating professionals of various disciplines in programs for students with multiple handicaps. *The Journal of the Association for Persons with Severe Handicaps, 12*(2), 107-116.

Castellani, P.J., Downey, N.A., Tausig, M.B., & Bird, W.A. (1986). Availability and accessibility of family support services. *Mental Retardation, 24*(2), 71-79.

Crapps, J.M., Langone, J., & Swaim, S. (1985). Quantity and quality of participation in community environments by mentally retarded adults. *Education and Training of the Mentally Retarded, 20*(2), 123-129.

Donder, D., & Nietupski, J. (1981). Nonhandicapped adolescents teaching playground skills to their mentally retarded peers: Toward a less restrictive middle school. *Education and Training of the Mentally Retarded, 16*(4), 270-276.

Education for All Handicapped Children Act of 1975. *Federal Register,* August 23, 1977.

Falvey, M.A. (1986). *Community-based instruction: Instructional strategies for students with severe handicaps.* Baltimore: Paul H. Brookes.

Fenrick, N.J., & McDonnell, J.J. (1980). Junior high school students as teachers of the severely retarded: Training and generalization. *Education and Training of the Mentally Retarded, 15*(3), 187-194.

Fernald, C.D. (1986). Changing Medicaid and intermediate care facilities for the mentally retarded (ICF/MR): Evaluation of alternatives. *Mental Retardation, 24*(1), 36-42.

Freagon, S., Wheeler, J., Brankin, G., McDannel, K., Costello, D., & Peters, W.M. (1983). *Curricular processes for the school and the community integration of severely handicapped students ages 6-21: Project replication guide.* DeKalb, IL: DeKalb County Special Education Association and Department of Learning Development and Special Education, Northern Illinois University.

Fredericks, B., Baldwin, J., & Grove, D.A. (1976). A home-center based parent training model. In D.L. Lillie & P.L. Trohanis (Eds.), *Teaching parents to teach.* (pp. 107-129). New York: Walker.

Fredericks, H.D., Anderson, R., & Baldwin, V. (1979). Identifying competency indicators of teachers of the severely handicapped. *AAESPH Review, 4*(1) 81-91.

Geiger, W. (1984). *A report on the cost of the Austin Independent School Districts' educational program for students with multiple handicaps.* Unpublished manuscript.

Geiger, W.L., Bradley, R.H., Rock, S.L., & Croce, R.V. (1986). Commentary. *Physical & Occupational Therapy in Pediatrics, 6*(2), 16-21.

Giangreco, M.F. (1986). Delivery of therapeutic services in special education programs for learners with severe handicaps. *Physical & Occupational Therapy in Pediatrics, 6*(2), 5-15.

Gilhool, T.K., & Stutman, E.A. (1978). Integration of severely handicapped students: Toward criteria for implementing and enforcing the integration imperative of P.L. 94-142 and Section 504. In S. Sarason, D. Geller & M. Klaber (Eds.), *Least restrictive alternatives: Moral, legal, and administrative dilemmas.* (pp. 191-227). New York: Free Press.

Goldenson, R.M. (1978). Rehabilitation professions. In R.M. Goldenson, J.R. Dunham, & C.S. Dunham (Eds.), *Disability and rehabilitation handbook.* (pp. 716-761). New York: McGraw-Hill.

Hamre-Nietupski, S., & Nietupski, J. (1981). Integral involvement of severely handicapped students within regular public schools. *The Journal of the Association for the Severely Handicapped, 6*(2) 30-39.

Hayden, A.H., & Haring, N.G. (1976). Early intervention for high risk infants and young children: Programs for Down's syndrome children. In T.D. Tjossem (ed.), *Intervention strategies for high risk infants and young children.* (pp. 573-607). Baltimore: University Park Press.

Hill, B.K., Lakin, K.C., & Bruininks, R.H. (1984). Trends in residential services for people who are mentally retarded: 1977–1982. *The Journal of the Association for Persons with Severe Handicaps, 9*(4), 243-250.

Horner, R.D. (1977). A competency-based approach to preparing teachers of the severely and profoundly handicapped: Perspective II. In E. Sontag, J. Smith, & N. Certo (Eds.), *Educational programming for the severely and profoundly handicapped.* (pp. 430-444). Reston, VA: The Council for Exceptional Children.

Huber, H., & Lynch, F. (1978). Teaching behavioral skills to parents. *Children Today, 7*(1), 8-10.

Jenkins, S., Stephens, W.B., & Sternberg, L. (1980). The use of parents as parent trainers of handicapped children. *Education and Training of the Mentally Retarded, 15,* 256-263.

Kenowitz, L.A., Zweibel, S., & Edgar, E. (1978). Determining the least restrictive opportunity for the severely and profoundly handicapped. In N. Haring & D. Bricker (Eds.), *Teaching the severely handicapped: Vol. III.* (pp. 49-61). Columbus, OH: Special Press.

Kregel, J., Wehman, P., Seyfarth, J., & Marshall, K. (1986). Community integration of young adults with mental retardation. Transition from school to adulthood. *Education and Training of the Mentally Retarded, 21*(1), 35-42.

Lehr, D.H. & Brown, F. (1984). Perspectives on severely multiply handicapped. In E.L. Meyen (Ed.), *Mental Retardation: Topics of today—issues of tomorrow* (pp. 41-65). Lancaster, PA: Lancaster Press.

Lehr, D., & Haubrich, P. (1986). Legal precedents for students with severe handicaps. *Exceptional Children, 50*(4), 358-365.

McKenzie, R.G., & Houk, C.S. (1986). The paraprofessional in special education. *Teaching Exceptional Children, 18*(4), 246-250.

National Information Center for Handicapped Children and Youth, (1986a). The least restrictive environment: Knowing one when you see it. *News Digest, 5,* pp. 1-8.

National Information Center for Handicapped Children and Youth, (1986b). Alternatives for community living. *News Digest,* April, pp. 1-8.

Office of Special Education and Rehabilitative Services, U.S. Department of Education. (1985). *Children and youth with severe handicaps: Effective communication.* Washington, DC.

Reid, B., & Johnston, M. (1978). Paraprofessionals in education for the severely/profoundly handicapped. In N.G. Haring & D.D. Bricker (Eds.), *Teaching the severely handicapped: Volume III.* (pp. 77-93). Seattle, WA: American Association for the Education of the Severely/Profoundly Handicapped.

Sailor, W., & Guess, D. (1983). *Severely handicapped students: An instructional design.* Boston: Houghton Mifflin.

Scheerenberger, R.C. (1982). Public residential services, 1981: Status and trends. *Mental Retardation, 20*(5), 210-215.

Sears, C.J. (1981). The transdisciplinary approach: A process of complying with Public Law 94-142. *Journal of the Association for the Severely Handicapped, 6*(1), 22-29.

Slater, M.A., & Black, P.B. (1986). Urban-rural differences in the delivery of community services: Wisconsin as a case in point. *Mental Retardation, 24*(3), 153-161.

Smith-Davis, J., Burke, P.J., & Noel, M.M. (1984). *Personnel to educate the handicapped in America: Supply and demand from a programmatic viewpoint.* College Park, MD: Institute for the Study of Exceptional Children and Youth.

Snart, F., & Hillyard, A. (1985). Staff ratios and allocated instructional time for multihandicapped students. *Exceptional Children, 51*(4), 289-296.

Stainback, S., & Stainback, W. (1985). *Integration of students with severe handicaps into regular schools.* Reston, VA: The Council for Exceptional Children.

Sternberg, L. (in press). Curriculum for profoundly handicapped students: A response to a critique. *Physical and Occupational Therapy in Pediatrics.*

Sternberg, L., & Caldwell, M.L. (1982). Parent involvement and training. In L. Sternberg & G.L. Adams (Eds.), *Educating severely and profoundly handicapped students.* (pp. 27-43). Rockville, MD: Aspen.

Sternberg, L., Taylor, R.L., & Schilit, J. (1986). *So you're not a special educator: A general handbook for educating handicapped children.* Springfield, IL: Charles C Thomas.

Stetson, F. (1984). Critical factors that facilitate integration: A theory of administrative responsibility. In N. Certo, N. Haring, & R. York (Eds.), *Public school integration of severely handicapped students: Regional issues and progressive alternatives.* (pp. 65-81). Baltimore: Paul H. Brookes.

Tawney, J.W. (1977). Educating severely handicapped children and their parents through telecommunications. In N.G. Haring & L.J. Brown (Eds.), *Teaching the severely handicapped: Volume II.* (pp. 315-340). New York: Grune & Stratton.

Tawney, J.W., Aeschleman, S.R., Deaton, S.L., & Donaldson, R.M. (1979). Using telecommunications to instruct rural severely handicapped children. *Exceptional Children, 46,* 118-125.

Taylor, S. (1982). From segregation to integration: Strategies for integrating severely handicapped students in normal school and community settings. *The Journal of the Association for the Severely Handicapped, 7*(3), 42-49.

Thomason, J., & Arkell, C. (1980). Educating the severely/profoundly handicapped in the public schools: A side-by-side approach. *Exceptional Children, 47*(2), 114-122.

Tucker, D.J., & Horner, R.D. (1977). Competency-based training of paraprofessional teaching associates for education of the severely and profoundly handicapped. In E. Sontag, J. Smith, & N. Certo (Eds.), *Educational programming for the severely and profoundly handicapped.* (pp. 405-417). Reston, VA: The Council for Exceptional Children.

Turnbull, A.P. (1978). Parent-professional interactions. In M.E. Snell (Ed.), *Systematic instruction of the moderately and severely handicapped.* (pp. 458-476). Columbus, OH: Charles E. Merrill.

Turnbull, A.P. (1983). Parental participation in the IEP process. In J.A. Mulick & S.M. Pueschel (Eds.), *Parent-professional partnerships in developmental disability services* (pp. 107-122). Cambridge, MA: Academic Guild.

Turnbull, A.P., Strickland, B., & Goldstein, S. (1978). Training professionals and parents in developing and implementing the IEP. *Education and Training of the Mentally Retarded, 13,* 414-423.

Wacker, D.P., & Berg, W.K. (1985). Use of peers to train and monitor the performance of adolescents with severe handicaps. *Education and Training of the Mentally Retarded, 20*(2), 109-122.

Watson, L.S., & Bassinger, J.F. (1974). Parent training technology: A potential service delivery system. *Mental Retardation, 12,* 3-10.

Wehman, P., Renzaglia, A., & Bates, P. (1985). *Functional living skills for moderately and severely handicapped individuals.* Austin, TX: PRO-ED.

Wershing, A., Gaylord-Ross, C., & Gaylord-Ross, R. (1986). Implementing a community-based vocational training model: A process for systems change. *Education and Training of the Mentally Retarded, 21*(2), 130-137.

Wiegerink, R., & Parrish, V. (1976). A parent-implemented school program. In D.L. Lillie & P.L. Trohanis (Eds.), *Teaching parents to teach.* (pp. 149-162). New York: Walker.

Williams, W., Fox, W., Christie, L., Thousand, J., Conn-Powers, M., Carmichael, L., Vogelsberg, R.T., & Hull, M. (1986). Community integration in Vermont. *The Journal of the Association for Persons with Severe Handicaps, 11*(4), 294-299.

Wolfensberger, W. (1972). *The principle of normalization in human services.* Toronto: National Institute on Mental Retardation.

Chapter 3

Classroom-Based Medical Interventions

Patricia L. McDonald, Ruth Wilson, Ruth Turner,
and Marilyn Mulligan Ault

PROBLEM AND PAST PRACTICES

Bill Coronado is four and one-half years old and was developing normally until his third birthday. Since surviving a motor vehicle accident, he is nonverbal, nonambulatory, has restricted range of motion, no head control, and an overall developmental level of less than one year. Due to extensive injuries, a gastrostomy tube has been placed through the abdominal wall into his stomach for feedings and medication. Bill breathes through an opening in his windpipe called a *tracheostomy.* Suctioning and mist treatments are required during the day to allow healthy, unrestricted breathing. Medications for Bill's seizure disorder are required morning and evening. A multidisciplinary team at the local children's hospital has determined that Bill is strong enough to tolerate transportation to and from and full-day placement outside the home. His father is an unskilled construction worker. His mother does not drive and cares for Bill's two preschool-age siblings in the home. The family's insurance has limited service and equipment provisions. The family has contacted the local school district's special education department for Bill's placement in public school.

Students with serious medical problems present innumerable questions regarding how their medical *environment* can best be maintained. In many respects, the concerns involving that environment are just as crucial as, if not more crucial than, any other environmental concerns. This is certainly the case when one is considering appropriate delivery of educational services. Public schools increasingly are receiving students with profound handicaps like Bill Coronado with medical and nursing needs. These increases are attributable, in part, to advances in medical technology and increases in child population (Wood, Walker, & Gardner, 1986). The passage of the Education for All Handicapped Children Act of 1975 (P.L.

94-142) has also contributed to the increase in the number of students with severe medical problems becoming eligible for education services. The "zero-reject" aspect of this law mandated services to students previously excluded from schools because school personnel did not feel equipped to handle them (Bryan, Warden, Berg, & Hauck, 1978).

Before P.L. 94-142, many states denied public school placement to students with complex medical problems and high levels of dependency. The law was a landmark, providing a "bill of rights" for persons with handicaps and mandating that schools find and serve all children with handicaps (Martin & Richmond, 1980).

Other legislation changing the level of services available to students who are profoundly handicapped includes the Rehabilitation Act of 1973. Section 504 of this law prohibits discrimination against handicapped individuals and guarantees them equal access to programs available to other students (Vlasak, 1980).

The provision of medically related services necessary to ensure a free and appropriate education in the least restrictive environment has been clarified through the courts by parents and concerned citizens using the due process procedure outlined in legislative actions. In spite of the fact that these medical services seem to be required, controversy and confusion continue regarding who is to perform these services and what training they should receive. Wood et al. (1986) reported that currently no federal statutes of health care codes govern health practices in public schools. In a national survey of state education and public health agencies, they found that only 6 of the 50 states have written guidelines for most medically related services. Thirteen states have guidelines for medication only, and 13 have no written guidelines at all.

The lack of guidelines and clarity does not offset the fact that non–medically trained educators increasingly will be required to understand complex medical conditions in their students. The teacher's responsibility may range from alerting a nurse or medical technician that a procedure needs to be performed to serving as the primary caregiver using input from school and community health professionals (Sailor & Guess, 1983).

How can non–medically trained school personnel begin to understand complex student health needs? How can these services be provided and the providers trained? How should implementation of medical services relate to the overall provision of education? How does one view a student as a student and not relate to him or her as a "patient" (Lehr, 1987). This chapter includes definitions, describes specific treatment techniques, and discusses environmental adaptations. Documentation and preplanning activities are stressed. Other practical information designed to implement classroom-based medical interventions is also offered. *It is imperative that the reader understand that in order for a practitioner to carry out many of the interventions described in this chapter, he or she must commit to in-depth initial and continuous training by qualified individuals.*

SUGGESTED METHODS

Management of medically involved students will necessitate that school-based personnel become more familiar with terminology, equipment, and supplies needed to provide health-related procedures at school. Parents, school staff, and members of the community will also need to work together to ensure the ongoing safety of special needs students. The school environment, staffing needs, and transportation may need to be adapted to serve students who are not only profoundly handicapped but medically involved. To understand the target focus of these services, a number of preliminary definitions are necessary:

- *Chronically ill* describes children or youth whose disorder of body functions, systems, or organs is of long duration. Other terms, such as medically fragile, medically complex, and technically intensive, have been used to describe this group (Health Advisory Committee, 1986).
- Students with profound handicaps who have a disease process that affects their health to the point of being life-threatening are described as *medically fragile.* An uncontrolled or poorly controlled seizure disorder or a long-term illness, such as leukemia or muscular dystrophy, may be the cause of a student's increasing disability or death.
- *Medically complex* might describe the student with several medical conditions, conditions that are poorly understood, or those that exhibit system-wide symptoms such as neurofibromatosis.
- *Technically intensive* may refer to students who require special services by trained individuals on a daily basis. These services require more time from the classroom teacher, as procedures include the use of supplies that must be cleaned and stored, and sophisticated equipment. Unless the classroom teacher receives additional help, he or she is not able to care for as many students who are profoundly handicapped.

Medical services required at school are *related services,* just as physical therapy, occupational therapy, audiology, speech, and psychological services are often considered related services. Many medical services, therefore, are *not defined* as medical treatments. In part, this is because parents and possibly certain students could perform the procedure.

Parents as the Student's Primary Care Providers

Caring for chronically ill children expands parental roles and responsibilities. Physicians depend on parental input to adjust treatment schedules and to notice and report adverse medical reactions. Teacher observations, provided to parents through systematic documentation, are helpful to the parents and the physician for monitoring medical intervention.

Parental responsibilities generally include completion of all required forms and provision of supplies and equipment necessary for school staff to provide health-related services. Families who have endured extraordinary financial and emotional hardships caring for their chronically ill child may need more than traditional school/family interaction. To obtain required information, school staff may need to make home visits, provide interpreters, arrange for transportation for parents to attend meetings, and accompany the parents and student to the physician. To acquire the necessary supplies and equipment, school staff may determine that referral of the family to community social services agencies is appropriate. Parents unable to provide duplicate equipment, such as a suctioning machine or humidifiers, and disposable equipment, such as catheters, should be referred to state agencies for grants. Referrals, however, should never be made without parental permission.

School staff must be aware that patience and the passage of time will be required to "settle" a student who is profoundly handicapped and medically involved into the school routine. Some parents participate fully in the give and take of school activities. A few seem afraid to step back and allow the teacher to coordinate teaching and health-related activities without providing daily input. In such cases, several demonstrations of competence may be necessary before parents can get on with their life during the school day. Other parents must be firmly guided, supported, and occasionally pushed to become effective members of the team.

Preliminary Assistive Concerns

The student's physician may make the initial referral for school placement. It is essential that scheduled, ongoing communication with the physician be established and maintained by the teacher coordinating the related services of the student. The name of a backup physician should be available. Many students are seen in hospital clinics that are not open every day. It is essential to determine who can respond if a problem occurs on a nonclinic day. Occasionally, questions may be addressed to the emergency room physician or nurse in another health care facility. After obtaining parental permission in writing, a call for information before the need arises is essential.

School nurses may be available; however, training and expertise are highly variable. The "traditional" school nurse may require training and backup services from community health care consultants. The physician may recommend that a private nursing consultant, visiting nurse, or home health agency be contacted for training, telephone consultation, or visits to the school. Qualified professionals can be provided on a contractual or as needed basis. However, annual inservice for staff by qualified health-related professionals should help decrease the need for ongoing consultant services.

It is important that the teacher determine how to access community emergency services and contact the administrator of the appropriate facility. He or she can advise staff of how long it would take for the emergency squad to arrive and what services would be available. The emergency squad administrator may be interested in a tour of the educational facility to locate the classroom in reference to the school entrance.

Volunteers can provide assistance in monitoring students or implementing medical interventions when properly trained and supervised. Delegation of duties, however, should depend on state and local guidelines regarding in-classroom care for students who are profoundly handicapped. Volunteers may be found by contacting nonprofit agencies, such as the American Red Cross, Volunteer Grandparents, or other local volunteer groups. High school students in extracurricular health-related service clubs expressing an interest in learning about medically involved individuals might also serve as volunteers during study periods or before and after school when students arrive early or leave late. Volunteers can help provide services to students on a limited, supervised basis by interacting directly or by helping with supplies and equipment. It is necessary to notify parents that volunteers will be assisting in the classroom.

Churches, service clubs, and PTAs are excellent sources of funds for backup disposable supplies or to help parents purchase needed duplicate equipment for the classroom. In this regard the teacher can expand the classroom role into one of advocating for the needs and rights of persons with handicaps in the school.

Many hospital personnel, private physicians, and rescue workers are still uninformed about medically involved individuals attending school. A school philosophy that actively seeks to educate the public regarding health care needs in the educational setting is to be commended. Articles in the school paper and presentations at PTA meetings, at an open house, and at health fairs carry the word to the community that public schools are for everyone.

Establishing a Comprehensive Medical Services Program

As a first step in establishing an appropriate program, school administrators will need to identify or develop guidelines regarding the provision of specialized health care services to students who are profoundly handicapped and require classroom-based medical interventions. Wood et al. (1986) reported that "74% of all states and territories have some written guidelines governing nursing procedures performed in public school settings" (p. 216). A number of states, however, address the issues only at the local level or only with standard or common procedures. State departments of education and of health can supply information regarding requirements for standardized procedures and identification of appropriate providers and trainers in the school setting. If no state guidelines exist regarding provision of specialized physical health care services to students with exceptional needs by unlicensed individuals during the school day, local policies should be instituted. Local school and/or agency administrators must address the legal and financial problems that may occur. Local policies should address who is qualified to train, who is qualified to provide direct service, and to whom the supervising provider may delegate responsibility. Regulations should not lock staff into rules that could harm the school's ability to provide services. For example, during unplanned multiple absences or in an *emergency situation,* previously unidentified personnel who have basic knowledge of hygiene and emergency procedures may be required to step in.

Staffing Needs

When determining staffing needs for classrooms, buildings, or districts providing education service to students with medically fragile or complex conditions, flexibility must be built into the plan. Chronically ill children may be absent frequently, and their need for special procedures may change. A student who is fed through a tube may require less time to feed than a student who has poor oral musculature coordination or neuromuscular involvement. Collecting the equipment and supplies, performing the procedure, and cleaning and storing the equipment will be time-consuming.

When routine care is provided or when emergencies occur, two staff members are often needed. Students who are not severely motorically involved may need to be restrained when certain treatments are provided. During emergencies, one staff member must work with the student while another activates the emergency medical system. Professionals and paraprofessionals who are required to follow precise medication and treatment regimens should be as free from *overwhelming situations* and *stress* as possible. The ability to concentrate fully on the task at hand is critical for the life and well-being of the student with a medically complex condition. High student-teacher ratios reduce this ability in classrooms with students having complex medical needs.

The teacher coordinating the medically complex student's related services should also be involved when additional student placement in the class is planned. With the placement of additional students, the teacher should be able to request additional part-time personnel. Full-time staff requirements would ideally include one teacher and three paraprofessionals for eight to ten students (Mulligan, 1984). The exact ratio of staff to students depends on current health needs and may fluctuate to one-to-one using part-time help during critical periods. When students are required to stay at home due to episodes of acute illness or after debilitating special medical procedures, a short-term home-based program should be provided at the teacher's or therapist's direction. This could be implemented by a qualified home care paraprofessional or by classroom staff allowed release time from school responsibilities. Delegation of duties to the paraprofessional will depend on state and local guidelines and the discretion of the teacher.

In addition to full-time personnel, related service providers must be available on a consultant basis to develop a team approach for intervention. A truly transdisciplinary approach is necessary in a classroom having students with medically complex or fragile conditions. Personnel in each related discipline must train all individuals in direct contact with students in critical management or intervention techniques (Sailor & Guess, 1983). This results in an educational staff prepared to meet the physical and medical needs of the student. Classroom personnel must also have speedy access to appropriate consultants when problem solving is required.

Consultant services would include professionals who provide physical, occupational, and speech therapy for educationally relevant instructions regarding motor, positioning, and feeding techniques. The services of a social worker, nutritionist, physician, and qualified nurse as consultants are also recommended for students who are profoundly handicapped and medically involved. Parents are also an integral part of the team of consultants.

Classroom Environment

The major function of the classroom is the education of the student. Educational programming should be developed and implemented to lead each student toward independent functioning or partial participation in daily activities. The student's medical conditions must be addressed, however, in order for many students to benefit from the educational program. Attention to classroom environment, proximity of the classroom to resources in the building and exits, and arrangement of classroom equipment are important.

The classroom serving students with medically fragile conditions, as well as those with severe or multiple handicaps, should be placed strategically in the school building to access emergency as well as frequently used settings. For emergency purposes the classroom should be located as near as possible to the emergency exit, the nurse's office, and the accessible exits. The major concern addressed with this location is providing access for the community emergency medical services and equipment as well as immediate access by medical personnel. The classroom should also be located near other settings in the school building that are frequently or daily accessed by the students. These areas may include the bus loading site, lunchroom, bathrooms, library, and gym.

The classroom itself should be large enough to accommodate several ongoing activities. These may include physical therapy, instruction, and the use of medical equipment. Partial carpeting is recommended for units with students requiring a variety of positions and opportunities to move on the floor. Bathroom facilities are recommended adjacent to the classroom. The bathroom should contain adapted commodes and changing facilities. Access to a shower with an adapted tube would provide additional facilities for excellent health-related care. It should be noted that many classrooms contain sinks for food preparation, medication preparation, and preparing activities. Any sink used for these purposes *should not* be used for cleaning medical equipment or disposing of liquid body waste. They *should not* be used adjacent to a diapering area. Since it is highly possible to spread infection when changing diapers, two separate sinks and associated areas should be available.

The instructional materials selected for the development of skills for independent or partial participation in present and future environments would not differ from those selected for a similar student without medically fragile or complex conditions. Additional equipment to meet their noneducational needs should include positioning equipment, a food blender, a hot plate or microwave, related medical equipment, and, when possible, a clothes washer and dryer. Disposable items are, however, always preferable, including disposable diapers and eating utensils. Medical equipment required will depend on the procedures required by the student and many include suctioning machines, vaporizers, misters, intravenous (IV) drips, etc. Battery operated equipment may require a generator for emergency backup use.

Cribs and playpens are usually, and appropriately, banned from most classrooms for students with severe and multiple impairments. Classrooms with medically involved students may require an area of the room reserved for a student who suddenly becomes ill. The student would use a mat, crib, or bed while waiting for emergency personnel or a parent or guardian. A student could also use the area while receiving a specialized treatment or if he or she is experiencing a prolonged seizure. The bed or mat should be clearly visible to the teacher, separate from interaction with other students, and easily accessible from the main entrance of the classroom.

Certain adjustments to the school environment may also be required, including lighting, air conditioning, vaporizing, air freshening, and temperature and/or humidity control. Safety accommodations may include equipment attached to the walls and ceiling. Materials typically attached and away from the paths of students are lamps, IV poles, cords, and stationary medical equipment.

Pre-Entrance Activities and Procedures

Attention to and completion of certain preparation activities will minimize potential problems and facilitate classroom-based medical interventions. After the initial referral is made and parents are contacted regarding placement, the school or special education administrator should determine who will manage the case. A *qualified* building health professional, whose job description allows for off-campus duties, would be ideal. Other experienced personnel who are not campus restricted can also function effectively as "nurse" case managers by working with the student's physician and the physician's staff. When the decision is made, parents should be notified regarding the identity of their primary contact. Appointing a case manager to coordinate pre-entrance planning and activities will decrease the time required for placement, prevent duplication of effort, and foster parental cooperation and trust. Use of the same case manager for the intake of students who are medically involved increases the accuracy and efficiency of the process as terminology and community medical contacts become familiar. If qualified medical personnel are not available, the parents and the physician need to take a more active role and advise the nonmedical case manager providing the health-related activities. The case manager should also inform parents about the other professionals who will be involved with the student during eligibility assessment and the admission meeting, and after placement.

The same information obtained for all school enrollees must be obtained for a child with medically fragile or complex conditions before the child attends school. This includes immunization records and general emergency information.

Often, medication(s) and treatment(s) can be provided for students either before they come to school or after they return home. When that is impossible, a parent must bring a request for medication and/or specialized procedures from the student's physician. Ideally, the physician should provide enough information so that school personnel will be able to (1) plan a school program that would not further injure the student; (2) allow staff to anticipate trouble areas or activities that could lead to trouble; (3) recognize signs that something is going wrong; and (4) recommend provision for prompt, effective emergency care (Bryan, 1979). Protocols for treatment and information written for lay persons regarding the specific illness process should be obtained and kept readily available for teachers, aides, and consulting professionals. This information will provide a base for school staff to work from as they learn to interact with the student, the primary caregivers, and the physician or his or her designee.

Additional information from the physician may be requested including a copy of the last physical assessment with recent height, weight, and results of vision and hearing testing. The medical report will delineate existing pathologic conditions and hopefully identify the remaining physical potential (Gray & McDonald, 1980). School staff may encourage the parent and family to request further testing by specialists if findings are inconclusive. For example, determination of the student's ability to hear and see are imperative when developing the education plan. New techniques for testing hearing can help determine if a hearing loss is possibly correctable by medication or surgery, or if nerve deafness is present. Hearing aids can be provided for students with profound handicaps when indicated. Students who do not respond visually deserve an opthalmologic evaluation by a specialist to ensure that medication or surgery is not indicated. Many students seem to use their eyes and ears commensurate with their ability to use the cognitive process. The physician may diagnose "cortical" blindness, indicating that although the organs of sight are present, the brain is unable to process what the eye sees.

Medical reports may be difficult to understand. The teacher is encouraged to ask parents what they have been told and ask the physician how this information will affect the student's ability to learn and function in the classroom. A partially sighted student will need visual stimulation. A student with partial hearing, with or without aids, will need special attention to auditory stimulation.

Pre-entrance procedures should also include training staff in special techniques before student arrival. Employees should keep records of any training they receive. Parents should be considered a source of training. Although parents may disrupt the usual classroom procedure, watching parents interact with the student during treatments may prove invaluable.

A plan should be adopted for daily documentation of medications administered and treatments given. It would be helpful to have an additional "diary" for reactions or problems. Any note regarding a problem should be followed by a note describing efforts to correct it and who was notified. Parents must always be notified when problems occur. Some treatments are given on an "as needed, but not to exceed a total number of treatments a day" basis. A notebook in which treatments are recorded should be used and sent back and forth each day between home and school.

An additional pre-entrance procedure for school personnel should include a statement in the student's folder regarding who may view the records. Parents should be notified regarding their rights to privacy. A sign-in sheet for those who view the student's records is recommended. Medical records, when copied completely, can be very specific and contain information parents would not like shared indiscriminantly. Other school or agency personnel, physicians, etc. who request records from the facility should be sent only information obtained during the placement. They can be notified that other records exist but must be requested directly from the previously attended facilities. Parents should be advised to request copies of medical records directly from providers and not from the facility.

Time lines for placement, when required by the state education agency for placement of students with profound handicaps, must be observed. Changes in the student's health status, however, may necessitate extending the time period from referral to placement. Other medical problems should not be allowed to delay placement unduly.

The final phase of pre-entry procedures includes a transdisciplinary meeting. The parent and student should be present, as well as any community members who can provide information relevant to eligibility or the student's individualized education program (IEP). Provision for the required treatments and medications should be included in the student's IEP.

Transportation

Transportation is a vital part of any school-based program. If concerns arise regarding the safety of transporting a student, the first step involves asking the caregivers how their child is transported to physicians or clinics. Many seemingly "fragile" students do quite well for hours in a vehicle or in a clinic or hospital waiting room without special procedures. Equipment and/or supplies required when the student is transported currently must be provided by the parent. Provision by the school staff must be made for transporting and using portable equipment when necessary for the student's safety and comfort.

Innovative transportation may include paying the parent by the mile for transporting the student to and from school. All transportation must be portal to portal, from the home door to the school. Direct routes are preferable. When not possible, time spent transporting must be considered, and extra routes may be needed. Attention to wheelchair safety on the bus and on the lift should not be overlooked when selecting buses, drivers, and bus monitors. In addition to safeguards previously mentioned, the following recommendations are offered:

- Drivers should maintain current certification in first aid and CPR.
- Monitors, who are also trained, should be provided to observe students for potential problems and give emergency care when needed.
- Transporting vehicles should be equipped with two-way radios.
- Vehicle heating and cooling systems should be provided to help maintain students' even body temperature throughout the year.
- Flashing red lights on the rear of the vehicles will provide protection for unscheduled off-road emergency stops.
- Providing annual physicals for drivers, including vision and hearing screening, is suggested.
- Providing ongoing and as needed training in special procedures, such as tracheostomy suctioning and emergency care, will help ensure safety for the students. Inclusion of the driver and monitor during the admission meeting would enable them to understand better the student's needs.

Hygiene and Precautions

Personnel who work with school-age individuals must understand their risk for increased exposure to infectious disease. Every educational facility should establish guidelines for dealing with the problems of transmission of communicable diseases. Local and state public health agencies, the National Education Association, and the Centers for Disease Control in Atlanta publish current information regarding communicable diseases. A quality lay publication written in nonmedical language is *Infections in children: A source book for educators and childcare providers* (Anderson, Bale, Blackburn, & Murph, 1985).

Immunization requirements have decreased the number of infectious diseases that may spread from one individual to another. Vaccines, however, do not exist or are not routinely required for such communicable diseases as the common cold, mononucleosis virus, gastrointestinal viruses, cytomegalovirus (EMV), and the acquired immune deficiency virus (AIDS). Recent information by Smego and Halsey (1987) suggests that routine hepatitis B vaccines may be recommended for susceptible populations.

Routine activities such as diapering, wiping runny noses, and cleaning vomitus in educational facilities expose personnel to bodily fluids of students. Usually, contact with these fluids presents a very small risk of infection. One exception is exposure to hepatitis B. If direct skin contact occurs, hands should be washed with soap and running water. *Soap* will suspend microorganisms, and *running water* will carry the debris away. Disposable wipes products are not recommended for thorough cleaning. Where possible, disposable plastic gloves may be worn, especially if the provider has cuts, scratches, or lesions on the hands. Cleanliness techniques must be followed in centers for students who are profoundly handicapped *whether or not* individuals are known to carry harmful organisms. Some individuals carry diseases although they are symptom-free. Because simple precautions like handwashing are not always carried out, transmission of communicable diseases from *unknown carriers* may be more frequent than transmission from students who are *known* to be contagious.

Policies and guidelines developed for communicable disease control should include consideration of the following information:

- Personnel should be excluded from direct contact with students if they are known to have communicable diseases or fever. Personnel must be trained in proper handwashing techniques and be provided with equipment and supplies that encourage handwashing.

- Care of the environment includes proper disposal of bodily waste while diapering, suctioning, wiping respiratory secretions, or controlling a nosebleed. Trash containers must be lined with plastic bags. If tightly fitted tops are not provided for receptacles, the liner bags should be closed with twist ties or other devices. The securely closed bags should be removed and replaced during the day to cut down on odor.

  Environmental cleanliness also includes cleaning of surfaces of equipment, floors, and carpets. Disinfectants used may include selected commercial cleaners, a 10% solution of laundry bleach (one part bleach to nine parts water), or 70% isopropyl alcohol. Spray disinfectants are primarily deodorizers and should *not* be used in place of liquid disinfectants. Disposable towels should be used when cleaning. Clothing soiled with bodily fluids should be soaked and bagged to be sent home.

- Recognizing infection in students and excluding the student from contact with others helps prevent the spread of infection. Look for fever, a change in activity level, vomiting, diarrhea, cough, rash, etc. However, fever may not always correlate with seriousness of illness (Anderson et al., 1985).

- Backup equipment should include toilet facilities that allow a view of the classroom, running water (carries away dirt and debris), liquid soap (bars may carry contamination), and disposable paper towels. Alcohol hand foams and wipes may be recommended in specific cases *after* handwashing but should not be used instead of handwashing unless water is not available, as on the playground or during home visits, etc.

- All activities of daily living should be *preceded* by handwashing. *After* completing an activity such as eating, diapering, tooth brushing, or dental hygiene, hands should be washed again. Appropriate printed and posted handwashing techniques must be observed by staff *before and after* each student contact (see Figure 3-1). In the classroom, pathogenic organisms (germs) travel in bodily fluids from one individual to another. Organisms that travel in feces, urine, respiratory secretions (saliva, nasal discharge), and vomitus are transmitted (passed) by oral inoculation (to the mouth) *from contaminated hands*. Infections passed via the bloodstream occur through cuts and abrasions on the hands.

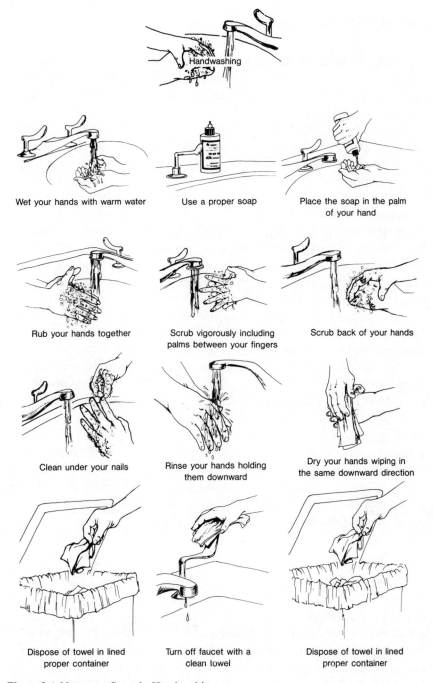

Figure 3-1 Necessary Steps in Handwashing.

General Medication Administration

It is best that all medications be given at home. Physicians who are made aware of the problems of giving medication at school may be able to change time schedules so medications can be given before and after school hours. If a student must take medication to attend school, *local school policy* or state law regarding administration of medication should be followed. Contact state education and health agencies to determine *who is qualified to give medication and to whom the activity may be delegated in the school setting.*

Prescription drugs are especially prepared for certain conditions and designed to be given to specific individuals. *Over-the-counter drugs,* such as cold or cough preparations, aspirin, and salves, do not require a prescription. Prescription medication provides many safeguards for school personnel. Whereas prescription drugs are specific to the disease process and the individual, *over-the-counter drugs* are not and should not be administered by school personnel unless accompanied by a label, a parental request in writing, and a physician's written order to do so. Upon receiving medication to be dispensed, school personnel should note the original date the medication was prescribed, requirements for storage, and the amount of medication in the container. If there are any questions regarding dosage information or out-of-date medication, immediate contact should be made with the pharmacist or physician.

Medications may be prescribed and given in various ways. Drugs can be dispensed as liquids, drops, pills, capsules, suppositories, or ointments. Liquids and/or drops may be prescribed as respiratory treatments. Ointments and salves may be used for treatment or *prophylaxis* (prevention). A brief description of some of the ways medication may be prescribed and given in the classroom for students who are profoundly handicapped follows.

Oral Administration

Medication to be given by mouth may be prescribed as a liquid, pill, or capsule and given by spoon, syringe, dropper, or cup. The measurement may be by teaspoon or cubic centimeters (cc). *With the physician's permission,* capsules may be emptied and pills crushed and mixed with water. A mortar and pestle is appropriate for crushing and mixing medication. Before giving any liquid, correct positioning is required. If the student vomits or spits out a medication, do not attempt to readminister the medication unless you are sure none has been retained. Parents should be notified should vomiting occur.

Tube Administration

Students may have a gastrostomy or nasogastric tube in place. Administering medication through a tube already in place will necessitate that one appropriately *position the student, check for tube placement, administer the medication,* and then *flush the tube* with a small amount of water. If medication must be given this way at school, obtain physician's orders, parental permission in writing, and request that training be provided with a written protocol.

Respiratory Administration

One manner of administering medication through the respiratory route is well known to most adults. A *vaporizer* will reduce medicated liquids to vapor (fine particles of liquid) fit for inhalation or application to the accessible mucous membranes. Many times, the administration of water vapor is required for types of respiratory congestion or dryness. Vapor or mist with or without medication may need to be provided continuously, on an as needed basis, or on a regularly set schedule for a specified time period. The vapor may simply flow from an apparatus or may be pumped at a specified rate in precise doses. A physician's written prescription, recommendations for dispensing the medication, parental permission in writing, and training to use the equipment must be required. A respiratory therapist or other trained health professional can provide this training.

Respiratory treatments may change the student's respiratory status. Provision must be made by staff to have time to observe the student after treatment. A student who receives mist or medicated mist must have suctioning equipment available. Training will be required for the staff to use the supplies and equipment correctly.

Rules for Accepting Medication

- Medication brought to school should be in the original container. Parents should be advised to ask the physician for one prescription bottle for home and one for school. Appropriate labeling includes the date the prescription was written, name of the student, name of the medication, method of administration, and dosage. The physician's name, name of the pharmacy, and telephone numbers must be present. Do not hesitate to call the parent and, if necessary, the pharmacist or physician if the prescription does not seem current, the medication looks or smells "wrong," or if information on the label is not sufficient.

Request for long-term medication administration (more than two weeks) should be accompanied by written orders from a physician. A form can be used that indicates the physician should include the student's diagnosis and reason(s) why the medication is to be given at school. Written permission from the parent or guardian requesting that the medication be given at school should also be included (see Exhibit 3-1).

- A locked cabinet should be provided for storage. If refrigeration is necessary, additional safety precautions may be required.

- Over-the-counter drugs should not be given unless they are in labeled dispensers with an accompanying written order from the physician and a note from the parent requesting the medication be given at school.

Rules for Medication Administration

- Wash hands thoroughly.

- Read the label *three times.* Read once when taking container from the storage area, read just before preparing to dispense, and read before returning medication to the shelf. Once medication is out of the container, do not leave it unattended. A liquid not used should never be poured back into the original container.

- Be sure you have the right student. Students who are profoundly handicapped often cannot tell you their name or even respond when their name is called. Designating one member of the staff to handle medications consistently is best.

- Give the medication, observe for any adverse reaction, and record that the medication was given on the medication record (see Exhibit 3-2).

- Immediately report any error in medication administration or any adverse reaction to the school administrator, parent, and physician. Knowledge of possible side effects of medications given at school should be obtained from the physician when the physician requests the medication be given at school.

Exhibit 3-1 Physician/Parent Request for Administration of Medicine or Special Procedure by School Personnel

Special health care procedures and medications may be prescribed for administration by school personnel as follows:

1. When such treatment cannot otherwise be accomplished

2. On receipt of this *completed* form along with prescription and/or special equipment items

Prescribed in-school medication/treatment may be administered by a non-health professional designate of the principal or school nurse.

1. Name of Pupil _____ Birth Date _____

2. Address _____ School _____

3. Condition for which prescribed treatment is required:

4. Specific medication or procedure: *

5. Dosage and method of administration/Instruction for procedure (include time schedule):

6. Precautions, unfavorable reactions:

7. Disposition of pupil following administration or procedure, if applicable, i.e., rest, home, hospital, doctor's office, return to class.

8. Date of Request _____ Date of Termination _____

9. _____/_____
    Physician's Name (printed)   *Signature*

_____/_____
    Physician's Address   *Telephone Number*

- -

(PARENT)

We (I), the undersigned, the parents/guardians of _____
                                                  (Student's Name)

request the above medication or procedure be administered to our (my) child.

_____/_____Telephone_____/_____
Name   *Relationship*   *Home*   *Business*

_____/_____Telephone_____/_____
Name   *Relationship*   *Home*   *Business*

* Please note which of the following statements is correct:
        Protocol attached_____
        Protocol provided by school is appropriate_____
        Protocol provided by the school is appropriate except for the following:

Exhibit 3-2 Medication or Special Procedure Record

STUDENT'S NAME_____GRADE _____

1. Medication_____Dosage _____Time _____

2. Medication_____Dosage _____Time _____

Special Instructions:_____

After giving medication(s) record time(s) administered and initials in the appropriate week of month/day and date of week space. All medications must be on prescription of physician. File this form in student's record, write summary on H-55.

SCHOOL NAME_____SCHOOL YEAR _____

Week	Dates M/F	Time	AUGUST					Week	Dates M/F	Time	SEPTEMBER					Week	Dates M/F	Time	OCTOBER				
			M	T	W	TH	F				M	T	W	TH	F				M	T	W	TH	F
1st								1st								1st							
2nd								2nd								2nd							
3rd								3rd								3rd							
4th								4th								4th							
5th								5th								5th							

Week	Dates M/F	Time	NOVEMBER					Week	Dates M/F	Time	DECEMBER					Week	Dates M/F	Time	JANUARY				
			M	T	W	TH	F				M	T	W	TH	F				M	T	W	TH	F
1st								1st								1st							
2nd								2nd								2nd							
3rd								3rd								3rd							
4th								4th								4th							
5th								5th								5th							

Week	Dates M/F	Time	FEBRUARY					Week	Dates M/F	Time	MARCH					Week	Dates M/F	Time	APRIL				
			M	T	W	TH	F				M	T	W	TH	F				M	T	W	TH	F
1st								1st								1st							
2nd								2nd								2nd							
3rd								3rd								3rd							
4th								4th								4th							
5th								5th								5th							

Week	Dates M/F	Time	MAY					Week	Dates M/F	Time	JUNE				
			M	T	W	TH	F				M	T	W	TH	F
1st								1st							
2nd															
3rd															
4th															
5th															

Disposition:
Prescription depleted_____
Medication discontinued_____
Medication returned to parents_____
Medication destroyed_____

COMMENTS: see attached sheet for additional comments._____

_____

_____

_____

Seizure Management

A comprehensive manual that addresses seizure disorders and includes a special section for teachers is the *Physician's Manual* prepared by the Dallas Epilepsy Association (1982). Epilepsy is a disorder of many causes. It is characterized by recurring seizures and is not a disease entity in itself. The seizures are a symptom of nervous system dysfunction or dysfunction of the body as a whole. A seizure is a spasm or convulsion which is brief and stereotyped, and results from abnormal electrical activity of the brain.

Many physicians will diagnose a *seizure disorder* and not use the word "epilepsy." If the *etiology* is unknown, there is no known cause of the seizures. Individuals may have seizures due to a variety of causes. From birth through adolescence, the most common causes of seizures are injury due to trauma or hypoxia (lack of oxygen), congenital malformation (abnormalities at birth), metabolic problems, genetic or inherited causes, disease processes, or infection.

Long-term treatment management of individuals with severe seizure disorders requires treatment of the seizures. Although not all seizures can be totally controlled, careful monitoring is often necessary particularly if a student enters into *status epilepticus,* a life-threatening medical emergency where an ongoing seizure does not stop. Depending on the individual seizure pattern, students who continue to have a seizure for more than 5 to 15 minutes should be transported to a facility where support for breathing and IV anticonvulsants may be used. Specific instructions from the student's physician and parents can assist the staff to know when such emergency instruction is necessary.

Anticonvulsant medications are prescribed for individuals with seizures. Many drugs are available. Physicians may select one or more drugs for the type of seizure exhibited. Physicians should notify the staff to be alert to abnormal reactions that may occur between the primary anticonvulsant and other anticonvulsant drugs, between anticonvulsants and other types of drugs, and the complications that may occur from anticonvulsant therapy. Even the time the drug stays active in the bloodstream will vary depending on whether it is used alone or in combination with other anticonvulsants.

When prescribing an anticonvulsant, a physician will look for *therapeutic* (helpful) effects and *side effects.* Documentation of medication administration and seizure episodes by school staff is a valuable tool that can be used by the physician for regulating medication. The student's family physician may refer the individual to a specialist for seizure control. A *neurologist,* a physician experienced in treating seizure disorders, may suggest that the seizure-disordered individual undergo an EEG (electroencephalogram) to help pinpoint the cause of the problem.

Some seizure medications are prescribed at low doses and then gradually increased; others are maintained at the initial dosage if results are positive. Appropriate dosage is monitored in two ways: (1) *clinically*, by observing the individual at home and at school for seizure activity and side effects; and (2) *chemically*, by measuring drug levels in the individual's blood via chemical analysis of blood samples. Parents are ideally given regular appointments to have their child's drug blood level evaluated. Occasionally, students may be hospitalized for a short time for the physician to regulate the anticonvulsants and attempt to decrease seizure activity.

Even though students with seizure disorders receive appropriate medical care and have been prescribed medications for seizures, seizure activity may increase. Infections, failure to take anticonvulsant medication, or the addition of other nonseizure medication to the medication regimen may exacerbate seizures. As the student grows and gains weight, dosages may need to be increased. Scheduled appointments should not be missed.

In general, the majority of students with seizure disorders maintain seizure control through daily medications. Seizures in students who are medically involved may be more difficult to control. Some of the most commonly used medications for seizure control are Clonopin, Depakene, Depakote, Dilantin, Mysoline, phenobarbitol, Tegretol, Tranxene, and Zarontin. Occasionally, students are placed on a ketogenic diet (containing large amounts of fats) for seizure control.

Side effects may occur from medications used to control seizures. Some may occur when a drug is first started and then stop when the body adjusts to the new medication. Side effects such as drowsiness, lethargy, confusion, irritability, agitation, and hyperactivity would be difficult to notice in a student who is profoundly handicapped. It may also be difficult to differentiate tremor or loss of usual muscle coordination in such a student. Sleep disturbance, nausea, stomach aches, and indigestion could be present but barely noticeable. Some side effects may occur after long-term use: gum overgrowth, anemia, hair loss, or increased body hair growth. Side effects may necessitate that dosages be adjusted or that medication be discontinued. If medications are well monitored, side effects should not impair the student's usual activities (see Table 3-1).

The following are suggestions for caring for a seizure-disordered student:

Table 3-1 Potential Side Effects from Various Medications

	Abdominal cramps	Constipation	Diarrhea	Dry mouth	Fatigue/tired	Gum hypertrophy (enlargement)	Hiccups	Headaches	Increase in body hair	Sore gums	Clumsiness, occasional	Nausea/vomiting	Drowsiness	Aggressive behavior	Anemia	Behavior deterioration	Bleeding or bruising	Clumsiness, frequent	Dizziness	Double or blurred vision	Edema (swelling)	Fever	Hair loss	High blood pressure	Hyperactivity	Irregular heartbeat	Jaundice	Joint pain	Low blood sugar	Sedation (extreme drowsiness)	Shortness of breath	Skin rash	Syncope (fainting)	Urination problems	Weight loss
	Minor Side Effects →																				**Major Side Effects** →														
Clonopin	X	X		X	X			X	X	X		X	X	X	X	X	X	X	X	X	X		X			X	X			X	X	X	X	X	X
Depakene	X	X	X	X	X			X				X	X	X		X	X	X	X	X			X		X		X	X		X		X	X	X	X
Depakote	X	X	X	X	X			X			X	X	X	X		X	X	X	X	X			X		X		X	X		X	X	X			X
Diamox	X			X							X	X		X	X	X	X	X	X	X		X	X				X			X	X	X	X	X	X
Dilantin		X				X		X	X	X		X	X		X	X	X	X	X	X		X					X	X	X	X		X	X		
Ketogenic diet	X	X		X		X		X			X	X	X	X	X	X	X	X	X	X	X	X					X	X	X	X					X
Mysoline	X				X			X			X	X	X	X	X	X	X	X	X	X					X		X	X	X	X		X	X		X
Phenobarbital (Mebaral)	X							X			X	X	X	X	X	X	X	X	X	X	X	X			X		X	X		X		X			
Peganone			X								X	X		X		X	X	X	X	X	X	X			X		X	X		X		X			
Serax	X				X			X			X	X	X	X	X	X	X	X	X	X	X	X			X		X		X	X		X	X		X
Tegretol	X	X	X	X	X			X			X	X	X	X	X	X	X	X	X	X	X	X		X		X	X			X		X	X	X	
Tranxene					X			X			X	X	X	X	X	X	X	X	X	X	X	X			X		X			X		X	X	X	
Zarontin	X							X			X	X	X	X	X	X	X	X	X	X		X			X		X	X		X		X	X	X	X

Source: Courtesy of Texas Scottish Rite Hospital, Dallas, Texas.

- Staff should have a physician's statement that includes type of seizure disorder and cause if known, medications required, request for school staff to give medication at school, and the medication's side effects. A dental statement should also be requested if teeth or gums may be affected by the medication.

- Staff should know the date of the next appointment and should encourage parents to keep appointments.

- Parental request for staff to give school medication at school should be obtained.

- A work sheet to log medications given and to describe any seizure activity should be provided. Staff should realize that although seizures can often be controlled, there is a possibility of life-long seizures. No one can be sure when the next seizure will occur.

- Staff should prepare for emergencies. *Define school policy regarding status epilepticus or seizures that cause injuries.* Communicate policy to staff.

- *Determine policy for active seizuring.* Staff should be informed that the student's head should be protected from hitting hard objects. Many students wear helmets during the school day. Nothing should be forced between the teeth. If secretions collect in the mouth, support the student and turn him or her so that the individual is supported but turned to the side to help clear the airway. Postical (after seizure) sleep is common. If the student does not breath after a seizure, start mouth-to-mouth resuscitation and activate the school emergency medical plan.

Physical Management Treatment Techniques

As stated previously, before providing intensive medical therapies, school officials must determine what policies or guidelines exist at the state level. If state education or health agencies have no policies, schools must develop their own. After determining who may train, who may provide therapy, and to whom the provision of services may be delegated, school staff members should be encouraged to visit health care facilities for information, and school administrators should consider hiring appropriate community health care professionals as consultants. The courts "have almost consistently upheld the necessity of the school district to provide a health care procedure when it is vital to assure an appropriate educational program" (Pathfinder and the School Nurse Organization, 1986, p. 2).

Physical management of students who require intensive medical therapies at school will necessitate that related service providers learn a set of skills that are impossible to teach through written materials alone. Each case that requires classroom-based medical interventions will be unique, and the provider must have directions from the managing health professional. Existing written procedures appropriate for the school setting can be adapted to the individual student. Many excellent protocols exist (e.g., those recommended by Pathfinder and the School Nurse Organization of Minnesota, 1986; California Department of Education, 1983). It is strongly recommended that written protocols be available if only to be used as a basis for a worksheet that may be developed for each student by the provider as the need arises.

It is imperative that the classroom health-related services provider completely unfamiliar with specialized procedures learn from an experienced parent or qualified health practitioner. If training is provided by a parent, it is still suggested that the supervising physician provide, or approve in writing, all steps of the procedure. It is preferable that the physician or his or her designee be present during the training to ensure accuracy and completeness. Proper guidance would include providing appropriate protocols, demonstrating techniques required, and providing an opportunity for the learner to perform the skills in a return demonstration. A written request for services at school signed by the physician and parent must be requested.

While learning new skills, it is natural for a learner to be concerned and afraid of the differences in appearance and care required to support medically involved students. These feelings are quite normal. The results will be rewarding as the student becomes more alert and comfortable. As Hammer (1986) suggested, although the school is not a treatment center, it provides special services so that students become more efficient, not only to survive, but to flourish. Providing health-related services in situations that otherwise might interfere with learning is a part of providing the opportunity for students to attend school.

Tube Feedings

The normal route for eating is the mouth, where food is chewed and mixed with saliva, through the *esophagus,* or swallowing tube, and into the stomach. After mixing with gastric juice in the stomach, the mixture

Figure 3-2 Nasogastric Tube. **A**, Tube securely taped to nose. (Never pull up on nose and tape to forehead.); **B**, Esophagus (swallowing tube); **C**, Stomach.

---

is moved to the *small intestine* for nutrient absorption and then on to the *large intestine,* where the bowel movement is formed.

Students who have abnormalities of the nerves that control the muscles allowing them to eat, or of the central nervous system, such as severe cerebral palsy, may have problems obtaining enough nutrients to stay healthy. An individual who exhibits extreme and continual gagging or coughing and ongoing difficulty in swallowing with associated failure to maintain appropriate weight *may* be a candidate for a feeding tube.

Feeding tubes may be placed through the nose or mouth into the stomach (usually temporary) or through the skin in the abdominal wall directly into the stomach (more permanent). Tubes inserted through the nose, and occasionally through the mouth, are called *nasogastric (NG) tubes* (see Figure 3-2). These tubes may be placed before each feeding and then removed, or may be left for longer periods. The reason for the tube placement and the material the tube is made of will determine how long the NG tube may remain in place without being changed (usually three days to one month).

Tubes placed through the skin in the abdominal wall go directly into the stomach. These tubes are usually placed for extended periods of time. However, they must be changed routinely (usually once a week to once a month) and may accidentally be pulled out (see Figure 3-3). However, a new button device made of silicon (AEI Button; Bard Interventional Products, 1987) has been designed to minimize the need for frequent

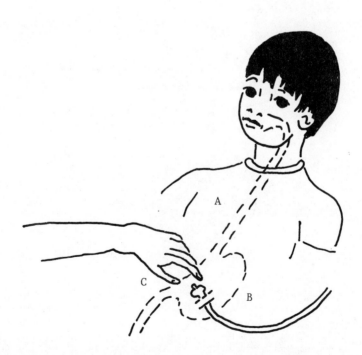

Figure 3-3 Gastrostomy Tube. **A**, Esophagus (swallowing tube); **B**, Stomach with opening through abdominal wall; **C**, Bulbous, open end of tube may be felt through abdominal wall.

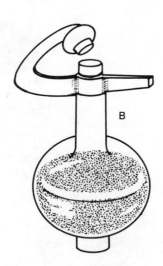

Figure 3-4 Gastrostomy Button™. **A,** Button device that has been inserted by the physician through the skin of the abdomen into the stomach. Safety plug is in place; **B,** Button device unplugged to allow a syringe or adaped tube to be inserted for feeding. Courtesy of Bard Interventional Products, Billerica, MA.

feeding tube replacements. A tube or syringe is attached for each feeding and then removed leaving only the "button" and the plug in place. The dome is distended by the physician for original placement and does not have a balloon device which may break or leak allowing the button to fall out (see Figure 3-4).

The physician must answer the following questions:

- Is it important that the NG or gastrostomy tube be replaced immediately if it comes out while the student is at school? If so, who should replace it?
- How long can it remain out before problems begin (gastrostomy openings may start to close in two hours)? How can feeding and medication be given if there is no route to the stomach?
- Are any liquids, solids, or medications allowed by mouth? If so, should oral feedings be encouraged?

Replacing an NG tube takes considerable skill after training and return demonstrations. Replacing *certain types* of gastrostomy tubes is relatively easy. The parent, a relative, a friend, a community health professional, or a qualified school nurse may be designated to replace the tube. Many teachers may desire to learn the skill.

If the decision is made to replace the tube at school, parents should provide supplies and equipment. The physician should provide or approve a protocol for tube insertion. Training should be comprehensive, and written requests and permission forms from the physician and parent should be obtained.

Routine tube changes and routine tube care should always be done at home. However, if a child is accepted for an extended day, such as from 7 AM to 6 PM, school staff will be required to provide more of the routine care than if the student arrives at 9 AM and leaves at 2:30 or 3:00 PM. School staff who are qualified and desire to learn tube replacement that may be required unexpectedly can learn the skill during a routine tube placement with the parent.

Students admitted to school with tubes in place usually require nutrients, and occasionally medications, through the tube. *In general,* the physician's protocol should include answers to the following:

- Why is the procedure needed during school hours?
- What type of formula is needed, how must it be stored, mixed, etc.? (Many parents bring premixed formula to school in a closed plastic baby bottle. The formula should be refrigerated when required and

warmed when necessary. Formula must be at room temperature for feeding.)

- How much extra fluid may be used to thin the formula or to follow the formula to clear the tube?
- What type of medication should be given, and is it to be given before feeding or at a different time? Is feeding by mouth also allowed? If so, how much and what kind of food or liquid may be given?
- In what position should the student be placed before feeding? (Usually *the head and chest* are elevated to 30 to 40 degrees. This helps keep the formula in the stomach to promote digestion.)
- How long should the elevated position be maintained? (Usually 30 minutes after feeding is adequate. The physician may also recommend the student be placed on his or her side.)
- How should one check to see that the tube remains in the right place? (An NG tube should be taped in a downward position on the nose. It should not be allowed to travel in or out of the nose. The entering end of a gastrostomy tube goes directly under the skin and into the stomach. Usually, if the tube is held in a taut position, the bulbous end, in the stomach, can be felt through the skin of the abdomen. The gastrostomy tube may be taped or otherwise secured so that it does not travel down the intestines.)
- Before feeding, how should one check to be sure the tube is actually in the stomach? (The physician may direct that a trained individual withdraw [with a syringe] some of the stomach contents or, if an NG tube is in place, listen with a stethoscope to the stomach as a small amount of air is inserted into the stomach through the tube.)

The supplies and equipment needed, depending on the type of tube, nutrients, and medication recommended, will usually include formula, syringe, adapter (if tubing and syringe do not fit), measuring and mixing utensils, and warm water to warm formula gently, and after formula is given, to clear the tubing. Other supplies that may be needed are a feeding bag with tubing, a clamp or rubber band, and a hook or IV pole on which to hang the formula bag. After the feeding, the end of the tube should be plugged or clamped. If a clamp or a plug is not provided, the end of the tube may be covered with clean gauze held in place with a rubber band and pinned to the shirt. *Do not push the secured end of a tube down into a diaper.*

Some students will require continuous feedings. A pump, electrically operated, can provide a continuous drip of formula throughout the day. It is preferable that parents supply a separate pump for the school. Ask the physician how long the student may go without the pump for travel and/or field trips or in the event the pump should fail to operate properly.

There are common problems associated with tube feeding, including skin irritation around the site of the tube; blocked tube; leaking around opening in the abdominal wall; and gastrointestinal distress such as loose bowel movements, nausea, cramps, and constipation. The protocol for tube feeding approved by the physician should address these problems and provide the information necessary to prevent and/or correct them.

All tube feeding equipment should be washed with a water and liquid soap solution, rinsed well, and allowed to dry thoroughly. All supplies should be placed on a clean tray covered with paper towels and covered with more paper towels. The supplies should then be stored in a closed cabinet.

Ostomy Care

An *ostomy* creates an opening to allow for the elimination of bodily wastes. The actual opening is called a *stoma*. A *colostomy* is an artificial opening created in the colon or large intestine; an *ileostomy* is an opening in the small intestine. An ostomy may be needed for conditions that occur at birth, for tumors that require removal of organs or parts of an organ, and for conditions that follow severe injury. Ostomies may be temporary or permanent.

The stoma is doughnut-shaped, shiny, wet, and dark pink. It is located on the skin of the abdomen. The location depends on what type of procedure was performed for the student's individual problem. A bag or pouch collects the wastes and may need to be emptied at school. There are many types of attachments and bags that hold the bag over the stoma. Many bags can be opened, emptied, and reclosed (see Figure 3-5).

Ostomy bags are attached to the skin with special protective adhesives. They will usually remain secure for one to seven days. Belts may or may not be used. Changing the entire device, removing the adhesive, and applying new adhesive should be done at home as should routine irrigation of the bowel.

Leakage may occur around the stoma during the school day. If this occurs, the pouch size may need to be changed by the parents. After surgery, the stoma shrinks, and the pouch size must be adjusted. If the attachment is too large or the adhesive comes loose, leakage will occur. If leakage does occur, the enzymes and acid in the digestive fluid will irritate the skin around the stoma. Wash the area with soap and water and dry it thoroughly to prevent damage to the skin. The physician may recommend a medicated skin barrier be applied around the area of the

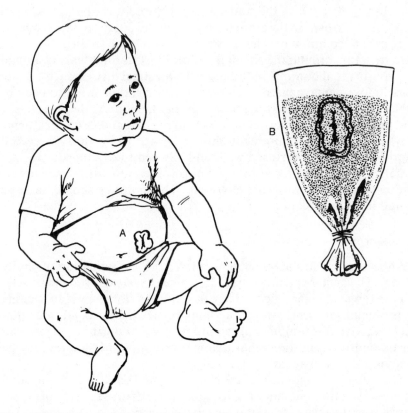

Figure 3-5 Colostomy. **A**, Stoma; **B**, Bag for collection of waste material.

stoma. The procedure for school staff to follow for ostomy care should be recommended by the student's physician.

Other Physical Management Concerns

Medically, correct *positioning* stimulates circulation and helps prevent pressure sores and *edema* (swelling due to fluid accumulation) in the extremities. Appropriate positioning may also facilitate good muscle tone and better breathing and lessen contractures. When students have tubes or other devices attached to or protruding from the body, be careful to position them so that they are not lying on the object, for pressure and injury to the skin may occur.

Decubitus ulcers (bed sores or pressure sores) may be caused by tissue or nerve injury due to the student's inability to move. Appropriate handling and positioning stimulate the circulation and help relieve pressure on body areas. Examine a new student or one who has been absent for an extended period of time for areas of tenderness or redness, especially over bony prominences such as heels, knees, lower back, and buttocks. Document by size and location any areas that appear abnormal, and then communicate concern to the parents and physician immediately. *Follow physician's written orders* regarding positioning and use of powders, creams, or supportive devices. The use of an *egg-crate* mattress 96-5 instead of a mat for floor positioning can be beneficial. This is a foam rubber mattress with elevated and depressed sections resembling an egg carton. All students may be susceptible to pressure sores. Sores may be caused by continual pressure from lying or sitting in one place too long, from dampness due to perspiration or urine and stool, or from friction under braces.

Basic care procedures, such as *vital sign measurements* (temperature, respiration, and blood pressure [BP]), are being done by more and more individuals in their homes. Equipment has improved. Taking a temperature by digital readout or BP by an automatic device may require no more training than reading the package insert. Resource materials are available at medical and nursing school libraries, equipment supply firms, home health care agencies, and medical book stores. Textbooks used for training nurses aides and home health care workers are excellent references.

Respiratory Therapies

Certain chronic health problems may require respiratory therapy programs at school. Kacmarek and Thompson (1986) stated that more infants born with respiratory problems are surviving. The decrease in deaths over the last century has been associated with an increase in the number of infants surviving with respiratory complications. Children saved by the advances of technology may also be dependent on technology and related equipment for extended periods of time (Raulin & Shannon, 1986).

During normal breathing, the lungs expand, and air is drawn in through the mouth and nose, down through the *trachea* (windpipe) and *bronchi* (tubes in the lungs that carry air in and out), and into the *alveoli* (air sacs). At this point, oxygen is in contact with blood *capillaries* (blood vessels surrounding the air sacs), and oxygen is carried to all parts of the body. Another set of blood vessels carries carbon dioxide (a waste gas) back from all parts of the body to the alveoli so that exhalation removes the waste gas from the body. When disease processes interfere with these functions, the individual will need assistance to survive.

Mucus is a normal byproduct of respiration. It is the fluid produced in the lining of the lungs. When normal, it is clear and slippery. Many times during the day the average person will cough slightly to clear the throat and swallow the small amount of mucus produced. Matter produced by the respiratory tract that is yellow or green may be pus and will probably indicate an infection. Disease processes may affect mucous production and provide opportunities for respiratory infections. Problems such as cerebral palsy, muscular dystrophy, and pulmonary disorders may prevent certain individuals from swallowing or coughing effectively. At times, chronic or acute conditions produce thick, sticky secretions that are difficult to remove from the airway. A physician may prescribe postural drainage, percussion, and possibly suctioning to remove secretions that cannot be coughed up.

Postural drainage is a therapy that encourages the secretions in the lungs to move into the large airways, by gravity, where they can be coughed out. The physician may recommend the student be positioned for drainage two to four times daily. *Percussion* is done by clapping the cupped hands with moderate pressure over the lungs, which creates a hollow sound and facilitates removal of secretions. The physician will determine which position the student should assume during percussion. *Suctioning* may be prescribed. As secretions build up in the airways, they pool and cause gurgling sounds and difficult breathing. Suctioning through the nose or mouth may be accomplished by a bulb syringe, a mucous trap, or a suction machine. If a student is identified who seems to have problems clearing secretions, parents should be asked if the physician discussed suctioning.

Most parents are familiar with a *bulb syringe*. Babies usually come home from the hospital with one of their own. Bulb syringes should not be shared at school. A *mucous trap* is more effective than a bulb syringe for tiny individuals or for suctioning tracheostomies. The provider supplies the suction power by sucking on the mouthpiece, and the mucus is trapped in the container (see Figure 3-6).

Ideally, suction machines should not be shared because of the danger of contamination from one child to another. Suctioning may also be prescribed after postural drainage and/or percussion. Suctioning will help the student get rid of loosened secretions.

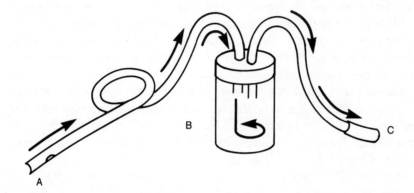

Figure 3-6 A, Suction tip of catheter, B, Trap to collect mucus; C, Mouth piece for provider to provide suction.

Each of these therapies promotes effective respiration for individuals who are unable to clear their own secretions. Each therapy must be prescribed by a physician. Training should be given by a respiratory therapist or other qualified health professional.

When caring for students with respiratory problems, physicians will usually mention the amount of water and humidity the student needs. Drinking water and clear liquids are usually encouraged. In a process called *humidification* (providing dampness in the air), use of a vaporizer or mist-producing equipment may be prescribed. Cigarette smoking near the student should be forbidden. Smoke coats the breathing tubes and limits the normal action of mucus, which leads to lung congestion, infection, and shortness of breath.

Respiratory Health Problems

Several health problems involving the respiratory tract affect school-age children. One of these is *asthma,* a chronic disease in which air passages become temporarily narrowed or blocked. An asthma attack impedes breathing, interrupts activities, or necessitates a procedure for the student to breathe normally again (Plout, 1983). Attacks may be triggered by colds, pulmonary infections, and allergins, such as dust, animal dander, foods, medications, cigarette smoke, powders, etc. School staff need to provide freedom from allergins as much as possible, medication administration and therapies as prescribed by a physician, appropriate fluid intake, and prompt identification of pending emergency situations. Medications are given to help the bronchial tubes relax. Medication sent directly to the lungs by special equipment will help liquify or thin mucus so it can be coughed up.

Students with *cystic fibrosis* need to cough often to force out mucus. Medication and respiratory therapy, including postural drainage and percussion, will help mucus drain. In *aerosol therapy,* the child breathes into a special machine. Because cystic fibrosis is an inherited disease, other students will not "catch" the lung problem from the cough.

Muscular dystrophy is an abnormality of muscles associated with dysfunction and ultimate deterioration. When weakening of the musculature occurs, the student may not be able to cough and swallow appropriately, and respiratory therapy will be required.

Many premature infants are born with *bronchopulmonary dysplasia.* Abnormal tissue development in the lungs may cause breathing problems that necessitate respiratory therapy. Individuals may also be born with or acquire certain conditions that cause a problem with the delivery of air through the mouth and nose into the lungs. Congenital (birth) defects, including *tracheoesophageal fistula* (connection of the feeding and breathing tubes) and narrow or small airway problems will directly affect air flow. Tumors in the respiratory tract, a crushing injury to the airway tract, or problems with the *neurologic* (brain-nerve) center may cause breathing problems. Some types of injuries may make normal air

Figure 3-7 A, Stoma; **B,** Bifurcation of the bronchus (breathing tube); **C,** Tracheostomy tube tied securely in place; **D,** Path of suction catheter tip.

exchange impossible. Certain problems may indicate a tracheostomy be performed.

Tracheostomies

A *tracheostomy* is a minor surgical procedure used to create an opening in the lower neck. The hole is called a *stoma*. The opening is usually kept open by a small metal or plastic tube called a *tracheostomy tube* or *trach tube* (see Figure 3-7). A trach tube will help ensure than an individual can continue to breathe. However, some conditions are so complex that the individual requires *ventilatory assistance.* In this case, assistance to breathe in and out is provided by a machine that produces measured amounts of air or pure oxygen at a prescribed rate.

Tracheostomies may be placed permanently because the reason the trach was required will probably never change, or it may be placed on a temporary basis to help an individual while he or she recovers from an acute health problem. New trachs will cause increased mucous production, which will usually decrease as the body adjusts to the change. Students with new tracheostomies (less than three months old) will possibly require more suctioning and supervision than students who have had trachs in place for a longer time.

Several changes occur in the respiratory tract when a trach tube is placed including weakening of the voice, loss of filtering action by the nose (foreign material such as soap, water, powder, aerosols, and food can be accidentally inhaled directly into the trachea through the tracheostomy), loss of normal humidification and warming by nasal passages, and increased loss of body water.

Tracheostomies provide an opening for air, medications (including oxygen), and respiratory treatment. They also provide an opening for used air and mucous accumulations to exit.

The best way to remove extra mucous accumulations is to cough them up and out through the trach. A student who can cough deeply and well may only need to have the mucus wiped from the outside of the tube with suctioning provided as needed. Students who cannot cough, or cough weakly, will need to be suctioned regularly. Suctioning can be quickly learned; however, *life-threatening conditions* may occur while caring for a student with a tracheostomy. Learning only the technique of suctioning is not enough. Special considerations for the student with a tracheostomy include:

- staff preparation in CPR and knowledge of community medical emergency services

- an understanding of hygiene (what is dirty and what is clean)
- availability of supplies and suctioning equipment
- routine for cleaning equipment and replacing supplies
- emergency kit with duplicate supplies near the student at all times
- ability to look for changes in general health status and condition of the tracheostomy
- provision of an environment as free as possible from respiratory irritants and programming that is not harmful to the student's compromised airways

Many types of trach tubes are used. Plastic tubes are usually one piece when they are in place, although a guide or obturator is placed in the tube *only* for insertion (see Figure 3-8). Metal trach tubes have an extra piece, a smaller tube that fits inside. The plastic trach tube must be changed at least once a week and sometimes once or twice a day. Metal trach tubes can stay in place longer because there is an inner cannula (tube) that can be taken out, cleaned, and replaced. Tubes need cleaning because mucous secretions build up in them. With enough fluid intake and humidity in the air, the mucus tends to become thin and watery and is

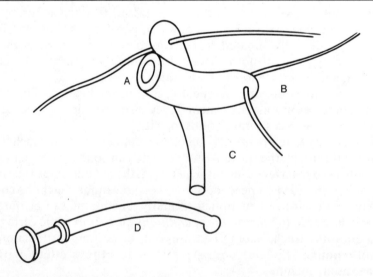

Figure 3-8 One Piece Tracheostomy Tube. **A,** Opening for air exchange and suctioning; **B,** Ties to secure trach tube; **C,** Tube that extends down into trachea. **D,** Obturator used *only* when first inserting new trach tube (must be removed immediately or air will not pass through trach tube). Courtesy of Shiley Incorporated, Irvine, CA.

usually easy to remove. If the air is dry, the mucus becomes thick and may form a plug of crusty material. If mucous plugs occur in a trach tube, they are difficult to remove. *Normal saline* ("body correct" sterile salt water) may be needed in the opening before the student is suctioned. Occasionally, the extra fluids and suctioning may not loosen the secretions, and respiration will become difficult. If this occurs, the trach tube must be removed and replaced with a clean tube immediately. This is the rationale for learning to do an emergency tracheostomy replacement for students *who have a stoma (opening) that will close unless the trach tube is replaced immediately.*

Routine tracheostomy replacement is the parents' responsibility. The schedule for changing the tube will depend on the health problem and type and size of the trach tube being used. The *ties* that hold the trach in place should be changed by the parents at least once a day. Parents must also provide daily skin care, which will include cleaning around the trach with a solution of mild liquid soap and water or a weakened hydrogen peroxide solution.

In preparation for leaving the home, a travel kit must be prepared to go on the school bus and stay with the student during the day. It should include the following supplies:

- mucous trap (or a battery operated portable suction machine)
- bulb syringe
- extra trach tube with ties in place
- scissors (to cut ties of tube that becomes plugged)
- box of tissues or gauze
- normal saline (individual disposable plastic ampules are available for travel)

Educational planning for students with trachs will differ in some ways from other students who are profoundly handicapped. Students with tracheostomies *cannot go swimming* and *cannot play in sand boxes* or *boxes filled with very small styrofoam pellets.* Clothing, toys, and blankets should not be fuzzy. Collars should not be tight around the neck and the tracheostomy. A loosely worn handkerchief or cotton scarf will conceal and protect a tracheostomy opening during the day. When the student arrives for classes, check general health, condition or respiration, trach site, and ties.

The trach site should be observed frequently to ensure it is functioning appropriately. A number of cautions are in order:

- Well-tied *trach ties* should be tight but allow the provider to slip in the little finger between neck and ties. The knot should be securely tied at the *side* of the neck.
- If *secretions* have an appearance that is different, such as very thick, odorous, yellow, green, or bloody, parents should be advised to seek medical advice.
- *Reddened skin* around the site or *bleeding* from the site necessitates a referral to a physician.

All students who are profoundly handicapped require appropriate positioning when eating and drinking. Correct positioning before and after meals for students with tracheostomies will help decrease *aspiration* (the sucking into the airway of fluids such as vomitus). The student should be held upright with a cotton, not plastic, bib covering the trach opening. The opening must be protected from small portions of food or drops of liquid that could go into the trach. With the student upright, feeding should be accomplished slowly with small portions. The head should be kept upright or tipped slightly forward to provide more room in the esophagus. After the meal, the student should be supported on his or her back side on a wedge for at least 30 minutes to facilitate emptying of the stomach. The student's physician should be asked what to do if vomiting during or after feeding occurs. It is usually recommended that you turn the child to the side and suction out the tracheostomy and the mouth after vomiting stops.

Individuals who do not have tracheostomies pass air from the lungs up the trachea to the *larynx,* or voice box, to produce sound. When a trach has been performed, air is diverted out the trach opening and sounds cannot be produced in the usual way. However, *with parents' and physician's approval,* and if the developmental age is appropriate, some students with tracheostomies may be encouraged to attempt vocalizations. A clean finger momentarily placed over the trach opening can encourage the student to make a few sounds. The parents should be asked if the physician has discussed this possibility with them for their child. Written permission must be obtained from the primary caregivers and the supervising physician before attempting this procedure. Consultation with a speech clinician is also recommended.

Suctioning

Indications that the student is having respiratory difficulty and that suctioning is needed include rapid labored breathing; gurgling noises; excessive coughing; bluish gray skin and fingernails that look dark;

anxiety, restlessness, or a frightened look; flared nostrils; and/or skin "pulling in" around the ribs or the trach. Suctioning will usually be required four to six times in a 24-hour period. During respiratory infection or after medical procedures, the need for suctioning may be increased. However, *too frequent* suctioning may be harmful. If suctioning seems to be required more often than usual, contact the parent and the primary care physician.

Routine suctioning can be performed using sterile gloves or with very clean hands. The student's physician makes this decision. Good hand-washing is required before either technique. For either technique, *the suction tip and solution (water or normal saline) must be sterile and used only for one suctioning episode.*

Equipment for suctioning may be rented or purchased new or used. Suction machines come in many styles. They may plug in with backup battery packs, plug in only, or operate by battery alone. Medical and respiratory therapy equipment supply firms are sources. Although local school districts are not required to purchase equipment for students, administrators may choose to purchase equipment as part of the district's "special needs" equipment. While transporting students or on extended day trips, a battery-operated suction machine or mucous trap is required. The plastic or rubber catheter tips that attach to the suction machine tubing may be used during only one suctioning episode (one to three passes into the trach opening). However, the suction machine tubing, which is rinsed after each episode, may be used for an extended period. Plastic collection jars may also be used for extended periods when cleaned appropriately (see Figure 3-9). Students who require sterile suctioning with sterile gloves will need special disposable packs that include sterile supplies such as gloves, a suction catheter tip, and a disposable container used to hold the rinsing solution. The supplies may be used for only one suctioning episode (two or three passes).

A protocol for suctioning without sterile gloves would include attention to the following procedures:

- Wash hands.
- Collect supplies.
- Gently restrain student if necessary. The presence of two adults will facilitate the activation of the school emergency procedure if required.
- Turn on suction machine.
- Fill sterile container with at least one-half cup of sterile solution recommended by the physician (usually normal saline).

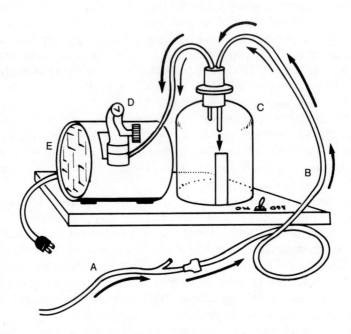

Figure 3-9 Electric Suction Machine. **A,** Suction catheter tip, which must be changed after each suctioning episode; **B,** Tubing, which may be rinsed after each use and used again until the end of the day when it should be washed and disinfected; **C,** Collection bottle, must be washed and disinfected at the end of the day; **D,** Regulator must be set as physician recommends to adjust amount of suction produced; **E,** Engine, which produces vacuum to provide suction.

- Connect suction catheter to suction machine tubing. *Do not touch the tip.*
- Lubricate suction catheter by dipping it into the solution. *Test suction* by placing thumb over the opening in the suction catheter (or adapter if red rubber catheter is used) to engage the suction from the machine to the catheter tip.
- *Remove thumb,* and *without suction,* pass suction catheter into trach opening following the curve of the trach tube. Usually the catheter is passed gently until resistance is felt; then the tip is withdrawn slightly.
- Place thumb over the opening, creating a suction, and remove suction tip *in a back and forth twirling motion or while twirling the*

catheter back and forth between the thumb and forefinger. Do not move the catheter up and down (see Figure 3-10).

- Suction for only five seconds at a time.
- Repeat suctioning with the same catheter tip after allowing the student to catch his or her breath.
- Record procedure. Note time, results, and name of provider. If problems arise and the parent or physician is notified, record that information.

When performed correctly, suctioning is usually a simple procedure. The student is relieved, and the provider can be pleased that the student has been helped. However, certain conditions may occur that will necessitate emergency procedures. For example, a "plugged" trach will not

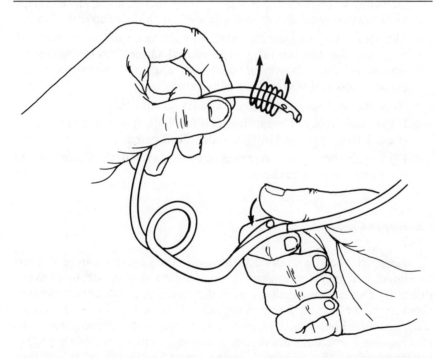

Figure 3-10 Suction Catheter Tip. **A,** Port hole or opening, which must be closed for suction to activate after the suction machine is turned on. Do not activate suction while inserting the tip; wait until tip is being withdrawn. **B,** Suction catheter tip. While suctioning and withdrawing the tip, twirl back and forth between the fingers. Never move up and down.

allow a catheter to pass, even after instilling normal saline and repeated attempts at suctioning. Depending on the type of tracheostomy tube, one will probably need to remove the plugged tube and replace it with the spare in the emergency pack.

Attempting emergency placement of a trach tube can be a terrifying experience if the provider has not previously participated in this procedure. An excellent way to gain this experience is to participate in the routine tracheostomy change provided daily or weekly by the parent. The parent can be asked to perform the procedure at school for school staff to observe. Training with a written protocol and parents' and physician's permission can then occur in a nonthreatening atmosphere.

In general, a protocol for *emergency tracheostomy replacement* will include the following information:

- Always have a clean trach tube with ties in place close at hand, including when the student is being transported, going on field trips or to the play yard. Position the student with the head tilted back.
- The clean tube will usually have a guide or obturator in place. If possible, moisten the tube with normal saline. Insert the tracheostomy tube in a *downward position.* If you insert the tube with the guide in place, it *must be removed immediately.*
- Hold the tube securely in place and replace the ties.
- If the student is not breathing, call for help, start rescue breathing (mouth to stoma), and initiate CPR if indicated.
- During any emergency, one person must stay with the student while someone else goes for help.

Emergency Care

Emergencies can be grouped according to the time that can be allowed to elapse before intervention is required to save a life or prevent disability (American Academy of Pediatrics, 1981). Medical emergencies may occur in the school, on the school bus or van, on field trips, or during other school-related activities. *Extreme life-threatening emergencies* require immediate intervention. Some examples include asphyxia (obstruction of the airway), cardiac arrest (cessation of heartbeat), drowning, internal poisoning, and neck or back injury with the possibility of spinal cord injury while being transported. *No practical plan can assure that health professionals can arrive within the critical minutes in which definitive action is required.* Therefore, school personnel should be able to provide first aid for extreme emergencies and should have training and competence in CPR. A CPR course will include instructions for removing foreign bodies from the airway, and mouth-to-mouth or mouth-to-stoma (for a tracheostomy patient) resuscitation.

During an emergency situation, do not waste time calling the school nurse, physician, or next of kin. After the victim is en route to a medical care facility by emergency transportation and the medical care facility has been alerted regarding the nature of the injury or illness, other inter- ested parties should be called.

Many emergencies may be out of the province of on-campus first aid management. Without special supplies and equipment, neither a physi- cian nor a nurse could provide appropriate care during certain situa- tions. For cases such as severe asthma, prolonged seizures (five to fifteen minutes), unconscious states of more than short duration, drug overdose or reactions, or teeth that have been accidentally and forcefully removed, the victim should be transported to a treatment facility immediately. School staff *who have been alerted to the possibility of such emergencies occurring* and who have emergency numbers available will be able to act quickly and confidently.

Other emergencies will require medical management, available from information that may be received by telephone. When there is a *question* of a fracture (except spine), burns, moderate reactions to drugs, fever, or other injuries, there is time to telephone the managing health profes- sional for advice. If the situation worsens, call for an emergency vehicle or initiate lifesaving measures.

School staff who work with students with medical conditions such as diabetes, epilepsy, and asthma should be alerted to specific problems that may occur before an emergency occurs. All staff should be trained to anticipate emergencies. Emergency numbers should be posted in full sight, and telephones must be readily available. All emergency arrange- ments must be reviewed and updated annually.

Needs of Staff

Staff protection is an important consideration for any school program. For example, school personnel are often in danger of musculoskeletal injuries due to the need for lifting and transferring students to and from wheelchairs and from place to place in the school. Staff should be instructed how to transfer students with the least danger to themselves. The use of mechanical lifts or extra personnel should be provided when needed. Bus drivers and bus monitors who desire to work during the school day can provide such assistance. Instruction and demonstration of proper transfer techniques and the proper use of lift equipment should be provided by physical or occupational therapists for new personnel, and on an annual basis for all employees.

Teachers and other school personnel should feel comfortable in their roles as education and related service providers. They should thoroughly understand local and state guidelines regarding training, provision of services, and delegation of various procedures. Staff should be encouraged to follow written procedures exactly for the comfort and safety of the student and for self-protection. The American Academy of Pediatrics (1981) recommended that "school districts assuming responsibility for giving medications during school hours should provide liability coverage for the staff" (p. 216). Most professionals feel that similar liability protection is warranted when staff are required to provide specialized procedures at school.

Training will help every staff member feel and accept the responsibility for protecting and caring for students who are profoundly handicapped and medically involved. Before providing training, however, determine what local or state policies exist regarding who is qualified to teach. "Qualified" for medically related personnel may mean only an individual with specialized training for certain procedures.

Administrators should determine basic requirements for all staff. Training in hygiene procedures, basic first aid, CPR, and how to access community medical services should be provided before employees are placed in a classroom with students who are medically involved. Other training to be considered would include information relating to specific medical conditions, disaster planning, therapy procedures, operation of medical equipment, and legal and liability issues.

Ideally, training for school staff should be provided by individuals currently providing therapies to individuals with problems similar to those of the students who require care. Trainers may be obtained through hospitals, public health agencies, and visiting nurse associations. Private health and therapy professionals, known to the education and medical community, are also available as consultants. Trainers can be asked to provide protocols that can later be adopted for individual students with the supervising physician's permission.

Training may be provided for staff through career and continuing education programs before the school year begins, on an annual basis, or episodically throughout the school year. New employees should have opportunities to obtain training on an as-needed basis. Individuals should keep records of training received. Instructors should observe students for performance accuracy during the school year.

Some training will be needed as specific special needs students present themselves for admission (e.g., using apnea monitors and performing catheterizations; Lehr, 1987). *Preneed training* or at least *exposure* to such techniques may help *lessen apprehension* and even identify staff who have previously provided these services to relatives or friends and, therefore, will help other school personnel feel comfortable when actually providing these services. In large school districts, preneed training will help administrators identify personnel with prior experience in providing medical interventions. This may necessitate changes in staffing assignments, as administrators should be responsible for serving students with the most capable and willing related service providers available.

CONCLUSION

Students who are profoundly handicapped and medically involved require an integrated service delivery model to have their needs met in school. Preneed planning by parents and professionals from the school and community should ensure that written protocols, delegation of duties, and emergency management are provided to facilitate placement of special needs students into public schools.

Sailor and Guess (1983) recommended that the classroom teacher become the program *facilitator* with the responsibility of coordinating and integrating the provision of service from various professionals. Ideally, in a transdisciplinary approach, all professionals provide services to the student. Regardless of which model of delivery is chosen, however, each person must commit to working as a member of the team and supplying input into the educational and medical needs of each and every student.

REFERENCES

American Academy of Pediatrics (1981). *School health: A guide for health professionals.* Evanston, IL: Author.

Anderson, R.D., Bale, J.F., Blackburn, J.A., & Murph, J.R. (1985). *Infections in children: A sourcebook for child care providers.* Rockville, MD: Aspen.

Bard Interventional Products (1987). *Care of a percutaneous endoscopic gastrostomy (P.E.G.) and the Button replacement gastrostomy.* Billerica, MA: C.R. Bard, Inc.

Bryan, E. (1979). Administrative concerns and school's relationship with private practicing physicians. *Journal of School Health, 49*(3), 157-163.

Bryan, E., Warden, M.G., Berg, B., & Hauck, G.R. (1978). Medical considerations for multiple-handicapped children in the public schools. *Journal of School Health, 48*(2), 84-85.

California Department of Education (1983). *Guidelines and procedures for meeting the specialized physical health care needs of students* (rev. ed.). Sacramento, CA: Author.

Dallas Epilepsy Association (1982). *Physician's manual: Epilepsy.* Dallas: Author.

Gray, C.C., & McDonald, P. (1980). Medical assessment of the child with a handicap. *Journal of School Health, 50*(5), 250-251.

Hammer, E.K. (1986). *Staff development for teachers of staff intensive classrooms.* Dallas: Dallas Independent School District. Unpublished manuscript.

Health Advisory Committee (1986). *Issue paper on medically intensive students.* Dallas: Texas Council of Urban School Districts, Dallas Independent School District.

Kacmarek, R.M., & Thompson, J.E. (1986). Respiratory care of the ventilator assisted infant in the home. *Respiratory Care, 31*(7), 605-614.

Lehr, D. (1987). *Considerations in providing education to students with fragile medical conditions.* Cedar Rapids, IA: State Conference On Innovative Practices in Special Education.

Martin, E.W., & Richmond, J.B. (1980). A historical perspective. *Journal of School Health, 50*(5), 244-245.

Mulligan, M. (1984). *Recommendations for teachers of staff intensive classrooms for medically fragile students.* Dallas: Dallas Independent School District. Unpublished manuscript.

Pathfinder and the School Nurse Organization (1986). *Managing the student with a chronic health condition: A practical guide for school personnel.* St. Paul: Author.

Plout, T.F. (1983). *Children with asthma.* Amherst, MA: Pedipress.

Raulin, A.M., & Shannon, K.A. (1986). PNPs: Case managers for technology dependent children. *Pediatric Nursing, 12*(5), 338-340.

Sailor, W., & Guess, D. (1983). *Severely handicapped students: An instructional design.* Boston: Houghton Mifflin.

Smego, R.A., & Halsey, N.A. (1987). The case for routine hepatitis B immunization in infancy for populations at increased risk. *Pediatric Infectious Disease Journal, 6*(1), 11-19.

Vlasak, J.W. (1980). Mainstreaming handicapped children: The underlying legal concept. *Journal of School Health, 50*(5), 285-287.

Wood, S.P., Walker, D.K., & Gardner, J. (1986). School health practices for children with complex medical needs. *Journal of School Health, 56*(6), 215-217.

Part III

Assessment Concerns

Chapter 4

Assessment Policies and Procedures

Ronald L. Taylor

PROBLEM

Timothy is a twelve-year-old boy who has been classified as profoundly handicapped as a result of "congenital encephalopathy." He is nonverbal, nonambulatory, and has a very restricted range of motion. You are responsible for an evaluation to determine Timothy's abilities and disabilities and to establish his educational objectives. Where do you begin? What techniques do you employ? What instruments should you use? To what extent can you adapt tests or the testing environment and still consider the results valid and reliable? These questions and many more are usually raised when assessment of individuals with severe or profound handicaps is discussed.

PAST PRACTICES

The assessment of individuals with severe or profound handicaps requires the participation of a number of professionals. Usually included on the evaluation team are a physician, physical therapist, speech therapist, social worker, psychologist, and teacher. Other specialists might also be involved.

The physician is often the first person to identify the individual with severe or profound handicaps. This is accomplished through a medical diagnosis using neurologic, biochemical, or other appropriate procedures and a comprehensive medical history. The physician might also initially administer vision and hearing tests although further testing is frequently required. The physical therapist usually performs an in-depth analysis of the child's motor skills. This information can aid in the development of programs for establishing appropriate positioning and therapy, and designing necessary adaptive equipment. The speech/communication therapist evaluates prelanguage, language, prespeech, and speech areas. Results from this evaluation could be used to develop a speech or language-based communication therapy program or to help initiate a nonverbal communication system. The social worker might evaluate the home situation in areas outside the realm of the educational setting. The psychologist is primarily responsible for meeting eligibility requirements, and the teacher is primarily responsible for developing and monitoring educational programs. In an ideal situation, the psychologist and teacher will work together, integrating their information with that from other team members.

Wolery and Dyk (1984) identified several assessment approaches that involve the participation of a variety of professionals. In the *multidisciplinary* approach, the roles of the team members are clearly established, but since communication among members is limited, efforts may be duplicated. In the *interdisciplinary* approach, there is clear role definition and more communication among team members. The *transdisciplinary* approach offers even more communication, and reports and other information are typically released to other team members. The last approach noted by Wolery and Dyk is *arena assessment* in which there are participants and active spectators. One person is usually responsible for the assessment, and the other team members observe, take notes, and make suggestions. Whichever approach is used, the importance of team cooperation and communication cannot be minimized.

The Effects of Legislation

The assessment of individuals with severe or profound handicaps did not receive serious attention until the mid 1970s. If for no other reason, this attention was due to the fact that individuals with more serious handicaps finally received their opportunity to receive an *educational* rather than a *custodial* program. Previously, their assessment was not considered important because, for the most part, they were not in appropriate educational programs that required assessment.

The passage of the Education for All Handicapped Children Act (P.L. 94-142) brought added attention to the assessment and subsequent education of such individuals. There are six principles mentioned in P.L. 94-142 that elaborate on the basic premise of the right to a free and appropriate education for all children with handicaps. One of them, the nondiscriminatory evaluation section, contains six parts that specifically address the issue of assessment:

1. Tests and other evaluation materials (a) are provided and administered in the child's native language or other dominant mode of communication, unless it is clearly not feasible to do so; (b) have been validated for the specific purpose for which they are used; and (c) are administered by trained personnel in conformance with the instructions provided by the producer.

2. Tests and other evaluation materials include those that are tailored to assess specific areas of educational need and not merely those that are designed to provide a single general IQ.

3. Tests are selected and administered so as best to ensure that when a test is administered to a child with impaired sensory, manual, or speaking skills, the test accurately reflects the child's aptitude or achievement level or whatever other factors the test purports to measure, rather than reflecting the child's impaired sensory, manual, or speaking skills (except where those skills are the factors that the test purports to measure).

4. No single procedure is used as the sole criterion for determining an appropriate educational program for a child.

5. The evaluation is made by a multidisciplinary team or group of persons, including at least one teacher or other specialist with knowledge in the area of the suspected disability.

6. The child is assessed in all areas related to the suspected disability, including, where appropriate, health, vision, hearing, social and emotional status, general intelligence, academic performance, communication status, and motor abilities (*Federal Register*, pp. 42496-97).

Before the passage of P.L. 94-142, the few attempts to assess students with severe or profound handicaps were usually limited to informal (and usually nonsystematic) observation, or to the modification and administration of infant intelligence and developmental scales. Theoretically, the latter procedure was followed because the "functioning level" of these students is similar to that of younger children. Tests such as the Bayley Scales of Infant Development (Bayley, 1969) and the Cattell Infant Intelligence Test (Cattell, 1950) were used. Unfortunately, this practice violated basic assessment principles. Most notably, the tests were usually administered to a population outside of the age range for which the test was intended. Thus the scores were rendered useless. At best, a rough developmental level could be determined. In addition, most infant scales consist of items in a wide variety of areas such as sensorimotor development, fine motor skills, and beginning language skills. The developmental level yielded depends on the number of items passed in all of the *combined areas.* Because of the relatively high incidence of sensory and motor problems of students with severe, and in particular, with profound handicaps, this approach is inconsistent with the principles stated in P.L. 94-142. More specifically, this practice violated the mandate of P.L. 94-142 that requires that "the test accurately reflects the child's aptitude or achievement level or whatever other factors the test purports to measure, rather than reflecting the child's impaired sensory, manual, or speaking skills."

Another approach was the use of other types of tests designed for "normal" children but that had items appropriate for individuals with severe or profound handicaps. These included adaptive behavior scales, behavior checklists, and developmental scales. A number of these instruments are discussed in the next chapter. Other attempts at assessment included the adaptation of test items of existing instruments, the use of response-fair tests, and the use of tests designed for and standardized on individuals with handicaps (Salvia & Ysseldyke, 1985).

At best, the assessment of this population is difficult, frustrating, and often a seemingly impossible task. The fact that students with severe or profound impairments comprise a very heterogeneous group makes the task even harder (Simeonsson, Huntington, & Parse, 1980). The purpose of this chapter, however, is not simply to discuss the difficulties of assessing this population. Rather, the intent is to present an assessment model for special education and how it must be modified when assessing students with severe or profound handicaps.

SUGGESTED METHODS

An Assessment Model for Special Education

Assessment refers to the gathering of relevant information that will improve educational decision making. As such, it is extremely important that the *purpose* of the assessment is clearly identified so that appropriate *techniques* or *procedures* can be used: different purposes for assessment will dictate that different procedures, techniques, or instruments be used.

Among the many reasons prospective special education students are assessed include screening for present or potential problems, meeting eligibility requirements for receiving special education services, determining the appropriate individualized education program (including goals and objectives), and evaluating student progress in the educational program.

Assessment for *screening* purposes is conducted for several possible reasons. Taylor (1984) noted that screening might be used to identify individuals (1) who are in need of further evaluation, (2) who might develop problems, and (3) who require special education or additional services. Assessment for *eligibility* involves the administration of tests to document an educational need, and to help in decisions regarding the most appropriate label, if any, to assign to the student. The information can also be used to help determine the best educational placement for the student. Determination of the *individualized education program* (IEP) involves, among other things, the careful identification of the student's educational goals and objectives. This part of the assessment process is critical for the teacher. Also important are the methods for *evaluating* the educational goals and objectives.

With most special education students, assessment involves the regular education teacher, special education teacher, school psychologist, and various diagnostic specialists such as speech and language therapists. Figure 4-1 shows a model that incorporates the purposes for assessment into a meaningful process. This model must be adapted when applied to students with severe or profound handicaps.

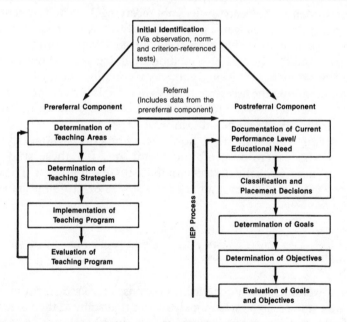

Figure 4-1 An Assessment Model for Students with Handicaps. *Source:* From *Assessment of Exceptional Students: Educational and Psychological Procedures* (p. 20) by R. Taylor, 1984, Englewood Cliffs, N.J.: Prentice-Hall, Inc. Copyright 1984 by Prentice-Hall, Inc. Reprinted by permission.

There are two major components of the assessment model—
prereferral and postreferral. The goal of the *prereferral component* is to
determine, develop, implement, and evaluate a teaching program before
a formal referral to special education. This component is heavily
weighted toward informal assessment such as observation and is usually
implemented by the regular education teacher in the student's current
educational setting.

The *postreferral component* includes the documentation of the student's
educational need and a decision about labeling, classification, and placement of the student. It might also involve auxiliary assessment by
specialists in such areas as vision, hearing, or speech. It would also include
information to help develop the student's IEP if a special education
program is warranted. An interdisciplinary or transdisciplinary approach
to assessment is stressed in the postreferral component.

There has been a trend in recent years to stress the prereferral component if at all possible: it is desirable to attempt to deal with the student's
problem(s) before making a referral for special education. This is particularly important since the majority of these students will "qualify"
(Ysseldyke, Algozzine, Regan, & McGue, 1981). This situation could
result in students who need services not receiving them and students who
do not really need them, getting them. Clearly, there is a need to establish
priorities so that available resources can go to appropriate students;
prereferral intervention is one method of doing this. Many times the
prereferral component will yield enough information to deal with the situation that required the assessment to begin with. If further information is
necessary, the prereferral information can also be used in the postreferral
component to avoid redundant testing.

The prereferral component, however, is practically nonexistent for
students with severe or profound handicaps. For these students, a
referral is justified as the first step in the assessment process. Therefore,
the assessment model for students with severe or profound handicaps
must be modified.

An Adapted Assessment Model

If you examine closely the various purposes for assessment of special
education students, you will quickly realize that some of them need to be
modified for students with severe or profound handicaps. At the very
least, the *emphasis* needs to be changed. For example, screening, particularly for identification of present and potential problems, becomes a
rather meaningless endeavor. The administration of formalized screening

instruments will provide little, if any, additional information about a student's need for special education. Since these students are already identified, the purpose of screening procedures should be modified to help determine *general program goals.* It is in this area that screening techniques and tests will pay the most dividends with this population.

The issue of assessing for eligibility for special education is also somewhat moot with this population. While the issue of labeling has important implications (and provides significant controversy) for students with mild handicaps, it is much more clearly defined with students with severe or profound handicaps. There is, however, the need to go through this process to receive funding for special education services. Again, the information gathered during this step might help document the student's functioning level in a variety of areas and determine general program goals.

The development of the IEP is an extremely important purpose of assessment with this population. As noted before, information gathered routinely for other purposes might be useful in determining *general* goals. The need for *precise, specific, and sequential objectives* for these students cannot be minimized, however. It is at this level that the focus of the assessment efforts should be addressed. Similarly, the evaluation of the student's progress with respect to the goals and objectives is very important. Knowing when to move forward (or perhaps when to change the goals and objectives or break them down into even smaller steps) is crucial to the success of a student's educational program.

Hupp and Donofrio (1983) noted three types of information that should be gathered when assessing individuals with severe or profound handicaps: *general goal areas,* such as sensory, physical, behavioral, and cognitive skills; *strengths and weaknesses in curriculum areas,* such as self-help and communication skills; and the *functional needs of the student* that will allow him or her to function in the environment.

If one examines the model presented in Figure 4-1, several changes should come to mind. First, the prereferral component is eliminated; these students have problems that need immediate and additional attention. Second, the importance of "auxiliary" assessment becomes significant. Because of the multidimensional nature of the handicaps of these students, what is considered auxiliary for most students becomes an integral component. A modified assessment model is found in Figure 4-2.

It is also important to realize that a new emphasis has emerged that utilizes an *individualized transition plan* (ITP) as a subcomponent of the IEP. A major problem facing practitioners is how to provide effective transition programming for students with severe or profound handicaps (Kiernan & Stark, 1986; see Chapters 12 and 13 for a more in-depth

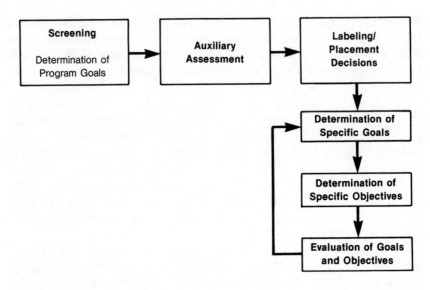

Figure 4-2 An Adapted Model of Assessment for Students with Severe or Profound Handicaps.

---

discussion of concerns related to transition programming). Therefore, goals and objectives for transition can now be seen in IEPs. This requires that an effective assessment be directed toward the area of transition needs and skill development for students with severe or profound handicaps.

A point should also be made about the *inappropriateness* of many available tests for this population and the general difficulty in assessing these students. The following discussion provides a look at previous attempts at this difficult process and suggested procedures to follow.

Assessment Techniques: Availability and Purpose

Assessment of students with severe or profound handicaps usually involves a combination of approaches. In general, these approaches can be categorized as either *formal* or *informal*.

Formal Assessment

Formal assessment involves the use of a *test or instrument*. This could include standardized inventories in the auxiliary areas of vision and hearing assessment, and scales, surveys, or tests to document cognitive, physical, and behavioral performance levels and/or to determine appropriate goals and objectives for the student. Formal approaches may also be used to determine the effectiveness of the educational program.

The Use of Instruments: What is Available? More and more, instruments are being used in the evaluation of students with severe or profound handicaps. These include both *norm-referenced tests* to determine eligibility and general goals, and *criterion-referenced tests* to determine specific strengths and weaknesses and educational objectives.

Norm-referenced tests compare an individual's score with others who have taken the test. The reference group with which the scores are compared is called the *standardization sample* or *standardization population*. Usually, raw scores (number of items passed) are converted to one of a variety of derived scores (scores that compare the individual's performance with those of a group with known demographic variables). Common derived scores are age equivalents, grade equivalents, percentiles, scaled scores, and stanines. A criterion-referenced test does not allow direct comparison of a person's performance with that of other individuals. It measures a person's mastery of content and typically is more concerned with what an individual can and cannot do as opposed to how much he or she can do compared with others of the same sex, age, socioeconomic status, and the like.

Crucial Statistical Components. Two important qualities that all tests must have are reliability and validity. *Reliability* is the consistency or dependability of a test. The most common type, *test-retest*, is the degree to which the test will yield the same or similar results if administered to the same population more than once. Other types are *split-half*, which is the test's internal consistency, and *alternative form*, which indicates how similar scores are when the test is given in an equivalent form, such as form A and B of an instrument, both of which measure the same thing.

The *validity* of a test is the degree to which it measures what it is designed to measure. For instance, does an intelligence test really measure "intelligence" or something else? There are three types of validity: criterion-related, content, and construct. Both reliability and validity are usually stated in terms of correlation coefficients. Correlation coefficients range from -1.0 (perfect negative correlation) to +1.0 (perfect positive correlation) and are expressed by a two-decimal number, such as .68, .92, or .57. The closer to +1.0, the greater the validity or reliability.

For example, to determine the test-retest reliability of a test, it would be administered twice to a group of subjects. The two scores for each subject would then be correlated. The resulting coefficient would be an indication of how consistent the test is over time. Although there is no cutoff point, a correlation below .60 indicates that the test results should be interpreted with caution. Similarly, to establish the criterion-related validity of an instrument, it would be administered with another test (the criterion measure) to a group of students. Scores from the two tests would be correlated to yield the validity coefficient. Again, a coefficient below .60 indicates the results must be interpreted cautiously. It is also important to remember that in determining criterion-related validity, the criterion measure itself must be valid.

For norm-referenced tests, another technical characteristic is important: the standardization population on which the test is based. The standardization sample should be both sufficiently large and representative. The characteristics (sex, socioeconomic status, intellectual level, and the like) of the individuals of the sample are also extremely important since scores are compared with their performance on the same test. For instance, if a person scored at the 50th percentile on a test that was normed on children without handicaps of average intelligence, his or her performance would be quite different from that of a child who scored at the 50th percentile on a test standardized on children who were deaf-blind and severely retarded.

Tests for Students with Severe or Profound Handicaps. The technical characteristics of many tests used with such students are inadequate. Cicchetti and Sparrow (1981) indicated that many instruments do not contain enough items to differentiate among lower functioning individuals, that most scales for this population have deficient reliability and validity estimates, and that many of the norm- and criterion-referenced tests do not report reliability and validity data in the manuals. This makes it difficult to determine their technical adequacy.

More and more tests are being developed specifically for those with severe or profound handicaps. Both norm- and criterion-referenced instruments are currently on the market. One must remember, however, that when a norm-referenced test is used, the scores must be compared with those of the standardization sample; if a test is normed on a population of individuals with profound handicaps, a person's score on the test is compared with scores of that population. There are times when this is advantageous, as in program development or program evaluation, and other times when it is disadvantageous, as with classification.

When tests are used that were not specifically developed for individuals with severe or profound handicaps, two approaches are usually considered: adapting test items or administration procedures and selecting a test that is "response fair."

Adaptation of Test Items and Administration. Existing instruments (usually norm-referenced) can be adapted by changing the mode of presentation, eliminating or modifying certain test items, or changing the scoring procedures. In changing the mode of presentation, one might give instructions through the subject's dominant mode of communication (e.g., sign language with deaf students), or use verbal cues or physical prompts indicated in the test manual. It might also be necessary to change the mode of response. For instance, on an instrument requiring a pointing response, a student who is extremely spastic might need to use a head pointer or respond in a nonpointing mode. It is important in assessing this population to determine how a student communicates a functional yes or no response. If you can discriminate the yes and no response, many tests can be adapted to accommodate a yes/no format. If a standardized test is used, however, these modifications violate the "standard" format and thus invalidate the scores from the tests. Nonetheless, it might provide valuable information that can be used informally.

Eliminating or modifying test items also violates the standardization procedures. Usually, a derived score cannot be obtained, and the results can be used only informally. The modification of scoring procedures involves prorating or extrapolating test scores when the individual's performance is outside of those included in the standardization.

Response-Fair Tests. The use of response-fair tests involves the careful selection of instruments that minimize the child's handicaps when measuring aptitude or determining educational objectives. This approach is consistent with P.L. 94-142. It should be noted, however, that the use of this approach depends on the initial reason for assessment. There are many times when you might want to measure the "degree of handicap." For instance, you might want to find out the amount of motor control a child has in order to initiate the most effective program for self-help skills. Whatever the purpose for assessment might be, it is extremely important for persons involved in assessment to be aware, for each instrument, of the prerequisite skills necessary for a student simply to perceive the instructions and to give a response.

Informal Assessment

Informal assessment of students with severe or profound handicaps provides invaluable information that will assist in the development of an educational program. As noted in the previous section, because of the severity and complexity of the handicaps in this population, most attempts at formal assessment must be so adapted that the results become virtually meaningless. There is, in fact, a tremendous reliance on informal techniques. It should be noted, however, that "informal" does not mean "nonsystematic." In reality, the more systematically informal techniques are applied, the more meaningful the results will be. Typically, observation is the primary source of informal assessment information with this population. For example, it is frequently used, in conjunction with behavioral techniques, to assess the functional vision and hearing of students who might be considered "untestable" using traditional techniques. Systematic observation can also be used to help determine and prioritize goals and objectives (target behaviors), and to provide a system to evaluate the effectiveness of a given educational program or procedure.

Observation in Auxiliary Assessment. The determination of the hearing and vision abilities of students is extremely important because most individuals who are severely or profoundly handicapped have disabilities in many areas. Specifically, the amount of *functional* vision and hearing is important for at least two reasons. First, it gives some indication of the ways in which further testing must be modified to accommodate their sensory limitations. Second, the information provides educational implications regarding the most efficient method of presenting information to the students.

In audiologic testing, specific techniques can be used to determine if certain pathologic conditions exist. For example, impedance audiometry, including tympanography (which evaluates the mobility and intactness of the eardrum), can be used to identify middle ear problems that might require medical management. These procedures, however, provide little educational implications since they give limited information about functional hearing ability (Spradlin, 1985). Behavioral observation can be used to help determine the hearing level of the student and to provide implications for educational management. For example, sounds of various amplitudes can be presented to see if the individual will turn his or her head to localize them or will simply respond in some way (e.g., an eyeblink). Other techniques combine observation and operant conditioning procedures, including the use of auditory stimuli as both discriminative or reinforcing stimuli (Spradlin, 1985). For example, the student might be trained (through reinforcers) to press a button or provide some other response whenever there is a change in the auditory stimulus. In this way, the auditory stimulus can be monitored to determine the student's hearing ability. When using the auditory stimulus as a reinforcer, the student is presented with an auditory signal after a designated response. By determining if the response rate increases after the contingent auditory stimulus is presented, one can determine if the individual is hearing. Unfortunately, the lack of increase in the response rate might also be attributed to the ineffectiveness of the auditory stimulus as a reinforcer rather than to the lack of hearing ability (Spradlin, 1985).

In visual testing, techniques are available to determine pathologic conditions that might have medical implications. It is important, however, to determine the *visual acuity* of an individual to provide educational implications. Unfortunately, traditional methods of determining visual acuity (e.g., the use of the Snellen chart) are extremely limited with students with severe or profound handicaps. There have been attempts to devise standardized procedures with this population (e.g., the *Functional Vision Inventory* discussed in the next chapter) although observation is frequently used to provide important information.

One observational technique evolved from the literature on *preferential looking* (Cress, 1985). Preferential looking refers to the finding that infants prefer to look at patterned rather than plain visual stimuli (Fantz, 1963). By varying the visual stimuli, one can observe the preference of the student and subsequently determine visual ability. Although the technique was developed initially for infants, it has been used with older individuals with handicaps (e.g., see Lennerstrand, Axelsson, & Andersson, 1983).

Observation in Making Educational Decisions. Observation can be a powerful assessment technique for educational decision making. Systematic observation, if done appropriately, can provide valuable information regarding the appropriateness of specific objectives chosen for a given student as well as the student's performance level in relation to them.

The first step in using observation for educational decision making is identifying the target behaviors: it is important to determine *what* behavior(s) to target and, subsequently, to teach. Unlike when a student is given a specific test that measures specific areas, the behaviors to be evaluated using the observational model are typically selected by the observer. However, one should not assume that such selection is accomplished without a critical analysis of what the student needs. Currently, the emphasis is on identifying skills that will be *functional* for the student (i.e., immediately useful in and frequently demanded by the student's present and future environments). As a rule, an *ecological assessment* approach is used to determine these targets. The various environments in which the student exists or will exist are investigated. The specific behaviors that will allow improved adaptation and independence in these environments are then identified and targeted for the student (see Chapter 8 for a more complete description of this process).

Other attempts at identifying what functional behaviors to assess use various theoretical models such as the *Component Model of Functional*

Life Routines (Brown, Evans, Weed, & Owen, 1987). This model identifies areas such as personal management, leisure activities, and vocational activities and provides information related to their functional use (see Chapter 8 for a more in-depth description of this model).

In general, initial observation might take the form of a list of targeted skills or behaviors that the person can and cannot do. Taken a step further, it might include the conditions under which the person can perform certain tasks (e.g., with verbal prompts or physical guidance). In general, observation should be one of the first procedures to gather information because it provides information about the performance level of the individual *in the natural environment*. Observation also has an important part in determining what other assessment procedures are necessary.

Once targeted skills are identified, more intensive and systematic observation is necessary. This might range from determining what steps of the behavior the student can or cannot accomplish (i.e., a task analysis) to a comprehensive assessment of the student's performance level. For example, one might be interested in determining how many times the student commits the behavior, what percentage of time the behavior occurs, or how long the behavior occurs. Adams, Sternberg, & Taylor (1982) outlined a number of systematic observation strategies and accompanying data collection devices that can be used to determine these types of levels. The reader is also referred to Chapter 8 for discussions concerning how systematic observation can be effectively used.

CONCLUSION

The assessment of individuals with severe or profound handicaps is a serious, and sometimes frustrating, challenge for the educator. The assessment model used in most special education programs must be adapted because of the unique needs of this population. The general lack of appropriate instruments or the misuse of existing tests makes matters more difficult. Adequate assessment is *difficult*, but not *impossible*. By carefully identifying the purpose for assessment and matching it with available techniques, meaningful information can be gathered. A revisit to the steps in the assessment model noted in Figure 4-2 serves as a summary of the information presented in this chapter.

1. *Initial identification:* Because of the severity of the handicaps involved, parents and physicians are usually the first to identify the individual as needing special education.
2. *Referral.*

3. *Preliminary assessment:* It is crucial to determine at least a consistent yes-no response so that tests and the testing environment can be modified accordingly. Duncan, Sbardellati, Maheady, and Sainato (1981) noted that the response should be physically possible, under voluntary control, and relatively easy to perform. They also identified a continuum of responses to look for (from most desirable to least): (1) expressive language, (2) pointing, (3) motor (e.g., kick, head nod), (4) inconsistent, and (5) nonexistent. Once this information is obtained, decisions can be made concerning the most appropriate procedure to use in any further assessment.

4. *Auxiliary assessment:* The determination of an individual's functional vision and hearing is necessary before further assessment is possible. By using the informal observation techniques discussed in this chapter, both alone and in combination with operant procedures, valuable information regarding the input mode of the individual can be determined and used to adapt further assessment. It can also be used with information about output modes to help determine instructional planning regarding preferred input/output channels.

5. *Documentation of current performance level:* In some cases, this is accomplished through the use of a standardized, usually norm-referenced, instrument. Such information is not particularly helpful other than in documenting the general functioning level of the individual in cognitive, self-help, communication, or other areas. Systematic observation is extremely helpful in documenting the current performance level.

6. *Classification and placement:* Assessment information is analyzed to determine the educational label to be assigned to the student. This is necessary among other reasons to receive federal and state funding. In reality, this step and step 7 are done simultaneously.

7. *Development of the IEP:* This involves the careful identification of goals and objectives. Sometimes, goals can be identified through the use of the gathered norm-referenced information. Observational data (e.g., through ecological assessments) are used more and more to assist in goal determination. Specifications of objectives can require the use of both observation and criterion-referenced tests.

8. *Evaluation of goals and objectives:* This involves using the same procedures and instruments administered to develop the IEP *after* the IEP is implemented. It is an extremely important step that is all too often overlooked and is especially crucial in determining the validity of any program implementation.

REFERENCES

Adams, G.L., Sternberg, L., & Taylor, R.L. (1982). Social skills training. In L. Sternberg and G.L. Adams (Eds.), *Educating severely and profoundly handicapped students* (pp. 97-132). Rockville, MD: Aspen.

Bayley, N. (1969). *Bayley scales of infant development.* Atlanta: The Psychological Corporation.

Brown, F., Evans, I.M., Weed, K., & Owen, V. (1987). Delineating functional competencies: A component model. *Journal of the Association for Persons with Severe Handicaps, 12* (2), 117-124.

Cattell, P. (1950). *Cattell infant intelligence scale.* Atlanta: The Psychological Corporation.

Cicchetti, D., & Sparrow, S. (1981). *Some recent research on adaptive behavior scales: Toward resolving some methodological issues.* Paper presented at the 105th meeting of the American Association on Mental Deficiency, Detroit, Michigan.

Cress, P. (1985). Visual assessment. In M. Bullis (Ed.), *Communication development in young children with deaf-blindness: Literature review 1* (pp. 31-47). Monmouth, OR: Oregon State System of Higher Education.

Duncan, D., Sbardellati, E., Maheady, L., & Sainato, D. (1981). Nondiscriminatory assessment of severely physically handicapped individuals. *The Journal of the Association for the Severely Handicapped, 6,* 17-22.

Fantz, R. (1963). Pattern vision in newborn infants. *Science, 140,* 296-297.

Federal Register, Washington, D.C.: U.S. Government Printing Office. August 23, 1977.

Hupp, S., & Donofrio, M. (1983). Assessment of multiply and severely handicapped learners for the development of cross-referenced objectives. *The Journal of the Association for the Severely Handicapped, 8,* 17-28.

Kiernan, W.E., & Stark, J.A. (Eds.) (1986). *Pathways to employment for adults with developmental disabilities.* Baltimore: Paul H. Brookes.

Lennerstrand, G., Axelsson, A., & Andersson, G. (1983). Visual acuity testing with preferential looking in mental retardation. *Acta Opthalmologica, 61,* 624-633.

Salvia, J., & Ysseldyke, J. (1985). *Assessment in special and remedial education* (3rd ed.). Boston: Houghton-Mifflin.

Simeonsson, R., Huntington, G., & Parse, S. (1980). Assessment of children with severe handicaps: Multiple problems—multivariate goals. *AAESPH Review, 1,* 55-72.

Spradlin, J. (1985). Auditory evaluation. In M. Bullis (Ed.), *Communication development in young children with deaf-blindness: Literature review 1.* (pp. 49-59). Monmouth, OR: Oregon State System of Higher Education.

Taylor, R. (1984). *Assessment of exceptional students: Educational and psychological procedures.* Englewood Cliffs, NJ: Prentice-Hall.

Wolery, M., & Dyk, L. (1984). Arena assessment: Description and preliminary social validity data. *The Journal of the Association for the Persons with Severe Handicaps, 9,* 231-235.

Ysseldyke, J., Algozzine, B., Regan, R., & McGue, M. (1981). The influence of test scores and naturally occurring pupil characteristics on psychoeducational decision making with children. *Journal of School Psychology, 19,* 167-177.

Chapter 5

Assessment Instruments

Ronald L. Taylor

PROBLEM

There are hundreds of instruments currently being used to evaluate students with severe or profound handicaps. Many, however, are nothing more than checklists or sequential lists of behaviors. Others contain items more appropriate for use with students with moderate, and in some cases, mild handicaps; there simply are not enough items in many tests that adequately measure the skills of individuals with severe or profound handicaps. Still other instruments, most notably norm-referenced tests, have inadequate technical characteristics such as validity, reliability, and representation of the standardization sample. Clearly, the practitioner is faced with a dilemma and a monumental decision when asked to choose a test or battery of tests for the population with severe or profound handicaps.

PAST PRACTICES

Attempts to assess this population formally are relatively recent phenomena. In the past, these individuals were, more often than not, considered "untestable." As noted in the last chapter, when they were evaluated, they were given standardized tests designed for infants such as the *Bayley Scales of Children's Development* and the *Cattell Infant Intelligence Scale*. These instruments were designed and standardized on children from birth to roughly age three. The inappropriateness of this procedure cannot be minimized. Even though many older students with severe or profound handicaps function at a chronologically younger age, this does not justify the use of a *norm-referenced* test designed for younger children. The results are uninterpretable, and it would be inappropriate to determine a score at all if individuals of the same age were not included in the standardization sample.

Other attempts have been to combine items from different tests and to use the resulting instrument more informally. Typically, "rough" developmental ages were associated with all or many of the items, although the test was not "scored" in a traditional sense. The Developmental Pinpoints (Cohen, Gross, & Haring, 1976) is an example of this approach (see Exhibit 5-1).

Exhibit 5-1 Developmental Pinpoints

two buttons in 19 sec	61.4 mo	MPS
Buttons coat or dress	40 mo	LAP/F/Den
(two-50 sec-38.8 mo-MPS)		MPS/Ges/Vin
(two-34 sec-44.6 mo-MPS)		
(four-76 sec-45 mo-MPS)		
Buttons four buttons	48-60 mo	MPS
(51 sec-50 mo)	50 mo	LAP
(42 sec-57.9 mo)		
3. Unbuttons		
Unbuttons accessible buttons	36-48 mo	LAP/Ges
III. Toileting		
A. Establishes general toileting schedule, habits		
Usually dry after nap	12 mo	LAP/Ges
Fusses to be changed after having bowel movement	12 mo	Ges/LAP
Indicates wet pants	15 mo	LAP/Sher/Ges
Has bowel control	15 mo	LAP/Ges
Bowel control usually attained	18-23 mo	Sher
Bladder control in transitional stage (usually wet after naps)	18-23 mo	Ges
Indicates toilet needs by restlessness and vocalization (or fetches the pot-Ges)	22.5 mo	Sher/Ges/Slos
Verbalizes toilet needs fairly consistently	24 mo	LAP/Sher/Vin
Dry at night if taken up	24 mo	LAP
	24-29 mo	Ges
	30-35 mo	Sher
Wakes wet but tolerates condition	24-29 mo	Ges
Dry during day: muscles of bladder coming under control	24-29 mo	Sher/Ges
Usually dry all night (no accidents)	36-48 mo	Ges/Sher/LAP
Dry through night	48-60 mo	Sher
B. Carries out toileting routine		
Pulls down pants at toilet, but seldom able to replace	24-29 mo	LAP
	30-35 mo	Sher
Cares for self at toilet; pulls down clothing and can replace	45 mo	Vin/II
Sits down on toilet without reminder, or moves to face toilet without reminder	45 mo	LAP

Exhibit 5-1 continued

Wipes self with toilet paper	45 mo	LAP
Flushes toilet by self	45 mo	LAP
Cares for self at toilet (pulls down clothing, sits, wipes, flushes)	45 mo	LAP
Goes into bathroom by self and does all of the above	60-72 mo	Ges/LAP

IV. Grooming

A. Washes self

Presents hands to be washed; stands quietly while face washed	No norms	
Washes hands and face unaided	36-48 mo	LAP
	42 mo	Ges/Vin
	54 mo	LAP/Vin
Needs help and supervision washing other than hands and feet; washes only hands and feet alone	60-72 mo	Sher
Washes face and hands without getting clothes wet	60-72 mo	Sher/II

B. Dries self

Dries face, hands (with supervision)	23 mo	Sher/Den
	31 mo	Vin
	42 mo	Ges/LAP
	48-60 mo	LAP
Dries hands	24-36 mo	LAP
	31 mo	Vin
Washes and dries face and hands without getting clothes wet	60-72 mo	Sher/II

C. Brushes teeth

Brushes teeth	42 mo	II/LAP
	48-60 mo	Sher/Ges

D. Brushes hair

Brushes and combs hair unassisted	60-72 mo	LAP/II

Source: From *Teaching the Severely Handicapped*, Vol. 1 (p. 74) by N. Haring and L. Brown (Eds.), 1976, Orlando, FL.: Grune & Stratton, Inc. Copyright 1976 by Grune & Stratton, Inc. Reprinted by permission.

More recent attempts (discussed in the previous chapter), have been to adapt existing instruments by changing the way in which the material is presented, eliminating certain test items, or allowing the student to respond in an alternate method (e.g., sign language instead of verbally). As previously mentioned, this approach is inappropriate with standardized tests because it violates the "standard" method in which the scores are given their meaning.

With the passage of P.L. 94-142, attempts were made to be more selective in the choice of instruments in keeping with the nondiscriminatory evaluation aspect of the law. For example, determining the overall developmental level of a deaf-blind student using a test primarily audiovisual in nature was avoided. These attempts were often futile because so few instruments existed that allowed for any reasonable choice. More tests were eventually designed for this population, however, and perhaps more importantly, professionals became more concerned with the *specific reasons* for evaluating these students so that appropriate assessment would indeed be possible.

SUGGESTED METHODS

As we become more informed about the educational needs of individuals with severe or profound handicaps, we are in a better position to know when to assess and what type of instrument to use. Norm-referenced tests are typically used for classification and placement and to determine general goals, while criterion-referenced tests are used to determine specific objectives.

The norm-referenced tests used with this population are generally *adaptive behavior scales*. "Adaptive behavior" is difficult to define and measure, but it is nonetheless receiving a great deal of attention in the area of special education. The American Association on Mental Deficiency (AAMD) includes "a deficit in adaptive behavior" as one of the criteria for the classification of mental retardation. The AAMD gives as examples of adaptive behavior sensorimotor, communication, self-help, and socialization skills. These skills are generally concerned with an individual's ability to adapt to the social and cultural demands of the environment and to function independently in the environment.

Most criterion-referenced tests for this population are generally developmental inventories. For the most part, they provide more detailed skill sequences in the areas of communication, self-help, sensorimotor skills, etc. than do norm-referenced tests. Some of these instruments have been specifically designed for use with students with severe or profound handicaps.

As noted in the previous chapter, another important area for these students is auxiliary assessment. Instruments are available (although limited in number) that can be used to evaluate the sensory deficits, most notably vision, frequently found in this population.

The instruments described in this section were chosen because of their present popularity, past usage, and, in some cases, their future potential. The tests are classified according to type (norm-referenced, criterion-referenced, auxiliary, other), purpose, and target population.

Survey of Tests

AAMD Adaptive Behavior Scale

  Purpose: Classification and *general* goal determination
  Target Population: Persons with handicaps (all levels of individuals who are mentally retarded)
  The *American Association on Mental Deficiency Adaptive Behavior Scale* (ABS) (Nihira, Foster, Shellhaas, & Leland, 1975) is an individually administered rating scale used with individuals who are mentally retarded, emotionally maladjusted, or have other handicaps. Norms are provided for individuals age 3 to 69. Adaptive behavior as measured by this instrument refers to "the effectiveness of an individual in coping with the natural and social demands of his or her environment" (p.5). According to the authors, the ABS can be used to identify areas of deficiency in individuals in different situations, compare ratings of different evaluators, provide a means of communication among professionals, stimulate research, and facilitate administrative decisions.
  The ABS has two parts. Part One measures personal independence in daily living skills. Part Two measures maladaptive behavior. For both parts, information is collected by one of three methods. The first is first person assessment. This is used when the evaluator is thoroughly familiar with the person being evaluated. The second is third party assessment. In this approach, the evaluator asks other individuals, such as a teacher, parent, or ward attendant, about each item on the scale. This is usually very time-consuming. The last method is the interview. The evaluator using this approach asks more open-ended questions ("Tell me about your child's toileting skills."), and completes the scale based on the information obtained during the interview.

  Part One and Part Two. Part One includes ten domains measuring the degree of independence in daily living skills. Each item in a given domain is scored in one of five ways. For some items, there is a breakdown of skills on a dependent-independent continuum. The examiner determines which behavioral description best fits the individual being evaluated. For the other items, a list of behaviors is provided, and the examiner must check all that apply. Descriptions of the ten domains are as follows:

  1. *Independent Functioning* (21 items): includes eating, toilet use, cleanliness, appearance, care of clothing, dressing and undressing, travel, and general independent functioning.
  2. *Physical Development* (6 items): includes items measuring sensory (vision and hearing) and motor (gross and fine) abilities.

3. *Economic Activity* (4 items): measures money handling, budgeting, and shopping skills.
4. *Language Development* (9 items): includes measures of language reception and expression plus two items concerning social language development (such as conversational behavior).
5. *Numbers and Time* (3 items): measures the ability to understand and manipulate numbers and to understand time concepts.
6. *Domestic Activity* (6 items): includes items concerning meal preparation and cleaning skills.
7. *Vocational Activity* (3 items): measures work habits and job performance.
8. *Self-Direction* (5 items): measures initiative, perseverance, and use of leisure time.
9. *Responsibility* (2 items): measures dependability.
10. *Socialization* (7 items): includes measures of cooperation, consideration for others, and social maturity.

Part Two was designed to measure the degree of an individual's maladaptive behavior. There are 14 domains, though the last domain, "Use of Medications," is not really a measure of maladaptive behavior. For each item in a given domain, there are a number of behaviors listed. The examiners must determine if each behavior occurs frequently (scored a 2), occasionally (scored a 1), or not at all (not scored). Unfortunately, no guidelines are provided that operationally define "frequently" and "occasionally." The 14 domains are summarized below.

1. *Violent and Destructive Behavior* (5 items): includes such items as "threatens or does physical violence" and "damages personal property."
2. *Antisocial Behavior* (6 items): includes such items as "bosses and manipulates others," "is inconsiderate of others," and "uses angry language."
3. *Rebellious Behavior* (6 items): includes measures of impudence, resistance to instructions, and absenteeism.
4. *Untrustworthy Behavior* (2 items): measures lying, cheating, and stealing behavior.
5. *Withdrawal* (3 items): includes measures of inactivity and shyness.
6. *Stereotyped Behavior and Odd Mannerisms* (2 items): measures stereotypic and repetitive behavior.
7. *Inappropriate Interpersonal Mannerisms* (1 item): includes behavior such as "kisses or licks others."

8. *Unacceptable Vocal Habits* (1 item): includes behavior such as "giggles hysterically."
9. *Unacceptable or Eccentric Habits* (4 items): includes items such as "has unacceptable oral habits" and "removes or tears off own clothing."
10. *Self-Abusive Behavior* (1 item): includes behavior such as "bites or cuts self."
11. *Hyperactive Tendencies* (1 item): includes behavior such as "talks excessively."
12. *Sexually Aberrant Behavior* (4 items): measures such behaviors as masturbation in inappropriate settings and indecent exposure.
13. *Psychological Disturbances* (7 items): includes items such as "reacts poorly to criticism," "demands excessive attention or praise," and "has hypochondriacal tendencies."
14. *Use of Medications* (1 item): indicates the degree to which an individual uses prescribed medications.

Interpretation of Scores. Each item is scored using one of the three methods previously mentioned. Each item in a given domain is summed to obtain a raw score for that domain. On Part One, it is also possible to obtain a raw score for various subdomains. The domain raw scores can then be transformed into percentile ranks, which are then plotted on the Profile Summary to provide a visual representation of the individual's adaptive behavior functioning.

Technical Characteristics. The ABS was standardized on 4,014 persons in residential settings who were mentally retarded. The subjects represented all levels of retardation. The ABS was administered to 133 residents at three training schools to obtain reliability data. Each subject was rated independently by two staff members and the scores correlated. For Part One, the correlation coefficients ranged from .71 (Self-Direction) to .93 (Physical Development), with a mean coefficient of .86. The correlations for Part Two were considerably lower, ranging from .37 (Unacceptable Vocal Habits) to .77 (Use of Medications), with a mean coefficient of .57. Validity studies of the ABS are generally lacking.

Summary. The ABS has received tremendous attention in recent years. Much of the research on the ABS constructively criticized its scoring system. Most notably, the rather subjective scoring format, particularly for Part Two, was noted. In addition, Part Two has low reliability and does not take into account in the scoring system the severity of the maladaptive behavior (Taylor, Warren, & Slocumb, 1979). The ABS does not have enough items that measure lower level skills to be considered an effective tool with the population with severe or profound handicaps. This instrument along with the Vineland (VABS) (to be discussed) has been used primarily for classification purposes.

Balthazar Scales of Adaptive Behavior

Purpose: Determination of goals and objectives

Target Population: Persons with severe or profound retardation

The *Balthazar Scales of Adaptive Behavior* (BSAB) (Balthazar, 1976) consist of two sections designed for assessing individuals with severe or profound retardation. Section One is Scales of Functional Independence, and Section Two is Scales of Social Adaptation. The first section assesses self-help skills such as eating, dressing, and toileting. Section Two assesses coping behaviors such as play activities and verbal communication. Unlike most adaptive behavior measures, information for the BSAB is collected via direct observation rather than from interviews. Another feature of the BSAB is two scoring systems for each section, one for the professional supervisor and one for the rater technician.

Scales of Functional Independence. The Eating Scale assesses five specific behaviors (or classes) further broken down into sequential steps used as test items. The classes are dependent feeding (9 items), finger feeds (9 items), spoon usage (13 items), fork usage (13 items), and drinking (13 items). For each item, the examiner must determine how many times out of a possible ten trials the individual did or could do each behavior. For instance, for the item "drinks from cup independently," the examiner would estimate how many times out of ten the individual manipulated the cup with no direct assistance with one or both hands. There is also a supplementary eating checklist that includes items pertaining to rate of eating, knife usage, etc. This part is not scored. Throughout the administration of the Eating Scale, the examiner is not allowed to initiate or respond to the individual's behavior.

The Dressing Scale measures the degree of independence in dressing and undressing. Several articles of clothing are used including shoes, socks, briefs, T-shirt/undershirt, regular shirt or blouse, pants, skirts, and dresses. The examiner must observe the person putting on and taking off each relevant article of clothing and rate him or her on a 0 (no participation) to 6 (independent, perfect performance) scale.

The Toileting Scales, unlike the rest of the BSAB, use an interview and questionnaire format. There is both a daytime questionnaire and night-time supplementary sheet.

Scales of Social Adaptation. These measure self-directedness and sociability. Unadaptive Self-Directed Behavior includes five items: failure to respond, stereotypy and posturing, repetitious verbalization and isolated smiling or laughing, inappropriate self-directed behavior, and disorderly nonsocial behavior. Unadaptive Interpersonal Behavior includes inappropriate contact with others and aggression or withdrawal. Adaptive Self-Directed Behaviors consists of exploratory searching activities, recreational activities, and self-interest or self-regard. Adaptive Interpersonal Behaviors assesses fundamental social behaviors, such as precommunication, social vocalization, and gesturing. Verbal Communication includes nonfunctional, repetitious, or inarticulate verbalization as well as articulate, meaningful speech. Play Activities measures the ability to manipulate objects and engage in playful activity. Response to Instructions measures cooperativeness and willingness to follow "instructions checklist" items. This is simply a checklist of behaviors that might interfere with the rating process for the other items.

Interpretation of Scores. Scores from Sections One and Two are interpreted in different ways. Section One yields percentile tables for each of the Scales of Functional Independence. The author suggests that these percentile tables be used as guidelines and not as strict normative information. Section Two yields information that is *not* standardized. This section includes a tally sheet that measures each item in terms of frequency on a one-minute interval basis. There is also a scoring summary sheet included. Data from Section Two (and Section One) are used informally for program development and evaluation. Scoring, for the most part, is tedious and overly complicated.

Technical Characteristics. The BSAB was standardized through observational studies that began in 1964 and continued to 1971. The population included 451 ambulant institutional residents from Wisconsin who were severely or profoundly retarded, although the manual notes that additional studies were conducted in other states and European sites. The age range of the sample was 5 to 57, with a median age of 17.27.

For Section One of the BSAB, no reliability or validity data are presented. The author suggests that these be established by the person using the instrument for finer instructional purposes. Section Two reports inter-rater reliability data from two studies. The percentage of agreement is extremely variable and is based on a limited sample size.

Summary. While the BSAB can technically be considered a standardized test, it is best not to use it in this manner. The author continually downplays the normative aspects of the test and stresses its use for program development and evaluation. Section One does include a sequence of behaviors that could easily be considered objectives in developing individual educational plans.

Callier-Azusa Scale

Purpose: Determination of goals

Target Population: Persons with multiple handicaps

The *Callier-Azusa Scale* (Stillman, 1978) is an individually administered instrument designed to assess the developmental level of deaf-blind children and those with severe or profound handicaps. The scale is comprised of 18 subscales in five major areas, and is designed to be administered by teachers or other individuals who are thoroughly familiar with the child. The author states that the child should be observed for at least two weeks, preferably in a classroom. The age range for the scale is from birth through approximately nine years. Descriptions of the five major areas follow. The items referred to are actually sequential steps measuring the particular developmental milestone of each subscale. In some cases, the step is further broken down into as many as five separate items.

1. *Motor Development:* includes the subscales of postural control (18 steps), locomotion (17 steps), fine motor skills (20 steps), and visual motor (21 steps).
2. *Perceptual Development:* includes the subscales of visual development (15 steps), auditory development (6 steps), and tactile development (13 steps).
3. *Daily Living Skills:* includes the subscales of undressing and dressing (16 items), personal hygiene (13 steps), feeding skills (16 steps), and toileting (13 steps).
4. *Cognition, Communication, and Language:* includes the subscales of cognitive development (21 steps), receptive communication (18 steps), expressive communication (20 steps), and development of speech (10 steps).
5. *Social Development:* includes the subscales of interaction with adults (16 steps), interactions with peers (17 steps), and interactions with environment (10 steps).

Interpretation of Scores. To give a child credit for a particular step, he or she must perform all the behaviors described in all items in that step. If a behavior is emerging, occurs only infrequently, or occurs only after prompting or in specific situations, credit is not given. Some items in the scale are starred (*). These items can be omitted if "a child cannot be expected to exhibit behavior because of a specific sensory or motor deficit" (p. 4). To score the scale, the steps in each subscale exhibited by the child are noted (the format for scoring is discussed in the manual). Each subscale score can be converted to a "rough" age equivalency. The author notes, however, that the behavior sequences for a child, not the age norms, provide the most important information.

Summary. The Callier-Azusa is one of a few scales specifically designed for use with individuals with sensory and/or motor deficits. There are also a number of items designed for lower functioning individuals. The test should be used for the determination of strengths and weaknesses and educational goals rather than an individual's development level. For example, it has been noted that passing or failing one test item might change test results 12 months because of the lack of easily measured behaviors in a given category (Cole, Swisher, Thompson, & Fewell, 1985).

Assessment Log and Developmental Progress Chart

Purpose: Determination of goals
Target Population: Infants with handicaps
The *Assessment Log and Developmental Progress Chart* (Johnson-Martin, Jens, & Attermeier, 1986) is part of the *Carolina Curriculum for Handicapped Infants and Infants at Risk*. It includes items correlated with 24 curriculum sequences and is in a checklist format. In general, cognition (using primarily a Piagetian approach), language/communication, self-help/social skills, and fine motor and gross motor skills are assessed. In each of the 24 areas is a number of sequential or ordinal items. The manual notes that "although every effort has been made to achieve this ordinal structure, the authors are well aware that moderately and severely handicapped infants, who manifest unusual developmental patterns, will undoubtedly show erratic patterns of achievement within the sequence on occasion" (p. 13). The 24 areas and examples of the first and last item in each follow.

1. *Tactile Integration and Manipulation* (11 items): "responds differently to warm/cold, rough/smooth" to "pokes or plays with clay."
2. *Auditory Localization and Object Permanence* (10 items): "quiets when noise is presented" to "turns head and looks back for two sounds"; there are alternative items for visually impaired children.
3. *Visual Pursuit and Objective Permanence* (7 items): "visually fixates for at least three seconds" to "looks at cover under which object has disappeared."

4. *Object Permanence–Visual Motor* (12 items): "pulls cloth from face" to "finds object after systematic search under 3 covers."
5. *Spatial Concepts* (14 items): "shifts attention from one object to another" to "uses tools to deal with spatial problems (e.g., extends reach with a stick)."
6. *Functional Use of Objects and Symbolic Play* (12 items): "moves hand to mouth" to "talks to dolls or animals or makes them interact with one another."
7. *Control Over Physical Environment* (9 items): "repeats activity that produces an interesting result" to "uses tools to solve problems."
8. *Readiness Concepts* (7 items): "matches simple geometric shapes" to "understands concept of big."
9. *Responses to Communication from Others* (23 items): "quiets to voice" to "follows 3 different 3-part commands."
10. *Gestural Imitation* (10 items): "looks at person talking and gesturing" to "imitates sequence of 2 signs that stand for words."
11. *Gestural Communication* (15 items): "shows anticipation of regularly occurring events in everyday care" to "combines signs to communicate."
12. *Vocal Imitation* (12 items): "vocalizing in response to person talking" to "imitates 3-syllable words."
13. *Vocal Communication* (22 items): "differentiates cries" to "combines 2 or more words in sentences."
14. *Social Skills* (19 items): "can be comforted by talking to, holding or rocking" to "shares spontaneously with peers."
15. *Self-Direction* (6 items): "moves away from Mom in same room" to "explores unfamiliar places with mother present."
16. *Feeding* (19 items): "sucks from nipple smoothly" to "distinguishes between edible and nonedible substances."
17. *Grooming* (4 items): "cooperates in hand-washing" to "wipes nose if given a handkerchief."
18. *Dressing* (6 items): "cooperates in dressing and undressing" to "puts on loose shoes or slippers."
19. *Reaching and Grasping* (11 items): "moves arms actively when sees or hears object" to "uses neat pincer grasp."
20. *Object Manipulation* (9 items): "looks at hand (or toy) to one side" to "looks toward object and visually directs reach or adjusts reach to get noisy object"; there are also modifications for visually impaired children.
21. *Object Manipulation (continued)* (30 items): items relate to form manipulation, block patterns, drawing, placing pegs, and putting in and taking out objects.

22. *Bilateral Hand Activity* (14 items): "bats at objects at chest level" to "strings three large beads."
23. *Gross Motor Activities: Prone* (16 items): "lifts head, freeing nose; arms and legs flexed" to "crawls downstairs backward."
24. *Gross Motor Activities: Supine* (7 items): "turns head from side to side in response to visual and/or auditory stimuli while in supine position" to "rolls from back to stomach."
25. *Gross Motor Activities: Upright* (10 items): "head steady when held" to "moves from hands and knees, to hands and feet, to standing."
26. *Gross Motor Activities: Upright (continued)* (15 items): measures stair climbing, balance, jumping, posture, and locomotion.

Interpretation of Scores. The authors suggest that an individual be evaluated in each of the 24 areas, usually beginning with the first item and continuing until he or she fails three consecutive items. The obvious exception are those areas that cannot be measured because of the nature of an individual's handicap (e.g., auditory localization for a person with a significant hearing impairment). The results are placed on the Developmental Progress Chart (see Exhibit 5-2). Items are scored as passed, failed, or emerging. Determination or prioritizing of instructional goals can then be accomplished. General age ranges for the various items can be determined from the results placed on the Developmental Progress Chart. These are grouped in 3-month clusters from birth to 24 months. These age ranges, particularly when interpreted with students with severe or profound handicaps, must be viewed with caution.

Summary. The *Assessment Log and Developmental Progress Chart* is used in conjunction with the Carolina Curriculum. It is a well-researched model that shows promise in determining instructional goals and in providing instructional procedures. It should be noted that the model was designed for infants, although there is information related to use with older individuals mentioned in the manual. In general, that information suggests that many items might need to be adapted, and that care should be taken to choose areas that are adaptive (functional) for the individual. There is a general lack of data available about the use of the curriculum, and subsequently the assessment component, with older students with severe or profound handicaps. There is mention in the manual to field test data that did not find the use of the curriculum effective with this population on a short-term (3 to 6 months) basis. Clearly, more research with the model is necessary.

Exhibit 5-2 Developmental Progress Chart

☒ No norms available.   ■ Items beyond this point are necessary only for certain populations (see Assessment Log).

Name: _____
Dates: _____

Domain	Sequence	0 – 3 mo.	3 – 6 mo.	6 – 9 mo.	9 – 12 mo.	12 – 15 mo.	15 – 18 mo.	18 – 21 mo.	21 – 24 mo.
Cognition	1. Tactile Integration and Manipulation	a b c		d e f	g h	i		k	
	2. Auditory Localization and Object Permanence	a b c	d	e	f g	h h	i	j k	
	3. Visual Pursuit and Object Permanence	a b c d e	f	g	h	i	j	k	
	4. Object Permanence (Visual-Motor)	a b c	d	d e f g	h	h	i	j k	l m n
	5. Spatial Concepts	a b	c	d	e f	g		h i	j k l
	6. Functional Use of Objects and Symbolic Play	a b	c d e	f g	h		g	h	i j
	7. Control over Physical Environment	a	b c	d	e	f	g	h	i
	8. "Readiness" Concepts						a b	c d	e f g
Communication/ Language	9. Responses to Communication from Others	a b	c d e f g	h i	j k ■	l m	n o p	q r s	t u v w
	10. Gestural Imitation	a	b	c d e	d e	f g h ■	i	m n	o
	11. Gestural Communication	a b	c d e f	g h i		h i	i	k	
	12. Vocal Imitation	a b c d	e f g h	i j	k	l m n o	o p	q r s	t u v
	13. Vocal Communication	a b c	d e f	g h	i j k	l m n	n o p	q r s	r s
S.S./A.*	14. Social Skills	a b c	d e f	g h i j k l	m	m n o	n o	o p	r s
	15. Self-Direction				m	n o	p q	r	s
Self-Help	16. Feeding	a b	c d e f	g h i j k l	m	n o	p	q r	d
	17. Grooming					a	a b	b c	d
	18. Dressing					b	c	c d e	e f
Fine Motor	19. Reaching and Grasping	a b	c d e f	g h i j k	l	a	b c	c d	e f g
	20. Object Manipulation	a b c d	e	f g h	i	j k	a b c d	d e	f g
Gross Motor	21. Bilateral Hand Activity	a b	c d e	f	g	h i	i j k	l m	n
	22. Gross Motor Activities: Stomach	a b	c d e f g h	i j k l	m n o	o p	a b	c	d
	23. Gross Motor Activities: Back	a b c d	e f g		a	b	a	b	c d
	24. Gross Motor Activities: Upright	a	b	c	d e f g h i	j			e

*S.S./A. = Social Skills/Adaptation.

Source: From *The Carolina Curriculum for Handicapped Infants and Infants at Risk* (p. 17) by N. Johnson-Martin et al., 1986, Baltimore: Paul H. Brookes Publishers. Copyright 1986 by Nancy M. Johnson-Martin, Kenneth G. Jens, and Susan M. Attermeier. Reprinted by permission.

The Functional Vision Inventory for the Multiple and Severely Handicapped

Type: Auxiliary
Purpose: Vision testing
Target Population: Persons with severe handicaps

The *Functional Vision Inventory* (Langley, 1980) is the result of a model vision project housed at the John F. Kennedy Center at George Peabody College. The Inventory has two basic purposes: first, to determine if a visual problem is interfering in an individual's learning process, and second to allow teachers and other professionals to determine the amount of functional vision an individual has so that educational programs can be developed. The test was designed for individuals with multiple handicaps; therefore nontraditional assessment techniques are used. For example, two individuals are involved in the evaluation, one to administer the items and the other to record the responses. The Inventory measures seven specific areas of vision:

1. *Structural Defects* (11 items): The examiner carefully studies the individual's eyes for structural defects such as cataracts or muscle imbalance. Questions concern incompatible behaviors such as stereotypic behaviors in which the eyes are involved. Other questions relate to wearing glasses and mobility (e.g., running into objects not seen).
2. *Reflexive Reactions* (9 items): The examiner notes the pupillary response to a penlight and the blinking response when a hand is waved in front of the eyes.
3. *Eye Movements* (9 items): Convergence, visual tracking, and the ability to shift a gaze from object to object are measured.
4. *Near Vision* (10 items): The individual is asked to focus on objects, locate dropped objects, match pictures, and thread beads.
5. *Distance Vision* (5 items): The individual tracks objects at a distance, visually matches objects that are at least 10 feet away, and is measured in the area of visual acuity using the New York Flash Card Vision Test (cards with an apple, umbrella, or house on one side and the number 200, 100, 40, 30, 20, 15, or 10 on the other side).
6. *Visual Field Difference* (3 items): The examiner notes if the individual turns the head to look at a toy or light brought around from the back of the head. Also noted is whether the individual prefers one eye and whether there is any visual field loss.

7. *Visual Perception* (13 items): This subtest requires the individual to perform a series of eye-hand coordination exercises. It also tests form and color perception.

Interpretation of Scores. The scoring system allows the examiner to record the *presence, emergence,* or *absence* of various visually related behaviors. Ten columns provide space for a detailed sketch of the individual's visual skills (see Exhibit 5-3):

1. *Present Column:* indicates whether or not individual is currently displaying the visual behavior
2. *Response Column:* allows examiner to record visual behavior not noted in the scoring criteria, e.g., if individual reacts to a visual stimulus but does not see it well enough to meet criteria for inclusion in the Present Column, it is noted here
3. *Fixation Column:* allows recording of the amount of time individual fixates on the stimulus
4. *Monocular/Binocular Column:* notes whether individual uses one or both eyes to focus on the visual stimuli
5. *Field Column:* allows examiner to record whether individual was using central or peripheral vision to attend to the stimuli
6. *Tracks Column:* includes information about the degree and type of visual tracking the individual exhibits
7. *Distance Column:* notes the distance at which the individual consistently focuses on objects
8. *Size Column:* notes approximate size of objects an individual focuses on
9. *Reaches Column:* measures the accuracy of eye-hand coordination
10. *Scans Column:* notes whether individual scans objects to the left of midline, at midline, or to the right of midline.

Summary. The *Functional Vision Inventory* is one of the few formal instruments available for testing the visual deficits of individuals with severe handicaps. The scoring system is somewhat tedious, but the results are helpful in educational programming decisions by indicating the amount of functional vision an individual has.

Assessment in Infancy: Ordinal Scales of Psychological Development

Type: Other (ordinal scale)
Purpose: Determine developmental level; aid in educational planning
The purpose of the *Ordinal Scales of Psychological Development* (Uzgiris & Hunt, 1975) is to measure cognitive and perceptual develop-

Exhibit 5-3 An Example of a Response Recording Device for the Near Vision Area

IV. Near Vision	Pres.	Response	Fix	Mon/Bin	Field CEN / PER	Tracks − / + / 0	Distance <11" / <23' / <5' / <10' / >10'	Object Size <1" / <2' / <5' / <10'	Reaches acc O U	Scans L M R
1. Reaches for Stationary Toy Materials: any assessment materials, cup of juice					L R					
2. Regards a Cube Materials: bright one inch cube or Weeble										
3. Regard ¼" Objects Materials: cereal, cookie bits, M & M's, bells										
4. Bead/Thread Test Materials: Cake decorations, 1mm, 3mm in size, 2" length red thread										
5. Locates dropped Object Materials: ¼" pegs or pellets, small bells, 1" cube, 2" toy or shape		Peg, Pellet, Bell, Cube, Shape			L 18"–24"R					
6. Matches Pictures Materials: simply drawn pictures no larger than 2-3" in size										

Source: From *Educational Vision Inventory for the Multiple and Severely Handicapped* (p. 28) by M. B. Langley, 1980, Chicago: Stoelting Company. Copyright 1980 by Stoelting Company. Reprinted by permission.

ment using a Piagetian approach. The scales are based on the assumption that individuals go through specific identifiable sequences of development. Rather than using a norm-referenced model of intellectual assessment in which the chronological age at which a specific skill is attained is crucial, the ordinal model determines developmental level regardless of age. The ordinal model is based on the assumption that there is an invariant sequence of behaviors, not linked with a specific age. Although the Ordinal Scales were originally developed for use with infants, they have been used with older individuals who are mentally retarded. In fact, a manual was provided by Dunst (1980) that offers additional items (called *steps*) to make the Ordinal Scales more sensitive to the intermediate levels that individuals with severe or profound handicaps pass through during development.

The Ordinal Scales assess development in six areas. These areas are broken down into *steps*, or test items. The steps involve an activity or directions for eliciting responses including the location of the activity and the materials to be used (a list of 34 items such as stacking rings and string is included in the manual). Exhibit 5-4 is an example of some steps. The behavior necessary to meet the criteria for passing each step is specified. A description of the six scales follows:

1. *Development of Visual Pursuit and the Permanence of Objects* (15 steps): requires individual to perform tasks ranging from "following a slow moving object through a 180 degree arc" to "finding object following a series of invisible displacements by searching in reverse of the order of hiding."
2. *Development of Means for Obtaining Desired Environmental Events* (12 steps): includes items ranging from "appearance of hand-watching behavior" to "foresight in the problem of the solid ring."
3. *Development of Imitation: Vocal and Gestural* (10 steps): items range from "use of vocalization other than crying" to "imitation of new words" (vocal), and "systematic imitation of familiar simple schemes" to "imitation of unfamiliar gestures invisible to the infant" (gestural).
4. *Development of Operational Causality* (7 steps): items include "behavior in a familiar game situation" and "behavior to a spectacle created by an agent."
5. *Construction of Object Relations in Space* (11 steps): items range from "observing two objects alternately" to "indicating absence of familiar persons."

Exhibit 5-4 Sample Examination Record Form

SCALE I: THE DEVELOPMENT OF VISUAL
PURSUIT AND THE PERMANENCE OF OBJECTS

Name:

Birthdate:

Date of Examination:

PRESENTATION

(Suggested number of presentations
for each situation is indicated in
parentheses)

Situation	1 2 3 4 5 6 7

1. Following a Slowly Moving Object through a
   180° Arc (3-4)
    a. Does not follow object
    b. Follows jerkily through part of arc
    c. Follows smoothly through part of arc
    *d. Follows object smoothly through complete
        arc
       Other:

2. Noticing the Disappearance of a Slowly Moving
   Object (3-4)
    a. Does not follow to point of disappearance
    b. Loses interest as soon as object disappears
    *c. Lingers with glance to starting point after
        several presentations
    d. Returns glance to starting point after
       several presentations
    e. Searches around point of disappearance
       Other:

3. Finding an Object Which Is Partially Covered
   (3)
    a. Loses interest
    b. Reacts to the loss, but does not obtain object
    *c. Obtains the object
       Other:

4. Finding an Object Which Is Completely Covered (3)
    a. Loses interest

Source: From *Assessment in Infancy: Ordinal Scales of Psychological Development* (p. 206) by I.
Uzgiris and J. Hunt, 1975, Champaign, IL: University of Illinois Press. Copyright 1975 by University of Illinois Press. Reprinted by permission.

6. *Development of Schemes for Relating to Objects* (3 steps): the items are "acting on simple objects," "acting on several objects available together," and "acting on objects with social meaning."

Interpretation of Scores. For each item, or step, several behaviors are possible. For example, for the item "follows a slowly moving object through a 180 degree arc," the following behaviors are possible: "does not follow object," "follows jerkily through part of arc," "follows smoothly through part of arc," and "follows smoothly through complete arc." A student's performance is scored using the following categories: (+) critical behavior is exhibited, (✔) critical behavior is exhibited after demonstration, (±) critical behavior is emerging, and (-) critical behavior is not demonstrated. Only the (+) and the (✔) are counted in determining the highest developmental attainment in each scale. Perhaps the most valuable use of the test results is provided in Dunst's manual in which intervention activities are suggested. These activities are based on the assumption that consideration of the relations between sensorimotor domains and the development of general cognitive functioning is more important than the development of an isolated skill.

Technical Characteristics. The Ordinal Scales were developed through the careful observation of at least four infants at each month of age from 1 to 24 months. Since this is not a norm-referenced test, there is no standardization sample. Inter-rater reliability data indicate that observer agreements range from 93.0 to 98.5%. The Ordinal Scales have *intrinsic validity* (Gorrell, 1985). This is the statistical determination that the scales are sequential.

Kahn (1976) investigated the reliability and validity of the instrument with 63 individuals with severe or profound handicaps. Inter-rater reliability ranged from .78 (Development of Schemes) to .95 (Development of Visual Pursuit and Permanence of Objects). Test-retest coefficients were .88 or above for each scale. He also noted that the ordinal nature of the scales was maintained when used with the population with severe or profound handicaps.

Summary. The *Ordinal Scales of Psychological Development* can provide important information regarding the cognitive functioning of individuals with severe or profound handicaps, especially when used in conjunction with the Dunst (1980) manual. A major limitation, however, is the reliance in some test areas on intact gross and fine motor capabilities. Major adaptations are necessary for students with severe motor limitations.

Project MEMPHIS

Type: Criterion-referenced
Purpose: Determination of goals and objectives
Target Population: Preschool children with handicaps

As a part of *Project MEMPHIS* (acronym for Memphis Educational Model Providing Handicapped Infant Services) (Quick, Little, & Campbell, 1974), a three-step developmental-educational evaluation and program evaluation is provided. The assessment model includes the MEMPHIS Comprehensive Developmental Scale, the Developmental Skill Assignment Record, and the Continuous Record for Educational-Developmental Gain.

MEMPHIS Comprehensive Developmental Scale. This scale assesses developmental skills in five areas. It is designed for preschool exceptional children between birth and age five. Information for the scale can be gathered through either direct observation (by someone who is familiar with the child) or interview. The scale gives only rough estimates of developmental levels and should be considered more of a screening and programming instrument rather than a diagnostic device.

There are a total of 260 items on the scale. Each item in the various subscales is correlated with developmental age levels and is therefore presented sequentially. Descriptions of the five areas are as follows:

1. *Personal-Social Skills* (60 items): includes such items as "drinks from glass or cup unassisted" (18-month developmental age), "dries hands well" (33-month), and "distinguishes front from back of clothes" (51-month).
2. *Gross Motor Skills* (40 items): includes "rolls over to side from back position" (3-month developmental age), "stands on one leg momentarily" (30-month), and "walks distances on tiptoe or skips alternating feet" (60-month).
3. *Fine Motor Skills* (40 items): includes "good grasp and release are present" (12-month developmental age) and "copies a cross from an example" (51-month).
4. *Language Skills* (60 items): includes "imitates words" (12-month developmental age), "knows last name and sex" (33-month), and "repeats a five-word sentence" (51-month).
5. *Perceptual-Cognitive Skills* (60 items): includes "responds to bye-bye" (9-month developmental age), "counts two objects" (30-month), and "recognizes and names common coins" (60-month).

Interpretation of Scores. An item is considered passed if it is regularly a part of the child's behavioral repertoire. Each item administered (you discontinue testing after six consecutive failures) is marked either passed or failed. The raw score is simply the number of items passed. There is a raw score for each subscale. This raw score is converted to a developmental age. Each developmental age can then be plotted on a profile available in the scale.

Developmental Skill Assignment Record. This record helps the teacher plan individual programs. Based on the results of the Comprehensive Developmental Scale, skills to be taught for a particular child are identified and placed on the Developmental Skill Assignment Record. A description of each skill, including criteria for passing the skill, must then be made by the teacher. In addition, an estimated time period for programming a child on the pinpointed skills is recorded. This section simply provides a standard format for prioritizing educational objectives and offers a guideline for meeting them.

Continuous Record for Educational-Developmental Gain. This record assists a teacher in keeping ongoing records of the skills identified on the Developmental Skill Assignment Record. There are five pages (one for each subscale). Each page allows for the evaluation of four skills. Information on the Continuous Record includes date evaluated, a pass or fail category, and a quality category. The quality category involves the recording of the degree of competence with which a child demonstrates a skill. There is a completion record on the cover sheet that summarizes the number of skills assigned from each subscale, the number mastered, and the percent mastered.

Summary. The assessment section of Project MEMPHIS offers a systematic and accountable method for evaluating preschool children with handicaps. One criticism is that the skills on the Comprehensive Developmental Scale are not well defined and necessitate some degree of subjectivity.

Pennsylvania Training Model Individual Assessment Guide

Type: Criterion-referenced
Purpose: Determination of goals and objectives
Target Population: Persons with severe or profound handicaps
The *Pennsylvania Training Model* (Somerton-Fair & Turner, 1979) was developed to meet the educational requirements of the population with severe or profound handicaps. In addition to a Curriculum Assessment Guide, which serves as a gross screening instrument in several behavioral

domains, there are sections on Developmental Taxonomies and Skill Observation Strategies. Also included is an Individual Prescription Planning Sheet.

Curriculum Assessment Guide. The purpose of this section is to provide information in four areas: how an individual (1) receives and expresses information; (2) moves about in his or her environment; (3) socializes; and (4) processes and retains information. There are 70 items broken down into 14 skill areas, each 14 containing five major behavioral items representing the range considered "traditional" among the population with severe or profound handicaps. Information for the assessment is usually obtained through direct observation. There are well-defined criteria for each item. Descriptions of the 14 skill areas are as follows:

1. *Tactile Skills:* Items range from "responds to tactile stimulation" to "ability to discriminate objects."
2. *Auditory Skills:* Items range from "reacts positively or negatively to loud noise" to "changes activity with change of sound."
3. *Visual Skills:* Items range from "responds to light" to "identifies familiar objects through sight."
4. *Gross Motor Skills:* Items range from "holds head in prone position" to "brings self to standing position."
5. *Fine Motor Skills:* Items range from "claps hands" to "strings beads."
6. *Feeding and Drinking Skills:* Items range from "swallows when stimulated externally" to "eats independently using spoon."
7. *Toilet Training Skills:* Items range from "retains urine for one hour" to "toilets independently."
8. *Dressing and Undressing Skills:* Items range from "takes sock off" to "buttons."
9. *Washing and Bathing Skills:* Items range from "attempts to wash with washcloth" to "washes and dries self independently."
10. *Nasal Hygiene Skills:* Items range from "wipes nose" to "cleans nose independently."
11. *Oral Hygiene Skills:* Items range from "opens mouth for toothbrushing" to "brushes teeth independently."
12. *Communication Skills:* Items range from "responds to 'look at me'" to "spontaneously verbalizes."
13. *Perceptual-Cognitive Skills:* Items range from "lifts cups to obtain object underneath" to "copies circle."
14. *Social Interaction Skills:* Items range from "smiles in response to facial expression of others" to "takes turns."

Each item can be scored in one of four ways depending on the item: the number of days the task was presented, the number of trials to reach criterion, the total time spent on the item, or the total number of correct responses. This information can be used as a rough guide for identifying areas to consider for educational programming and to indicate the modality strengths and weaknesses and motivational factors pertinent for each individual educational plan.

Developmental Taxonomies. This section was developed to give detailed sequences of behaviors in each of the 14 skill areas. These behavioral sequences are intended to assist the teacher/trainer in determining the appropriate curriculum by giving a much more detailed breakdown of the skill areas. For instance, the gross motor area is broken down into 43 behaviors, the feeding and drinking area into 80, and the toileting area into 43. For each behavior in the sequence, an individual can be scored in one of six ways. An "O" is given if the behavior was observed. An "X" is given if the behavior was not observed. A "U" is given if the behavior was unknown (unable to be observed). A "P" (physical prompt), "G" (gestural prompt), or "V" (verbal prompt) is specified if it was necessary to initiate the child's behavior.

Skill Observation Strategies. This section was developed to incorporate the information from the Curriculum Assessment Guide and the Developmental Taxonomies sections into functional lesson plans. This information gives the teacher/trainer instructional suggestions after developmental pinpoints (skill area and specific behaviors) have been identified.

Individual Prescriptive Planning Sheet. This Planning Sheet provides for the systematic planning of the student's curriculum (see Exhibit 5-5). Included are antecedents (preparation procedures necessary before teacher intervention), the behavior itself (including definitions of correct and incorrect behavior), the consequences given by the teacher of both correct and incorrect behaviors, and the criteria necessary to master a particular behavioral item.

Summary. The Pennsylvania Training Model Individual Assessment Guide has many positive characteristics, including well-defined test items and a means of translating assessment information into functional educational plans.

Exhibit 5-5 Individual Prescriptive Planning Sheet from the Pennsylvania Training Model

Student's Name		Date		Area Involved		Terminal Objective		Educator
ANTECEDENTS (GIVENS)		BEHAVIOR		CONSEQUENCES		CRITERIA	COMMENTS	
Preparation	Procedures	Correct	Error	Correct	Error			
1) Mash food.	1) Place Dennis' right hand around handle of spoon.	1) Dennis takes food from spoon with lips.	1) More than half the food is left on the spoon.	1) Pat on left shoulder paired with "Dennis eats nicely". 1:1	1) Ignore unsuccessful trial. 1:1	8 out of 10 correct trials for 3 consecutive days.		
2) Place food in yellow bowl.	2) Instructor should place her right hand over Dennis' right hand.							
3) Place Dennis' therapy spoon in bowl.	3) Instructor's left hand supporting right elbow.							
4) Place Dennis in chair with feet & side support.	4) Guide Dennis' hand to scoop small amount of food from bowl.							
5) Place chair at lunch table with no other children present.	5) Direct full spoon to mouth.							
6) Instructor should sit to Dennis' right side.	6) Give verbal command "eat your food".							
	7) Instructor should withdraw spoon from Dennis' mouth & guide his hand & spoon back to bowl.							

Source: From *Pennsylvania Training Model* by E. Somerton-Fair and K. Turner, 1979, Pennsylvania Department of Education.

Vineland Adaptive Behavior Scales

Type: Norm-referenced
Purpose: Classification decisions and determination of general goals
Target Population: Test was standardized on a national representative sample (approximately 10% enrolled in special education)

The Vineland Adaptive Behavior Scales (VABS) (Sparrow, Balla, & Cicchetti, 1984) is a revision and modification of the Vineland Social Maturity Scale (Doll, 1965). Doll made a significant contribution to the area of adaptive behavior assessment, and the authors of the VABS have incorporated many of his concepts in designing the new instrument. The VABS is a much more comprehensive test than its predecessor.

The VABS, designed for use with individuals aged 3 to 18, has three editions that can be used separately or in combination: the classroom edition, which allows teachers to assess adaptive behavior in the classroom, and two interview editions that are administered in a semistructured format with the parents or primary caregiver as the respondent. The *Interview Edition—Survey Form* is most like the original Vineland and measures an individual's strengths and deficits. The *Interview Edition—Expanded Form* is more comprehensive and is the edition that has the most relevance for individuals with severe handicaps. Both interview editions measure 5 domains that are broken down into 12 subdomains.

Interview Edition—Expanded Form. There are a total of 574 items on the Expanded Form in 5 areas:

1. *Communication Domain* (133 items): The three subdomains are: (1) Receptive measures areas such as "beginning to understand" and "listening and attending"; (2) Expressive has areas such as "prespeech sounds" and "articulating"; (3) and Written measures reading and writing skills.
2. *Daily Living Skills Domain* (200 items): There are three subdomains: (1) Personal measures areas such as eating and toileting; (2) Domestic measures such areas as housecleaning and food preparation; and (3) Community includes such areas as safety and understanding money.
3. *Socialization Domain* (134 items): The three subdomains are (1) Interpersonal Relationships (e.g., "recognizing emotions" and "initiating social communication"), (2) Play and Leisure Time (e.g., "playing with toys" and "sharing and cooperating"), and (3) Coping Skills (e.g., "following rules").

4. *Motor Skills Domain* (71 items): This section assesses gross and fine motor skills.
5. *Maladaptive Behavior* (36 items): This optional domain allows for rating a number of maladaptive or inappropriate behaviors.

Interpretation of Scores. A variety of scores are available from the VABS including standard scores, percentile ranks, stanines, and age equivalents. These are available for the domains, subdomains, and a composite of the Communication, Daily Living Skills, Socialization, and Motor Skills domains. One nice feature is a summary report for parents, although this is used to provide meaning to the test scores and does not provide specific information for parents of children with severe or profound handicaps.

Technical Characteristics. The VABS was standardized on a national representative sample of 3,000 individuals aged 0 to 18 years; approximately 10% were receiving special education. Only the Survey Form was administered to the sample; the norms and the technical data (primarily validity) of the Expanded Form were determined using statistical calibration and estimate techniques. Test-retest reliability for the Survey Form was high (.98 to .99) although no estimated coefficients for the Expanded Form were given. The inter-rater reliability for the Survey Form ranged from .62 (Socialization) to .78 (Motor Skills). A discussion of the content and construct validity of the VABS is provided in the manual. Criterion-related validity of the Survey Form was established by correlating its scores with the original Vineland Social Maturity Scale (.55). The VABS correlated relatively low (.32) with an intelligence test: the *Kaufman Assessment Battery for Children.* The authors suggest this provides additional evidence of the test's validity since adaptive behavior scales and intelligence tests measure different areas of functioning. Similarly, they report low correlations (.12 to .37) with the *Peabody Picture Vocabulary Test—Revised*, with the highest correlation coefficient being with the Communication Domain. The estimated validity coefficients of the Expanded Form were almost identical with or slightly higher than those reported for the Survey Form.

Summary. The VABS promises to be one of the most widely used adaptive behavior instruments. The standardization and technical aspects are good, and it is based on a sound theoretical model. The test will have its greatest use with students with mild or moderate handicaps, although the Expanded Form contains many items appropriate for individuals with severe handicaps.

Vulpé Assessment Battery

Type: Criterion-referenced
Purpose: Determination of objectives
Target Population: Persons with or without handicaps

The *Vulpé Assessment Battery* (Vulpé, 1979) is a developmentally based system for measuring behaviors of children ages birth to six years. Information from the Vulpé can be used to determine an appropriate specific teaching approach, to indicate program goals and objectives, and to provide an accountability system for individual programs. The Vulpé is sequentially based in a number of developmental skill areas, and the author states it is applicable to all children, including multihandicapped, at-risk, and normal. She further states that the battery is comprehensive, individualized, and competency oriented. The Vulpé is divided into various developmental skill areas or sections, and further divided into subskill areas or subsections. An appendix includes a developmental reflex test and functional tests of muscle strength, motor planning, and balance.

There are eight skill areas included. Many items appear in more than one section. To eliminate the need to administer an item more than once, those included in more than one section are cross-referenced on the assessment form. All listed equipment necessary and the instructions for administering each item are on the record form. Descriptions of the skill areas are as follows:

1. *Basic Senses and Functions* (16 items): measures central nervous system functions considered important in performing basic activities, including vision, hearing, olfaction, balance, muscle strength, range of motion, and reflexes.
2. *Gross Motor Behaviors* (206 items): includes items that measure such behaviors as standing, jumping, lying down, sitting, kneeling, skipping, and running.
3. *Fine Motor Behaviors* (177 items): includes items concerned with behaviors of small muscle movements such as eye coordination, eye-hand coordination, reaching, manipulation, and use of toys and utensils.
4. *Language Behaviors* (241 items): divided into two subsections: Auditory Expressive Language (160 items) includes items ranging from vocalizing noises to saying one-word sentences to using free expression. Auditory Receptive Language (81 items) ranges from hearing sounds to comprehending sentences.

5. *Cognitive Processes and Specific Concepts* (245 items): divided into 13 subsections: (1) Object Concepts (17 items) measures understanding of objects from a developmental (for example, Piagetian) framework; (2) Body Concepts (32 items) includes items regarding self-image and knowledge of body parts; (3) Color Concepts (9 items) includes items ranging from matching and sorting to naming and discriminating colors; (4) Shape Concepts (22 items) includes items that require a child to identify shapes and discriminate three-dimensional objects and parts of objects; (5) Size Concepts (6 items) includes items measuring the understanding of such concepts as "bigger," "longer," and "shorter"; (6) Space Concepts (36 items) includes items related to the child's understanding of relations of his or her own body to objects in space and the abstract understanding of space not directly related to self; (7) Time Concepts (16 items) includes items measuring understanding of events occurring in the immediate present as well as more abstract concepts of past and future; (8) Amount and Number Concepts (22 items) includes counting and understanding quantitative concepts; (9) Visual Memory (12 items) includes items requiring rote memory and more complex sequential memory; (10) Auditory Discrimination (12 items) requires a child to discriminate consonants, words, sounds, and tones; (11) Auditory, Attention, Comprehension, and Memory (25 items) includes items such as "follows one-step command," "repeats four words," "follows three-step command," and "repeats four digits"; (12) Cause/Effect or Means/End Behavior (12 items) includes items such as "understands relationship of adult's presence to being lifted" and "uses parts of objects for specific purposes"; (13) Categorizing/Combining Scheme (24 items) includes items requiring the child to integrate information and to organize it into meaningful thoughts and actions.

6. *Organization of Behavior* (79 items): divided into four parts: (1) Attention and Goal Orientation (18 items) is concerned with the ability to orient and react to sensory stimuli, and to attend, selectively focus, and maintain attention; (2) Internal Control to Environmental Limits (20 items) includes recognition of boundaries or behavioral limits in the environment and the desire and ability to control behaviors to function effectively in the environment; (3) Problem Solving and Learning Patterns (17 items) includes items measuring the ability to react appropriately to the environment, to imitate others, and to solve problems of different complexity; (4) Dependence/Independence (24 items) measures behavior along a dependence/independence continuum.

7. *Activities of Daily Living:* includes subsections on feeding (47 items), dressing (32 items), social interaction (48 items), playing (50 items), sleeping (16 items), toileting (17 items), and grooming (12 items); items are similar to those in most adaptive behavior scales measuring daily living skills.
8. *Assessment of Environment:* This section is somewhat unique for a developmental skill instrument such as the Vulpe'. It measures the interaction of the child and the environment to discover whether the child's physical and emotional needs are met by the physical environment. There are also items that measure the characteristics and knowledge level of the "primary caregiver."

Interpretation of Scores. Each item is scored in one of seven ways. A *no* score is given if the child has no apparent interest or motivation to participate or cannot attend to the task. An *attention* score is given if the child shows interest in any part of the activity but does not actively participate because of physical incapacity or insufficient attention. A *physical assistance* score is used if the child actively participates in the activity when the task or environment is modified. A *social-emotional assistance* score is used when the child is given feedback, reinforcement, or reassurance to participate in the task. A *verbal assistance* score is given if the child's performance changes when verbal cues are given or the instructions repeated. An *independent* score is given when the child succeeds with no assistance in familiar surroundings. A *transfer* score is given if the child can perform tasks of similar complexity in different environments.

These scores can be marked directly on the Performance Analysis/ Developmental Assessment scoring pad (see Exhibit 5-6). Using this system, an objective might be written for a specific skill that would allow the student to move from left (more dependent) to right (more independent). Comments about a child's performance can be included. Age levels are provided for the items, but they represent gross indicators and should be used only to determine relative strengths and weaknesses.

Summary. The Vulpé offers a comprehensive assessment of developmental skills of children aged birth to six years. Its comprehensiveness, in fact, might be considered one of its drawbacks: it takes time to administer and score all the appropriate items. The results, however, are more meaningful than those yielded from most developmental tests, particularly for educational programming purposes. Another limitation is the relatively few items in certain subsections.

Exhibit 5-6 Scoring Sheet from the Vulpé Assessment Battery

VULPÉ ASSESSMENT BATTERY ★ SCORING PAD

PERFORMANCE ANALYSIS/DEVELOPMENTAL ASSESSMENT

Name _____ Birthdate: _____

Developmental Area: _____

Date: _____ Manual page: _____

| | COMMENTS |
| SCALE SCORE | INFORMATION PROCESSING AND ACTIVITY ANALYSIS |

No	Attention	Phys. Assis.	Soc./Emot. Assis.	Verbal Assis.	Independent	Transfer	1. Analyse activities considering component parts of each and relationship to: Basic Senses & Functions Organizational Behaviors Cognitive Processes & Specific Concepts Auditory Language Gross & Fine Motor	2. Information Processing Consider: Input Integration Feedback Assimilation Output
1	2	3	4	5	6	7		

Activity (Item number)

1 2 3 4 5 6 7

Activity (Item number)

1 2 3 4 5 6 7

Activity (Item number)

1 2 3 4 5 6 7

Activity (Item number)

1 2 3 4 5 6 7

Activity (Item number)

1 2 3 4 5 6 7

Source: From *Vulpé Assessment Battery* by S.G. Vulpé, 1979, National Institute on Mental Retardation. Copyright 1977 for use with the *Vulpé Assessment Battery* by Shirley German Vulpé. Reprinted by permission.

A Model of Assessment: Choosing the Best Instrument

There are indeed a number of instruments available to the teacher or specialist for assessing students with severe or profound handicaps. The question of "which test do I use?" is a very important one. Before this question is answered, however, a more fundamental one must first be addressed. That question, addressed in the previous chapter, is "What is the purpose for the assessment?" (Taylor, 1984).

Screening (Determination of Goals)

As noted previously, *screening* is a procedural term that has multiple meanings. For the population with severe or profound handicaps it usually involves the identification of *general* program goals. The Interview Edition—Survey Form from the VABS, the *AAMD Adaptive Behavior Scale*, the Comprehensive Developmental Scale from *Project MEMPHIS*, and the Curriculum Assessment Guide from the *Pennsylvania Training Model* could all be used for this purpose, as might the Callier-Azusa, the *Ordinal Scales of Psycological Development*, and the Assessment Log and Developmental Progress Chart.

Auxiliary Assessment and Programming

This step of the assessment model involves the development and integration of programs from the other members of the assessment team. For instance, the physical therapist, speech therapist, and social worker might develop specific programs that are integrated with the teacher's information in the student's overall educational program. In this chapter, the Functional Vision Inventory was discussed as an example of an instrument used in auxiliary assessment.

Classification Decisions

Although a student might have a medical diagnosis before receiving educational programming, eligibility requirements for special education must also be met. This is accomplished through the administration of instruments that establish an educational need and determine the most appropriate "label" to assign the student to receive the most appropriate program. For students with severe or profound handicaps, an adaptive behavior scale is usually administered as part of the battery to determine the label and the potential placement. The *AAMD Adaptive Behavior Scale* and the VABS have been used for this purpose. These instruments are not sensitive enough for determining specific objectives; rather they compare an individual's general adaptive behavior level with others. Thus, degrees of handicap can be determined.

Determination of Educational Objectives

For the teacher of children with severe or profound handicaps, the determination of educational objectives is probably the most important purpose of assessment. To help the teacher choose the best instrument, the tests discussed in this chapter will be further divided into three categories: tests designed for special populations, comprehensive tests requiring preselection, and assessment systems.

Two tests were specifically designed for special populations. The *Balthazar Scales* were standardized using individuals with severe or profound mental retardation. As a result, compared with most other instruments, there are fewer areas measured (functional independence and social adaptation), with more items in each area. The *Callier-Azusa Scale* was designed for use with children who are deaf-blind or who have severe or profound handicaps. The scoring system thus allows for the omission of certain items if a child has a sensory or motor deficit.

Several tests are comprehensive, requiring the examiner to administer only portions or certain areas. This requires either that the examiner is familiar enough with the student to know the priority areas of assessment or that screening measures are obtained to determine the target areas. The *Vulpé Assessment Battery* measures eight major areas and includes approximately 6,000 items; it also has a rather detailed scoring system that further necessitates limiting the number of items. For this test, the amount of usable information is largely dependent on the ability of the examiner to determine and prioritize assessment need areas.

Finally, some tests used to determine educational objectives are actually assessment systems. The *Pennsylvania Training Model* includes a Curriculum Assessment Guide that serves as a screening instrument in a number of skill areas as well as a Developmental Taxonomies section to give detailed behavior sequences for each of the skill areas. The *Pennsylvania Training Model* also includes a Skill Observation Strategies section to aid in the development of functional educational programs and an Individual Prescriptive Planning Sheet section to monitor the program. *Project MEMPHIS* includes a Comprehensive Developmental Scale that measures five areas, a Developmental Skill Assignment Record to help prioritize objectives, and a Continuous Record for Educational-Developmental Gain.

Implementation of the Educational Program

A total educational program involves the integration of all assessment data to develop the most appropriate program. Included in the program are such factors as general program goals, specific program objectives, personnel involved, adaptive equipment (if needed), and criteria for successfully meeting the program objectives.

Evaluation of the Education Program

This evaluation is, in reality, nothing more than the evaluation of the student's progress toward attainment of objectives. Typically, documentation of this progress is accomplished through pre-, post-, or continuous evaluation. Usually, the instrument used to establish the objectives is also used to test progress.

Certain instruments deserve additional comment. The *Adaptive Behavior Scale* and the VABS, because they are norm-referenced, are sometimes used to measure global progress, usually annually. Typically however, because of their lack of sensitivity with students with severe or profound handicaps, little if any progress is documented. As a result, the instrument used to determine the educational objectives is readministered to determine the success of, or the need to revise, the educational program. In addition, the *Pennsylvania Training Model and Project MEMPHIS* both include a system of accountability to measure progress.

CONCLUSION

It is imperative that new tests for this population be developed and older tests be improved. The lack of adequate technical characteristics of many currently available instruments makes the difficult task of assessing individuals with severe or profound handicaps even more difficult.

Finally, the importance of knowing what test to use in a given situation cannot be minimized. The information included in this chapter emphasizes the importance of carefully designating the purpose for assessment.

REFERENCES

Balthazar, E. (1976). *Balthazar scales of adaptive behavior.* Palo Alto, CA: Consulting Psychologists.

Cohen, M., Gross, P., & Haring, N. (1976). Developmental pinpoints. In N. Haring & L. Brown (Eds.), *Teaching the severely handicapped* (Vol. 1) (pp. 35-110). New York: Grune & Stratton.

Cole, K., Swisher, V., Thompson, M., & Fewell, R. (1985). Enhancing sensitivity of assessment instruments for children: Graded multidimensional scoring. *Journal of the Association for Persons with Severe Handicaps, 10,* 209-213.

Doll, E. (1965). *Vineland social maturity scale.* Circle Pines, MN: American Guidance Service.

Dunst, C. (1980). *A clinical and educational manual for use with the Uzgiris and Hunt scales of infant psychological development.* Baltimore: University Park Press.

Gorrell, J. (1985). Ordinal scales of psychological development. In D. Keyser & R. Sweetland (Eds.), *Test critiques* (Vol. 2, pp. 543-549). Kansas City: Test Corporation of America.

Johnson-Martin, N.M., Jens, K.G., & Attermeier, S.M. (1986). *The Carolina curriculum for handicapped infants and infants at risk.* Baltimore: Paul H. Brookes.

Kahn, J. (1976). Utility of the Uzgiris and Hunt scales of sensorimotor development with severely and profoundly retarded children. *American Journal of Mental Deficiency, 80,* 663-665.

Langley, M.B. (1980). *Functional vision inventory for the multiple and severely handicapped.* Chicago: Stoelting.

Nihira, K., Foster, R., Shellhaas, M., & Leland, H. (1975). *Adaptive behavior scale.* Washington, DC: American Association on Mental Deficiency.

Quick, A., Little, T., & Campbell, A. (1974). *Project MEMPHIS: Memphis comprehensive development scales.* Belmont, CA: Fearon.

Somerton-Fair, E., & Turner, K. (1979). *Pennsylvania training model.* Harrisburg, PA: Pennsylvania Department of Education.

Sparrow, S., Balla, D., & Cicchetti, D. (1985). *Vineland adaptive behavior scales.* Circle Pines, MN: American Guidance Service.

Stillman, R. (1978). *Callier-Azusa scale.* Dallas: University of Texas at Dallas, Callier Center for Communication Disorders.

Taylor, R.L. (1984). *Assessment of exceptional students: Educational and psychological procedures.* Englewood Cliffs, NJ: Prentice-Hall.

Taylor, R., Warren, S., & Slocumb, P. (1979). Categorizing behavior in terms of severity: Considerations for part two of the adaptive behavior scale. *American Journal of Mental Deficiency, 83,* 411-414.

Uzgiris, I., & Hunt, J. (1975). *Assessment in infancy: Ordinal scales of psychological development.* Urbana, IL: University of Illinois Press.

Vulpé, S.G. (1979). *Vulpé assessment battery.* Toronto, Canada: National Institute on Mental Retardation.

Part IV

Behavior Management Concerns

Chapter 6

Systems and Procedures for Managing Behavior

Les Sternberg and Ronald L. Taylor

PROBLEM

Many students with severe or profound handicaps experience significant difficulties in managing their behaviors. In many respects, these difficulties may not be inherent in the individual but rather due to his or her environment. Because of the past tendency to isolate students with severe or profound handicaps into segregated and extremely restrictive settings, expectations for more normalized types of behaviors were almost nonexistent; therefore, opportunities for their acquisition were often not provided (Renzaglia & Bates, 1983).

In terms of managing behaviors, two areas of concern are noteworthy. The first relates to development and control of *social skills.* Social skills are those behaviors that, when acquired and performed successfully, can assist the individual in becoming more independent and better able to adapt to a variety of appropriate environments. Included in this category would be behaviors related to appropriate social interaction and interpersonal skills, communication skills in a social context, and independent living skills. The second area relates to *aberrant behaviors.* For the most part, these behaviors are considered extremely abnormal and are often very disturbing to others (Gaylord-Ross, 1980). Such behaviors can be self-directed (e.g., self-abuse) or other-directed (e.g., biting others). A student's type and level of aberrant behavior can negatively affect his or her ability to acquire and display various social skills. When students with severe or profound handicaps exhibit excessive aberrant behaviors, those behaviors interfere with the student's ability to attend to relevant aspects of social skills training situations (Gaylord-Ross, 1980).

PAST PRACTICES

If there is one intervention area for students with severe or profound handicaps that has received significant and noteworthy attention in the literature, it is the area of behavior management. The literature is replete with documentation concerning various techniques used to remedy social deficits (Adkins & Matson, 1980; Bates & Renzaglia, 1982; Cuvo, Jacobi, & Sipko, 1981; Doleys, Stacy, & Knowles, 1981; Johnson & Cuvo, 1981; Koop, Martin, Yu, & Suthons, 1980; Matson, 1980; Matson & Adkins, 1980; Matson & Andrasik, 1982; Risley & Cuvo, 1980; Schleien, Ash, Kiernan, & Wehman, 1981; Walls, Crist, Sienicki, & Grant, 1981; Walls, Ellis, & Zane, 1981) or decrease aberrant behaviors exhibited at excessive levels (Carey & Bucher, 1981; Carr, Newsom, & Binkoff, 1980; Dorsey, Iwata, Ong, & McSween, 1980; Harris & Wolchik, 1979; Polvinale & Lutzker, 1980; Rincover, Cook, Peoples, & Packard, 1979; Roberts, Iwata, McSween, & Desmond, 1979; Rose, 1979). Until recently, however, two major problems existed. The first was the lack of a coherent and consistent decision-making plan for not only initiating behavior control programs but for changing them when failure was evident. The second was the paucity of behavior change research pertaining to students with intractable aberrant behaviors.

SUGGESTED METHODS

When there are questions raised about either developing social skills or decreasing or eliminating aberrant behavior, the answers revolve around behavior change. Behavior change is typically viewed from the standpoint of either remedying *behavior deficits* (desired behaviors that do not occur at an acceptable level or rate) or decreasing *behavior excesses* (undesirable behaviors that occur too frequently). In many cases with students with severe or profound handicaps, behavior deficits can be manifested in depressed social skill levels, and behavior excesses are often represented by frequent displays of aberrant behaviors. As indicated previously, there is often a relation between the behavior deficits and excesses (e.g., when a student's level of self-abuse prevents him or her from exhibiting specific on-task behavior). Given this interactive quality, programs developed to effect behavior change must often be designed so that both behavior deficits *and* excesses are dealt with simultaneously. Options for behavior change programs are considerable and have necessitated that practitioners advocate and use a more systematic approach to determining the best fit between the expressed behavioral needs of the student and the range of options available.

A number of approaches provide model frameworks for establishing behavior change programs.

Models for Behavior Change Programs

Evans and Meyer

Evans and Meyer (1985) provided a comprehensive and detailed decision-making system for selecting an appropriate behavior change strategy for behavior excesses. In their system, two conditions must be met before determining what type of behavior change program might be necessary.

The first is a *functional analysis* of the behavior. This involves determining if any environmental events are currently acting to "cause" the behavior. This analysis usually takes the form of systematically charting events that precede (*before events* or *antecedents*) and immediately follow (*after events* or *consequences*) the behavior. The observer then looks for consistencies that can probably account for the behavior. For example, a child might begin self-abuse incidents each time a certain adult comes in close proximity (an antecedent "cause") or display more self-abuse as a result of someone telling him or her to stop the incident each time it occurs (a consequence "cause"). A functional analysis can provide direction in choosing a specific behavior change strategy. It also is an effective tool to generate ideas concerning the *intent* (function), if any, of the behavior. Recently, a number of researchers (Carr & Durand, 1985; Donnellan, Mirenda, Mesaros, & Fassbender, 1984; Durand & Carr, 1985; Iwata, Dorsey, Slifer, Baumann, & Richman, 1982) developed comprehensive functional analysis schemes to determine whether certain types of aberrant behaviors actually serve functional purposes (e.g., when self-injurious behavior is used intentionally to communicate a desire for or against physical or social interaction).

Evans and Meyer cautioned that, in certain situations, consistencies may be difficult to establish. This is especially the case when certain environmental events might be hard to observe. Examples would be antecedent *setting events*, where an environmental event that took place considerably before the behavior occurrence affects the behavior, and consequent *intrinsic reinforcers*, where the behavior continues to occur because of its self-reinforcing quality (e.g., self-stimulation).

Functional analysis can also prove extremely worthwhile in helping set up programs for social skills training, especially in regard to antecedent effects on social skills development. Renzaglia and Bates (1983) reviewed potential antecedent factors that can be used to increase social skills. These include expanding the environmental opportunities for increased interaction between students with severe handicaps and their peers without handicaps, changing the quality of materials students with severe handicaps are required to interact with, and more carefully controlling the types of prompts and prompt sequences used with students.

The second major condition that must be met before a behavior change program is formalized is *prioritizing the behaviors that should be changed.* As Evans and Meyer (1985) pointed out, it is very rarely the case that a person with severe handicaps exhibits only one behavior excess. What is necessary is to determine how serious the behavior actually is, for this will determine if and what type of intervention plan will be followed. Although there are many types of systems for determining the severity of behavior excesses, Evans and Meyer provided a number of categories of behavior excesses:

- behaviors in urgent need of reduction due to their potential for self-harm (e.g., self-abuse)
- behaviors that are a concern to others in that they most probably will be used to hurt others (e.g., aggressive acts)
- behaviors that may negatively affect one's adjustment to people and environments (e.g., excessive self-stimulation behavior in public)
- behaviors incompatible with or that prevent more positive behavior (e.g., when self-stimulation may prevent on-task behavior)
- behaviors that, if changed, could increase functionality for the individual in more than one way (e.g., increasing appropriate tooth brushing skills so as to prevent tooth decay and afford the individual a better appearance)
- behaviors that, if changed, assist the teacher in more easily carrying out his or her instruction (e.g., decreasing masturbation so that the student will more appropriately interact with objects during instructional episodes)

These categories of behavior are associated with priority levels. Behaviors that are life-threatening are Level I. Behaviors that are potentially harmful to others are Level II. All other behaviors are Level III.

Evans and Meyer refer practitioners to a decision-making procedure (flow chart) for designing and implementing behavior change programs. The crux of most of the suggested procedures is the concept of *positive alternatives.* This implies that one can decrease a behavior excess by providing intervention or instruction toward developing a more positive behavior. Often this positive alternative will serve the same function as the inappropriate behavior. Emphasis, then, is on the development of this alternative, especially in that it will typically be reinforced because it is behavior preferred and desired by others. Evans and Meyer do not, however, preclude the possibility of using *negative consequences* (punishment) for behavior excesses. They typically recommend that, if at all possible, such consequences be delivered for a very short time with the positive alternative reinforced simultaneously. They discuss alternatives in the event simultaneous programming is not possible.

Sternberg and Schilit

Sternberg and Schilit (1986) also provided a system for developing behavior change programs for social skills training and aberrant behavior reduction. The purpose of their model is three-fold: (1) to provide descriptions of specific consequent behavioral strategies and everyday examples of how those strategies might be used; (2) to describe a decision-making process for identifying what type of behavioral strategy to start with; and (3) to outline a procedure of what to do if a technique does not seem to be working.

The system describes prerequisites to the establishment of any behavior change program, including:

- a concise and accurate description of the behavior one wishes to change and whether the desire is to increase or decrease the behavior (for the purpose of communication to others)
- a functional analysis of the behavior, including a determination of the intent, if any, of the behavior
- a measure of the degree or level of the behavior (requires knowledge of various types of observation strategies and corresponding data collection systems)

Sternberg and Schilit recommended that, when one is at the point of selecting a consequent behavioral technique, the "flow" of behavioral options be outlined. This outline is necessary so that the practitioner can see the options that might be available for dealing with any targeted behavior. A range of behavioral options is provided based on the concept that the least intrusive (least restrictive) technique should always be opted for initially: always select a procedure that is as *natural, non-disruptive, and non-aversive* as possible to the student and to others. Also, any other technique considered as a result of the student not reaching the criterion should proceed from less restrictive to more restrictive.

Table 6-1 is a summary of some options, with their progression based on a *hypothetical* sequence of least to most restrictive. The techniques are general classes or categories of procedures, and headings above each column indicate the basic intent of their implementation (i.e., to reduce or increase behavior).

Sternberg and Schilit provided definitions of each technique, with examples of how each might be operationalized with a sample targeted behavior. The following are composites of those definitions and descriptions.

Positive Reinforcement. This is one technique to use when the intent is to increase a behavior. If the student displays the behavior, he or she receives something that has the potential to increase the probability the behavior will occur again. However, never assume that something is reinforcing or a reinforcer; you can only determine it is reinforcing if, as a result of its application, the behavior increases.

> *Example*: Kenny can sit in his seat. However, he doesn't sit in his seat for sustained periods of time. You know that Kenny likes to play with a certain toy. What you decide to do is to let Kenny play with the toy for a short period of time if he stays in his seat for at least _____ seconds. Once he does this for a number of times (you have already established a reasonable criterion), you let him play with the toy if he stays in his seat for progressively longer periods of time.

Response Differentiation. This procedure is used to teach a new behavior. It is only used if one is sure that the student can actually produce the behavior but does not because the behavior is "hidden" or masked by other behaviors. Using this technique, the student receives reinforcement only when he or she commits the correct behavior, but not when the student either produces the target behavior with other behaviors or when he or she produces only the other behaviors.

> *Example*: Linda can produce vocalizations. However she doesn't vocalize when she wants something; she only points. You decide to give her something she wants only if she vocalizes. If she vocalizes when she points or if she still only points, you do not give her what she wants. (You are assuming that she *really* wants the thing she is pointing to.)

Shaping. This procedure is also used to teach a new behavior. But in this case, the student has never displayed the targeted behavior. In shaping, one typically breaks down immediate expectations of behavior. Instead of expecting the student to display the entire targeted behavior, the student is

Table 6-1 Hypothetical Sequence of Least to Most Restrictive Behavioral Techniques

	Increase	*Increase*	*Reduce*	*Reduce*	*Reduce*	*Reduce*	*Increase*	*Reduce*	*Reduce*	*Reduce*
Positive reinforcement		DRH	Extinction	DRO	Contingent observation	Response cost	Negative reinforcement	Positive practice	Over correction	Positive punishment
Teach new behaviors				DRI		Exclusion time-out			Seclusion time-out	
Response differentiation				DRL						
Shaping										
Maintainance										
Scheduling										

Least Restrictive ⟶ **Most Restrictive**

only expected to demonstrate a small predetermined part or step. If it is displayed, a reinforcer is delivered. Slowly, expectations are increased, and reinforcers are delivered based on the demonstration of improved performance.

Example: It is decided that Beth must learn how to feed herself with a spoon. At the present time, she can hold the spoon and scoop food with it but does not lift it from the plate or move it to her mouth. What you decide to do is to reward her for better and better "lifting spoon behavior." Once she shows appropriate lifting, you will reward her for better and better "moving the spoon to the mouth."

Scheduling. This procedure is used to maintain a behavior once the student has shown it consistently. What is involved in this procedure is a change from continuous to more intermittent reinforcement delivery. Reinforcers are no longer delivered each time the student commits the behavior. The student must eventually understand that he or she will receive a reinforcer only intermittently because this is a more natural way that reinforcers are delivered and obtained.

Example: Dwayne has been displaying very consistent task completion behavior as long as you reward him at the end of each completed task. You decide you want to maintain this behavior but reinforcing him each time is not only time-consuming, it is not helping him to exhibit the behavior under more "natural" reinforcement time frames. You decide to begin to *lean* the reward schedule (not reinforcing as frequently) by at first only reinforcing for every two tasks completed. Once he displays appropriate "two-task completion behavior," you will lean the schedule even more (e.g., one reinforcer for every three tasks, for every five tasks, etc.).

Differential Reinforcement of High Rates of Behavior (DRH). This procedure is used to increase behaviors. With a DRH technique, the intent is to have the student display behaviors *more rapidly*.

Example: Billy is currently working under a sheltered workshop contract. He is reinforced each time he sorts one bag of assorted bolts. This usually takes him about 1/2 hour. A more acceptable rate would be ten bags in 1/2 hour. You decide to reinforce him for faster and faster performance. For example, you start by giving him a reinforcer only when he starts sorting the second bag before the 1/2 hour period is over. You might set a timer on his desk and indicate to him that if he starts the second bag before the timer goes off, he'll get his reward. Then you'll begin reinforcing him only when he completes two bags within 1/2 hour, etc.

Extinction. This is a procedure used to reduce behaviors. It is based on the assumption that if the student desires attention, he or she will reduce inappropriate behavior if the behavior is ignored.

> *Example*: Jennifer produces many inappropriate vocalizations during instructional periods. In the past, you have paid attention to these by either telling Jennifer or gesturing to her (e.g., pointing to your mouth) to stop the noises. Jennifer not only continues to produce the noises but the frequency seems to have increased. You decide to ignore her when she produces inappropriate vocalizations.

Differential Reinforcement of Other Behaviors (DRO). This is a procedure used to reduce a behavior. In this procedure, *all* other behaviors *except* the one targeted for reduction are reinforced usually at specific predetermined points in time or after predetermined durations (as long as the target behavior is not occurring or has not occurred). Using this procedure, one is usually interested in reducing only *one* behavior and not concerned about reinforcing any other behavior the student might display.

> *Example*: Bruce frequently ruminates. You decide to start to try to reduce this behavior by selecting a period of time when he is most likely to do so (e.g., the 1/2 hour directly after lunch). You know he likes to interact with a certain toy. During this time, you decide to reinforce him every 10 seconds with opportunities to play with the toy if he is showing any behavior other than rumination.

Differential Reinforcement of Incompatible Behaviors (DRI). This is a procedure used to reduce a behavior. In this case, only behaviors that are opposite to (or incompatible with) the targeted behavior are reinforced according to the same type of time frames used in the DRO procedure. This procedure is often used as an alternative to the DRO technique. One is willing to accept only certain behaviors to reinforce (those that are incompatible with the targeted behavior) rather than merely any other behavior.

> *Example:* Jeffrey often bites the cuticles around his fingernails. You find that even during tasks, he bites his cuticles approximately 30 seconds every minute with an average duration of 5 seconds per episode. You decide to use the task situations and reinforce him by stroking his back (something he really likes) only when he shows correct hands behavior (i.e., any hands behavior incompatible with or opposite to fingers in the mouth). To start with, you decide to reinforce him for 5 seconds of "appropriate hands." If he begins to show success, you will increase the criterion.

Differential Reinforcement of Low Rates of Behavior (DRL). This is a procedure to reduce behavior. The assumption is that certain behaviors are "allowable" if they occur at low rates.

   Example: Ron leaves to go to the bathroom every 5 minutes. You know there is no medical or physical problem causing this behavior. You know that going to the bathroom is an appropriate behavior as long as it is done at a lower rate. You decide to try to reduce the rate by reinforcing Ron only when he goes to the bathroom less than 5 times in a 1/2-hour period. You might give him partial reinforcement (e.g., tokens or social praise) during segments of the 1/2-hour period if he is meeting the criterion (e.g., every 5 minutes, telling him how pleased you are he is staying in the room). If he meets the 1/2-hour criterion, he may receive his major reinforcer (e.g., a preferred short-term activity). If he consistently shows he is meeting this criterion, you'll begin to reinforce lower and lower rates of this behavior (e.g., reinforcing him for less than four times, less than two times, etc.).

Contingent Observation. This procedure is used to reduce behavior. If the student displays an inappropriate behavior, he or she is moved to another area of the classroom to observe the behaviors of other students that are appropriate and that receive reinforcement.

   Example: Although you have observed him comply with various verbal requests, Randy very rarely responds to them during small group training. Based on the fact that this is a desired behavior from the group, you decide to remove Randy to any area of the room where he can observe his peers being reinforced for complying with verbal requests.

Response Cost. This procedure is used to reduce behavior. In this case, something that is reinforcing to the student is taken away as a result of the display of the inappropriate behavior.

   Example: Barbara has a tendency to eat her food very quickly so that she can get her dessert, something she really likes. You decide to let her have half of her dessert in individual bites during her meal if she decreases the rapid rate of her eating (slows down her utensil from plate to mouth to plate behavior). If she meets the criterion for approximately 30 seconds, she can have a bite of dessert. If not, she doesn't get the bite of dessert. If the majority of 30-second periods for meal eating are successful, she can have the remaining half of her dessert. If they are not, the remaining half of the dessert is taken away from her.

Exclusion Time-Out. This is a procedure used to reduce a behavior. If a student displayed an inappropriate behavior he or she would be removed from the immediate situation but remain in the same room. The student is not permitted either to observe or participate in the classroom activities but may hear what is going on. This time-out procedure is based on the assumption that if a potential reinforcer is removed (e.g., the teacher's attention or the attention of the class) the inappropriate behavior will decrease.

> *Example:* Gary can't seem to keep his hands to himself in small group training sessions. You know that he enjoys working with other students. You decide that if he either inappropriately touches or hits another student, he will be removed from the situation and placed behind a screen in the classroom for about 5 minutes. After this period of time-out, he can come back to work if he exhibits appropriate behavior in the group.

Negative Reinforcement. This is a procedure used to increase a behavior. It is based on the premise that if an unpleasant situation or stimulus is removed from the student when he or she exhibits an appropriate behavior, then that behavior will increase.

> *Example:* John dislikes certain types of food (e.g., green vegetables). You know that he'll at least take a couple of bites of some green vegetables (such as peas) before he gives up on them. Because he very rarely eats green vegetables, he is on vitamin supplements. John does understand the verbal command "eat your _____." Unfortunately, whenever you really try to force him to eat the vegetables, he really gets upset. What you decide to do is set up a program where there are two types of green vegetables on his plate; one type he'll eat a little of, and the other type he won't try. You tell him that if he eats the more "preferred" green vegetable, he won't have to eat the other. You slowly increase the criterion over a period of time (i.e., you ask him to eat more and more of the "preferred" vegetable so he won't have to eat the other).

Positive Practice. This procedure is typically used to reduce a behavior. If a student displays an inappropriate behavior, the student "overpractices" an appropriate or preferred behavior (to others).

> *Example:* Beth is responsible for putting pen parts together in an assembly type of contract task. What has been happening is that the bottom parts of the pen tube have not been turned enough, and the majority of them fall off the top. What you decide to have her do is

overpractice the behavior by completing many more of the tasks than would normally be required during a typical assembly period of time.

Overcorrection. This is a procedure used to reduce a behavior. It can be used with inappropriate behaviors that disrupt the environment. As the name implies, in overcorrection one typically requires the student not only to correct what he or she has done wrong to the environment but to "overcorrect" it. Usually, positive practice accompanies this technique.

> *Example:* Katie wets her pants frequently. She has no medical or physical problems that might account for the behavior. She is capable of being toilet trained, and you believe she should be on a natural toileting schedule. You have tried to reinforce her for both going to the bathroom on schedule and keeping her pants dry, but she still is having many accidents. You decide that each time she has an accident, she must rinse out her clothing, hang her wet clothing in an appropriate area, change into dry clothing, and (the overcorrection) clean both the sink area and her immediate classroom area.

Seclusion Time-Out. This is a procedure used to reduce a behavior. In this method, if a student displays an inappropriate behavior, he or she is removed from the situation and placed in a truly isolated area. While in seclusion, the student interacts with no one and cannot observe or hear anything going on in the classroom. This procedure is based on the assumption that if a potential reinforcer is removed (e.g., the teacher's attention or the attention of the class), the inappropriate behavior will decrease.

> *Example:* Matthew cannot seem to keep his hands to himself in small group training situations. You have tried exclusion time-out, but it doesn't seem to have any effect. You feel this may be because he can still hear what is going on and this, in and of itself, is providing reinforcement to him. You know that Matthew enjoys being in the small group. You decide to remove Matthew to an isolated time-out room if he either inappropriately touches or hits anyone. He will spend 5 minutes in this room under close (but outside the room) supervision. The time-out room is very close to the classroom and is well ventilated, well lit, and easily accessible to observation.

Positive Punishment (Contingent Application of an Aversive). This is a procedure used to reduce behavior. If the student displays an inappropriate behavior, one administers an unpleasant or aversive event or stimulus to the student. Just as is the case with positive reinforcement, one cannot assume that something is punishing to a student. If behavior decreases as a result of the stimulus being applied, the stimulus would be considered punishing.

Example: Scott frequently hits himself in the head with his fist. You have tried other procedures to stop this behavior (such as reinforcing him for correct hands behavior) but the behavior seems to be getting worse. You decide that each time he hits himself you are going to yell very loudly at him "no hitting." When he puts his hand down, you will say "that's good hands." The yelling may be considered positive punishment (if it has the effect of decreasing the behavior). The "that's good hands" is actually an attempt at rewarding the opposite appropriate behavior.

Sternberg and Schilit noted that some of these techniques may not be appropriate for certain students. For example, a time-out procedure would have limited, if any, positive effect on a student with considerable self-stimulatory behavior, or on a student whose overall awareness behavior was severely limited.

Merely knowing that certain techniques are less restrictive than others does not necessarily dictate which specific procedure should be used. Sternberg and Schilit provided a decision-making framework for determining which procedure to start with as well as which procedure to opt for in the event the student is not making progress. These decisions are typically based on accurate and representational data concerning the present level of the behavior, what one expects to happen to the behavior once a procedure is implemented, and the effect the handicapping condition might have on the range of options (again, it would probably be impossible to use contingent observation or an exclusion time-out procedure for a student who is both deaf and blind).

The Sternberg and Schilit model does differ in a number of respects from the Evans and Meyer approach in regard to behavior excesses. Principally, these differences involve the assumption that reductive procedures may have to be used at the initial intervention stage (rather than attempting the positive alternatives procedure as a first step) and that the full range of reductive procedures may be necessary. However, and as described previously, they caution that any reductive procedure will produce diminishing returns if positive alternatives are not quickly provided.

Results of Previous Investigations

As noted previously, the choice of which behaviors to change first necessitates systematic prioritizing. Consistent with the Evans and Meyer model, Level I behaviors are those that have typically been the target of most behavior change programs. As a result, the vast majority of the research literature pertaining to the management of social behaviors is concerned with attempts to eliminate or reduce *socially inappropriate, maladaptive, or aberrant behaviors.* Further, the majority of that body of literature focuses on attempts to decrease *self-injurious behavior* (SIB). This attention is due to the fact that engaging in SIB is potentially life-threatening. Many intervention programs are designed around this as a first priority.

Self-Injurious Behavior

Several approaches have been used to reduce SIB. These include punishment, overcorrection, DRO, the use of protective equipment, and various combinations of these approaches. Several issues emerge regarding the choice of which approach(es) to use. These primarily depend on ethical considerations (e.g., when to use severe punishments) and the various theories regarding the cause of SIB.

Treatment approaches might differ depending on the perceived cause of the SIB. Durand and Carr (1985) noted four potential "motivating conditions" to consider when designing intervention techniques for reducing SIB: *social attention, tangible consequences, escape from aversive situations,* and *sensory consequences.* If, for example, it was viewed that SIB was a result of social attention, extinction might be used to eliminate it. On the other hand, if the SIB was thought to be a method to produce sensory stimulation for an individual, providing alternative and more appropriate methods of stimulation might be suggested. Interestingly, even with the ethical and theoretical considerations, the use of punishment ranks among the most prominently used approaches to reduce SIB.

Punishment. The majority of the literature supports the notion that punishment is successful in reducing SIB. Further, it seems that the success of the program, in part, is due to the intensity of the punishment. Durand (1982) found, for instance, that mild punishment was not successful in reducing the SIB of an adolescent with profound mental retardation. On the other hand, Singh, Dawson, and Gregory (1980) found that the use of ammonia was successful in reducing face-hitting. Similarly, Rapoff, Altman, and Christophersen (1980) noted that the use of ammonia was the most effective among several approaches, including DRO and overcorrection, in reducing SIB.

Another punishment that has proven effective is the use of water mist. Dorsey et al. (1980) found that spraying water into the face was effective in reducing a variety of SIBs. Further, pairing of the water mist with a verbal cue allowed the subsequent use of the verbal cue alone to reduce the SIB. Bailey, Pokrzywinski, and Bryant (1983) also found that the use of water mist reduced SIB and noted no physical side effects or avoidance behaviors after its use.

Physical activity has also been used contingently as a punishment to reduce SIB. Borreson (1980) found that forcing a 22-year-old man with severe retardation to run when he engaged in SIB reduced that behavior and resulted in positive side effects, such as increased smiling. Finally, in one study (Bates & Smeltzer, 1982), electroconvulsive therapy was used to control SIB. It should be noted, however, that the SIB under investigation was of a life-threatening nature.

Overcorrection. When research on overcorrection first appeared in the professional literature, many felt it would be the most effective and appropriate procedure to reduce SIB and other negative behaviors. Gorman-Smith and Matson (1985) conducted a meta-analysis of selected research on SIB and found that overcorrection procedures were used more than any other approach. This popularity of overcorrection is probably due to the claim that it combines the reduction of inappropriate behaviors with the "educative" aspects of training appropriate behaviors (positive practice). Unfortunately, the research on overcorrection is somewhat equivocal concerning its effectiveness.

While many studies have supported the use of overcorrection, particularly regarding its short-term effectiveness, others have found general problems in using the procedure. These problems include the development of negative side effects and the lack of generalization and maintenance of treatment effects. On the positive side, Singh et al. (1980) found that overcorrection was helpful in reducing the jaw hitting of two girls with profound retardation. Similarly, Halpern and Andrasik (1986) noted that the procedure was effective in decreasing head banging in a 23-year-old individual with profound retardation. They also noted that follow-up data indicated long-term effectiveness of the overcorrection procedure. In another study, Duker and Seys (1983) compared the effectiveness of overcorrection with extinction and found overcorrection superior. They also noted long-term maintenance in five of their six subjects followed; that the effectiveness of the overcorrection seemed to be greater for behaviors that occurred infrequently; and that the procedure in general was very time-consuming. Barton and Lagrow (1983) also found that the SIBs of three individuals who were deaf-blind were decreased, and that the treatment gains were maintained at follow-up.

On the other hand, there are data suggesting that overcorrection is not so effective in reducing SIB as other procedures, and/or the effects of overcorrection are not generalized or maintained over time. Gorman-Smith and Matson (1985), for example, found in their meta-analysis of the SIB literature that, even though overcorrection was the most frequently used procedure, it was not the most effective. In one study, Rapoff et al. (1980) found that overcorrection was not effective in reducing SIB. Other studies (Agosta, Close, Hops, & Rusch, 1980; Czyzewski, Barrera, & Sulzer-Azaroff, 1982) found that, while overcorrection was effective in the short-term, the results did not generalize or were not maintained over time.

The issue of generalization and maintenance of treatment effects was addressed by Foxx and Livesay (1984). They examined overcorrection programs over a ten-year period and concluded that maintenance seemed to be related to the level of retardation, with lower functioning individuals demonstrating less maintenance effects. They also noted that because of the complexity of the procedure and the subsequent time involvement, overcorrection programs are frequently reinstated after the initial treatment phase. Their suggestion was to build-in generalization components in the initial treatment and to keep the overcorrection programs as short as possible.

DRO. The research literature regarding the use of DRO to reduce SIB is somewhat contradictory. Lockwood and Bourland (1982) found that reinforcement for toy play decreased SIB in two nonambulatory young adults with profound mental retardation. Similarly, Favell, McGimsey, and Schell (1982) found that reinforcement for appropriate toy play reduced SIB in six individuals with profound handicaps. Interestingly, they noted that when the toys were presented without external reinforcement, the SIB decreased but was replaced by self-stimulation with the toys. Heidorn and Jensen (1984) also found that DRO was effective when trying to reduce forehead gouging. However, and as noted previously, Rapoff et al. (1980) found that DRO was ineffective in reducing SIB.

Other Procedures. A variety of other procedures have been used to reduce SIB in individuals with severe or profound handicaps. These include *response interruption* (Slifer, Iwata, & Dorsey, 1984) and *physical restraint* (Gaylord-Ross, Weeks, Lipner, & Gaylord-Ross, 1983; Rapoff et al., 1980; Singh, Dawson, & Manning, 1981). Gaylord-Ross et al. (1983) found, in fact, that contingent physical restraint was the most effective of four procedures used, including positive reinforcement. Additionally, Singh et al. (1981) found that the *duration* of the physical restraint was an important variable; the shorter intervention (one minute) was more effective than the longer (three minutes). Other procedures include the *use of protective clothing* (Silverman, Watanabe, Marshall, & Baer, 1984), *arm splints* (Ball, Datta, Rios, & Constantine, 1985), *contingent physical stimulation* (Hirama, 1982), and *noncontingent physical stimulation* (Wells & Smith, 1983). All of these approaches were reported to be successful in reducing SIB. In that there appears to be no clearcut difference in effectiveness between the use of physical and mechanical restraint, Hill and Spreat (1987) have analyzed the effect of implementing various forms of contingent restraint on those who administer such restraint. They concluded that less staff injury was evident when mechanical restraint (e.g., arm splints) was used in place of physical restraint (e.g., holding an individual's arms down).

Yet another technique used to decrease SIB is *facial screening*. This involves the placement of an opaque screen (usually a bib) over the individual's face when the SIB occurs. Lutzker and Wesch (1983) reviewed the literature on facial screening and noted that it was a harmless yet effective method for decreasing SIB. A variation of this approach is *visual screening*, in which just the eyes are covered briefly. Watson, Singh, and Winton (1986), in fact, found visual screening to be more effective than facial screening. Similarly, Winton, Singh, and Dawson (1984) found that facial screening was more effective when combined with visual blocking (screening) than when used alone.

Combination of Procedures. There is growing evidence that various combinations of procedures might be more effective than single isolated procedures. Altmeyer, Williams, and Sams (1985) noted, for example, that a combination of DRO, time-out, physical restraint, and the contingent application of an aversive resulted in the rapid decrease of SIB in a 16-year-old individual with severe retardation. They further noted that the treatment effects were maintained after 20 months.

One procedure frequently used in combination with others is DRO. Parrish, Iwata, Dorsey, Bunck, and Slifer (1985) reported success when DRO was used in combination with protective equipment. Similarly, Dorsey, Iwata, Reid, and Davis (1982) found that DRO and protective equipment were successful in reducing SIB in three adolescents who were retarded. They also reported that the amount of time the equipment was necessary decreased as the SIB decreased. Augustine and Cipani (1982) found that while DRO was effective alone in reducing SIB, the treatment effects were enhanced when it was used with response cost.

Stereotypic Behavior

Another behavior frequently the target of a number of intervention programs is stereotypy. Stereotypic behavior can be defined as ritualistic repetitive behavior that essentially is purposeless. A variety of procedures are effective in decreasing stereotypy, both alone and in combination. These include the use of punishment in the form of contingent application of water mist (Friman, Cook, & Finney, 1984); visual screening (McGonigle, Duncan, Cordisco, & Barrett, 1982); sensory awareness training (Storey, Bates, McGhee, & Dycus, 1984), and time-out (McKeegan, Estill, & Campbell, 1984). A number of combinations of procedures are successful in decreasing stereotypy. These include sensory reinforcement and punishment (Lancioni, Smeets, Ceccarani, & Goossens, 1983); DRO and response interruption (Barton & Lagrow, 1983; Fellner, Laroche, & Sulzer-Azaroff, 1984); and positive practice and social praise (Denny, 1980).

In a comparative and summative review of the various techniques used to decrease stereotypy, LaGrow and Repp (1984) found that, when separate treatments were employed, punishment or differential reinforcement techniques were most effective (with punishment being somewhat more effective). Positive reinforcement of alternative responses proved to be the least effective. However, when combinations of techniques were employed, they proved more effective than any procedure alone. Especially effective was restraint combined with either overcorrection or DRO, and overcorrection combined with DRI.

Other Inappropriate Behaviors

Many other inappropriate behaviors are frequently exhibited by individuals with severe or profound handicaps. Among these are *pica* and *rumination,* which have been successfully decreased using aversive taste procedures (Beukelman & Rogers, 1984; Marholin, Luiselli, Robinson, & Lott, 1980); overcorrection (Barton & Barton, 1982); and a treatment package consisting of verbal reprimands, physical restraint, response interruption, and overcorrection (Paniagua, Braverman, & Capriotti, 1986). In addition, disruptive behavior has been decreased in individuals with severe or profound handicaps using DRO (Luiselli, Pollow, Colozzi, & Teitelbaum, 1981); physical restraint (Bluestone, 1984); and a combination of time-out and positive reinforcement (Miles and Cuvo, 1980). Other inappropriate behaviors that have been the target of intervention programs include inappropriate verbalizations (Konczak & Johnson, 1983); public disrobing (Durana & Cuvo, 1980); and spitting (St. Lawrence & Drabman, 1984).

Use of Medication

Although the prior section of this chapter has dealt with behavioral procedures that have been used to decrease aberrant behaviors, pharmacological or drug intervention should be discussed. Apparently there is overwhelming evidence that indicates that proper implementation of behavioral techniques can decrease various forms of SIB (Schroeder, Schroeder, Rojahn, & Mulick, 1981). This has not prevented the continued use of medication to decrease SIB and other aberrant behaviors even though there does not appear to be a consensus or database for the utility of such practices (Poling, Picker, & Wallace, 1984). Altmeyer, Locke, Griffin, Ricketts, Williams, Mason, and Stark (1987) indicated that whether one receives pharmocological interventions is often based on variables that have little to do with the target behavior. For example, they found there was a greater likelihood for females and ambulatory individuals to be medicated, and that staff convenience often played a role as to whether an individual received medication. They concluded that, just as with many other practices, the use of pharmacological interventions must be based upon clinical research findings. Until such are available, the use of medication to decrease aberrant behavior should be handled judiciously.

Socially Appropriate Behavior

Fewer studies have been conducted on increasing appropriate behaviors than on decreasing inappropriate behaviors. As noted before, the focus on inappropriate behaviors is probably due to the potential consequences of actions such as self-abuse and aggression. For the most part, the studies on increasing social skill deficits have used techniques considered nonintrusive and least restrictive (e.g., shaping, response differentiation, and positive reinforcement). Some social behavior deficits of individuals who are severely or profoundly handicapped that have received noteworthy attention include leisure skills, such as playing pinball (Hill, Wehman, & Horst, 1982) and darts (Schleien, Wehman, & Kiernan, 1981), and job-related behaviors, such as interviewing (Hall, Sheldon-Wildgen, & Sherman, 1980) and prevocational task performance (Gola, Holmes, & Holmes, 1982).

CONCLUSION

The material presented in this chapter can be considered to be a rather formal look at systems and procedures for managing behaviors. So as not to lose sight of the purposes of education, however, one should be advised that managing behavior should not be looked upon from an isolated point of view. Evans and Meyer (1985) pointed out a number of crucial considerations for designing and implementing all behavior change programs for students with severe handicaps. First, the program must take into account each student's individualized *education* program. Merely running a formal behavior reduction program without regard for the educational ramifications of such change is meaningless. Second, one must never lose sight of the social and empirical validity of what one is trying to accomplish. *Social validity* refers to how important other people think the targeted behavior is and how acceptable the method to change that behavior is considered. *Empirical validity* refers to the actual measures that prove a change will make a difference. If social and empirical validity are not established, the direction of any behavior change program is suspect.

In regard to social validity, especially the point concerning the acceptability of any chosen method of behavior change, there are certainly differences of opinion within the professional community. On the one hand, certain groups (such as The Association for Persons with Severe Handicaps, The Association for Retarded Citizens of the United States, The American Association on Mental Deficiency, and the National Association of School Psychologists; see Meyer (1987) for a compilation of the position statements) have stated that aversive procedures that have the potential to inflict bodily harm or pain should be discounted as viable techniques for use with any type of behavioral excess.

Others have opted for the position that such use of extreme aversives may indeed be justified in cases where all other data-based, less intrusive options would prove ineffective (Favell, Azrin, Baumeister, Carr, Dorsey, Forehand, Foxx, Lovass, Rincover, Risley, Romanczyk, Russo, Schroeder, & Solnick, 1982). As has been discussed previously, in relation to intractible types of aberrant behaviors that would "typically" necessitate a decision to use or not to use extreme aversives (for example, SIB), most of the research indicates that applications of strong aversives do reduce or eliminate the behavior. Gast and Wolery (1987) indicated that, given the current nonresearch base for the use of nonpunitive alternatives, it may very well be necessary to use extreme aversives. However, they caution that such use must be predicated on four points: (1) that a least intrusive to most intrusive behavior paradigm be adopted if the behavior is not life-threatening to the individual or others; (2) that movement from a less intrusive to more intrusive procedure be based on a data base; (3) that punishment can be rendered as a first choice if the behavior is life-threatening (and if there is no data base to indicate that a less intrusive procedure would be successful); and (4) when punishment is indicated, that levels of punishment should also follow a less intrusive to more intrusive pattern if data support that such movement is possible and efficacious.

A final consideration that is important to behavior change programs is empirical validity. Many times, behavior change programs have been evaluated through the use of single-subject designs (Adams, Sternberg, & Taylor, 1982; Tawney & Gast, 1984). Voeltz and Evans (1983) and Evans and Meyer (1985) specify a number of problems with using single-subject designs, one of which is the underestimation of the actual effect of certain skill development (for example, whether the behavior has any potential for affecting collateral or covariate behaviors). The issue of whether single-subject designs should be used has produced an ongoing debate, with one side insisting that modifications to these designs can answer all questions concerning educational validity (Test, Spooner, & Cooke, 1987); and the other insisting that such is not plausible (Evans & Meyer, 1987).

Regardless of these differing viewpoints, it is still important to realize that any system or procedure for managing behavior of students with severe or profound handicaps will eventually have its worth judged through evaluation data. As Evans and Meyer (1985) stated, however, the evaluation system should never take precedent over the meaning and ramifications of all behavior change:

> As an *evaluation* approach, the charting of individual responses leaves much to be desired. It will not answer the question of whether the change documented is clinically or educationally significant; it will not answer the question of what other collateral effects (good or bad) have taken place; it will not answer the question of whether the intervention strategy itself was appropriate, humane, and in keeping with philosophical or legal assumptions regarding the handicapped child's rights (p. 161).

REFERENCES

Adams, G.L., Sternberg, L., & Taylor, R.L. (1982). Social skills training. In L. Sternberg & G.L. Adams (Eds.) *Educating severely and profoundly handicapped students* (pp. 97-128). Rockville, MD: Aspen.

Adkins, J., & Matson, J.L. (1980). Teaching institutionalized mentally retarded adults socially appropriate leisure skills. *Mental Retardation, 10*(3), 249-252.

Agosta, J., Close, D., Hops, H., & Rusch, F. (1980). Treatment of self-injurious behavior through overcorrection procedures. *Journal of the Association for the Severely Handicapped, 5,* 5-12.

Altmeyer, B.K., Locke, B.J., Griffin, J.C., Ricketts, R.W., Williams, D.E., Mason, M., & Stark, M.T. (1987). Treatment strategies for self-injurious behavior in a large service-delivery network. *American Journal of Mental Deficiency, 91*(4), 333-340.

Altmeyer, B., Williams, D., & Sams, V. (1985). Treatment of severe self-injurious and aggressive biting. *Journal of Behavior Therapy and Experimental Psychiatry, 16,* 169-172.

Augustine, A., & Cipani, E. (1982). Treating self-injurious behavior: Initial effects, maintenance, and acceptability of treatment. *Child and Family Behavior Therapy, 4,* 53-69.

Bailey, S., Pokrzywinski, J., & Bryant, L. (1983). Using water mist to reduce self-injurious and stereotypic behavior. *Applied Research in Mental Retardation, 4,* 229-241.

Ball, T., Datta, P., Rios, M., & Constantine, C. (1985). Flexible arm splints in the control of a Lesch-Nyhan victim's finger biting and a profoundly retarded client's finger sucking. *Journal of Autism and Developmental Disorders, 15,* 177-184.

Barton, C., & Barton, L. (1982). Reduction of rumination in a six year old severely retarded institutionalized child through overcorrection procedures. *British Columbia Journal of Special Education, 6,* 121-130.

Barton, L., & Lagrow, S. (1983). Reducing self-injurious and aggressive behavior in deaf-blind persons through overcorrection. *Journal of Visual Impairment and Blindness, 77,* 421-424.

Bates, P., & Renzaglia, A. (1982). Language game instruction: Use of a table game. *Education and Treatment of Children, 5*(1), 13-22.

Bates, W., & Smeltzer, D. (1982). Electroconvulsive treatment of psychotic self-injurious behavior in a patient with severe mental retardation. *American Journal of Psychiatry, 139,* 1355-1356.

Beukelman, F., & Rogers, J. (1984). Noncontingent use of alum in the reduction of rumination. *Psychology in the Schools, 21,* 500-503.

Bluestone, M. (1984). *Decreasing aggression using four-point restraints and symbol programs.* Paper presented at the annual convention of the American Psychological Association, Toronto, Canada.

Borreson, P. (1980). The elimination of a self-injurious avoidance response through a forced running consequence. *Mental Retardation, 18,* 73-77.

Carey, R.G., & Bucher, B. (1981). Identifying the educative and suppressive effects of positive practice and restitutional overcorrection. *Journal of Applied Behavior Analysis, 14*(1), 71-80.

Carr, E.G., & Durand, V.M. (1985). Reducing behavior problems through functional communication training. *Journal of Applied Behavior Analysis, 18,* 111-126.

Carr, E.G., Newsom, C.D., & Binkoff, J.A. (1980). Escape as a factor in the aggressive behavior of two retarded children. *Journal of Applied Behavior Analysis, 13,* 101-117.

Cuvo, A.J., Jacobi, L., & Sipko, R. (1981). Teaching laundry skills to mentally retarded students. *Education and Training of the Mentally Retarded, 16,* 54-64.

Czyzewski, M., Barrera, R., & Sulzer-Azaroff, B. (1982). An abbreviated overcorrection program to reduce self-stimulatory behaviors. *Journal of Behavior Therapy and Experimental Psychiatry, 13,* 55-62.

Denny, M. (1980). Reducing self-stimulatory behavior of mentally retarded persons by alternative positive practice. *American Journal of Mental Deficiency, 84,* 610-615.

Doleys, D.M., Stacy, D., & Knowles, S. (1981). Modification of grooming behavior in adult retarded: Token reinforcement in a community-based program. *Behavior Modification, 5,* 119-128.

Donnellan, A.M., Mirenda, P.L., Mesaros, & Fassbender, L.L. (1984). Analyzing the communicative functions of aberrant behavior. *Journal of the Association for Persons with Severe Handicaps, 9*(3), 201-212.

Dorsey, M.F., Iwata, B.A., Ong, P., & McSween, T.E. (1980). Treatment of self-injurious behavior using a water mist: Initial response suppression and generalization. *Journal of Applied Behavior Analysis, 13,* 343-354.

Dorsey, M., Iwata, B., Reid, D., & Davis, P. (1982). Protective equipment: Continuous and contingent application in the treatment of self-injurious behavior. *Journal of Applied Behavior Analysis, 15,* 217-230.

Duker, P., & Seys, D. (1983). Symposium on behaviour modification treatments: II. Long-term follow up effects of extinction and overcorrection procedures with severely retarded individuals. *British Journal of Mental Subnormality, 29,* 74-80.

Durana, I., & Cuvo, A. (1980). A comparison of procedures for decreasing public disrobing of an institutionalized profoundly mentally retarded woman. *Mental Retardation, 18,* 185-188.

Durand, M. (1982). A behavioral/pharmacological intervention for the treatment of severe self-injurious behavior. *Journal of Autism and Developmental Disorders, 12,* 243-251.

Durand, V.M., & Carr, E.G. (1985). Self-injurious behavior: Motivating conditions and guidelines for treatment. *School Psychology Review, 14*(2), 171-176.

Evans, I.M., & Meyer, L.H. (1985). *An educative approach to behavior problems.* Baltimore: Paul H. Brookes.

Evans, I.M., & Meyer, L.H. (1987). Moving to educational validity: A reply to Test, Spooner, and Cooke. *Journal of the Association for Persons with Severe Handicaps, 12*(2), 103-106.

Favell, J.E., Azrin, N.H., Baumeister, A., Carr, E.G., Dorsey, M.F., Forehand, R., Foxx, R.M., Lovass, O.I., Rincover, A., Risley, T.R., Romanczyk, R.G., Russo, D.C., Schroeder, J.R., & Solnick, J.V. (1982). The treatment of self-injurious behavior. *Behavior Therapy, 13,* 529-554.

Favell, J., McGimsey, J., & Schell, R. (1982). Treatment of self-injury by providing alternative sensory activities. *Analysis and Intervention in Developmental Disabilities, 2,* 83-104.

Fellner, D., Laroche, M., & Sulzer-Azaroff, B. (1984). The effects of adding interruption to differential reinforcement on targeted and novel self-stimulatory behaviors. *Journal of Behavior Therapy and Experimental Psychiatry, 15,* 315-321.

Foxx, R., & Livesay, J. (1984). Maintenance of response suppression following overcorrection: A 10-year retrospective examination of eight cases. *Analysis and Intervention in Developmental Disabilities, 4,* 65-79.

Friman, P., Cook, W., & Finney, J. (1984). Effects of punishment procedures on the self-stimulatory behavior of an autistic child. *Analysis and Intervention in Developmental Disabilities, 4,* 39-46.

Gast, D.L., & Wolery, M. (1987). Severe maladaptive behaviors. In M.E. Snell (Ed.) *Systematic instruction of persons with severe handicaps* (pp. 300-332). Columbus, OH: Charles E. Merrill.

Gaylord-Ross, R. (1980). A decision model for the treatment of aberrant behavior in applied settings. In W. Sailor, B. Wilcox, & L. Brown (Eds.), *Methods of instruction for severely handicapped students* (pp. 135-158). Baltimore: Paul H. Brookes.

Gaylord-Ross, R., Weeks, M., Lipner, C., & Gaylord-Ross, C. (1983). The differential effectiveness of four treatment procedures in suppressing self-injurious behaviors among severely handicapped students. *Education and Training of the Mentally Retarded, 18,* 38-44.

Gola, T., Holmes, P., & Holmes, N. (1982). Effectiveness of a group contingency procedure for increasing prevocational behavior of profoundly mentally retarded residents. *Mental Retardation, 20,* 26-29.

Gorman-Smith, D., & Matson, J. (1985). A review of treatment research for self-injurious and stereotyped responding. *Journal of Mental Deficiency Research, 29,* 295-308.

Hall, G., Sheldon-Wildgen, J., & Sherman J. (1980). Teaching job interview skills to retarded clients. *Journal of Applied Behavior Analysis, 13,* 433-442.

Halpern, L., & Andrasik, F. (1986). The immediate and long-term effectiveness of overcorrection in treating self-injurious behavior in a mentally retarded adult. *Applied Research in Mental Retardation, 7,* 59-65.

Harris, S., & Wolchik, S. (1979). Suppression of self-stimulation: Three alternative strategies. *Journal of Applied Behavior Analysis, 12,* 185-198.

Heidorn, S., & Jensen, C. (1984). Generalization and maintenance of the reduction of self-injurious behavior maintained by two types of reinforcement. *Behavior Research and Therapy, 22,* 581-586.

Hill, J., & Spreat, S. (1987). Staff injury rates associated with the implementation of contingent restraint. *Mental Retardation, 25*(3), 141-145.

Hill, J., Wehman, P., & Horst, G. (1982). Toward generalization of appropriate leisure and social behavior in severely handicapped youth: Pinball machine use. *Journal of the Association for the Severely Handicapped, 6,* 38-44.

Hirama, H. (1982). *The effect of tactile stimulation on self-injurious behavior.* Doctoral dissertation, Lehigh University.

Iwata, B.A., Dorsey, M.F., Slifer, K.J., Baumann, K.E., & Richman, G.S. (1982). Toward a functional analysis of self-injury. *Analysis and Intervention in Developmental Disabilities, 2*(3), 3-20.

Johnson, B.F., & Cuvo, A.J. (1981). Teaching mentally retarded adults to cook. *Behavior Modification, 5,* 187-202.

Konczak, L., & Johnson, M. (1983). Reducing inappropriate verbalizations in a sheltered workshop through differential reinforcement of other behavior. *Education and Training of the Mentally Retarded, 18,* 120-124.

Koop, S., Martin, G., Yu, D., & Suthons, E. (1980). Comparison of two reinforcement strategies in vocational skill training of mentally retarded persons. *American Journal of Mental Deficiency, 84,* 616-626.

Lagrow, S.J., & Repp, A.C. (1984). Stereotypic responding: A review of intervention research. *American Journal of Mental Deficiency, 88,* 595-609.

Lancioni, G., Smeets, P., Ceccarani, P., & Goossens, A. (1983). Self-stimulation and task-related responding: The role of sensory reinforcement in maintaining and extending treatment effects. *Journal of Behavior Therapy and Experimental Psychiatry, 14,* 33-41.

Lockwood, K., & Bourland, G. (1982). Reduction of self-injurious behaviors by reinforcement and toy use. *Mental Retardation, 20,* 169-173.

Luiselli, J., Pollow, R., Colozzi, G., & Teitelbaum, M. (1981). Application of differential reinforcement to control disruptive behaviors of mentally retarded students during remedial instruction. *Journal of Mental Deficiency Research, 25,* 265-273.

Lutzker, J., & Wesch, D. (1983). Facial screening: History and critical review. *Australia and New Zealand Journal of Developmental Disabilities, 9,* 209-223.

Marholin, D., Luiselli, J., Robinson, M., & Lott, I. (1980). Response-contingent taste aversion in treating chronic ruminative vomiting of institutionalized profoundly retarded children. *Journal of Mental Deficiency Research, 24,* 47-56.

Matson, J.L. (1980). A controlled group study of pedestrian skill training for the mentally retarded. *Behaviour Research and Therapy, 18,* 99-106.

Matson, J.L., & Adkins, J.A. (1980). A self-instruction social skills training program for mentally retarded persons. *Mental Retardation, 18,* 245-248.

Matson, J., & Andrasik, F. (1982). Training leisure-time and social-interaction skills to mentally retarded adults. *American Journal of Mental Deficiency, 86,* 533-542.

McGonigle, J., Duncan, D., Cordisco, L., & Barrett, R. (1982). Visual screening: An alternative method for reducing stereotypic behavior. *Journal of Applied Behavior Analysis, 15,* 461-467.

McKeegan, G., Estill, K., & Campbell, B. (1984). Brief report: Use of nonexclusionary timeout for the elimination of a stereotype behavior. *Journal of Behavior Therapy and Experimental Psychiatry, 15,* 261-264.

Meyer, L. (Ed.) (1987). *Newsletter of The Association for Persons with Severe Handicaps, 13*(5), 3,9.

Miles, C., & Cuvo, A. (1980). Modification of the disruptive and productive classroom behavior of a severely retarded child: A comparison of two procedures. *Education and Treatment of Children, 3,* 113-121.

Paniagua, F., Braverman, C., & Capriotti, R. (1986). Use of a treatment package in the management of a profoundly mentally retarded girl's pica and self-stimulation. *American Journal of Mental Deficiency, 90,* 550-557.

Parrish, J., Iwata, B., Dorsey, M., Bunck, T., & Slifer, K. (1985). Behavior analysis, program development, and transfer of control in the treatment of self-injury. *Journal of Behavior Therapy and Experimental Psychiatry, 16,* 159-168.

Poling, A.D., Picker, M., & Wallace, S. (1984). Psychopharmacological research with the mentally retarded: A methodological analysis of thirty-nine studies published from 1970-1982. In J.C. Griffin, M.T. Stark, D.E. Williams, B.K. Altmeyer, & H.K. Griffin (Eds.), *Advances in the treatment of self-injurious behavior* (pp. 89-122). Austin: Department of Health and Human Services, Texas Planning Council for Developmental Disabilities.

Polvinale, R.A., & Lutzker, J.R. (1980). Elimination of assaultive and inappropriate sexual behavior by reinforcement and social-restitution. *Mental Retardation, 18,* 27-30.

Rapoff, M., Altman, K., & Christophersen, E. (1980). Suppression of self-injurious behavior: Determining the least restrictive alternative. *Journal of Mental Deficiency Research, 24,* 37-46.

Renzaglia, A.M., & Bates, P. (1983). Socially appropriate behavior. In M.E. Snell (Ed.), *Systematic instruction of the moderately and severely handicapped* (2nd ed., pp. 314-356). Columbus, OH: Charles E. Merrill.

Rincover, A., Cook, R., Peoples, A., & Packard, D. (1979). Sensory extinction and sensory reinforcement principles for programming multiple adaptive behavior change. *Journal of Applied Behavior Analysis, 12,* 221-233.

Risley, R., & Cuvo, A.J. (1980). Training mentally retarded adults to make emergency phone calls. *Behavior Modification, 4,* 513-525.

Roberts, P., Iwata, B., McSween, T., & Desmond, E. (1979). An analysis of overcorrection movements. *American Journal of Mental Deficiency, 83,* 588-594.

Rose, H. (1979). Effectiveness and generalization of overcorrection procedures with the stereotyped behavior of a severely retarded adult. *AAESPH Review, 4,* 196-201.

Schleien, S.J., Ash, T., Kiernan, J., & Wehman, P. (1981). Developing independent cooking skills in a profoundly retarded woman. *Journal of the Association for the Severely Handicapped, 6,* 23-29.

Schleien, S.J., Wehman, P., & Kiernan, J. (1981). Teaching leisure skills to severely handicapped adults: An age-appropriate darts game. *Journal of Applied Behavior Analysis, 14,* 513-519.

Schroeder, S.R., Schroeder, C.S., Rojahn, J., & Mulick, J.A. (1981). Self-injurious behavior: An analysis of behavior management techniques. In J.L. Matson & J.R. McCartney (Eds.), *Handbook of behavior modification with the mentally retarded* (pp. 61-116). New York: Plenum.

Silverman, K., Watanabe, K., Marshall, A., & Baer, D., (1984). Reducing self-injury and corresponding self-restraint through the strategic use of protective clothing. *Journal of Applied Behavior Analysis, 17,* 548-552.

Singh, M., Dawson, M., & Gregory, P. (1980). Self-injury in the profoundly retarded: Clinically significant versus therapeutic control. *Journal of Mental Deficiency Research, 24,* 87-97.

Singh, N., Dawson, M., & Manning, P. (1981). The effects of physical restraint on self-injurious behavior. *Journal of Mental Deficiency Research, 25,* 207-216.

Slifer, K., Iwata, B., & Dorsey, M. (1984). Reduction of eye gouging using a response interruption procedure. *Journal of Behavior Therapy and Experimental Psychiatry, 15,* 369-375.

Sternberg, L., & Schilit, J. (1986). *Behavioral guidelines manual: Programs for students with profound handicaps.* Ft. Lauderdale, FL: Broward County Public Schools.

St. Lawrence, J., & Drabman, R. (1984). Suppression of chronic high frequency spitting in a multiply handicapped and mentally retarded adolescent. *Child and Family Behavior Therapy, 6,* 45-55.

Storey, K., Bates, P., McGhee, N., & Dycus, S. (1984). Reducing the self-stimulatory behavior of a profoundly retarded female through sensory awareness training. *American Journal of Occupational Therapy, 38,* 510-516.

Tawney, J.W., & Gast, D.L. (1984). *Single-subject research in special education.* Columbus, OH: Charles E. Merrill.

Test, D.W., Spooner, F., & Cooke, N.L. (1987). Educational validity revisited. *The Journal of the Association for Persons with Severe Handicaps, 12*(2), 96-102.

Voeltz, L.M., & Evans, I.M. (1983). Educational validity: Procedures to evaluate outcomes in programs for severely handicapped learners. *The Journal of the Association for Persons with Severe Handicaps, 8,* 3-15.

Walls, R.T., Crist, K., Sienicki, D.A., & Grant, L. (1981). Prompting sequences in teaching independent living skills. *Mental Retardation, 19,* 243-246.

Walls, R.T., Ellis, W.D., & Zane, T. (1981). Forward and backward chaining, and whole task methods: Training assembly tasks in vocational rehabilitation. *Behavior Modification, 5,* 61-74.

Watson, J., Singh, N., & Winton, A. (1986). Suppressive effects of visual and facial screening on self-injurious finger-sucking. *American Journal on Mental Deficiency, 90,* 526-534.

Wells, M., & Smith, D. (1983). Reduction of self-injurious behavior of mentally retarded persons using sensory-integrative techniques. *American Journal of Mental Deficiency, 87,* 664-666.

Winton, A., Singh, N., & Dawson, M. (1984). Effects of facial screening and blindfold on self-injurious behavior. *Applied Research in Mental Retardation, 5,* 29-42.

Part V

Curriculum Concerns

Chapter 7

Components of Instructional Technology

Paul A. Alberto and William Sharpton

PROBLEM AND PAST PRACTICES

In the not too distant past, students with severe or profound handicaps were often considered incapable of profiting from education. If an "education" was provided, it was typically comprised of elements that could normally be found in early infant or preschool programs. Often, no actual education was provided. Caregivers tended to emphasize a "custodial" approach to meeting the needs of these students.

Fortunately, this situation has changed. The change reflects not only an increased awareness of professionals and other interested parties in the present and future quality of life for individuals with severe or profound handicaps, but an increased commitment toward research and concomitant best practice implementation.

SUGGESTED METHODS

While the content of an educational program is operationalized through curriculum design, the implementation of the curriculum is dependent on the use of an effective instructional technology. For students with severe or profound handicaps, the foundation upon which effective instructional technology rests include the following components:

- an understanding of learning theory (e.g., principles of reinforcement) and the relation of instruction to the levels of learning or response competence (acquisition, fluency, and generalization)

Table 7-1 Examples of Nonfunctional Materials and Activities

Skill Domain	Functional Task	Nonfunctional Because of Materials	Nonfunctional Because of Activity
Domestic/self-help	Student attending to instructions of how to put on winter hat	Student attending to instructions of how to put on a play police chief's hat	Student attending to instructions to look at a magazine picture of a woman putting on a hat
Leisure	Student being manually guided in operating a video game	Student being manually guided in operating a play video game made from a milk carton	Student being manually guided in putting toy pegs in a pegboard
Vocational	Student following instructions to sort like-sized nuts and bolts into a package	Student following instructions to sort plastic toy nuts and bolts into slots on a form board	Student following instructions to fill up egg cartons with cotton balls
Community living	Student attending to teacher demonstration of counting out 50 cents in change	Student attending to teacher demonstration of counting toy coins	Student attending to teacher demonstration of matching a real coin with a magazine picture of a coin
Social/communication	Student being manually guided in signing "Hi" when first greeted by teacher	Student being manually guided in holding up a cartoon of "Smokey the Bear" waving "Hi"	Student being manually guided in drawing a picture of someone signing "Hi"

Source: From "Providing a More Appropriate Education for Severely Handicapped Persons: Increasing and Validating Functional Classroom Tasks" by D. Reid et al., 1985, *Journal of Applied Behavior Analysis*, 18, p. 292. Copyright 1985 by the Society for the Experimental Analysis of Behavior, Inc. Reprinted by permission.

- an affirmation that all students with severe or profound handicaps, regardless of their presenting needs or perceived level of functioning, should be taught to participate fully or partially in a wide range of school and nonschool activities and environments, resulting in the student being perceived as a valuable and contributing member of society (Baumgart, Brown, Pumpian, Nisbet, Ford, Sweet, Messina, & Schroeder, 1982)

- planning that coordinates the scheduling of individual and group instruction for each class member; and scheduling of the various professionals considered part of the essential educational team (e.g., physical, occupational, and speech/language therapists)

- assurance that, to the maximum extent possible, instructional materials and tasks are functional, age appropriate, and socially validated (Brown, Branston, Hamre-Nietupski, Pumpian, Certo, & Gruenewald, 1979; Reid, Parsons, McCarn, Green, Phillips, & Schepis, 1985; see Table 7-1)

- selection of appropriate community settings for generalized learning

- consistency of instruction and contingencies across various instructional personnel, including parents

- class grouping such that there is a mix of levels of functioning and physical disability (allows opportunities for pairing more and less capable students during instruction, and prevents a teacher from spending the majority of classroom time in activities of attending to the presenting physical needs of students)

- the ongoing use of an accurate and useful system of documenting learning

A Trial as the Basic Unit of Instruction

A *trial* is an instance of instruction or an opportunity for performance by the student. Operationalized, a trial has three components as illustrated in Table 7-2: (1) the behavior itself; (2) the *antecedent*, or the event(s) that immediately precede(s) the behavior; and (3) the *consequence*, or the event(s) that immediately follow(s) the behavior.

For the purpose of skill instruction, "behavior" refers to *operant* behavior. Operant behavior is voluntary, as opposed to involuntary or reflexive behavior (*respondent* behavior). Operant behaviors include activities such as communicating, eating, walking, reading, and attending to a task. Antecedents to a behavior include those arrangements that facilitate student performance: the instructional setting, instructional materials, verbal or written instructions, prerequisite skills, task analysis, etc. Consequences of a behavior during skill instruction include those arranged by the teacher, as well as those that occur naturally as a result of performance of the behavior. Reinforcement and correction are the primary forms of consequences.

Table 7-2 Components of an Instructional Trial

A Antecedent	B Behavior	C Consequence
Setting Materials Instruction Prerequisites Task analysis		Reinforcement Correction

Reinforcement during the Trial

Reinforcement serves two major purposes in the instructional process. First, it provides a motivator for student performance. The student is motivated to comply with the instructional cue in order to obtain the reinforcing item or event being offered. If the item/event is truly a reinforcer, it will increase the future rate and/or probability of the student producing the behavior. If the item/event does not have this effect, it may be only a one-time satisfying occurrence, but one that is not a useful instructional tool over time.

The second purpose of reinforcement is to train the understanding of cause and effect. The student learns that the response he or she makes (cause) results in the reinforcer (effect). For the student to make this connection, the delivery of the reinforcer must immediately follow the requested behavior (or, at times, occur during the behavior), and its delivery must be contingent upon performance of the behavior. This understanding is the underpinning of the instructional interaction between a teacher and a student. The student is, in effect, learning the process of learning.

It is not our purpose to provide a full review of reinforcement theory; however, several critical points need to be remembered. The greater the level of a student's disability, the more difficult reinforcer identification becomes. Such a situation may challenge a teacher's creativity and problem-solving skills, but every student is reinforced by something. There is no one item or event that will reinforce every student. An attempt to use a single item as the reinforcer for all members of the class dooms instruction to failure. When using primary reinforcers (e.g., edibles) during the initial stage of learning a new behavior (i.e., acquisition), the teacher must be aware that once the student has satiated on the edible, responding and its accuracy will decrease. This is not a function of an inability to learn, but a function of the student's satiation on the reinforcer.

Pairing of primary and secondary reinforcers (e.g., praise, preferred activities, tokens) should begin as soon as possible. It must be remembered that in teaching students with severe or profound handicaps, the ultimate goal is for the student to be motivated by reinforcement that naturally occurs due to performing a behavior. Therefore, activities that have naturally occurring reinforcing consequences should be included in instruction. For example, when teaching name and function of "cup," there should be some juice in the cup so the student may experience the reinforcing result of using the cup appropriately; or when teaching the use of "on/off," one should use items such as a radio or table lamp.

Finally, it is essential to reduce the amount of reinforcers provided a student systematically. Such thinning of the schedules of reinforcement delivery will train a student to accept delayed gratification for increasing amounts of performance.

Correction during a Trial

When the student's attempt at behavior performance is not correct, it should not be reinforced. Rather, it should be corrected by the teacher in such a manner that the student experiences the correct performance and its resulting reinforcement. Correction often requires the teacher putting the student through the requested behavior in a "hand over hand" manner. There are several variations of correction procedures. Following are two examples.

The first procedure is recommended when the student is being trained on a single step of a task analysis (Wuerch & Voeltz, 1982):

1. Immediately interrupt the student's incorrect response.
2. Repeat the instructional cue paired with the activity cue that preceded the incorrect response.
3. Give whatever additional assistance is necessary to ensure a correct response by the student.
4. Immediately reinforce the correct response.
5. Repeat the procedure, this time fading the additional assistance, to provide additional practice on the missed step.
6. If the student meets the performance criterion for that step, continue on to the next step.

The following is recommended when the student is being trained on a number of steps of a task analysis concurrently (e.g., in vocational training procedures; Bellamy, Horner, & Inman, 1979).

1. Immediately interrupt the student's incorrect response.
2. Go back two steps in the task analysis and give the appropriate instructional cue for that step.
3. Have the student repeat the two steps and the missed step, providing enough assistance to ensure correct responses on all three steps.
4. Reinforce each correct (assisted and unassisted) response.
5. Repeat the procedure to provide additional practice on the missed step.
6. Continue on to the next step in the task analysis.

Trial Management

In the past, it was assumed that trials should be arranged such that an instance of a given behavior was presented repeatedly in the belief that isolated repeated presentation more likely resulted in the acquisition of a new behavior. Such an arrangement of trials is known as *massed trials* presentation. It may be represented as :A-A-A-A-A-A. For example, a cup is placed in front of the student, and ten repetitions are presented of "Michael, give me cup." However, such trial management is inefficient when measured by the number of trials needed to reach the criterion and by the crucial and problematic concern for generalization of learning.

An alternative management is *distributed trials* presentation (Brown, Holvoet, Guess, & Mulligan, 1980; Mulligan, Guess, Holvoet, & Brown, 1980; Sailor & Guess, 1983). Distributed trial presentation interposes time and/or a related interaction with the material between each repetition of a particular trial. Such an arrangement of trials may be within a teaching session (*intrasession* trial distribution) or between sessions (*intersession* trial distribution). Distributed trials can be represented as follows: A-B-C-D A-B-C-D A-B-C-D.

Within a session, distributed trials may be conducted such that when the student is presented in the cafeteria with an array of functionally related instructional materials such as a cup, dish, and spoon, the following distribution of trials might occur for a student with severe handicaps (Holvoet, Brown, & Helmstetter, 1980).

A: "Point to cup" (requires receptive vocabulary skill)
B: "Hand me cup" (requires compliance skill)

C: "What is this" (requires expressive vocabulary skill)

D: "Show me what you do with cup" (requires functional use skill)

For a lower functioning student, a distribution might occur as follows:

A: Visual scan of materials array (requires attending skill)

B: "Find the cup" (requires receptive vocabulary skill)

C: "Do this with the cup" (requires imitation of functional use skill)

D: "Give me the cup" (requires compliance skill)

Intersession distribution of trials might be scheduled as follows. If instruction is designed to teach functional use of a towel, instructional trials would take place during scheduled activities of the day whenever the student would be required to use a towel (e.g., before and after toileting sessions; before and after snacks; after certain play or leisure-time activities; within a cooking session when asked to pour two glasses of milk, count two slices of bread; and within a play session when he or she is asked to count two balls, two playmates). In such an arrangement, the trials are separated by time and arc designed to promote generalization from the regular instructional session.

Prompting

When instructing a new behavior, an immediate problem will occur after delivery of the instructional cue for performance if the student does not respond. This is to be expected when asking a student to perform a response that is not part of his or her behavior repertoire. Skinner (1968) referred to this as the "problem of the first instance." This first instance must be occasioned so that it can be reinforced to increase the probability of continued performance, or so that an incorrect response can be corrected or an approximation of the response can be shaped. First instances of a new behavior can be effected by teacher assistance known as *prompting*.

A prompt may be placed in relation to different components of a trial. Various *antecedent prompts* can augment the antecedent event(s), and various *response prompts* can be paired with the instructional cue to assist response performance. Although multiple options are available, until recently there has been very little research comparing the effectiveness of these two prompt classes on the acquisition of various skills (Adams, Matlock, & Tallon, 1981; Billingsley & Romer, 1983; Day, 1987).

Antecedent Prompts

Antecedent prompts are alterations of, or additions to, the instructional material to focus student attention on the natural cue(s) for making correct responses. There are at least six categories of antecedent prompts: relevant feature prompts, proximity prompts, context prompts, associative prompts, errorless prompts, and modeling.

Relevant feature prompts are those by which the teacher "cues" the feature of the task materials on which the student should focus to make the correct response. Use of this procedure teaches the student to distinguish the features that define a correct response. For example, if the student is being instructed to discriminate a spoon from a fork, the relevant feature of the spoon is the bowl portion, and of the fork, the tines. In teaching this discrimination, these are the places the antecedent prompt should be placed, instead of the handle. If instruction is in use of a vending machine the relevant features are the coin slot and the array of brand selections. In teaching a student how to put on a sweater or T-shirt, the prompt for determining front from back should be placed on the label at the back. Once the prompt has been faded, the label on the back is still there and acts as the natural cue that one normally uses to judge the front from the back.

The teacher may use color, size, and shape as tools to focus or prompt the student's attention by highlighting the relevant feature. For example, a brightly colored piece of ribbon is placed on the label of the sweater as the relevant feature antecedent prompt.

Proximity prompts are employed by varying the placement of materials on the instructional plane (Lovass, 1981). If the student is being taught the spoon/fork discrimination (with "fork" the correct response), during initial training trials the two materials should be placed on the table such that the fork is immediately in front of the student, with the spoon several inches above it. Over trials, the distance between the two materials should be reduced until they are finally presented in parallel.

Context prompting is presentation of instructional materials in an array as similar as possible to that in the natural setting. For example, if the student is being taught "fork," the array within which the student should learn to select the fork is one containing a fork, spoon, and knife (such as a utensil tray in a cafeteria, as this is the array from which he or she must select the item in the natural environment).

Associative prompts are exemplified by the typical flash cards used in many classroom activities. The target concept, such as the number two, is presented in association with a more concrete or representational display, as seen in a flash card with the number two on one side and two boys on the other, or in the case of sight word instruction where the word "milk" appears above the picture of a glass of milk.

Errorless prompts are exaggerated, external, and basically irrelevant cues that dramatically draw the student's attention to the correct response. For example, in the spoon/fork discrimination ("fork" being the correct response), a large sheet of colored paper is placed under the fork as trials are conducted. Once the student stabilizes correct responding, the size of the errorless cue is reduced over successive trials/sessions until it is removed altogether.

A *modeling prompt* is when another individual, such as a teacher or peer, demonstrates the behavior to allow for student imitation. The student watches the teacher put toothpaste on a brush and is then asked to imitate the process.

For modeling to be effective, a teacher should follow some basic guidelines (Baer, Peterson, & Sherman, 1967; Bandura, 1969; Parton, 1976). First, gain the student's attention before presenting the model. The instructional cue for student imitation should be a simple generalizable cue such as a gestural or verbal "Do this." During modeling, the student must have a clear view of the demonstration. Carefully point out the positioning of any materials and how they are applied or handled. The pace of the demonstration should be such that the student can clearly discriminate the order and interdependence of each step. When modeling a series of actions initially, the length or complexity should be short and simple; extensions may be added as successful imitations occur. Finally, when directionality of the response is important, both the teacher and student should face the same direction.

Effective antecedent prompting is characterized by the following guidelines:

- Prompts should focus students' attention on the natural cue, not distract from it.
- Prompts should be as weak as possible. The use of strong prompts when weak ones will do is inefficient and may unnecessarily prolong instruction.
- Prompts should be faded as rapidly as possible. Continuing to prompt longer than necessary may result in artificial dependence on the prompt rather than on natural cues. However, abrupt removal of prompts may result in termination of the desired behavior. Fading is conducted by progressively and systematically providing less frequent intrusive or intense prompts over the course of instruction.

- Unplanned prompts should be avoided. A teacher may be unaware that students are being prompted by facial expression or vocal inflection (Alberto & Troutman, 1986): Consider the example of a teacher involved in street crossing instruction who consistently leans forward when the signal changes to a green light. The teacher may well not realize that his or her behavior, rather than the traffic light, is prompting the student's presumed correct response.

Response Prompts

Response prompts are types of assistance for actual behavior performance. They require the teacher to assist the student in his or her act of producing the response. There are at least six types of response prompts: full physical prompts, partial physical prompts, model prompts, signal prompts, verbal prompts, and self-operated prompts.

Full physical prompts provide total guidance to the student. The teacher actually puts the student through the entire behavior, thereby providing assistance for each movement necessary for successful performance. A *partial physical prompt* is physical assistance to initiate or provide direction for performance. As soon as the teacher feels the student engaging in the response, the assistance is terminated. A *model prompt* is a response prompt when its purpose is to occasion coactive imitation by the student. The procedure is implemented to increase a student's ability to imitate a response when given a concurrent (continuing) model presentation. This type of model prompt is particularly useful with students with profound handicaps (Sternberg, McNerney, & Pegnatore, 1985; Sternberg, & Owens, 1985). A *signal prompt* is a gesture to signal response initiation, as in pointing to or tapping the target instructional material(s). A *verbal prompt* is assistance provided beyond the initial verbal instruction (e.g., *encouragement* [" You are doing fine." "Go to the next step."]; *hints* ["It is what you sleep in?"]; *rules* ["When the light is red you should _____."]; or *questions* ["How do you start the washing machine?" "How much soap do you need?"]) that further stimulates student consideration and interest, or provides information for student initiation and performance of the response. *Self-operated* prompting systems are artificial systems that provide the student continuous performance cues and are operated by the student. They may take the form of pictorial prompt sequences (Connis, 1979; Johnson & Cuvo, 1981; Martin, Rusch, James, Decker, & Trytol, 1982; Thinesen & Bryan, 1981; Wacker & Berg, 1983; Wacker, Berg, Berrie, & Swatta, 1985), or auditory prompt sequences (Alberto, Sharpton, Briggs, & Stright, 1986).

Systematic Use of Response Prompts

To provide consistent assistance to students, a systematic use of response prompts should be employed. Guidelines for their systematic use have been proposed for both single prompts and coordinated multiple prompts (*prompt sequences*). One systematic use of a single response prompt is known as the *time-delay procedure*. The systematic use of multiple response prompts may be seen in the *system of maximum prompts,* or in the *system of least prompts.*

Systematic Use of a Single Prompt. When a teacher sits down with a student to instruct a skill, he or she may give a cue such as "Michael, show me the shirt," and then wait for the student to perform the response. After waiting, if the student does not respond, the teacher should help him perform the task. The time-delay procedure is an approach to systematizing the amount of time the teacher waits before providing assistance (Snell & Gast, 1981).

If the skill being taught is completely new to the student, the teacher may begin the instructional session at a *zero-second delay.* The teacher gives the instruction and the prompt simultaneously. In that way the student learns to associate the verbal instruction and the nature of the response called for. After several repetitions at zero-second delay, or simultaneous presentation, the teacher begins to give the student time to respond before he or she gives any prompt. The teacher systematically increases the length of delay between the verbal instruction and the assistance.

Table 7-3 Sequence of Components of a Time-Delay Procedure: Use of a Single Prompt

Antecedent	Delay	Prompt	Response	Consequence
(A) "Roll the ball"	0 sec .5 1	Teacher touches ball	Student rolls ball	(A) Primary or secondary reinforcer
(B) Object	2 3 4			(B) "Good you rolled the ball."
				(C) The ball rolls

Source: From "Applying Time Delay Procedure to the Instruction of the Severely Handicapped" by M. Snell and D. Gast, 1981, *The Journal of the Association of Persons with Severe Handicaps, 6,* pp. 3-14. Copyright 1981 by Association for Persons with Severe Handicaps. Reprinted by permission.

As illustrated in Table 7-3, a typical strategy is for the teacher to increase the time-delay at one-second intervals. The length of delay is increased once the student shows a pattern of anticipating the prompt (i.e., is correctly performing the behavior during the delay time, thereby no longer requiring the prompt). Indeed, the goal of the procedure is for the student to perform the correct response in the absence of a response prompt. Billingsley & Romer (1983) suggested that time-delay is as effective as, and may be more efficient than, the use of multiple prompts.

Systematic Use of Multiple Prompts. To use the *system of maximum prompts,* the teacher begins by providing the student with the most assistance possible. Gradually, the amount of assistance is reduced. The amount or intrusiveness of the prompt is faded as the student's independence increases over sessions. As seen in Figure 7-1, instruction begins with a full physical prompt where the teacher physically assists the student through the entire response while restating the instruction. The teacher performs the task hand-in-hand with the student, providing errorless practice. After an initial session(s) of guidance, the teacher reduces the amount of assistance by employing a partial physical prompt. After sessions in which the student can successfully respond with a partial physical prompt, the teacher reduces his or her level of assistance to the use of a less controlling prompt such as a signal or verbal instruction. The goal is for the student to perform the response without any assistance when given a verbal instruction.

The *system of least prompts* operates from the opposite perspective. Instead of beginning instruction with the greatest amount of assistance, the teacher begins by providing the student with the least amount of assistance necessary. The student is provided the opportunity to perform at his or her highest level of independence on each occasion before assistance is increased within a trial.

Instruction begins with a presentation of the materials and a request for the response. If after three to five seconds the response is not initiated, the teacher will increase the amount of assistance in a sequential manner (e.g., from just the instructional cue to the cue plus a signal delivered simultaneously). If the increased prompt is still insufficient to occasion the response, the level of assistance will be increased to a partial physical prompt, and so on, until the response is made by the student or until the teacher makes use of the most assistance possible, a full physical prompt. At each subsequent request (trial) for the response, the teacher again begins at the instructional cue and progressively increases assistance as needed.

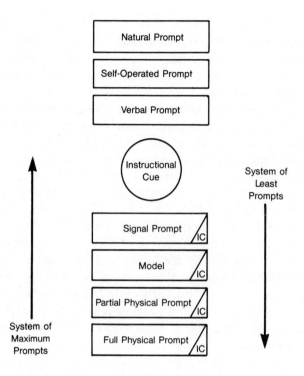

Figure 7-1 Components of the System of Maximum Prompts and the System of Least Prompts.

Response prompting systems are most often used in teaching activities that require a motor movement such as dressing, vocational tasks, play tasks, and academic tasks that involve material manipulation, as in sorting by size or color, or in selecting materials to indicate receptive language comprehension.

While the two prompting systems have common elements, there are several practical differences in their application. As noted, when using the system of maximum prompts each teaching session is conducted at one assistance level, though in subsequent sessions the assistance level will decrease. In the system of least prompts each opportunity for performance (trial) begins at the level of instructional cue, regardless of how much assistance was required on the previous trial. As maximum prompts initially provide greater physical assistance by the teacher, they are thought to be most appropriate for use during the acquisition stage of learning. Decreasing assistance provides more intensive instruction earlier, thereby minimizing errors and reducing time between the instructional cue and the student response (Schoen, 1986). Least prompts are thought most useful at higher levels of learning such as fluency and generalization (Csapo, 1981).

With either response prompting system, the goal of instruction is for the student to comply with the instructional cue when presented by the teacher. However, such a goal can result in a student who still relies on the teacher for initiation and/or correction of his or her performance.

Although response to a teacher-delivered cue may be appropriate in certain situations, such as the classroom or community, it does not provide sufficient independence for adolescents or adults. True independence is the ability to respond to cues that naturally occur in the environment that signal the student to perform a particular behavior or that a behavior is being performed incorrectly. For some students with severe or profound handicaps, the extent of our current knowledge of instruction is such that they may be unable to perform certain complex behaviors or series of behaviors independent of additional cueing. A possible solution to this problem is instruction in the use of *self-operated prompting systems.*

A self-operated system may be one that provides continuous picture cues or carefully timed auditory cues to prompt performance. *Picture cues* may be designed so that they depict each step in an activity. For example, the steps to operating a commercial dishwasher can be placed on the machine or may be in a book such that each page turned depicts the next step. *Auditory cues* are prerecorded audio tapes. They are arranged such that each step in a task analysis, in addition to self-evaluation/correction steps, are presented to the student via a "walkman" tape player to provide continuous cues. Teaching the student to use such permanent prompting systems allows performance without continuous supervision.

General Instructional Formatting

The precision of trial management is incorporated in various methodologic formats. One set of formats is used for instructing single-step behaviors, such as labeling functional objects or learning which restroom to use. Another set is used for learning multiple-step behaviors, such as self-help and vocational activities.

Table 7-4 Sequence of Instruction for the Match-to-Sample Format

	3	Model	The array consists of a single, identical choice.
	3	Instance	
	3	Model	The array consists of an identical match and a grossly dissimilar choice.
3	4		
Instance	Non-instance		
	3		The array consists of an identical match and two alternative selections.
4	3	7	
	3		The array consists of an identical match and two or more alternative selections of increasing similarity to the model.
5 8		2 3	

Formats for Single-Step Behaviors

Formats for single-step behaviors include at least the following procedures: match-to-sample, sort-to-sample, simple discrimination learning, and shaping.

Match-to-Sample. This format is used to teach the ability to select, from a variety of items, one that matches a sample item. The teacher is in effect saying: "Here is one of these (the item, correct choice) and an array consisting of an 'instance' and one or more 'non-instances' (incorrect choices) from which to select one similar to the model." The sequence of increasing complexity of a selection array is illustrated in Table 7-4.

The ability to match an item to a given sample is a useful skill in work (following an assembly sequence): home (selecting items for dinner); leisure (using a prosthetic device to select the various amounts of money necessary to take a bus to go to the movies); and community settings (selecting correct items in a grocery store).

Sort-to-Sample. This format is used to teach a student to sort an array of items into categories when two models are presented. The first step is sorting by dimensions in which the student sorts by the "likeness" of dimensional features such as color, size, and form. Initially the determination is based on a *single dimensional difference*. For example, socks or cups identical in all respects except color are sorted.

The next step is sorting with *multiple dimensional differences*. Multiple dimension sorting involves such items as various coins, screws, articles of clothing, and objects. Sorting moves then to categories such as function of objects as in sorting objects one wears versus things one eats, or things found in the kitchen versus things found in the bathroom. Include functional sorts such as broken versus unbroken, clean versus unclean, complete versus incomplete, and correctly assembled versus incorrectly assembled.

For both match-to-sample and sort-to-sample tasks, one begins with real objects before using pictures or some other form of representation. Klein & Stafford (1978) state that classification competence is enhanced by experience with concrete, familiar materials before the use of symbolic materials.

Simple Discrimination Learning. This format is used to teach differential selection of two items without an exemplar, such as correctly selecting a fork when requested or when needed, as at meal time. On another level, discrimination learning is said to occur when a student can tell whether two objects (e.g., socks and cups), symbols, or figures are the same or different.

During initial stages of discrimination learning, the relevant dimension should vary while the irrelevant dimensions remain constant (Zeaman & House, 1979). In a case such as discriminating forks and spoons, or cups and bowls, the relevant feature that varies is form. Therefore when teaching the spoon/fork or cup/bowl discrimination, only form should vary while all other dimensions, such as size and color, should not. Progress to concept learning occurs when sets of items can be correctly identified even though they vary in multiple dimensions such as size, color, position, etc. (Gagne & Briggs, 1979). The student has learned that a cup is a cup despite variations in color and/or size.

The tendency of some students to respond to only one component of a training procedure suggests that antecedent prompts of the relevant feature prompt variety should be employed in discrimination learning. Such prompts will tend to insure that the student is focusing on the appropriate natural cue for responding once the prompt is faded, as opposed to a response prompt that does not directly focus student attention to dimensions of the instructional material (Schriebman, 1975; Wolfe & Cuvo, 1978).

Figure 7-2 provides a simplified example of the progression from basic discrimination to generalized concept using "redness" as the example. Steps 1, 2, and 3 are basic discrimination where the only thing varied is the relevant dimension of color; size and shape are held constant. In Steps 4 and 5 it is generalized to a concept applicable across dimensional differences, complexities, and materials.

Shaping. This is instruction of a behavior by reinforcing successive approximations of the target behavior. The student has made some attempt at performance. Shaping molds a change or extension of the attempted topography of the response. By accepting small incremental steps, and assuring mastery of each approximation before moving on to the next, each step becomes the foundation upon which a more sophisticated response is established.

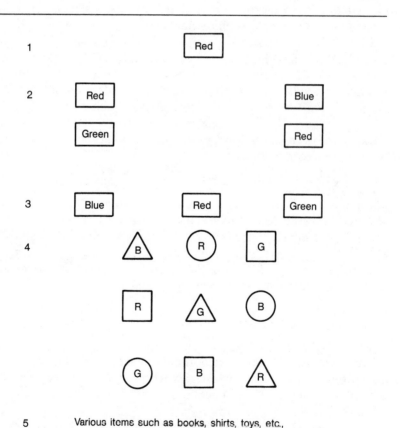

Figure 7-2 Sequence of Instruction for Discrimination Learning.

Many skills are acquired through shaping. Walking, imitation, reaching, and grasping are examples of complex skills that started from simpler, easier forms of behavior that were built upon until more extensive, complex performances developed. For typical children, certain skills, such as a toddler learning to walk, are learned through accidental or natural selection of the successive approximations. Shaping, as an instructional procedure with students with severe or profound handicaps, must be thoughtfully planned.

Shaping is a linear procedure. It always moves from current capability toward the target behavior. Performance criteria are shifted so as to drive this advancing capability. Criteria for step advancement may be qualitative (e.g., improved articulation) or quantitative (e.g., working for increasing periods of time or at a faster rate). As the steps move from easier/simple to harder/complex, one never progresses to a harder requirement until the easier has been mastered.

Shaping is a systematic procedure. The steps for shaping as a teaching procedure include (1) identifying the objective; (2) identifying the incremental steps; (3) determining the student's current level of ability; (4) teaching to the first criterion, providing the student reinforcement and correction until mastery of step 1; (5) teaching each successive step until the student can successfully perform the total objective; and (6) terminating reinforcement of previous accomplishments once the student has moved to succeeding steps.

When employing the shaping procedure, one must bear in mind that if the approximations are too small, the procedure may be needlessly time-consuming, inefficient, and boring to the student. If they are too large, instruction will be just as frustrating to the student as if he or she had been initially presented with the requirement of performing the original objective. If the teacher finds that some of the steps are indeed too large, he or she should return to the step of the student's last successful performance and advance again, but at smaller increments.

Formats for Multiple-Step Behaviors

Formats for *multiple-step behaviors* include three variations of *chaining*. Much of what we teach students makes use of skills or behaviors in various combinations or series to achieve new ends. These skills are related by their usefulness in obtaining new objectives. When sequenced, these related skills are known as *chains*.

Chains may allow a complex behavior such as toothbrushing, or a series of activities such as taking a bus to the store and returning home. Teaching how to form and make use of chains of behaviors is known as *chaining*.

The components of a chain may be individual behaviors already in a student's repertoire, or a combination of old and new behaviors. The various steps or components of a chain of a complex behavior are taught in a sequence. The variations in sequencing are known as *forward chaining, backward chaining,* and *total task* or *whole task programming.*

One way of approaching the teaching of a chained performance is to teach the first link in the chain and then each step in its natural order of succession. This is known as *forward chaining.* If the objective is to teach a student how to put on a sock, the teacher begins by identifying the sequential steps in putting on a sock as follows: (1) pick up sock; (2) lift foot; (3) insert thumbs at opening; (4) separate and open hole; (5) insert toe; (6) pull to heel; and (7) pull over heel and up to ankle. In forward chaining, the teacher instructs the student how to do step 1 until the student demonstrates acquisition. The student then is instructed in the performance of step 2 (with step 1 expected to occur). Once acquisition of step 2 is demonstrated, the teacher moves on to step 3 (with steps 1 and 2 expected to occur). This progression continues in succession until the student can perform all the steps in a coordinated series resulting in the ultimate objective of putting on the sock.

An alternate choice is *backward chaining.* In this case, instruction begins with the last step in the chain and proceeds in reverse order until the student can perform all the steps in succession. In the case of teaching the student to put on a sock, the first thing the teacher does is perform steps 1 through 6 and require the student to perform only step 7, the last step. Instruction would proceed on step 7. Once the student demonstrated acquisition of step 7, the teacher would perform steps 1 through 5 and require student performance of steps 6 and 7 (with instruction of step 6 only, and expectation of performance on step 7). The teacher would continue in this reverse order until the student had shown acquisition of the entire chain. Such instruction continues in reverse order until the student is finally presented with only the sock and must independently perform all the necessary steps. In Table 7-5, Falvey (1986) illustrates the procedural progress of a task when taught through forward and backward chaining.

Spooner and Spooner (1984) suggested a procedural modification of backward chaining they call *backward chaining with leap-aheads.* In this modification, the student is presented with a completed assembly except for the last step. If that step is completed with minimal or no assistance from the teacher, several steps are skipped and a step farther up the chain is selected for training. Although not every step in the chain is trained, each step must be performed correctly before the terminal criterion is met. The leap-ahead procedure is reported to speed up learning significantly.

Table 7-5 Examples of Forward and Backward Chaining Sequencing

Environment: Home (domestic)
Subenvironment: Food preparation area
Activity: Washing the dishes

Forward Teaching Order	Backward Teaching Order
1.	20. Put drain in sink.
2.	19. Turn on hot water.
3.	18. Adjust hot water flow.
4.	17. Turn on cold water.
5.	16. Adjust cold water flow.
6.	15. Put correct amount of soap in sink.
7.	14. Determine when sink is full.
8.	13. Turn off hot water.
9.	12. Turn off cold water.
10.	11. Place dirty dish in water.
11.	10. Pick up sponge.
12.	9. Use sponge to wash front of dish.
13.	8. Turn dish over.
14.	7. Use sponge to wash back of dish.
15.	6. Check front and back of dish for dirt.
16.	5. Place sponge in water.
17.	4. Rinse front of dish.
18.	3. Rinse back of dish.
19.	2. Check dish for remaining soap.
20.	1. Place dish in rack.

Source: From *Community-Based Curriculum: Instructional Strategies for Students with Severe Handicaps* (p. 52) by M. Falvey, 1986, Baltimore, Md.: Paul H. Brookes Publishers. Copyright 1986 by Paul H. Brookes Publishers. Reprinted by permission.

A final variation of chaining is *total task programming.* In this approach the student begins with the first step, but every step in the sequence is trained on every trial until the student performs the whole task to a predetermined criterion (Bellamy et al., 1979; Gold, 1976). A trial is defined as an opportunity to perform the entire chain, not just a single step or subset of steps of the chain. At the beginning of each trial, the student is given the instructional cue for performance of the entire chain. As the student begins with the first step, he or she is encouraged to continue with the succeeding steps. As the student confronts a step he or she cannot perform, the teacher provides assistance through that step. For each trial, the teacher records the number of steps the student performed independently and the number that required assistance. Bellamy et al. (1979) suggested that difficult steps be taught in isolation until an accuracy rate of 80% is achieved, at which point the responses may be chained together. This approach seems to include a reasonable use of massed trials for difficult steps.

In a review of various chaining options, Spooner & Spooner (1984) concluded: "In the final analysis, it may be that different learners do better with different procedures, and that when different tasks are used (e.g., dressing vs. vocational) different results are obtainable" (p. 123).

Task Analysis

All chaining formats just discussed are conducted in the framework of *task analysis.* Task analysis involves preparing three components: the objective, the steps of the task sequence, and identification of the prerequisite skills.

The *instructional objective* is derived from the information gathered through functional, behavioral, and ecological assessments (Browder & Snell, in press: Brown et al., 1979; Falvey, 1986). The objective should contain an operational definition of the behavior to be taught, the conditions under which it will be taught (e.g., materials, cues, setting), and the criterion required for acceptable performance.

The *component steps* are arranged in an ordinal listing required to accomplish the target behavior. The detail required in this listing should be determined by the student's ability level (Crist, Walls, & Haught, 1984; Gold, 1980). One student may learn to wash hands through a 10-step process, while another may need a 30-step process. There should be just enough steps to allow efficient and systematic teaching. It is often the case that a teacher will analyze a task to such a fine degree that unimportant or nonfunctional steps are included (Cuvo, Jacobi, & Sipko, 1981). If the student has special difficulty in successfully performing a step, the step can be further analyzed (Falvey, 1986). For example, a step that states: "sticks blade end of knife into butter container" may be sliced into steps that read: (1) "places knife in middle of butter container"; (2) "presses knife into butter"; (3) "pulls knife toward body to side of butter container"; and (4) "turns knife blade over so butter rests on top of knife blade."

Prerequisite skills can usually be identified by examining the first three or four steps of the task analysis and asking whether they can be performed without other skills already being in the student's repertoire. Be very careful when identifying prerequisites to instruction. It has been the case with students with severe or profound handicaps that identification of prerequisite skills results in never embarking on instruction, as we are continually diverted to instruction of prerequisites. Rather, think of the student's "task engagement capability" and be alert to "alternative performance strategies" to enable task instruction and performance (Wilcox & Bellamy, 1982). A student might use an alternative strategy that does not or does require special equipment. For example, he or she might use two hands on either end of a knife to cut butter; use special equipment or a prosthetic device, as with a special knife that accommodates the student's range of motion; or partially participate in the activity (a peer cuts the butter when given a signal by the student, or the student touches a plate for butter to be placed on the bread).

Fluency and Generalization

The focus to this point has been to ensure that the student can accurately perform a new behavior. This is the level of learning, or competence, known as *acquisition*. This is not the point at which instruction should end, as behaviors must be performed accurately and in a functionally reasonable time. Consider the student who takes five minutes to put on a coat or fifteen seconds to reply to a social greeting. After acquisition instruction, fluency instruction is designed to decrease duration (as in time to put on a coat), increase duration (as time on a vocational task), and/or decrease latency (as in replying to a greeting) (Liberty, Haring, & Martin, 1981). *Fluency instruction,* being based on a time criterion, necessitates that the teacher alter a performance criterion by setting a time limit: In order for the student's behavior to result in reinforcement, the behavior must be performed accurately within a time limit. White & Haring (1980) suggest that fluency of performance may be a better indicator of a student's ability to maintain, generalize, or apply a newly acquired skill than accuracy of performance alone.

Generalization refers to the performance of previously learned behaviors in new situations, in new settings, in response to new people, in response to new requests (instructional cues), or with new materials (e.g., different garments or vending machines). One methodology for generalization programming is *general case instruction* (Horner, McDonnell, & Bellamy, 1986; Horner, Sprague, & Wilcox, 1982).

General case instruction is a strategy for teaching skills that will be performed across people, places, and materials; or the efficient teaching of students to perform in nontrained situations. A general case has been taught when, after instruction on some tasks in a particular class, any task in that class can be performed correctly (Becker & Engelmann, 1978). General case instruction begins by examining the environment in which the student may be expected to perform the behavior to identify the range of variations that may be reasonably expected. For example, it may be appropriate to teach some students to shop in all grocery stores in their city, regardless of product arrangements and check-out operations. For other students, this goal may be unrealistic, and instruction might focus on just those stores in a particular neighborhood. In either case, two representative groups of examples of various stores are analyzed. To minimize errors in generalized settings, positive and negative training examples should be included in the general case (Horner, Eberhard, & Sheehan, 1986). One set of examples is used for direct instruction. The other set is used to probe generalization of the target activity to nontrained situations systematically, thus ensuring maintenance of the ability to perform the behavior.

As an example, Williams and Horner (1984) provided the following steps for applying general case instruction to street crossing.

1. Define the instructional universe (specifying all streets the student will be expected to cross after training).
2. Select the streets that will be trained and those that will serve as untrained probes (include streets that have features present in the student's instructional universe, such as stop signs, street lights).
3. Conduct the training, and collect the data reflecting the student's performance.
4. Modify the instruction based on an analysis of the "error patterns."
5. Train street crossing under exceptional traffic conditions (e.g., emergency vehicles with sirens, malfunctioning traffic signals).
6. Determine when to stop training based on verification of the student's performance on nontrained streets.

Group Instruction

A key element to efficient and effective instructional programming in public school classes for students with severe or profound handicaps is instruction in other than the clinical one-to-one student/teacher ratio. There now exists ample evidence that this population of students can benefit and learn in instructional arrangements that use larger student/teacher ratios, at rates comparable to or better than one-to-one instruction (Favell, Favell, & McGimsey, 1978; Kohl, Wilcox, & Karlan, 1978; Oliver, 1983; Storm & Willis, 1978; Westling, Ferrell, & Swenson, 1982). As a result of their review of the research on group instruction, Reid & Favell (1984) concluded: "The published research leaves virtually no doubt that useful skills can be taught to these individuals using a group format" (p. 175). Group instruction also provides opportunities for "a) increased control of motivational variables; b) opportunities to facilitate observational learning, peer interaction, and peer communication; and c) generalization of skills" (Brown et al., 1980, p. 353).

Students are often not automatically capable of participating as group members. There are a variety of procedures for preparing students for group instruction. One such procedure is suggested by Koegel and Rincover (1974) and Rincover and Koegel (1977). They took the members of a class and initially instructed each student in a one-to-one ratio. Each was taught on the one-to-one basis to familiarize them with the following instructional process: "I am going to ask you to do something, you are expected to do it, and I will reinforce you." A general class of activity, such as imitation, was the focus of instruction.

Once the students reached the criterion level of accuracy, they were grouped into a 2-to-1 ratio. The instructional content remained imitation, though a different sample of imitative behaviors was taught. The content matter remained the same because the focus of instruction was not the content (imitation capability) but the ability to be an attentive and active group member. Again, once the students reached a criterion of accuracy, they were reformed into a group with a ratio of 3-to-1. For reasons of management, three is the suggested maximum size for a group with targeted instructional goals. Reinforcement is suggested to start on a continuous reinforcement schedule of one reinforcement for each correct response and be thinned as the group size increases. Reinforcement is delivered to students for appropriate behaviors expected of a group member (attending, waiting turn, staying in seat).

Alternatively, Sobsey, McLarney, Missall, and Murphy (1985) suggested the initial formation of group instruction occur such that the students are in close proximity at a table but each is initially working on different instructional tasks with different instructional materials. As such, the teacher does a trial distribution with one student and then rotates to the next.

Though instruction may start with what is essentially one-to-one instruction in close proximity, this is not yet "group" instruction. It is critical to progress beyond merely one-to-one instruction with students placed in close proximity at a table. To assist in this progress, Brown et al. (1980) and Sobsey et al. (1985) suggested two variations on management of content for group instruction. These variations include teaching the same program to each group member. In such a case, the goal of instruction and the ensuring distribution of trials are identical for each group

Table 7-6 Example of Trial Distribution for Group Instruction Where the Instructional Program for Each Student Is Different, but the Theme Is the Same

Theme: APPLE

Student A

1. Say the word "apple."
2. Pick out the word when 1 distractor present.
3. Match word to picture presented with 2 distractor pictures of fruit.

Student B

1. Pick out apple when presented with 2 other fruits.
2. Point to pic-symbol of apple.
3. Pass apple of student C.

Student C

1. Take apple from student B.
2. Pick up knife from assorted cutlery in box.
3. Cut apple into pieces.

Student D

1. Hold piece of apple in hand.
2. Take a bite.
3. Chew it and swallow.

Source: From "Group Instruction: Theory and Application to Students with Severe Handicaps" by R. Sobsey et al., 1985, Boston, Mass. Paper presented at the 12th Annual Conference of the Association for Persons with Severe Handicaps. Reprinted by permission.

member. For example, each group member would engage in the following distribution of trials: (1) point to hairbrush; (2) verbalize "brush"; and (3) brush hair (Brown et al., 1980).

A second approach is different program/same theme (Sobsey, et al., 1985). In this case, group members may be working on different skills or different levels of the same skill, but the members are unified in that they are all being instructed with and interacting with the same materials. This is illustrated in Table 7-6.

Data Collection

An instructional session may be structured so that it contains a predetermined number of trials (usually 10 to 20) without regard to how long it will take to complete them, or a predetermined number of minutes (usually 10 to 20) within which a varying number of trials may occur. Generally, the first approach is used during the acquisition phase of instruction, and the second in a higher level of response competence (fluency and generalization). With the first approach, trial-by-trial data recording is usually employed: a data notation is recorded for each trial. With the second approach, a probe approach to data collection is usually employed: after the predetermined number of minutes of instruction, a

Exhibit 7-1 Adaptation of Dichotomous Data Sheet

Name: ____

Task: ____

Criterion: ____

DATE:

10	10	10	10	10	10	10	10	10	10	10	10	10	10	10	10	10	10	10	10	10	10	10	10	10	10	10	10	10
9	9	9	9	9	9	9	9	9	9	9	9	9	9	9	9	9	9	9	9	9	9	9	9	9	9	9	9	9
8	8	8	8	8	8	8	8	8	8	8	8	8	8	8	8	8	8	8	8	8	8	8	8	8	8	8	8	8
7	7	7	7	7	7	7	7	7	7	7	7	7	7	7	7	7	7	7	7	7	7	7	7	7	7	7	7	7
6	6	6	6	6	6	6	6	6	6	6	6	6	6	6	6	6	6	6	6	6	6	6	6	6	6	6	6	6
5	5	5	5	5	5	5	5	5	5	5	5	5	5	5	5	5	5	5	5	5	5	5	5	5	5	5	5	5
4	4	4	4	4	4	4	4	4	4	4	4	4	4	4	4	4	4	4	4	4	4	4	4	4	4	4	4	4
3	3	3	3	3	3	3	3	3	3	3	3	3	3	3	3	3	3	3	3	3	3	3	3	3	3	3	3	3
2	2	2	2	2	2	2	2	2	2	2	2	2	2	2	2	2	2	2	2	2	2	2	2	2	2	2	2	2
1	1	1	1	1	1	1	1	1	1	1	1	1	1	1	1	1	1	1	1	1	1	1	1	1	1	1	1	1
0	0	0	0	0	0	0	0	0	0	0	0	0	0	0	0	0	0	0	0	0	0	0	0	0	0	0	0	0

Comments:

DATE:

10	10	10	10	10	10	10	10	10	10	10	10	10	10	10	10	10	10	10	10	10	10	10	10	10	10	10	10	10
9	9	9	9	9	9	9	9	9	9	9	9	9	9	9	9	9	9	9	9	9	9	9	9	9	9	9	9	9
8	8	8	8	8	8	8	8	8	8	8	8	8	8	8	8	8	8	8	8	8	8	8	8	8	8	8	8	8
7	7	7	7	7	7	7	7	7	7	7	7	7	7	7	7	7	7	7	7	7	7	7	7	7	7	7	7	7
6	6	6	6	6	6	6	6	6	6	6	6	6	6	6	6	6	6	6	6	6	6	6	6	6	6	6	6	6
5	5	5	5	5	5	5	5	5	5	5	5	5	5	5	5	5	5	5	5	5	5	5	5	5	5	5	5	5
4	4	4	4	4	4	4	4	4	4	4	4	4	4	4	4	4	4	4	4	4	4	4	4	4	4	4	4	4
3	3	3	3	3	3	3	3	3	3	3	3	3	3	3	3	3	3	3	3	3	3	3	3	3	3	3	3	3
2	2	2	2	2	2	2	2	2	2	2	2	2	2	2	2	2	2	2	2	2	2	2	2	2	2	2	2	2
1	1	1	1	1	1	1	1	1	1	1	1	1	1	1	1	1	1	1	1	1	1	1	1	1	1	1	1	1
0	0	0	0	0	0	0	0	0	0	0	0	0	0	0	0	0	0	0	0	0	0	0	0	0	0	0	0	0

Comments:

Source: From "A Multi-Purpose Data Sheet for Recording and Graphing in the Classroom" by R. Saunders and K. Koplik, 1975, *The Journal of the Association for Persons with Severe Handicaps, 1,* p. 1. Copyright 1975 by Association for Persons with Severe Handicaps. Adapted by permission.

sample of the behavior is tested (probed), and the result of this performance is recorded as the data for the session.

Two basic forms of data can be taken during instruction. One is *dichotomous data*. When using dichotomous data, the teacher records only whether or not the student performed the requested behavior, correct or incorrect. One form of data sheet that can be used for dichotomous data collection is presented in Exhibit 7-1 and is a variation of one by Saunders & Koplik (1975). It may be used as follows:

1. Circle the trial number that corresponds to a correct response.
2. Slash (/) through the trial number that corresponds to an incorrect response.

After each instructional session
1. Total the number of correct trials (those circled).
2. Place a square around the corresponding number in the session column that corresponds to the number of correct trials.
3. To graph directly on the data sheet, connect the squared numbers across the sessions to yield a learning curve.

To collect dichotomous data when using a task analysis with the total task program format, the data sheet in Exhibit 7-2 is available (Bellamy et al., 1979). One column is for listing antecedents to be provided and another for a description of the steps of the chain. Each trial consists of an opportunity for the student to perform the entire chain of steps. For each trial, the teacher records the accuracy of the student's performance of each step using the same circle and slash procedure. This format also allows for graphing directly on the data sheet. The number corresponding to the number of correctly performed steps is indicated by a square, and the squares are connected across trials.

The other form of data collection indicates the instruction required for the student to perform the requested behavior. It is used when the teacher is employing a system of response prompting. Exhibit 7-3 presents such a data sheet (Alberto & Schofield, 1979). It depicts 20 sessions, each containing 10 trials. For each trial, the teacher can indicate the type of assistance that was necessary to enable the student to perform the response. After each trial, the trial number is marked on the row corresponding to the type of assistance provided (e.g., a gesture). This data sheet may also serve as a self-graphing sheet if the marked trial numbers are connected within and across sessions, thus yielding a curve that displays the increasing independence of the student to perform the response.

Exhibit 7-2 Data Sheet for Chain Instruction (Task Analysis)

SD	RESPONSE																			
25.	_____	25	25	25	25	25	25	25	25	25	25	25	25	25	25	25	25	25	25	25
24.	_____	24	24	24	24	24	24	24	24	24	24	24	24	24	24	24	24	24	24	24
23.	_____	23	23	23	23	23	23	23	23	23	23	23	23	23	23	23	23	23	23	23
22.	_____	22	22	22	22	22	22	22	22	22	22	22	22	22	22	22	22	22	22	22
21.	_____	21	21	21	21	21	21	21	21	21	21	21	21	21	21	21	21	21	21	21
20.	_____	20	20	20	20	20	20	20	20	20	20	20	20	20	20	20	20	20	20	20
19.	_____	19	19	19	19	19	19	19	19	19	19	19	19	19	19	19	19	19	19	19
18.	_____	18	18	18	18	18	18	18	18	18	18	18	18	18	18	18	18	18	18	18
17.	_____	17	17	17	17	17	17	17	17	17	17	17	17	17	17	17	17	17	17	17
16.	_____	16	16	16	16	16	16	16	16	16	16	16	16	16	16	16	16	16	16	16
15.	_____	15	15	15	15	15	15	15	15	15	15	15	15	15	15	15	15	15	15	15
14.	_____	14	14	14	14	14	14	14	14	14	14	14	14	14	14	14	14	14	14	14
13.	_____	13	13	13	13	13	13	13	13	13	13	13	13	13	13	13	13	13	13	13
12.	_____	12	12	12	12	12	12	12	12	12	12	12	12	12	12	12	12	12	12	12
11.	_____	11	11	11	11	11	11	11	11	11	11	11	11	11	11	11	11	11	11	11
10.	_____	10	10	10	10	10	10	10	10	10	10	10	10	10	10	10	10	10	10	10
9.	_____	9	9	9	9	9	9	9	9	9	9	9	9	9	9	9	9	9	9	9
8.	_____	8	8	8	8	8	8	8	8	8	8	8	8	8	8	8	8	8	8	8
7.	_____	7	7	7	7	7	7	7	7	7	7	7	7	7	7	7	7	7	7	7
6.	_____	6	6	6	6	6	6	6	6	6	6	6	6	6	6	6	6	6	6	6
5.	_____	5	5	5	5	5	5	5	5	5	5	5	5	5	5	5	5	5	5	5
4.	_____	4	4	4	4	4	4	4	4	4	4	4	4	4	4	4	4	4	4	4
3.	_____	3	3	3	3	3	3	3	3	3	3	3	3	3	3	3	3	3	3	3
2.	_____	2	2	2	2	2	2	2	2	2	2	2	2	2	2	2	2	2	2	2
1.	_____	1	1	1	1	1	1	1	1	1	1	1	1	1	1	1	1	1	1	1

Source: From *Vocational Habilitation of Severely Retarded Adults: A Direct Service Technology* (p. 75) by G.T. Bellamy, R. Horner, and D. Inman, 1979, Austin, Texas: PRO-ED. Copyright 1979 by PRO-ED. Reprinted by permission.

Exhibit 7-3 Data Sheet that Indicates Response Prompting

NAME: ______________________ MONTH: ______________

GOAL: ______________________

CRITERION: ______________________

COMMENTS: ______________________

	V.CUE	1 2 3 4 5 6 7 8 9 10	1 2 3 4 5 6 7 8 9 10	1 2 3 4 5 6 7 8 9 10	1 2 3 4 5 6 7 8 9 10	1 2 3 4 5 6 7 8 9 10
	SIGNAL	1 2 3 4 5 6 7 8 9 10	1 2 3 4 5 6 7 8 9 10	1 2 3 4 5 6 7 8 9 10	1 2 3 4 5 6 7 8 9 10	1 2 3 4 5 6 7 8 9 10
	MODEL	1 2 3 4 5 6 7 8 9 10	1 2 3 4 5 6 7 8 9 10	1 2 3 4 5 6 7 8 9 10	1 2 3 4 5 6 7 8 9 10	1 2 3 4 5 6 7 8 9 10
	PARTIAL	1 2 3 4 5 6 7 8 9 10	1 2 3 4 5 6 7 8 9 10	1 2 3 4 5 6 7 8 9 10	1 2 3 4 5 6 7 8 9 10	1 2 3 4 5 6 7 8 9 10
TRIALS	FULL	1 2 3 4 5 6 7 8 9 10	1 2 3 4 5 6 7 8 9 10	1 2 3 4 5 6 7 8 9 10	1 2 3 4 5 6 7 8 9 10	1 2 3 4 5 6 7 8 9 10
	INCORR	1 2 3 4 5 6 7 8 9 10	1 2 3 4 5 6 7 8 9 10	1 2 3 4 5 6 7 8 9 10	1 2 3 4 5 6 7 8 9 10	1 2 3 4 5 6 7 8 9 10
	V.CUE	1 2 3 4 5 6 7 8 9 10	1 2 3 4 5 6 7 8 9 10	1 2 3 4 5 6 7 8 9 10	1 2 3 4 5 6 7 8 9 10	1 2 3 4 5 6 7 8 9 10
	SIGNAL	1 2 3 4 5 6 7 8 9 10	1 2 3 4 5 6 7 8 9 10	1 2 3 4 5 6 7 8 9 10	1 2 3 4 5 6 7 8 9 10	1 2 3 4 5 6 7 8 9 10
	MODEL	1 2 3 4 5 6 7 8 9 10	1 2 3 4 5 6 7 8 9 10	1 2 3 4 5 6 7 8 9 10	1 2 3 4 5 6 7 8 9 10	1 2 3 4 5 6 7 8 9 10
	PARTIAL	1 2 3 4 5 6 7 8 9 10	1 2 3 4 5 6 7 8 9 10	1 2 3 4 5 6 7 8 9 10	1 2 3 4 5 6 7 8 9 10	1 2 3 4 5 6 7 8 9 10
	FULL	1 2 3 4 5 6 7 8 9 10	1 2 3 4 5 6 7 8 9 10	1 2 3 4 5 6 7 8 9 10	1 2 3 4 5 6 7 8 9 10	1 2 3 4 5 6 7 8 9 10
	INCORR	1 2 3 4 5 6 7 8 9 10	1 2 3 4 5 6 7 8 9 10	1 2 3 4 5 6 7 8 9 10	1 2 3 4 5 6 7 8 9 10	1 2 3 4 5 6 7 8 9 10
	V.CUE	1 2 3 4 5 6 7 8 9 10	1 2 3 4 5 6 7 8 9 10	1 2 3 4 5 6 7 8 9 10	1 2 3 4 5 6 7 8 9 10	1 2 3 4 5 6 7 8 9 10
	SIGNAL	1 2 3 4 5 6 7 8 9 10	1 2 3 4 5 6 7 8 9 10	1 2 3 4 5 6 7 8 9 10	1 2 3 4 5 6 7 8 9 10	1 2 3 4 5 6 7 8 9 10
	MODEL	1 2 3 4 5 6 7 8 9 10	1 2 3 4 5 6 7 8 9 10	1 2 3 4 5 6 7 8 9 10	1 2 3 4 5 6 7 8 9 10	1 2 3 4 5 6 7 8 9 10
	PARTIAL	1 2 3 4 5 6 7 8 9 10	1 2 3 4 5 6 7 8 9 10	1 2 3 4 5 6 7 8 9 10	1 2 3 4 5 6 7 8 9 10	1 2 3 4 5 6 7 8 9 10
	FULL	1 2 3 4 5 6 7 8 9 10	1 2 3 4 5 6 7 8 9 10	1 2 3 4 5 6 7 8 9 10	1 2 3 4 5 6 7 8 9 10	1 2 3 4 5 6 7 8 9 10
	INCORR	1 2 3 4 5 6 7 8 9 10	1 2 3 4 5 6 7 8 9 10	1 2 3 4 5 6 7 8 9 10	1 2 3 4 5 6 7 8 9 10	1 2 3 4 5 6 7 8 9 10
	V.CUE	1 2 3 4 5 6 7 8 9 10	1 2 3 4 5 6 7 8 9 10	1 2 3 4 5 6 7 8 9 10	1 2 3 4 5 6 7 8 9 10	1 2 3 4 5 6 7 8 9 10
	SIGNAL	1 2 3 4 5 6 7 8 9 10	1 2 3 4 5 6 7 8 9 10	1 2 3 4 5 6 7 8 9 10	1 2 3 4 5 6 7 8 9 10	1 2 3 4 5 6 7 8 9 10
	MODEL	1 2 3 4 5 6 7 8 9 10	1 2 3 4 5 6 7 8 9 10	1 2 3 4 5 6 7 8 9 10	1 2 3 4 5 6 7 8 9 10	1 2 3 4 5 6 7 8 9 10
	PARTIAL	1 2 3 4 5 6 7 8 9 10	1 2 3 4 5 6 7 8 9 10	1 2 3 4 5 6 7 8 9 10	1 2 3 4 5 6 7 8 9 10	1 2 3 4 5 6 7 8 9 10
	FULL	1 2 3 4 5 6 7 8 9 10	1 2 3 4 5 6 7 8 9 10	1 2 3 4 5 6 7 8 9 10	1 2 3 4 5 6 7 8 9 10	1 2 3 4 5 6 7 8 9 10
	INCORR	1 2 3 4 5 6 7 8 9 10	1 2 3 4 5 6 7 8 9 10	1 2 3 4 5 6 7 8 9 10	1 2 3 4 5 6 7 8 9 10	1 2 3 4 5 6 7 8 9 10

Source: From "An Instructional Interaction Pattern for the Severely Handicapped" by P. Alberto and P. Schofield, 1979, *Teaching Exceptional Children, 12,* p. 19. Copyright 1979 by Council for Exceptional Children. Reprinted by permission.

The three data sheets presented are examples of some that have proven useful for teachers; however, they are just models. Teachers should either adapt these examples or design a different data sheet they find easy to use and that provides the information required. Otherwise, data collection will be a cumbersome and neglected exercise. Data collection is a vital component of effective instructional programming for students with severe or profound handicaps.

Systematic review of program data allows the instructor to note the presence, absence, and rate of student progress. One strategy proposed for assisting in this evaluation is *trend analysis* or the *quarter-intersect method* (White & Liberty, 1976). As seen in Figure 7-3, evaluation is based on the

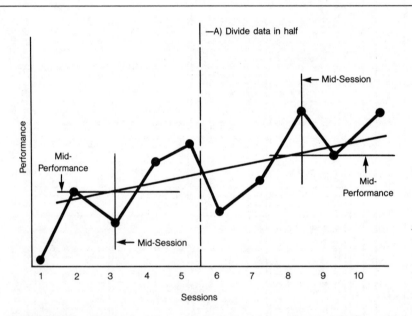

A. Divide the total number of data points in half and draw a vertical line between the two halves.
B. Now for each half of the graph:
    1. Find the mid-session point (the session or point where there is an equal number of sessions on both sides), and draw a vertical line.
    2. Find the mid-performance point (the data point that has an equal number of data points above and below it) and draw a horizontal line.
C. Connect the intersections of these points on both halves of the graph.

Figure 7-3. Constructing a Trend Line.

trend of the acquisition curve developed from median values of the data when graphed. Such an analysis of trend lines can indicate the direction of behavior change in the past and predict the direction of behavior change in the future. Such a prediction allows the teacher to consider the effectiveness and efficiency of the instructional program. When problems in an instructional program are reflected by the data, the teacher should review the major elements of instruction presented in this chapter to target the component in need of revision, whether it is the task selected, the materials used, the management of instructional trials, or the general methods format employed.

CONCLUSION

The major purpose of this chapter was to provide a framework for understanding the complexities involved in instruction of students with severe or profound handicaps. All appropriate instructional technology, however, should be effectively embedded in an overall curriculum design. The next chapter presents information on curriculum designs and development processes that are appropriate for use with these students.

REFERENCES

Adams, G., Matlock, B., & Tallon, R. (1981). Analysis of social praise given during the correction procedure of skill training. *American Journal of Mental Deficiency, 85,* 652-654.

Alberto, P., & Schofield, P. (1979). An instructional interaction pattern for the severely handicapped. *Teaching Exceptional Children, 12,* 16-19.

Alberto, P., Sharpton, W., Briggs, A., & Stright, M.H. (1986). Facilitating task acquisition through the use of a self-operated auditory prompting system. *Journal of the Association for Persons with Severe Handicaps, 11,* 85-91.

Alberto, P., & Troutman, A. (1986). *Applied behavior analysis for teachers.* Columbus, OH: Charles E. Merrill.

Baer, D., Peterson, R., & Sherman, J. (1967). The development of imitation by reinforcing behavioral similarity to a model. *Journal of the Experimental Analysis of Behavior, 10,* 405-416.

Bandura, A. (1969). *Principles of behavior modification.* New York: Holt, Rinehart & Winston.

Baumgart, D., Brown, L., Pumpian, I., Nisbet, J., Ford. A., Sweet, M., Messina, R., & Schroeder, J. (1982). Principle of partial participation and individualized adaptations in educational programs for severely handicapped students. *Journal of the Association for the Severely Handicapped, 7,* 17-27.

Becker, W., & Engelman, S. (1978). Systems for basic instruction: Theory and applications. In A. Catania & T. Brigham (Eds.), *Handbook of applied behavior analysis: Social and instructional progress* (pp. 325-377). New York: Irvington.

Bellamy, G.T., Horner, R., & Inman, D. (1979). *Vocational habilitation of severely retarded adults: A direct service technology.* Austin, TX: PRO-ED.

Billingsley, F., & Romer, L. (1983). Response prompting and the transfer of stimulus control: Methods, research, and a conceptual framework. *The Journal of the Association for the Severely Handicapped, 8*, 3-12.

Browder, D., & Snell, M. (in press). Assessment of students with severe handicaps. In E.S. Shapiro & T.R. Kratochwill (Eds.), *Behavioral assessment in schools: Approaches to classification and intervention.* New York: Guilford Press.

Brown, L., Branston, M.B., Hamre-Nietupski, S., Pumpian, I., Certo, N., & Gruenewald, L. (1979). A strategy for developing chronological-age–appropriate and functional curricular content for severely handicapped adolescents and young adults. *The Journal of Special Education, 13*, 81-90.

Brown, F., Holvoet, J., Guess, D., & Mulligan, M. (1980). The individualized curriculum sequencing model (III): Small group instruction. *Journal of the Association for the Severely Handicapped, 5*, 352-367.

Connis, R. (1979). The effects of sequential pictorial cues, self-recording and praise on the job task sequencing of retarded adults. *Journal of Applied Behavior Analysis, 12*, 355-361.

Crist, K., Walls, R., & Haught, P. (1984). Degrees of specificity in task analysis. *American Journal of Mental Deficiency, 89*, 67-74.

Csapo, M. (1981). Comparison of two prompting procedures to increase response fluency among severely handicapped learners. *Journal of the Association for the Severely Handicapped, 6*, 39-47.

Cuvo, A., Jacobi, L., & Sipko, R. (1981). Teaching laundry skills to mentally retarded students. *Education and Training of the Mentally Retarded, 16*, 54-64.

Day, H.M. (1987). Comparison of two prompting procedures to facilitate skill acquisition among severely mentally retarded adolescents. *American Journal of Mental Deficiency, 91*(4), 366-372.

Falvey, M. (1986). *Community-based curriculum.* Baltimore: Paul H. Brookes.

Favell, J., Favell, J., & McGimsey, J. (1978). Relative effectiveness and efficiency of group vs. individualized training of severely retarded groups. *American Journal of Mental Deficiency, 83*, 104-109.

Gagne, R., & Briggs, L. (1979). *Principles of instructional design.* New York: Holt, Rinehart & Winston.

Gold, M. (1976). Task analysis of a complex assembly task by the retarded blind. *Exceptional Children, 43*, 78-84.

Gold, M. (1980). *Try another way: Training manual.* Champaign, IL: Research Press.

Holvoet, J., Brown, F., & Helmstetter, E. (1980). *Writing functional group sequences using the ICS curriculum sequencing model.* Paper presented: 7th Annual Conference of The Association for Persons with Severe Handicaps. San Francisco, CA.

Horner, R., Eberhard, J., & Sheehan, M. (1986). Teaching generalized table bussing: The importance of negative teaching examples. *Behavior Modification, 10*, 457-471.

Horner, R., McDonnell, J., & Bellamy, G.T. (1986). Teaching generalized skills: General case instruction in simulation and community settings. In R. Horner, L. Meyer, & H.D. Fredericks (Eds.), *Education of learners with severe handicaps: Exemplary service strategies* (pp. 289-314). Baltimore: Paul H. Brookes.

Horner, R., Sprague, J., & Wilcox, B. (1982). General case programming for community activities. In B. Wilcox & G.T. Bellamy (Eds.), *Design of high school programs for severely handicapped students* (pp. 61-98). Baltimore: Paul H. Brookes.

Johnson, B., & Cuvo, A. (1981). Teaching mentally retarded adults to cook. *Behavior Modification, 5,* 187-202.

Klein, N., & Stafford, P. (1978). The acquisition of classification skills by trainable mentally retarded children. *Education and Training of the Mentally Retarded, 13,* 272-277.

Koegel, R., & Rincover, A. (1974). Treatment of psychotic children in a classroom environment: Learning in a large group. *Journal of Applied Behavior Analysis, 7,* 45-59.

Kohl, F., Wilcox, B., & Karlan, G. (1978). Effects of training conditions on the generalization of manual signs with moderately handicapped students. *Education and Training of the Mentally Retarded, 13,* 327-331.

Liberty, K., Haring, N., & Martin, M. (1981) Teaching new skills to the severely handicapped. *Journal of the Association for the Severely Handicapped, 6,* 5-13.

Lovass, O.I. (1981). *Teaching developmentally disabled children.* Baltimore: University Park Press.

Martin, J., Rusch, F., James, V., Decker, P., & Trtol, K. (1982). The use of picture cues to establish self-control in the preparation of complex meals by mentally retarded adults. *Applied Research in Mental Retardation, 3,* 105-119.

Mulligan, M., Guess, D., Holvoet, J., & Brown, F. (1980). The individualized curriculum sequencing model (1): Implications from research on massed, distributed, or spaced trial training. *Journal of the Association for the Severely Handicapped, 5,* 325-336.

Oliver, P. (1983). Effects of teaching different tasks in group versus individual training formats with severely handicapped individuals. *Journal of the Association for the Severely Handicapped, 8,* 79-91.

Parton, D. (1976). Learning to imitate in infancy. *Child Development, 47,* 14-31.

Reid, D., & Favell, J. (1984). Group instruction with persons who have severe disabilities: A critical review. *Journal of the Association for Persons with Severe Handicaps, 9,* 167-177.

Reid, D., Parsons, M., McCarn, J., Green, C., Phillips, J., & Schepis, M. (1985). Providing a more appropriate education for severely handicapped persons: Increasing and validating functional classroom tasks. *Journal of Applied Behavior Analysis, 18,* 289-301.

Rincover, A., & Koegel, R. (1977). Classroom treatment of autistic children: Individualizing instruction in a group. *Journal of Abnormal Child Psychology, 5,* 113-125.

Sailor, W., & Guess, D. (1983). *Severely handicapped students: An instructional design.* Boston: Houghton Mifflin.

Saunders, R., & Koplik, K. (1975). A multi-purpose data sheet for recording and graphing in the classroom. *AAESPH Review, 1,* 1.

Schoen, S. (1986). Assistance procedures to facilitate the transfer of stimulus control: Review and analysis. *Education and Training of the Mentally Retarded, 21,* 62-74.

Schriebman, L. (1975). Effects of within-stimulus and extra-stimulus prompting on discrimination learning in autistic children. *Journal of Applied Behavior Analysis, 8,* 91-112.

Skinner, B.F. (1968). *The technology of teaching.* New York: Appleton-Century-Crofts.

Snell, M., & Gast, D. (1981). Applying time delay procedure to the instruction of the severely handicapped. *The Journal of the Association for the Severely Handicapped, 6,* 3-14.

Sobsey, D., McLarney, P., Missall, P., & Murphy, G. (1985). *Group instruction: Theory and application to students with severe handicaps.* Paper presented: 12th Annual Conference of The Association for Persons with Severe Handicaps. Boston, MA.

Spooner, F., & Spooner, D. (1984). A review of chaining techniques: Implications for future research and practice. *Education and Training of the Mentally Retarded, 19,* 114-124.

Sternberg, L., McNerney, C., & Pegnatore, L. (1985). Developing co-active imitative behaviors with profoundly mentally handicapped students. *Education and Training of the Mentally Retarded, 5,* 260-268.

Sternberg, L, & Owens, A. (1985). Establishing prelanguage signalling behavior with profoundly mentally handicapped students: A preliminary investigation. *Journal of Mental Deficiency Research, 29,* 81-93.

Storm, R., & Willis, J. (1978). Small-group training as an alternative to individual programs for profoundly retarded persons. *American Journal of Mental Deficiency, 83,* 283-288.

Thinesen, P., & Bryan, A. (1981). The use of sequential picture cues in the initiation and maintenance of grooming behaviors with mentally retarded adults. *Mental Retardation, 19,* 246-250.

Wacker, D., & Berg, W. (1983). Effects of picture prompts on the acquisition of complex vocational tasks by mentally retarded adolescents. *Journal of Applied Behavior Analysis, 16,* 417-433.

Wacker, D., Berg, W., Berrie, P., & Swatta, P. (1985). Generalization and maintenance of complex skills by severely handicapped adolescents following picture prompt training. *Journal of Applied Behavior Analysis, 18,* 329-336.

Westling, D., Ferrell, K., & Swenson, K. (1982). Intra-classroom comparison of two arrangements for teaching profoundly mentally retarded children. *American Journal of Mental Deficiency, 86,* 601-688.

White, O., & Haring, N. (1980). *Exceptional teaching.* Columbus, OH: Charles E. Merrill.

White, O., & Liberty, K. (1976). Evaluation and measurement. In N. Haring & R. Schiefelbusch (Eds.). *Teaching special children* (pp. 31-71). New York: McGraw-Hill.

Wilcox, B., & Bellamy, G.T. (1982). *Design of high school programs for severely handicapped students.* Baltimore: Paul H. Brookes.

Williams, J., & Horner, R. (1984). *General case street crossing instructional package.* Unpublished manuscript, University of Oregon, Eugene.

Wolfe, V., & Cuvo, A. (1978). Effects of within-stimulus and extra-stimulus prompting on letter discrimination by mentally retarded persons. *American Journal of Mental Deficiency, 83,* 297-303.

Wuerch, B., & Voeltz, L. (1982). *Longitudinal leisure skills for severely handicapped learners.* Baltimore: Paul H. Brookes.

Zeaman, D., & House, B. (1979). A review of attention theory. In N.R. Ellis (Ed.). *Handbook of mental deficiency* (pp. 63-120). Hillsdale, NJ: Lawrence Erlbaum Association.

Chapter 8

Curriculum Development

Marilyn Mulligan Ault

PROBLEM

When a teacher of students with severe and multiple handicaps is provided with "the curriculum" used by a school district, institution, or agency, the package could contain a range of information. The curriculum could be very useful in planning individual programs for students, or it could be only a revised, and again revised, list of skills sequenced in approximate developmental order. It is not unusual for several students in a classroom to have different curriculum packages, or for the plans to be pulled from a number of different manuals. Generally, what the teacher will *not* receive is a plan or strategy to help organize and implement a *classroom curriculum:* a plan for the instructional day for all students in the classroom.

This inconsistency is due to the fact that many types of packages, with many levels of information, are presented as curricula. Each of them, to a greater or lesser degree, assists in identifying instructional objectives for individual students. Many provide instructional programs for the identified objectives. Few assist in identifying how the instruction should fall across the day. None presents a plan for developing the relation of one student's instructional day with the other students in the class.

What does the teacher need or want when selecting a curriculum? Should the curriculum be only a list of skills developmentally sequenced or based on some criterion-referenced checklist of adaptive skills? With this information, the teacher could assess the student's functioning level and identify educational objectives. The objectives would be derived by pinpointing skills on the checklist the student did not complete or completed incorrectly. The teacher could then task analyze the intermediate steps between the skills listed on the curriculum, generate instructional programs and evaluation procedures, and develop a plan for teaching the skills.

A more extensive and complete curriculum would provide not only a list of skills but methods for their optimal instruction. In this instance, the curriculum could also contain in-depth assessment information on the student's performance level and preferred instructional methodology. The curriculum could then assist the teacher in identifying appropriate instructional methodology and provide suggestions for manipulating the environment, materials, additional trainers, and evaluation procedures.

The selection of curriculum for a classroom should depend largely on the teacher's philosophical view of education, how the teacher feels development occurs, the primary purpose of instruction, and the general plan the teacher has for developing the school day. Most available curricula address the second and third issues. More complete curricula also address the teacher's philosophical view of education. Curricula, at best, only briefly discuss the organization of the student's instructional day in relation to other students in the classroom. Even with a more complete curriculum guide, the teacher is still left without a planning guide for the student's, and students', entire instructional day. The problem is that most curricula do not suggest that such planning is necessary for the instruction of objectives to be useful for the student. The organization of the student's instructional day is a major factor in the development, implementation, and evaluation of a student's instructional program.

A great deal of research in the instruction of persons with severe and multiple impairments addresses issues such as environments of instructions, functional materials and settings, functional time of day, group instruction, and integration into the community in proportions natural to the occurrence of persons with handicaps in the various settings. These are overall curriculum issues. Teachers are not generally provided commercially available curricula addressing these issues. The good teacher deals with these issues through developing his or her own sense of sequencing the instruction of educational objectives across the day. More often than not, the issues are not addressed.

PAST PRACTICES

The practice of selecting a curriculum and developing the instructional day from the domains on the curriculum has been the most adhered-to model for providing instruction for students with severe or profound impairments: Teachers first identified the specific domains or areas of the curriculum, e.g., language, motor, self-care, cognition, sensory integration, socialization, and work. Regardless of the name given to the area, the teacher divided the entire class into relatively even periods reflecting the number of major areas from the assessment or curriculum; there would be a "language time," a "gross motor time," or a "self-care time." These time designations might have reflected the actual time of day. More often than not they represented a random sequencing of times or were based on the needs and preferences of the staff.

The student was moved through the instructional day, experiencing specific domain-related instruction during different time periods. Often, the students would experience the different activities without changing settings or even moving from the table. The student or students were positioned around a table with language time, self-care time, and snack time following one right after the other. The only indication of an activity change was that the teacher would remove the materials and present a different set of materials without requiring the students to participate in the transition. The classroom appeared to be a disconnected series of unrelated instructional events.

Many times, the teacher interpreted the curriculum items, since they were written for one student, to imply that all students should receive one-to-one instruction. One-to-one instruction was the way to individualize instruction. Students would experience their individual sequence of the assessment areas, e.g., vision training, auditory discrimination training, and gross motor training, without interacting with other students and without direct attention being paid to why, where, or with what materials the skills were being taught. Students were placed in groups only as a last resort, with group time not considered direct instructional time.

Even with the more current practice of attending to functional settings, times, and materials, teachers still often insist on a student's separate experience of the instructional day. Persistently, most instructional methodology is presented with a one teacher–one student model. This approach fails to assist the teacher in establishing a cohesive sequence of experiences for the individual student across the educational day, and perpetuates a *model of isolated therapy*. This model has a medical orientation: the therapist removes the student from the class, performs the therapy, and then returns the student to the class without any correlation between the class and the therapy.

The *transdisciplinary approach* (Haynes, Patterson, D'Wolf, Hutchinson, Lowry, Schilling, & Siepp, 1976; McCormick & Goldman, 1979; Lyon & Lyon, 1980) has been relatively successful in bringing related therapies together with the teacher in the classroom. Unfortunately, many times the classroom teacher is unable to apply the same strategy to the instruction of educational objectives. The focus on individual (one-to-one) instruction, rather than individualization of instruction, ignores the literature emphasizing the benefits of group instruction (Brown, Holvoet, Guess, & Mulligan, 1980). Primarily it ignores the reality of the classroom situation. One-to-one instruction ratios necessitate that many students spend a significant portion of their day in unacceptable "down time" or noninstructional time.

Finally, the persistent use of commercial curriculum as the basis of classroom curriculum development does not assist the teacher in developing the use of the classroom as an optimum intervention strategy. Teachers tend not to attend to the environments of instruction, appropriateness of materials, or the relation of the student's experiences across the day.

This chapter addresses the issue of developing curricula to include relating a student's instructional events across the day and relating the instructional sequences of all students.

SUGGESTED METHODS

Curricula for Students with Severe or Profound Handicaps

A number of curricula have been developed to address the needs of students with severe or profound impairments. The teacher should become familiar with them to identify crucial areas to include in program development and implementation. They are also particularly helpful in determining the current performance levels of students, suggesting the sequence in which skills should be addressed, and identifying considerations when providing instruction. Most of the curricula state very clearly that a packaged curriculum is not sufficient for developing a student's curricula: They are intended as guidelines for the areas to address, and considerations to respond to when planning for a student. Many of the curricula provide an excellent review of specific techniques, discussions about development, the integration of motor programming, or the philosophy behind the instruction of persons with severe handicaps. Many should be considered valuable references and used for periodic review.

These commercially available curricula are briefly discussed in three groups: (1) primarily developmentally sequenced; (2) primarily sequenced according to environmental considerations; and (3) developed to address specific domains. The list is not comprehensive. The teacher is referred to additional sources for more complete discussions of alternative curricula (Gaylord-Ross & Holvoet, 1985; Sailor & Guess, 1983; Snell, 1983). The curricula are presented within a discussion of classroom curriculum development to emphasize that there is a great deal of information concerning the appropriateness of different types of skill sequences for teaching a range of skills. The information in any of these curricula can be used with the final recommended approach (the ICS model) in developing the classroom curricula.

Developmentally-Based Curricula

The following curricula were selected because they were written specifically for students with severe or profound handicaps and present sequences of skills primarily based on the normal developmental sequence. All have criterion-referenced components. Some skill sequences are basic task analyses of the skill rather than a strict listing of the developmental emergence of the skill. In this regard the curricula present a blend of the normal developmental model with an understanding of the basic needs of the student.

Programmed Environments Curriculum (Tawney, Knapp, O'Reilly, & Pratt, 1979). This curriculum is introduced as a sequence of skills, a conceptualization of the learning process, and a framework for developing additional and student-specific instructional programs. Its target population is students with severe or profound retardation whose general developmental skill acquisition is between birth and three years of age.

Even though the curriculum items blend a developmental approach with the requirements of the environment, the orientation is behavioral. Generally, the development of skills is seen as either response building or response shaping. The authors acknowledge that not all behaviors are in these two categories; however, the delineations guide the teacher within a general view of behavior.

The curriculum is divided into eight skill areas of assessment and instruction: receptive language, expressive language, cognitive, fine motor, gross motor, eating, dressing, and grooming. Within each are instructional programs describing techniques for arranging the environments and setting the occasion for the student to practice the skill. Most programs are written to be free of materials or environmental restrictions. The examples in the programs, even though not specifically written to be applied to young children, generally suggest a young child. The teacher needs to be careful in following the examples so as to avoid using only developmentally young materials.

The curriculum, as stated in the introduction, is not intended to be inclusive. Rather it is a framework for developing additional skills. The teacher, in the process of implementing the framework, will develop excellent skills in the analysis of objective and discrete units of behavior and will arrange the setting to elicit and reinforce the behaviors. The items begin with very immature responses, such as "responding to social interactions" or "making sounds." The size of the steps between skills, however, may be quite large (e.g., only eight items between "responding to social interactions" and "identifying people").

The curriculum is excellent in that it does raise significant issues about the nature of learning and skills that are pertinent to the learner. It is clear and easy to follow, with assessment, programs, and observation records provided in the same package.

A Curriculum for Profoundly Handicapped Students: The Broward County Model Program (Sternberg, Ritchey, Pegnatore, Wills, & Hill, 1986). This curriculum was developed to address the needs of students with profound handicaps. To this end it identifies many items concerning very low levels of responding. Because of this, the sequences are primarily developmental. Some criterion-referenced sequencing is included when the manual deals with higher levels of responding, particularly in communication.

The authors present an in-depth discussion of the characteristics of the student with profound handicaps, why certain curriculum items should be selected for instruction, and basic considerations in arranging the environments for instruction and selecting materials. The introduction is an excellent review of major issues and should be referred to frequently.

The manual presents an assessment device and a curriculum related directly to the assessment. The assessment is unique in addressing two factors usually ignored by the majority of assessments and curricula: both teacher and student behaviors, and a student's instructional objectives within a *range* of skills for a particular domain. The assessment form provides for scoring a student's independent responses to natural environmental cues. The teacher may also score the level of prompting required by the student to perform the skill as "verbal," "motor modeling," or "physical guidance." Scoring results in identifying a collection of skills within a range in the domain to target for instruction. Certain skills are then transferred to an *activity summary form.* The purpose of this option is to point out that it may be inappropriate to teach just one skill per area or activity; a concurrent instructional strategy may be more appropriate (Schroeder & Baer, 1972; Gold & Pomerantz, 1978).

The curriculum section provides instructional programs for each assessed skill that include a listing of the skill and objective, and a suggestion of materials to use. The materials recommendations describe the qualities of the object without specifying an object. Since a particular material is not specified, the program is not limited to a particular chronological age. For example, "three small objects" is listed rather than "pegs"; "brightly colored objects" rather than "colorful mobiles." Occasionally the teacher must further identify items that are also functional. Suggestions for the position of the trainer and the student are provided.

The program addresses basic instructional considerations usually omitted when providing a functional and age-appropriate curriculum for students with little or no generalization skills and very slow rates of learning. A category identified as "training setting" suggests whether the activity is best conducted in a 1:1, small group, or large group session. Most activities suggest the first two options. The program also lists other targeted opportunities. This listing proposes that the teacher not schedule the practice of the targeted skill in just one setting; other suggested activities and subactivities are listed.

Finally, each instructional program includes a suggested task analysis of the skill (or listing of expected student behaviors in certain domains) and addresses instructional concerns and training suggestions. A program-by-program review of each section leaves the teacher with a general understanding of the focus of instruction for the learner with profound handicaps. The emphasis is on natural schedules, age-appropriate materials, and the development of responses that are spontaneous and integrated across the student's environments.

The Carolina Curriculum for Handicapped Infants and Infants at Risk (Johnson-Martin, Jens, & Attermeier, 1986). This curriculum is based on Piaget's theory of normal development. The authors, however, emphasize that the curriculum was developed for students with mild to severe handicaps. The curriculum was not developed assuming even development, so it is considered applicable to the students with very atypical development. The items are sequenced, to a great degree, by the logical order in which a skill should be taught, rather than strictly adhering to a developmental progression. The authors recognize that the goal of instruction is not to make children with handicaps "normal." In many instances, they emphasize teaching skills that are highly adaptive, rather than adhering to the normal developmental sequence.

The curriculum presents an assessment and curriculum for students functioning from birth to 24 months. Even though the curriculum is titled "Infants and Infants at Risk," it was field tested with and recommended for infants as well as students older than four years of age, all functioning between birth to 24 months. In this regard it is well suited to meet some of the needs of students with profound handicaps.

The authors include instructional considerations at the beginning of the manual. In preparing to use the curriculum, the teacher should review this information. Many of the suggestions are excellent for developing the overall classroom. These include establishing a nurturing environment in which consequences must be individualized, natural, and functional to the student's own experiences; providing the environment with characteristics of sameness and change to maintain motivation; and building learning opportunities into the activities of the daily routine. The overriding emphasis is a concern for the learning of the student and fostering it through care of the child and the environment.

The manual also contains an excellent review of techniques to foster motor development. Abnormal motor development is addressed with discussions of positioning, handling, and precautions. The major emphasis is on the child participating in any motor activity. The students should, as much as possible, be a part of all phases of the movement.

The authors present the typical developmental domains in a different order and clustering, reflecting their strong Piagetian orientation. They provide the teacher with an expanded understanding of the components of language and cognitive development. The usual domain designation of "cognition" is divided into eight categories to include tactile integration and manipulation, auditory localization, visual pursuit, object permanence, spatial concepts, functional use of objects and symbolic play, control over the physical environment, and readiness. Language and social skill areas are similarly broken down into components. Each area, in turn, has specific assessment items and instructional programs developed for the identified skill.

Each instructional program includes suggestions for the position of the trainer and student, materials, teaching procedures, and steps for evaluation. The materials listed usually emphasize the significant characteristics of the items (e.g., "toys with openings" or "colorful objects"). The general tendency is to identify toys as the items to select. If the teacher is working with chronologically older students, attention must be paid to selecting functional and age-appropriate materials.

The curriculum is excellent for teaching teachers about normal cognitive, language, and motor development. The assessment and curriculum are developed with an understanding of the needs of students with handicaps and encourages the teacher to select items and adapt procedures to meet the needs of the individual student.

Environmentally-Based Curricula

A number of checklists and strategies delineate skills a student should acquire through an analysis of the student's present or future environments (Brown, Branston-McClean, Baumgart, Vincent, Falvey, &

Schroeder, 1979; Helmstetter, Murphy-Herd, Roberts, & Guess, 1984). These procedures lead the teacher through analyzing the student's environments, then identifying discrepancies between the requirements of the environment and the student's current level of performance. The *Learning in Functional Environments Curricula (LIFE)* by Stetson (1985) collects the basics of this information into a comprehensive curriculum sequence. The curriculum is accompanied by an extensive training package reviewing the major issues of instruction in the environments in which the skills will be used (e.g., on-site job training and basic housekeeping skills). The domains include vocational, leisure, and community integration mobility; skills are listed for different levels of independent functioning within each. Because the curriculum is based on potential environments, there is no "developmental" sequence. Skills in each environmental area are sequenced through a logical progression of least to most difficult (Freagon, Wheeler, McDannel, Brankin, & Costello, 1983).

The manual does not contain specific instructional programs or guidelines for the training of specific skills. There is, however, a teacher training packet accompanying the curriculum that uses videotapes, slides, and lectures to present the basic strategies for teaching in the community.

As with most curricula for training in actual environments, this one seems most suited for students who are moderately to severely handicapped. It does not address the needs of the teacher of students with profound handicaps. It does, however, present an excellent argument for and examples of training students with severe handicaps in functional environments.

Domain-Specific Curricula

A number of curricula address skill development in isolated domain areas, typically, leisure, self-care, vocational, and language. Usually they break down the components of the curriculum into subcomponents with task analyses of individual skills. All provide instructional programs for specific skills, instructional or training procedures, and performance monitoring forms. The more recent attend specifically to age-appropriate and functional materials. If selecting an older program, the teacher must be careful to expand the training suggestions to include considerations of functional materials, environments, settings, and times.

Sample curricula are (1) leisure: *Longitudinal Leisure Skills for Severely Handicapped Learners: The Ho'onanea Curriculum Component* (Wuerch & Voeltz, 1982); *Recreation Programming for Developmentally Disabled Persons* (Wehman, 1979); (2) language: *Functional Speech and Language Training for the Severely Handicapped* (Guess, Sailor, & Baer, 1976);

Early Communication: Development and Training (Bricker, 1983); (3)
self-care: *Adaptive Behavior Curriculum* (Popovich & Laham, 1981);
Project MORE (Lent, 1975); (4) vocational: *Curriculum for Developmentally Disabled Persons* (Wehman & McLaughlin, 1980); *Vocational Training for Mentally Retarded Adults: A Behavior Analytic Approach* (Rusch & Mithaney, 1980). All contain assessment and programming information. They are valuable in that they draw the teacher's attention to specific considerations in each domain. They generally tend to be designed for students with moderate to severe handicaps. They also provide minimal information on integrating other students into the educational objectives plan or on using the classroom itself as a curricular tool.

The Individualized Curriculum Sequence (ICS) Model

The focus of this section is on assisting the teacher in developing a comprehensive class curriculum to meet the functional and age-appropriate needs of all students in the class. The ICS Model is presented as a class curriculum development tool addressing the needs of students with either severe or profound retardation and multiple handicaps across the entire instructional day.

The ICS model is an individual curriculum development strategy. The classroom is viewed as a unique and optimal arrangement for the instruction of many skills necessary for developing a student's independent functioning. The "classroom" is defined as the students, instructional staff, related staff, and environments of instruction extending well beyond the four walls of the traditional classroom. The model emphasizes that the teacher can manage these components in relation to students' instructional objectives. The teacher can arrange the instructional day so the student is required to interact with peers, change settings, access real and functional environments, and interact with adults. The ICS model assists the teacher in understanding that these components can be manipulated to develop an appropriate curriculum. To implement the model, the teacher must spend a good deal of time in preparing and developing the class curriculum. Two of the major time-consuming processes are collecting relevant assessment information and developing the actual classroom plan. Both of these processes are discussed.

Assessment

The ICS model originated as a planning strategy for integrating all of a single student's educational objectives into the instructional day. It is most effectively used, however, as a curriculum development guide for an entire class of students with severe or profound handicaps. The quality of the class curriculum developed is based solely on the quality of information gathered about the needs of the student; the requirements of the students' present and future environments; and the identification of, development of, or access to appropriate environments for instruction. The model provides the teacher with a framework in which to decide what to teach and how to organize the student's instructional day. The plan for identifying what to teach was drawn from a five-step plan developed by Sailor and Guess (1983). The process of how to organize the instructional events across the students' school day was drawn from 10 years of research and experience with various implementation strategies in classrooms for early childhood through young adult students with severe and multiple impairments, deaf-blindness, and autism (Guess, Horner, Utley, Holvoet, Maxon, Tucker, & Warren, 1978; Mulligan, Guess, Holvoet, & Brown, 1980; Holvoet, Guess, Mulligan, & Brown, 1980; Brown et al., 1980; Helmstetter et al., 1984).

The five-step process developed by Sailor and Guess (1983) was designed to collect information about students from two sources, both of which are needed to develop a functional and age-appropriate curriculum: the requirements of the environments in which the students will live and work, and the current functioning level of the student. The five steps in the process are (1) determine each student's future environments; (2) assess the (or similar) environments to determine the skills crucial to independent functioning in these settings, (3) select and prioritize the critical skills to determine the order in which they should be presented to the student, (4) formally assess each student to identify the current level of functioning, either developmentally or in relation to the critical skills, and (5) construct a sequence of objectives that lead from the current level of performance to the attainment of each critical skill. The application of these procedures is also clearly outlined in an instructional manual by Helmstetter et al. (1984).

Step 1. The decision-making process of identifying potential placements for the student is necessarily a team decision. Helmstetter et al. (1984) developed a process for determining a "best possible" estimate of future placements. Table 8-1 is used to determine this estimate by using two factors: the age of the student, and the potential range of future placements in the student's community.

To use Table 8-1, first identify the student's current environment and age range. The intersection of the column indicating age and the row indicating "current environment" will result in either a number, series of

Table 8-1 Guidelines for Identifying Appropriate Future Environments

Current Environment	Appropriate Future Environment(s) if Current Age of Student Is		
	0-5 years	6-10 years	11-21 years
Living			
1. Home (natural/foster/adoptive)	1	1	2,3,4,5
2. Independent living	NA[a]	NA	2
3. Apartment cluster	NA	NA	2,3
4. Apartment cluster—supervised	1	1	2,3,4
5. Group home	1,5	1,5	2,3,4,5
6. Residential (5 days/week)	1,5	1,5	2,3,4,5
7. Institution (year round)	1,5,6	1,5,6	2,3,4,5
School			
1. Public	1[b]	1[b]	6,7
2. Other day program (e.g., private day school)	1	1	6,7
3. Residential (on grounds)	1,2	1,2	6,7
4. Institution (on grounds)	1,2,3	1,2,3	6,7
5. Home/hospital bound	1,2,3	1,2,3	6,7
6. Community college/vocational technical school	NA	NA	6,7
7. Postschool independent learning	NA	NA	6,7
Vocational			
1. Simulated work activities (e.g., in school, classroom, shop cafeteria, laundry, office)	NA	1	2,3,4,5,6,7
2. Volunteer jobs	NA	1,2	3,4,5,6,7
3. Work study	NA	NA	NA
4. Activity center	NA	NA	NA
5. Sheltered workshop	NA	NA	NA
6. On-job-training	NA	NA	NA
7. Competitive employment	NA	NA	NA

Community Areas

Future community environments depend on the domestic and vocational environments selected.

[a]NA is nonapplicable.
[b]Public school at a more advanced class level (e.g., from classroom for students with severe handicaps to classroom for students who are moderately handicapped), more integrated program, and/or closer to home.

Source: From *Individualized Curriculum Sequence and Extended Classroom Models for Learners who Are Deaf and Blind* (p. 26) by E. Helmstetter et al., 1984, Lawrence, Kansas: University of Kansas, Department of Special Education. Copyright 1984 by University of Kansas. Reprinted by permission.

numbers, or NA. The number(s) indicate the number given to each item listed under *Living, School,* or *Vocational.*

An alternate method is the use of the Life Skills Screening Inventory (Becker, Schur, Paoletti-Schelp, & Hammer, 1985), which identifies three levels of functioning with corresponding recommendations for potential placements.

Step 2. A number of assessment procedures are available for identifying the skills required in the student's present and potential environments. According to Helmstetter et al. (1984), informal assessment procedures consist of observational and interview techniques. "These procedures help teachers to survey environments for the skills required for successful participation in them, to interview families and professionals to identify additional critical skills and tasks, and to recognize student preferences for both learning activities and environmental conditions" (p. 27). Assessment should be made of all potential environments, including the living situation, work setting, community, and school or information-gathering areas. Techniques commonly used are interviews with significant individuals in the settings, checklists itemizing skills required as a result of specific environmental conditions (environmental inventories), or student preference inventories (Helmstetter et al., 1984). The reader is referred to the latter manual or to similar texts containing informal environmental survey procedures (Stetson, 1985; Freagon et al., 1983).

The informal assessment information can be summarized on a matrix (see Exhibit 8-1) identifying the particular critical requirements of each future environment across a collection of goals. The first ten items listed under *Goal Areas* are skills relevant to successful functioning in almost any environment. The remaining items are critical to success in specific settings only. The teacher focuses on pinpointing minimal entry skill requirements across all goal areas and settings for each student. In some cases a goal-per-setting summary is inappropriate. In these instances the box joining the column and the row would be left blank.

Step 3. Selecting and prioritizing the crucial skills involves proceeding through a decision-making sequence to identify those skills most crucial to the student's independent functioning. This process will identify more skills than should be included in an instructional day. Generally, the teacher must identify the most critical skills to reduce those to be taught to a manageable size. A manageable number is suggested to be a minimum of 8 and a maximum of 20, depending on the age and functioning level of the student (Helmstetter et al., 1984).

Exhibit 8-1 Critical Skills Matrix

Goal Areas	Future Environments			
	Living/ Domestic	Vocational	School	Community Area
Eat/Drink				
Toileting				
Dressing				
Mobility				
Expressive Communication				
Receptive Communication				
Hygiene/ Appearance				
Recreation/ Leisure				
Social				
Sensory/ Perceptual				
(Pre)vocational				
(Pre)academic				
Domestic				
Other				

Source: From *Individualized Curriculum Sequence and Extended Classroom Models for Learners who are Deaf and Blind* (p. 35) by E. Helmstetter et al., 1984, Lawrence, Kansas: University of Kansas, Department of Special Education. Copyright 1984 by University of Kansas. Reprinted by permission.

The teacher must address several questions to identify the most critical skills: (1) Is the skill necessary for moving to a less restrictive environment? (2) Will it be used in a variety of future environments? (3) Will it be used frequently across the day? (4) Is it age appropriate? (5) Would the student choose to learn it? (6) Would someone else have to perform it if the student could not? (7) Does it improve the quality of life of the student, resulting in better treatment by others? (Helmstetter et al., 1984). The list is not intended to be inclusive.

Step 4. To identify the student's current level of functioning, developmental assessments are typically used. Examples can be found in Chapter 5.

Sailor and Guess (1983) criticize the exclusive use of developmental assessments for developing instructional curriculum for students with severe and multiple handicaps for two reasons: the items rarely have direct relevance to independent functioning in the future environments of living, working, leisure, or gathering information, and few are normed for or address the learning characteristics of such students.

Sailor and Guess (1983) proposed an alternative use of assessment information. They suggested that such information be directly related to the critical skills necessary for functioning in future environments. There are four major ways to identify such skills: using traditional assessment information from adaptive behavior scales and possibly developmental scales; using information from related service providers; using task analysis procedures; and using baseline information. None of these techniques is new to teachers of students with severe and multiple impairments.

When *using traditional assessment procedures,* i.e., adaptive behavior assessment (Helmstetter et al., 1984) or developmental assessment information, the skills critical for success in future environments must be identified. The teacher does this by determining how the assessed item will contribute to attaining an environmentally critical skill. For example, if the skill of "assisting while dressing" is identified as a critical skill for an adolescent living in a group home, the teacher needs to identify assessed items that contribute to its attainment. Assessment items commonly found on adaptive behavior or developmental tests that could contribute include "extends arm to grasp," "raises head," or "recognizes activity from environmental cue."

Sailor and Guess (1983) emphasized that the individually identified assessed skill should never become a goal in itself, but rather a component of a more intricate and critical skill necessary for future partial or total independence. For example, "head up" or "visual tracking" should never be the sole intent of any instructional period. How these skills relate to the attainment of a skill critical to partial or total independence is the focus of curriculum development.

When *using related or support staff information,* professionals surveyed may include the language therapist, audiologist, physical or occupational therapist, nutritionist, nurse, orientation and mobility specialist, etc. For example, if the skill "requesting assistance or seeking help" is identified as critical for a student in a specific vocational setting, the language therapist could identify the student's current language skills and develop a sequence of skills to reach the critical skill level for communication. If independent mobility in a group living setting is critical, then an orientation and mobility specialist could identify the necessary sequence of instructional objectives.

When *using information from a task analysis* of the critical skill, test the student's performance relative to the task-analyzed items of the critical skill. The series of items performed incompletely or incorrectly would indicate the skills to be addressed during instruction.

Brown, Evans, Weed, and Owen (1987), in their Component Model of Functional Life Routines, expanded the traditional concept of the task-analyzed sequence to identify three components of the skill: core, extension, and enrichment. The levels of performance represented by each component indicate differences in the degree of participation and independence of the person completing the routine.

Core components of routines are skills that must be completed for the routine to be accomplished. For example, a sequence of core components for brushing teeth could include picking up the toothbrush, applying paste, moving the brush across the teeth, putting the brush down, and rinsing the mouth. This task analysis is very common in classrooms and tends to represent the series of skills usually instructed when teaching "toothbrushing."

This, however, is not all there is to toothbrushing. Additional skills listed by Brown et al. (1987) include knowing when to brush, going to the bathroom independently and at the appropriate time, and knowing what to do if a problem should arise, such as no toothpaste. They identified these additional behaviors as *extension components* of the targeted skill. Six extension components are identified as critical to performing the skill independently: initiating the routine, preparing the materials and setting, monitoring one's performance, problem solving, and terminating the routine.

The *enrichment components* are not crucial to the critical effect of the skill. They do, however, add to the competence. They reflect how well the student responds to demands of the environment when performing the skill. This category includes social and communication considerations as well as expressing choice. Examples are not entering the bathroom when someone is in it, selecting the type of toothpaste, or recognizing that an unscheduled "toothbrushing" is required. Each of these components, core, extension, and enrichment, should be addressed when developing the task analysis sequence for assessing a student's performance level. However, an analysis of past research indicates that extension and enrichment components have not consistently been a part of task analyses (Brown et al., 1987).

The discussion by Brown et al. (1987) of the development of the task analysis sequence centers on the concept of developing a series of set routines in which the student will learn to participate across the day while changing settings, materials, and people with whom to interact. The student's participation in a routine should include the ability to perform all the skills or steps leading from the natural and environmental cues to the critical effect desired by the action. This critical effect may be being completely dressed, having his or her supervisor come to answer a question, or tuning in favorite music on the radio. The routines are divided into four types: substitutable, fixed, daily, and episodic.

Substitutable routines are a collection of skills sequenced in order, any one of which would produce the desired result. Examples are meal preparation routines. The routine of fixing a sandwich is different than for fixing soup or baking a chicken. But they are all ways of completing the routine of fixing a meal. *Fixed routines* are a set sequence of skills that tend to be used repeatedly to achieve a desired result. Examples are toothbrushing, taking a shower, and washing the face; they tend to be done approximately the same way over and over. *Daily routines* occur daily, and *episodic routines* occur intermittently.

For purposes of assessing a student's competency level on the completion of a task, it is important for the teacher to identify whether the skill is substitutable or fixed. Second, the teacher must identify the core, extension, and enrichment components of the task. Then, an assessment of a student's performance in the completion of the task is possible.

When selecting a skill to target as an instructional objective, the teacher should first select the steps of the core components that were not performed or were performed incorrectly. A suggested method for doing so is first to teach initiating and terminating the routine, followed by preparing the setting, monitoring the quality of one's performance, problem solving, and finally monitoring the tempo of one's performance. The selection of skills included in the enrichment components depends largely on the routine and its social context. Some routines have more language-based enrichment components, others have more choice-based enrichment components.

A complete task analysis for a skill routine is obviously more than just a listing of observable events conducted in a limited area at a specific time. Competence and independence require that many additional skills, not specific to just one skill, be identified and instructed. When constructing the sequence of skills, it is important to focus on the purpose of the skill to the student, not the form in which the behavior is executed (White, 1980). This mind set will lead the teacher to seek alternative sequences for achieving a specific goal rather than insisting that the student "has to do it this way." If the purpose of a skill is to seek assistance, a variety of methods can be used. Selecting only a verbal approach postpones and limits the student's chances of becoming independent in the use of the skill.

If *using baseline information* to determine the skills to be taught, record the information on current levels of performance. Some skills identified for independent functioning in any of the future environments may already be present in the student's repertoire of behaviors. The problem may be that the student does not perform the skill often enough *or* performs it too often. For example, the student may already have the skill of remaining on task and assembling an object. The assessment of future environments may indicate that the student does not perform this skill for the desired duration. The instructional objective could be to increase the length of time on task. Sometimes a student performs a response too often, more than the rate the future environment will tolerate. For example, it may be identified that a community living arrangement will require the student to participate in an isolated leisure activity without disrupting others. The student may seek out others too frequently for this setting. The instructional objective could be to reduce the amount of contacts during a specified time in a certain setting.

After the teacher has identified the student's current level of functioning, he or she may have to reinterpret the targeted skills into functional and age-appropriate skills. This involves identifying the action implied by the assessment item, and omitting irrelevant variables. For example, assessment items on developmental tests in particular were not developed with the intent that all students should perform that exact behavior during a portion of their day. Rather, the items were selected to be standard examples of what students could do with different objects at different ages. Items such as "releases block into a can" does not imply that this should be a curricular item and that the student should be taught this exact skill. The teacher must adjust the item to be more educationally appropriate, to reflect a skill useful for the student. It could be translated to read "demonstrates a controlled release from a pincer or palmar grasp."

Step 5. After the behavior or skill is identified, the teacher then writes the instructional long-term goal and short-term objectives. According to Sailor and Guess (1983), this involves determining the discrepancy between the student's current level of performance and the skill level required in the future environment. Some critical skills may be acquired in a year or less; more often than not, it will take many years. A task analysis is helpful in identifying the discrete steps between the present and the future.

After the teacher has collected the required assessment information reflecting the student's current functioning level and the requirements of the future environments, the organization of the class curriculum is a matter of fitting the parts together into a functional and age-appropriate instructional day for all students.

Developing the Educational Day

The procedures for developing the educational day are divided into ten steps. These steps are most easily accomplished when approached in order. A necessary violation of the order, however, is when a student is placed in a class during the ongoing year. In these instances, the teacher will necessarily have to accommodate the student in the established class curriculum. Over time, the class curriculum can be modified to incorporate the new student's individualized education program (IEP) objectives into the ongoing daily activities.

The following steps are used to establish a class curriculum. Their purpose is to deal with all variables available to the teacher in developing a meaningful, functional, and comprehensive educational day for all students in the class.

Step 1: Review Student Files. The purpose of this review is to identify the special needs of each student and to establish a preliminary working schedule for the students when they enter the class. Pertinent information regarding special needs centers on medical information, toileting skills, functioning level, and mobility level. Information to be reviewed includes (1) medical conditions and procedures; (2) behavioral problems and interventions currently used; (3) current functioning level across all areas of development, particularly expressive and receptive language levels; (4) current or applicable IEP goals and objectives; (5) past IEP objectives and mastery levels; (6) dietary needs; (7) hygiene and toileting needs; and (8) mobility level or requirements. It is recommended that the teacher establish a file for each student with this information and the student's age, family's address, and relevant telephone numbers.

Step 2: Group Students. The review of the student files will also allow the teacher to divide the students into initial groups for instruction. Planning for groups of two to four students with one instructional person is recommended. Current best practice techniques in the instruction of students with severe handicaps support this concept.

Group instruction is defined as the individualization of instruction among a group of students with each student's skills acquisition addressed according to the IEP objectives. The students, while receiving individualized instruction, experience the activities of the instructional day together. The activities selected for a particular group are designed to provide practice for each student on IEP objectives. The other groups in the class experience the activities of the day in a different sequence.

Group instruction is selected over the traditional strategy of individual or isolated instruction for a variety of reasons. Grouping tends to provide a more natural experience for the student. The students also learn to share adult attention, interact with peers, and have the opportunity to incidentally learn portions of skills being practiced by other students. The most compelling reason for choosing this strategy, however, is that group instruction is a much more efficient use of teacher time. Given the same time period of instruction, students experiencing group instruction receive more opportunities to practice a skill and are less disruptive and less likely to engage in stereotypic behaviors than the same group of students experiencing a series of individual sessions (Brown et al., 1980).

Strategies used for grouping students usually depend on the type of students in the class. Generally, teachers try to group students who have very similar IEP goals and objectives and are likely to be instructed using the same type of daily activities; i.e., students with similar proposed future environments. Characteristics to consider when grouping students are age, size, functioning level, mobility needs, and strategy for communication. Suggested considerations for grouping are: (1) the students should be functioning at about the same level; (2) the students should be within three years of age of each other; (3) the students should be heterogenous in terms of mobility needs; and (4) the students should be responsive to each other's communication or communicative intent. This list is not inclusive. Teacher and student preferences and personalities should also be considered.

In some classes, there will be students with profound handicaps. Typically these students have no apparent communication system and little awareness of input from their environments. They may either be placed into one group or shared among several groups in the class. A heterogeneous grouping is preferable. There are *no* students for whom group instruction, a group experience of the day, is not appropriate and useful.

Step 3: Identify Educational Activities. Educational activities are those experiences the teacher uses to provide the student with practice on IEP objectives. For the student with severe and multiple impairments, they must be functional and age appropriate. Often, a teacher erroneously approaches the development of a class curriculum with the idea that the identified IEP goals and objectives describe the experiences the student should have during the day. For example, language is a skill area on an assessment and is often identified on the IEPs of students with severe and multiple impairments. Many teachers fulfill the requirement to teach language by establishing a "language period" during the class day. In doing so, the teacher is making a mistake in not differentiating the educational objective (language) from the activity used to teach it (snack, board game, custodial cleaning, meal preparation, etc.). Students without handicaps do not experience a "language time" as an instructional activity during the day to the exclusion of using language at any other time. Rather, language is a skill to be learned and used while participating in all of the day's activities. The same is true for a student with severe and multiple impairments.

For an activity or material to be age appropriate, it must be one in which an age-peer might engage. Preschoolers interact with busy-blocks, stacking cups, and primary books. Adolescents interact with stereos, radios, and magazines. Children go to the kiddie park; adolescents go to the library, mall, or city park.

For an activity to be functional it must meet one of two criteria: it must occur frequently in the student's future home, work place, and community *or* it must be performed by another individual if the student cannot perform the skill. The skill of picking up and putting items away is both a frequently occurring activity and one another person would have to do if the student did not complete it independently. Activities fulfilling the frequency requirement could be sitting in chairs, communicating needs, sharing space, and independent mobility. Most self-care and mealtime skills are obviously functional.

Instructional activities selected for the classroom are most easily developed if they are seen as components of four domains: leisure, vocational, domestic, and community. Other pertinent domains have also been identified as critical (Brown et al., 1987). The important element to recognize when determining the domains of instruction is that they should represent real life activities, not developmental characteristics. For purposes of clarity in discussing the implementation of the ICS model, the four domains suggested by Brown, Branston-McClean, Baumgart, Vincent, Falvey, and Schroeder (1979) will be adopted: leisure, vocational, community, and housekeeping.

The importance of *leisure activities* cannot be overstated. Their purpose is to teach the individual to participate in activities at his or her own initiation without direct intervention or supervision from an adult. Many parents identify this skill as crucial for maintaining the student in the family.

An opportunity to learn individual leisure activities is also appropriate for students with more profound handicaps. One of the major identified goals for such students is developing an awareness of input from the environment. The second most often identified goal is the development of some social interaction (Thompson, 1986). The opportunity to engage in individual leisure activities translates into the student using his or her senses to gather information from the environment and, in turn, acting upon that environment. Even though the range of activities available is much narrower for these students, leisure skill training should occur. During the training, the teacher could select materials that are interactive and age appropriate. Such material adaptations would include attaching mercury or pressure switches to mechanical devices (e.g., fan, massage pillow, lights, radio, battery-operated toys).

When planning and implementing group leisure (e.g., swimming), it is important to arrange the schedule so that not all students in the class participate at the same time. One of the three or four groups in the classroom should access a community setting at any one time. When accessing the community, it is important to maintain an appropriate ratio of persons with handicaps to persons without handicaps. The intent of these activities is to teach group participation in community recreation. Maintaining appropriate ratios in the community tends to lessen the attention paid to the student with a handicap, providing a less restrictive and more functional activity.

It should be noted that large outings to the skating arena or bowling alley for "Handicapped Day Out" are in direct contrast to the purpose of instructing recreation and mobility in the communities. These types of activities tend to be of little or no value instructionally, are inappropriate, and generally occur for the benefit of the staff rather than students.

The use of *vocational activities* in the classroom is appropriate for students even as young as five and six years of age (Clark, 1979; Brolin & Kokaska, 1979). They can be divided into two groups: those designed to replicate either sheltered or competitive employment. These activities are directly related to the projected vocational settings for the student and the skill criteria identified at those sites.

It is difficult to see vocational training as appropriate for students with profound handicaps, those who have little or no awareness of the environment, and those who make little or no attempt at interacting with others. Some professionals in the field of education argue that the person with profound handicaps has the right to participate in all activities of living to the fullest extent possible. In some instances, this means only that the student is present and attentive to the work site. There are no answers here. The field of special education needs to do a great deal more work before complete and meaningful vocational instruction for individuals with the most profound handicaps is clearly understood.

Activities in the *domestic domain* can be broken down into five areas: housekeeping, hygiene, dressing, grooming, and mealtime. Housekeeping activities may include sweeping, dusting, cleaning tables, washing dishes, and washing and folding clothes. They are very similar to vocational tasks; only the setting is different. The development of vocational activities for younger students often involves housekeeping activities. Hygiene activities can include bathing/showering, toileting, washing face and hands, brushing teeth, pedicare, and deodorant use. In addition to the dressing process, dressing and grooming can include clothes selection; clothes matching; adjusting clothing; grooming hands, face, and hair; etc. Mealtimes skills range from chewing and swallowing, to eating with a knife and fork, to simple meal preparation. Complete lists of activities in these domains can be found in several sources (Snell, 1983; Sailor & Guess, 1983).

Much of the instruction for students with profound handicaps should center on the domestic area. In addition to communication and socialization, the intent of instruction for these students is to make caregiving as easy as possible. To teach them to cooperate or reduce resistance will have a great effect on their quality of care and, therefore, their quality of life (Helmstetter et al., 1984; Thompson, 1986). Since much of the student's day is spent in mealtime and custodial tasks, a great deal of training should involve assisting the student in learning to participate in these activities. The focus should be especially on eating, toileting, bathing, and dressing.

Community access addresses activities involved in getting to and moving around in public places such as taking a walk in a neighborhood, going into public buildings and asking for assistance, riding public transportation, or attending community events. Activities available in the school setting include walking on or around the campus, using the auditorium, and attending school functions.

The guidelines for selecting activities in these four domains are (1) select those that are functional and age appropriate for the student; (2) select those that will transfer directly into the student's potential future placement; and (3) select those that are potentially available and accessible in the school setting or adjacent community.

Step 4: Assess Available Materials and Settings. One of the first things a teacher must do when developing a class curriculum is identify the settings in and around the school building and community that are accessible for instruction. Application of the ICS model is compatible with the current emphasis on instruction in the actual setting and with the actual materials the student will use in the future setting. The planning strategies discussed here can be implemented when using the *community intensive instructional model* developed by Sailor and his colleagues (Sailor, Halvorsen,

Anderson, Goetz, Gee, Doering, & Hunt, 1986). This model essentially proposes that the teacher's perception of the instructional environment extend far beyond the classroom. The degree of the extension is directly related to the student's chronological age. The older the student becomes, the more instruction should occur in environments outside the classroom.

Even if the teacher has initial difficulty in administratively adopting this view of the extended classroom, some application is possible. When the students are of late elementary, middle, and high school age, instruction should occur out of the classroom as much as possible. What is "as much as possible" can be determined by following Sailor et al.'s (1986) recommendation on the percentages of time in the school day required for instruction in the different settings. Areas to access *in the school* for the practice of vocational, leisure, housekeeping, and community skills are, for example, the gym, cafeteria, auditorium, hallways, offices, bathrooms, home economics suite, the teacher lounge, and the student "hang out." Materials to use for instruction in these settings are already there. For example, any custodial cleaning of the bathrooms, halls, or offices should involve building maintenance materials. Leisure activities taught in the home economics suite or lounge will use furnishings and materials already present (vending machines, sofas, magazines, record players, etc.).

Often, the teacher is unable to access settings in the school building immediately due to administrative problems or concerns. In these instances, while pursuing the opportunities to conduct activities in the natural setting, the classroom needs to be developed into areas simulating necessary but unavailable settings. Classrooms can establish centers or areas simulating a living room, bedroom, kitchen, and shop. The centers a teacher selects to establish depend on what other settings are available in the school. The typical classroom can be divided into three to five simulated settings. The settings must conform with specific guidelines: Each must have an established and clearly discernable boundary; there must be clear pathways between them; and the materials stored and used in a center must be specific to the activities simulated in the center.

As much as possible, the materials used for instruction in an area should be those typically found or already present in the natural area. Often these materials are not typically provided by a district's materials center. Examples may be a set of dishes, pots and pans, custodial cleaning rack and mops, a bed, and bed linen. The teacher is encouraged to use resources in the community to assist in furnishing the needed supplies.

Step 5: Develop Subactivities. Once the teacher has identified a list of appropriate instructional activities, possible settings of instruction, and potential materials for use in the settings, the list of subactivities for instruction can be developed. *Subactivities* identify the actual behavior engaged in by the student during the activity. They should first be determined by observing the student's potential future environment. For example, what housekeeping activities are conducted in a group home? What leisure activities occur during break at the workshop? What games are played at the local arcade? Subactivities may include, respectively, picking up, dusting, vacuuming, and washing floors; visiting; simple card games, checkers; and pinball and laser games.

Subactivities can also be determined by first identifying the activity and environment in which a domain will be addressed. An assessment of the materials available in the environment will lead the teacher to identify subactivities. For example, two settings in the school could be used in teaching vocational skills: the bathroom and the auditorium. Subactivities for the bathroom could be mopping the floor, washing the mirror, and washing the sinks. Subactivities for the auditorium could be sweeping the floor, wiping all the seats, and mopping the stage. The selection of subactivities depends on external factors: the requirements of the student's potential future setting and the availability of materials. The level of a student's participation in a subactivity is determined by his or her functioning level and sensory and motor abilities.

Table 8-2 Examples of Activities, Settings, and Subactivities in Different Domains

Domain	Activity	Setting	Subactivity
Domestic	Meal preparation	Kitchen	Make a sandwich, set the table, wash & put dishes away, fold napkins
Leisure	Individual leisure	Living room	Listen to records, read a magazine, watch movies on the VCR
		Canteen	Buy a soda & candy, read a magazine
	Take a walk	Community	Sit in the park, walk in the park, toss pennies in the fountain
Vocational	Custodial cleaning	Hall office	Sweep floor, dust furniture, wash windows

Some sample activities, settings, and subactivities are presented in Table 8-2.

Step 6: Develop a Class Schedule. The purpose of the classroom schedule is to establish, for each group of students, a complete, cohesive, and logical school day. Most importantly, the schedule should reflect activities a similar chronologically aged peer without handicaps might experience in the order and setting in which the events would occur. A separate daily schedule is established for each group of students. Group sizes of no more than four students are recommended. Each group will experience the school day together as they move from setting to setting and activity to activity. Students are provided individual instruction on their IEP objectives in group situations while interacting with different portions of the environment together, sharing materials, and interacting with each other. Across time the teacher can take advantage of the dynamics of the group and use social interaction as one strategy for maintaining interest and motivation. Typically, one classroom instructional person is assigned to provide appropriate instruction to each group of students as the day progresses. A class ratio of one adult to three or four students implies that paraprofessionals are totally utilized as instructional personnel.

Several strategies are used to develop a schedule. The first is the Premack principle (Premack, 1965). This principle implies that the teacher schedules activities according to the students' preferences. Since Premack found that activities can be powerful rewards for students, it is to the teacher's advantage to sequence activities using their reinforcing qualities. Activities the students tend to like should be scheduled after those that are difficult or disliked. This type of attention to scheduling will assist the teacher in maintaining higher levels of motivation and student interest. The students will learn to continue through disliked or hard activities because liked or favored activities will follow. Typical like activities are snacks, outdoor activities, and activities with other students or in exciting settings. These events should be scheduled after such activities as vocational custodial cleaning, housekeeping, or grooming and dressing.

A second strategy to use when developing a schedule is to arrange for activities to occur during their functional or natural times. For example, grooming and toileting activities should occur before snack, before work, and after play. All mealtime skill activities should occur during the snack, break, or lunch period. The third strategy requires that logic be applied to the schedule. For example, people typically work before playing, groom before and after eating, and clean up after meals or special activities.

Table 8-3 An Example of a Class Schedule for a Group of Adolescent Students

Time	Domain	Activity	Day	Setting	Subactivity
8:00	Domestic	Entry		Class	Put away materials Prepare for work
8:15	Vocational	Custodial cleaning	MWF	Bathroom	(a) Clean mirror & sinks (b) Sweep & mop floor
			TTH	Kitchen area	(a) Clean mirror & sinks (b) Sweep & mop floors
9:30	Leisure	Break		Lounge area	(a) Use vending machine & eat snack (b) Play board/card game & share information
9:45	Domestic	Grooming		Bathroom	(a) Wash face & hands, comb hair (b) Apply deodorant, make up, shave
10:15	Vocational	Prevoc		Sheltered shop	(a) Collate paper by number (b) Sort machinery items (c) Assemble hospital kits
11:30	Domestic	Grooming		Bathroom	(a) Wash face & hands, comb hair
11:45	Domestic	Lunch	MWF	Cafeteria	(a) Go through lunch line, obtain food, go to table (b) Bring lunch & eat from bagged lunch
			TTH	Home ec. suite	(a) Prepare simple meal, set table, eat meal, clean up (b) Eat bagged lunch at family style table
12:30	Community/ Leisure	Take a walk		Grounds around school building	(a) Take a walk (b) Cross streets at intersection (c) Sit on park benches & share information

continues

Table 8-3 continued

Time	Domain	Activity	Day	Setting	Subactivity
1:15	Domestic	Grooming		Bathroom	(a) Wash face & hands, comb hair
1:30	Vocational	Gardening	MWF	Greenhouse	(a) Watering (b) Sweeping aisle
			TTH	Lawn	(a) Rake leaves (b) Pick up trash
2:45	Domestic	Grooming		Bathroom	(a) Wash face & hands, comb hair
3:00	Domestic/ Community	Prepare to depart		Classroom	(a) Select appropriate clothing items, put away materials

During the process of classroom scheduling, the teacher should sequence events using all of these principles for each group in the class. Each group should experience a slightly different day so that only a small number of students share the same setting at the same time. The schedules should be relatively fixed so the students can expect certain activities after other activities. The scheduled consistency across the day will assist the student in becoming more independent in the environment. As he or she learns the schedule, the student can begin to move independently between settings without direct teacher instruction.

Variation in the instructional day is equally important. Systematic variation assists the teacher in maintaining a student's motivation for participation in the various activities that continue across the day (Dunlap & Koegel, 1980). Daily schedules should reflect both consistency and variation. The variation in the day is supplied by the different subactivities used during the different activities of the day. For example, from 9:00-10:00 the students in Group A may be engaged in housekeeping in the kitchen, under the domestic domain of instruction. On some days of the week, they may be folding and putting away laundry. On other days they may be cleaning the kitchen and putting away the dishes. Both activities involve sorting, matching, and following directions, yet the materials change to maintain a high interest level.

Incorporating the domain, activity, setting, and subactivity requirements, a typical class schedule for one group of adolescent students in a class might be as presented in Table 8-3. This schedule is designed for a group of three adolescents having severe and multiple handicaps, operating with one instructional person. Notice that the *Setting* column indicates the different environments that will be accessed to participate in the different subactivities. The settings should change across the day and indicate the actual setting in which the practiced skill will be used. The *Subactivities* column specifies separate subactivities; these could be addressed on different days of the week. For example, all (a)'s could be conducted on Monday and Wednesday; all (b)'s on Tuesday, Thursday, and Friday, unless there was a (c) indicated. All (c)'s would then be conducted on Fridays. This type of scheduling allows for variation in the predictability of the daily schedule. In the implementation of the schedule, the students will learn to anticipate vocational gardening at 1:30, but the location and task will change depending on the day (and probably the weather).

The same classroom may also have a group of students who are profoundly handicapped. The schedule of activities for this group may appear as in Table 8-4.

These students follow a separate schedule throughout the day, accessing the same environments as the other students but during different times. The primary goals of instruction for these students are obviously different than those for students with severe handicaps. Goals of instruction identified by teachers of students with profound handicaps tend to be (1) develop or increase environmental awareness; (2) develop or increase social interaction with a familiar person; (3) develop a consistent response (Thompson, 1986); (4) maintain or increase motor functioning; (5) develop mealtime skills to insure proper nutrition and use of oral mechanisms during eating; and (6) increase student participation in activities of daily living so that caregiving is more enjoyable for the student and the caregiver. To this end, the experiences of the student's day focus on domestic and leisure skills.

The focus of the subactivities is for the student to participate as much as possible in the activity. This is a direct application of the principle of partial participation (Brown, Branston, Hamre-Nietupski, Pumpian, Certo, & Gruenewald, 1979). For the most part, those students will not become totally independent in any activity of daily living. The goal, then, is to provide them with skills so they can participate as much as possible in the activities. Social interaction during caretaking is a very important skill for persons relying on others for most of their needs. Therefore the instruction of a social smile, reciprocal interactions, and relaxation techniques are appropriate skills to be included in instructing activities of daily living.

It is generally advisable to have instructional personnel alternate the groups they instruct each day. For example, if a classroom contains two groups of students, one following the first schedule, and the second

Table 8-4 An Example of a Class Schedule for a Group of Students with Profound Handicaps

Time	Domain	Activity	Day	Setting	Subactivity
8:00	Domestic	Entry		Class	Put away materials Undress
8:15	Domestic	Grooming	MWF	Grooming (in class)	(a) Wash face & hands (b) Comb & brush hair, brush teeth
9:15	Leisure	Sensory integration		Mat area (in class)	(a) Activiate mechan- ical items (b) Interact with age- appropriate mate- rials & peers
10:30	Domestic	Snack		Kitchen area (in class)	Self-feeding chewing, swallowing liquid consumption
11:30	Domestic	Grooming		Bathroom	Toileting, wash face & hands, comb hair, adjust clothing
12:00	Domestic	Lunch		Kitchen area (in class)	Self-feeding swallowing, monitor liquid consumption, position for interac- tion
1:00	Domestic	Grooming		Grooming area (in class)	Brush teeth, toilet, wash hands & face, comb hair
1:30	Leisure/ Community	Sensory integration	MW	Mat area (in class)	(a) Position for interaction, acti- vate materials in environment (b) Vestibular stimula- tion
			TTH	Outdoors	Position for interaction, respond to elements in envi- ronment
2:30	Domestic	Grooming		Grooming area	Toileting, wash face & hands
3:00	Domestic	Prepare to depart		Classroom	Dress appropriately

following the second, the teacher may instruct group 1 on MWF and group 2 on TTH. During the next week, the assigned groups may alternate.

Step 7: Develop an ICS Matrix for Each Student in Each Group. The ICS matrix is a form that, when completed correctly and completely, assists the teacher in developing a class curriculum addressing both the demands of the students' future environments and their current developmental levels. The form, Exhibit 8-2, is simply a collection of rows and columns forming a matrix. The intersection of the rows and columns joins the environmental concerns with the concerns of the functioning level. The columns under *Class Variables* include many of the decisions made in steps 1 through 6. The columns under *Educational Objectives* include a summary of the information gathered in steps 1 through 5 of the Assessment section of this chapter. The present step involves making decisions about how the two bodies of information should be translated into the actual educational day.

The teacher fills in the information required under *Class Variables.* All these decisions were made during the previous steps. The teacher should re-evaluate the schedule to make sure the principles for sequencing the daily activities were adhered to: the Premack principle, appropriate times, and logical relation between activities.

Next, the teacher lists the student's educational objectives in the columns with the heading of the same name. For decision-making and planning purposes, they should be listed in an order from left to right. The order may reflect the teacher's designation of the priority of the objectives or according to sensory, language, mobility, and hygiene objectives. Obviously, the sequencing depends on the teacher's preference and the student's characteristics.

The teacher completes the matrix by indicating whether a skill can and should be practiced (*Objective* column) in a specific environment, activity, and subactivity (*Class Variables* row). The teacher may record his or her decision by marking an "x" in the box where the column and row intersect, or by making instructional notes in the box.

While there is no one right way for filling out the matrix for a particular student, there are several considerations. Most objectives should have an opportunity to be practiced at least 10 times a day. Some objectives, however, are tied to specific materials and settings so that practicing the skill 10 times a day would be inappropriate. Toothbrushing, deodorant use, and toileting are some examples. Objectives considered a high priority (required most frequently in a student's future environment or critical for moving to a less restrictive environment) should be practiced

Exhibit 8-2 Blank ICS Matrix

			Class Variables				Educational Objectives
Time	Domain	Activity	Day	Setting	Subactivity		

Student ——— Group ——— ICS Matrix

Completed by ———

Semester ———

as much as possible across the day: language, mobility, and socialization may be examples.

A second consideration has to do with the clustering of skills. A cluster of skills is a group of two to five educational objectives that, when sequenced together, produce a functional unit of behavior for the student when interacting with the environment. Examples may be reach and grasp, maintaining visual fixation, auditory localization, and maintaining head in midline. The opportunity to practice these objectives may be sequenced so as to not only teach the individual skills to the student but to teach the relationship between the skills. With repeated opportunities the student could learn to locate an object by its sound, to turn to fixate visually while maintaining the head in midline, to reach/grasp, and to retain the grasp while looking at the object. If several objectives apparently fit into a cluster, the entire group should be repeated across selected settings and activities.

A third consideration is the appropriateness or ability of incorporating the educational objective into the instructional activity. For example, "rotary chewing" is only appropriate for mealtime activities; "works independently for five minutes" may only be appropriate for vocational activities; and "visual tracking" or "reach, grasp, and controlled release" are appropriate across a variety of activities and settings. After the matrix is completed for one student in a designated group, the matrices for the other students should be completed.

A final consideration for the appropriateness of designating a particular objective for a particular activity and setting for one student has to do with the objectives selected for the other students in the group. The teacher needs to determine if any objectives selected for any student in the group are incompatible for a specific setting and activity. While "sharing materials" may be appropriate in the kitchen during meal preparation, it may be incompatible with other student's objective of "working independently." The teacher must be aware of any difficulties and adjust activities, the selection of objectives, or the instructional management of the session accordingly.

The completed ICS matrices in Exhibits 8-3 and 8-4 are examples for an adolescent with severe handicaps and a youngster with profound handicaps. Again, there is no *one* right way. Variations in students, settings, materials, and activities make the identification of the best schedule or matrix possible.

Step 8: Develop Individual Programs. After the teacher develops and completes the ICS matrix for each student in the group, the teacher has information on which educational objectives will be taught as a part of

Exhibit 8-3 ICS Matrix for Student with Severe Handicaps

Student __Jan__ Group __B__ ICS Matrix

Completed by __Mark__

Semester __Fall 1987__

	Class Variables					Educational Objectives								
Time	Domain	Activity	Day	Setting	Subactivity	Follow 2 step direction	Use survival words	Express independent idea	Manipulate turn/ corner in chair	Pull with Strength	Match like items	Identify amount to 10	Use dollar amount to $5	Read survival words
8³⁰	Entry			Lockers	Hang up coat Prepare bks	X	X	X		X	X			
8⁴⁵	Vocational	Cleaning	MW	Cafeteria	Sweep floor	X			X	X	X			
			TTHF	Auditorium	a) Sweep floor	X			X	X	X			
					b) Wipe windows					X	X			
9³⁰	Leisure	Break		Cafeteria	Use vending machines	X	X		X			X	X	
					Socialize in canteen area			X	X					
					Play cards			X	X		X	X		

Exhibit 8-4 ICS Matrix for Student with Profound Handicaps

Student __Lisa__ Group __A__ ICS Matrix

Completed by __Mark__

Semester __Fall 1987__

| | Class Variables | | | | | Educational Objectives | | | | | | | | |
Time	Domain	Activity	Day	Setting	Subactivity	Respond to stimulation	Social interaction Smile	Consistent response	Maintain ROM	Auditory recognition	Visual fixation	Maintain grasp	Reduce Tongue Thrust	Increase fluid intake
8³⁰	Housekeep	Entry		Classroom	Remove coat Orient to room	X	X		X	X	X			
8⁴⁵		Grooming		BR	Wash face Comb hair	X	X				X	X		
					adjust Clothes	X	X		X					
					Toileting	X	X		X		X	X		
9¹⁰	Leisure	Individual investigation	MWF	Classroom	AV equipment with pressure switches	X		X		X				X
					Computer	X		X		X	X	X		
				TTH	Library	Audio tapes with pressure switches	X		X		X				

which subactivities in which settings. Reading across the matrix, from left to right, the teacher can identify all objectives to be addressed during a specific domain, activity, and subactivity on a particular day and in a specific setting.

The actual arrangement of the practice of these skills in that setting and with that subactivity depends, to a large degree, on the student and the objectives selected. For objectives that seem to cluster, the teacher could attempt to adhere to a set sequence in providing their practice. If there is no logic to an order in practicing these skills, the teacher should present practice to the student as he or she encounters the opportunity in the environment. For example, if an objective for a student is "uses pincer grasp" and the student is in the kitchen area participating in simple meal preparation, the teacher can provide practice in using the correct grasp as the student works through making the sandwich, soup, etc. Attempting to prearrange an exact sequence of opportunities in which to practice all objectives forces the student to follow the dictates of the teacher rather than responding to the demands of the environment.

Reading down the matrix, by column of individual objective, will show the teacher all the settings, activities, and subactivities in which a particular skill will be practiced. The teacher needs to develop an individual program for the instruction of a particular skill across all these settings and activities for a variety of reasons. First, written directions allow for consistent communication between the instructional staff in the classroom on how the student's opportunity to practice a skill will be provided. Second, it allows for consistent planning in the development or acquisition of a skill. Third, it allows for ease in evaluating or updating a student's educational day.

A number of models for the development of instructional or implementation programs are presented elsewhere (Snell, 1983; Sailor & Guess, 1983; Gaylord-Ross & Holvoet, 1985). The following format is an additional option. The teacher is encouraged to synthesize suggestions from as many sources as possible and develop a format most workable in his or her classroom. The important consideration is that it must be applicable for the instruction of the particular skill across *all* the activities and settings identified. The salient characteristics of the proposed instructional program format are its readability, adaptability, and brevity.

Exhibit 8-5 is a blank form, Exhibit 8-6 is a program completed for a student with severe handicaps, and Exhibit 8-7 is a program completed for a student with profound handicaps. After the initial information is written on the form, updating requires only a change in the column being modified; the other columns remain the same. *Date* indicates the date the program is initiated or the date of the revision. *Instructional Goal* identi-

Exhibit 8-5 Blank Individual Program Form

Student _____   Activities _____

Completed by _____   Settings _____

Date written _____   Subactivities _____

Date	Instructional Goal	Instructional Objective	Instructional Techniques	Reward/ Consequence	Record Keeping

Exhibit 8-6 Instructional Program for Student with Severe Handicaps

Student _____ Jan _____

Completed by _____ Mark _____

Date written _____ February 16, 1987 _____

Activities _____ Leisure _____

Settings _____ Lockers, canteen, outside _____

Subactivities _____ Socializing, entry, Playing cards, taking a walk _____

Date	Instructional Goal	Instructional Objective	Instructional Techniques	Reward/ Consequence	Record Keeping
2-20-87	Express independent idea	Will describe home event	Teacher/Student relays event — pause, ask Jan about "____" from the log	Verbal praise, encourage comments re: items not selected by trainer	3 – Jan initiates 2 – Responds to nonspecific cue 1 – Responds to specific cue 0 – Resists/no response
2-23-87		Will describe school event			

Exhibit 8-7 Instructional Program for Student with Profound Handicaps

Student ___Lisa___

Completed by ___Mark___

Date written ___February 16, 1987___

Activities ___Grooming, Leisure, Mealtime___

Settings ___All___

Subactivities ___Removing clothes, toileting, using A.V. equipment, oral desensitization___

Date	Instructional Goal	Instructional Objective	Instructional Techniques	Reward/ Consequence	Record Keeping
2-20-87	Uses consistent response to environment	Recognizes changes in environment	Present stimuli, continue for duration of 5 to 10 seconds. Stop stimulation.	Touching, rocking, re-present stimulation	Score + if she demonstrates any change in facial or body position/tone/ response
2-27-87			Do not use bright lights or moving/ vibrating visual stimuli		

fies the year or long-term goal. *Instructional Objective* identifies the short-term objectives for meeting the goal. *Instructional Techniques* identifies the procedures instructional personnel will use to teach or facilitate the objective. Items may include positioning needs, natural cues, and the additional prompts that may be necessary. *Consequences* indicates the reward the child is to receive for accomplishing the objective. This should include the positive consequence and some indication of how often it is to be received. *Record Keeping* indicates the monitoring procedures and the codes used. The procedures used in record keeping affect significantly the quality of the revisions made to the individual programs as well as to the student's entire instructional day.

Step 9: Monitoring Student Performance. The process of monitoring student performance receives mixed responses from classroom teachers. There are many strategies for monitoring student performance (Haring, Liberty, & White, 1980; Sailor & Guess, 1983; Gaylord-Ross & Holvoet, 1985). The following strategy may be a reasonable approach and requires that the teacher score the results of a student's performance on discrete trials of responses or quantify it on a trial-by-trial basis.

There are two approaches to trial-by-trial analysis of student performance, each with a different function. Data may be collected to provide either predictive or descriptive information. If the teacher is interested in collecting data to predict the speed at which a skill will be learned and the point of mastery, then rate data requiring a score on each discrete response are needed (Haring, et al, 1980). This involves continuous monitoring of student performance.

If, however, the teacher is primarily interested in describing a student's current level of performance, only samples of a student's performance will be needed. This requires only a portion of observational time across the entire school day and week. The purpose of descriptive data is to provide the teacher with a sample of the student's current performance on each educational goal and objective. Rather than continuously monitoring all discrete responses, the quantification of a small number of responses is needed. The key to sampling responses is recording observations on each objective across settings and materials. In collecting samples of responses across the day, the teacher is insuring a description of the generalized acquisition and use of a skill, not just skill acquisition in one setting.

Exhibit 8-8 is a suggested form to use when collecting such samples. The first column indicates the objective being monitored, the second column the setting in which the skill is being observed, and the third column the activities used in each setting to address skill acquisition. The coding (scoring key) suggested is only one of many options available. This partic-

Exhibit 8-8 Example of a Data Collection Form

Student _____

Goal _____

Objective	Setting	Activity
develop pincer grasp	housekeeping	sorting silverware
	quiet area	turning pages in book
		moving pieces on game
	mealtime	fingerfeeding
follow directions	vocational	going to station
		changing activities
	quiet area	playing alone
		sharing materials
	mealtime	where to sit
gesture for items	vocational	work at station
	mealtime	pointing to food
	bathroom	point to clothes
		point to towels
put away items	vocational	after work completed
	mealtime	clear eating area
	leisure	put away toys
	housekeeping	put away cleaning supplies
		put away dishes/utensils
step over objects	vocational	moving to work area

Scoring key: 4-independent   2-pointing, gesture

3-verbal prompt   1-hand over hand prompt

0-resists

ular code quantifies the amount of assistance needed by the student to perform the desired response. Other common scoring options are a 3-2-1-0 or 2-1-0 to represent levels of assistance required. As the teacher and student change instructional settings, the teacher scans the data sheet to identify objectives targeted for each area. A sample of student responses for each objective per area are then recorded.

The term "a sample of responses" indicates that only some of the many responses a student uses to practice a skill in a setting are scored. For example, in the housekeeping setting the student may use a pincer grasp to sort 10 to 20 items of silverware. Of these 20 discrete trials, the teacher only needs to score two or three responses. The teacher may only score the first three, and then proceed with the student as he or she completes the activity without scoring the remaining responses. For a reasonable sample of data to describe a student's level of response, the teacher only needs to score approximately 10 responses per week across settings. Exhibit 8-9 shows how this would appear. During the week of 9-2, performance on the pincer grasp was scored 10 times: 4 times in housekeeping, 3 times in the quiet area, and 3 times at mealtime. Even though this is not the number of times the student used the pincer grasp, it reflects the level of the student's response across three settings.

Many teachers are opposed to data collection during instructional or class time because they feel it interferes with the instructional flow of the student-teacher interaction. The activity of data collection, or testing, and the activity of teaching need to be clearly differentiated. Testing is a necessary process to evaluate the student's progress and the success of the instructional programs. During the testing periods, the teacher primarily observes the student's competence in a specific skill. When the testing is complete, the teacher is free to assume a teaching and facilitating role. Testing and teaching are different classroom operations and neither should be done halfheartedly. If the teacher tests only a small number of the total discrete trials, the process of testing will not interfere with the process of teaching.

Many other similar data collection strategies are applicable in the classroom (Helmstetter et al., 1984; Gaylord-Ross & Holvoet, 1985); the reader is encouraged to develop his or her own. A formative evaluation system, however, is needed to optimize the classroom experience for each student.

Step 10: Adapt Class Schedule and Programs as the Data Suggest. Many resources have invested many more pages than those used here in describing how to evaluate student performance (Helmstetter et al., 1984; Haring et al., 1980; Sailor & Guess, 1983; Gaylord-Ross & Holvoet, 1985).

Exhibit 8-9 Data Sheet for Noting the Level of Proficiency per Discrete Trial by Instructional Objective Across Settings and Activities

Student ___ Susan ___

Goal ___

Objective	Setting	Activity	9-2	9-3	9-4	9-5	9-9	9-10	9-11	9-12	9-16	9-17	9-18
develop pincer grasp	housekeeping	sorting silverware	1	2	1	2	1	2	2	2	3	2	3
	quiet area	turning pages in book	2	3	2						3	3	3
		moving pieces on game					2	2	2	2	2	3	3
follow directions	mealtime	fingerfeeding	3	3	3		3	3	4	3	3	3	3
	vocational	going to station	2	3			3	3			3	4	
		changing activities	2	3			2	2	3		3	2	3
	quiet area	play alone	2	2			2	2	2		2	2	2
		sharing materials	2	1	2		2	2	2	3	2	3	2
	mealtime	where to sit	3	3	3		3	4			4		
gesture for items	vocational	work at station	1	0	1	1	1	1	1	1	1	2	2
	mealtime	pointing to food	2	3	3		3	3	3	3	3	3	3
	bathroom	point to clothes	1	1	1		1	2	2	2	2	2	2
		point to towels	1	1	1		1	1	1	2	1	1	1
put away items	vocational	after work completed	1				1				1	1	
	mealtime	clear eating area	0				1				1		
	leisure	put away toys	1				1				1		
	housekeeping	put away cleaning supplies	1				1				1		
		put away dishes/utensils	1				1						
step over objects	vocational	moving to work area	1				2				2		

Scoring key:
4-independent
3-verbal prompt
2-pointing, gesture
1-hand over hand prompt
0-resists

The teacher is referred to them for discussions on how to interpret data and change instructional procedures as a result of the data analysis. Regardless of the procedures used, the teacher should review student progress data at least once every one or two weeks. At that time, teachers should make some decision about the instructional programs either remaining the same or being revised. Any component of the program can be revised to attempt to alter the direction of the performance graph. If the student's performance is represented by a flat or declining line (assuming that an ascending line is desirable), the teacher should first consider an alteration in either the teaching techniques or the consequences listed on the instructional program. If these alterations are unsuccessful, the appropriateness of the step reflected in the objective should be reanalyzed. If the instructional objective and overall long-term goal are deemed appropriate and within the student's competence, the teacher will need to analyze components of the educational day.

Every component of the class is a subject for analysis. The first consideration is to determine whether the student is receiving sufficient practice in the desired skill. A reanalysis of the activities and settings in which the skill is scheduled to be practiced will determine whether additional activities need to be targeted for practice.

If these analyses do not identify factors affecting flat or declining performance, the teacher should observe the training techniques of the various instructional staff. Inconsistencies in training procedures or "personalities" may contribute to the student's resistance to participating in the activity. The teacher is referred to Guess and Siegel-Causey's (1985) discussion of this topic.

CONCLUSION

This chapter focused on expanding the classroom teacher's concept of curriculum in the classroom. The entire classroom, including the students, instructional staff, and environments of instruction, can be manipulated to develop a functional and age-appropriate curriculum for all students in the class. The class curriculum can best be described by how the student's instructional day is organized. The ICS model assists the teacher in not only sequencing functional and age-appropriate activities but in integrating the students' objectives.

Although the ICS model is a fairly structured approach to curriculum development, it is unreasonable to expect, and undesirable to have, all teacher-student interactions structured in a predetermined discrete-trial format. A significant portion of the school day involves the opportunity for incidental instruction (Hart & Risley, 1982) and independent investigation of the environment. These situations occur when the teacher and the students are interacting in a functional environment but are not specifically engaged in a structured interaction. Much of this teaching involves the teacher responding to the initiations of the student. The teacher "follows the student" (Montessorri, 1967), identifies the teachable moment, and takes advantage of it by expanding on the student's current skill level. It is reasonable to assume that 60% to 70% of the teacher-student interactions should be in the form of discrete-trial interactions. The remainder of the instructional day should consist of the teacher creating the "teachable moment" for the student, as the student, regardless of functioning level, learns to interact with and seeks information from functional and age-appropriate instructional environments.

REFERENCES

Becker, H., Schur, S., Paoletti-Schelp, M., & Hammer, E. (1985). *Functional skills screening inventory*. Austin, TX: Functional Resources Enterprises.

Bricker, D.D. (1983). Early communication: Development and training. In M.E. Snell (Ed.), *Systematic instruction of the moderately and severely handicapped* (2nd ed.) (pp. 269-288). Columbus, OH; Charles E. Merrill.

Brolin, D.E., & Kokaska, C.J. (1979). *Career education for handicapped children and youth*. Columbus, OH: Charles E. Merrill.

Brown, L., Branston, M.B., Hamre-Nietupski, S., Johnson, F., Wilcox, B., & Gruenewald, L. (1979). A rationale for comprehensive longitudinal interactions between severely handicapped students and other nonhandicapped citizens. *AAESPH Review, 4*, 3-14.

Brown, L., Branston-McClean, M.B., Baumgart, D., Vincent, L., Falvey, M., & Schroeder, J. (1979). Using the characteristics of current and subsequent least restrictive environments in the development of curricular content for severely handicapped students. *AAESPH Review, 4(4)*, 407-424.

Brown, F., Evans, I.M., Weed, K.A., & Owen, V. (1987). Delineating functional competence: A component model. *Journal of the Association for Persons with Severe Handicaps, 12*(2), 117-124.

Brown, F., Holvoet, J., Guess, D., & Mulligan, M. (1980). The individualized curriculum sequencing model (III): Small group instruction. *Journal of the Association for the Severely Handicapped, 5*, 352-367.

Brown, L., Branston, M.B., Hamre-Nietupski, S., Pumpian, I., Certo, N., & Gruenewald, L. (1979). A strategy for developing chronological-age-appropriate and functional curricular content for severely handicapped adolescents and young adults. *The Journal of Special Education, 13*, 81-90.

Clark, G.M. (1979). *Career education for the handicapped child in the elementary classroom*. Denver: Love Publishing.

Dunlap, G., & Koegel, R.L. (1980). Motivating autistic children through stimulus variation. *Journal of Applied Behavior Analysis, 13*(4), 619-628.

Freagon, S., Wheeler, J., McDannel, K., Brankin, G., & Costello, D. (1983). *Individual student community life skill profile system for severely handicapped students.* Dekalb, IL: Northern Illinois University and the Dekalb County Special Education Association.

Gaylord-Ross, R., & Holvoet, J. (1985). *Strategies for educating students with severe handicaps.* Boston: Little, Brown, and Company.

Gold, M.W., & Pomerantz, E.J. (1978). Issues in prevocational training. In M.E. Snell (Ed.), *Systematic instruction of the moderately and severely handicapped* (pp. 431-440). Columbus, OH: Charles E. Merrill.

Guess, D., Horner, D., Utley, B., Holvoet, J., Maxon, D., Tucker, D., & Warren, S. (1978). A functional curriculum sequencing model for teaching the severely handicapped. *AAESPH Review, 3,* 202-215.

Guess, D., Sailor, W., & Baer, D.M. (1976). *Functional speech and language training for the severely handicapped.* Austin, TX: PRO-ED.

Guess, D., & Siegel-Causey, E. (1985). Behavioral control and education of severely handicapped students: Who's doing what to whom? and why? In D. Bricker & J. Filler (Eds.), *Severe mental retardation: From theory to practice* (pp. 230-244). Reston, VA: The Council for Exceptional Children.

Haring, N.G., Liberty, K.A., & White, O.R. (1980). Rules for data-based strategy decisions in instructional programs: Current research and instructional implications. In W. Sailor, B. Wilcox, & L. Brown (Eds.), *Methods of instruction for severely handicapped students* (pp. 159-194). Baltimore: Paul H. Brookes.

Hart, B.M., & Risley, T.R. (1982). *How to use incidental teaching for elaborating language.* Lawrence, KS: H. & H. Enterprises.

Haynes, U., Patterson, G., D'Wolf, N., Hutchinson, D., Lowry, W., Schilling, M., & Siepp, J. (1976). *Staff development handbook: A resource for the transdisciplinary process.* New York: United Cerebral Palsy Association.

Helmstetter, E., Murphy-Herd, M.C., Roberts, R., & Guess, D. (1984). *Individualized curriculum sequence and extended classroom models for students who are deaf and blind.* Lawrence, KS: University of Kansas, Department of Special Education.

Holvoet, J., Guess, D., Mulligan, M., & Brown, F. (1980). The individualized curriculum sequencing model (II): A teaching strategy for severely handicapped students. *Journal of the Association for the Severely Handicapped, 5,* 325-336.

Johnson-Martin, N., Jens, K.G., and Attermeier, S.M. (1986). *The Carolina curriculum for handicapped infants and infants at risk.* Baltimore: Paul H. Brookes.

Lent, J. (1975). *Project MORE.* Bellevue, WA: Edmark.

Lyon, S., & Lyon, G. (1980). Team functioning and staff development: A role release approach to providing the integral educational services to severely handicapped students. *Journal of the Association for the Severely Handicapped, 5,* 250-263.

McCormick, L., & Goldman, R. (1979) The transdisciplinary model: Implications for service delivery and personnel preparation for the severely and profoundly handicapped. *AAESPH Review, 4,* 152-161.

Montessori, M. (1967). *The Montessori method.* Cambridge, MA: Robert Bentley.

Mulligan, M., Guess, D., Holvoet, J., & Brown, F. (1980). The individualized sequencing model (l): Implications from research on massed, distributed, or spaced trial training. *Journal of the Association for the Severely Handicapped, 5,* 325-336.

Popovich, D., & Laham, S.L. (1981). *The adaptive behavior curriculum: Prescriptive behavioral analysis for moderately, severely, and profoundly handicapped students.* Baltimore: Paul H. Brookes.

Premack, D. (1965). Reinforcement theory. In D. Levine (Ed.), *Nebraska symposium on motivation.* Lincoln, NE: University of Nebraska Press.

Rusch, F.R., & Mithaney, D.E. (1980). *Vocational training for mentally retarded adults: A behavior analytic approach.* Champaign, IL: Research Press.

Sailor, W., & Guess, D. (1983). *Severely handicapped students: An instructional design.* Boston: Houghton Mifflin.

Sailor, W., Halvorsen, A., Anderson, J., Goetz, L., Gee, K., Doering, K., & Hunt, P. (1986). Community intensive instruction. In R.H. Horner, L.H. Meyer, & H.D. Fredricks (Eds.), *Education of learners with severe handicaps: Exemplary service strategies* (pp. 251-288). Baltimore: Paul H. Brookes.

Schroeder, G., & Baer, D.M. (1972) Effects of concurrent versus serial training on generalized vocal imitation in retarded children. *Developmental Psychology, 6,* 293-301.

Snell, M.E. (1983). *Systematic instruction of the moderately and severely handicapped,* (2nd Ed.). Columbus, OH: Charles E. Merrill.

Sternberg, L., Ritchey, H., Pegnatore, L., Wills, L., & Hill, C. (1986). *A curriculum for profoundly handicapped students: The Broward county model program.* Rockville, MD: Aspen.

Stetson, F. (1985). *L.I.F.E.: Learning in functional environments: A training program for teachers of severely handicapped students.* Houston, TX: Region IV, Educational Service Center.

Tawney, J.W., Knapp, D.S., O'Reilly, C.D., & Pratt, S.S. (1979). *Programmed environments curriculum.* Columbus, OH: Charles E. Merrill.

Thompson, B. (1986). *Messages from the field: Teachers' perceptions of educational practices for students who experience profound disabilities.* Paper presented at 1986 Annual TASH Conference. San Francisco, CA.

Wehman, P. (Ed.). (1979). *Recreation programming for developmentally disabled persons.* Baltimore: University Park Press.

Wehman, P., & McLaughlin, P. (1980). *Vocational curriculum for developmentally disabled persons.* Baltimore: University Park Press.

White, O.R. (1980). Adaptive performance objectives: Form versus function. In W. Sailor, B. Wilcox, & L. Brown (Eds.), *Methods of instruction for severely handicapped students* (pp. 47-70). Baltimore: Paul H. Brookes.

Wuerch, B.B., & Voeltz, L.M. (1982). *Longitudinal leisure skills for severely handicapped learners: The Ho'onanea curriculum component.* Baltimore: Paul H. Brookes.

Chapter 9

Physical Management, Handling, and Motor Programming

Bonnie L. Utley

PROBLEMS AND PAST PRACTICES

The problems that confront a teacher of students with severe or profound handicaps fall into four categories. The first is the sometimes overwhelming magnitude of the handicapping conditions. Many students exhibit little or no voluntary movement, present combinations of sensory handicaps in addition to their motor and intellectual deficits, and may be fragile with regard to their health.

The second category of problems is the range of service delivery models in operation. A teacher's responsibilities may range from conducting a "holding area" for therapists to being a primary programmer with input from therapy consultants. The latter model is more desirable, being more efficient in terms of the student's time as well as resulting in more consistent programming. To function effectively in this capacity, however, the teacher must be familiar with the terminology and some of the basic procedures of occupational and physical therapy.

The third category of problems relates to the theoretical model adopted by teachers of this population. It is not uncommon for educators to adopt theoretical models from other disciplines as the basis for educational services. An example of this is the impact of applied behavior analysis in special education. A similar phenomenon has occurred with regard to services for students with severe or profound handicaps. In contrast to applied behavior analysis, however, the literature describing theory and application of treatment approaches such as neurodevelopmental treatment is less accessible to special educators. Additionally, few therapists are taught task analysis, systematic instruction, or measurement, thereby limiting their ability to integrate this information within treatment. Primary service delivery personnel must all have knowledge and skills from multiple disciplines to serve students with severe or profound handicaps effectively.

The final category of problems relates to documentation of past practices. In the late 1970's Banerdt and Bricker (1978) published a study documenting the effectiveness of therapeutic positioning in promoting the acquisition of self-feeding skills by a young student with severe handicaps. Subsequently, however, an analysis of the literature revealed studies that show effects (Norton, 1975; Scherzer, Mike, & Wilson, 1976; Tyler & Kahn, 1976) but have problems with regard to methodology (Noonan, 1984) or that show weak or inconsistent effects (Kuharski, Rues, Cook & Guess, 1985; Sobsey & Orelove, 1984). Exceptions include the work of Campbell and Stewart (1986) and Noonan (1984) that show more dramatic treatment effects, at least for some subjects. Clearly, there is a continuing need for systematic evaluation of the effectiveness of physical management, motor programming, and feeding techniques to clarify which procedures are beneficial for students with severe or profound handicaps.

This chapter addresses some of these problems by providing information on physical management, motor programming, and feeding techniques. Suggested methods of measurement are included to facilitate data collection. *As with classroom-based medical interventions, a word of caution is in order. Many of the methods that are described in this chapter should not be attempted without initial training, continuous follow-up, and supervision by physical and occupational therapists.*

SUGGESTED METHODS

Physical Management

The classic volume by Finnie (1975) remains the best source for clear, concise, and comprehensive information regarding general physical management of students with severe or profound handicaps. It is strongly recommended that the information in the chapters related to movement, principles of handling, carrying, and dressing be mastered, as they provide guidance for solving most of the practical problems (such as putting on shoes and socks) a teacher might encounter throughout the school day. Refer also to Fraser and Hensinger (1983) as another source for general physical management techniques and for information regarding good body mechanics during performance of wheelchair transfers.

A number of preliminary definitions should be given. *Tone* is the degree of tension in a muscle. *Hypertonia* exists when tone is higher than normal.

Hypotonia is the condition in which reduced muscle tone is evident. Tone can fluctuate from one extreme to the other. The amount exhibited by a student is influenced by a variety of factors including position (and the resultant effects of gravity), amount of sensory stimulation, and whether the student is resting or attempting to engage in goal-directed behavior. See Campbell (1987a) for additional information regarding tone normalization.

Flexion is the bending of a joint, and *extension* the straightening of a joint. *Supine* is a postural position where one lays horizontally on the back with face upward. In the *prone* position, one lays horizontally on the stomach with face downward.

In *midline positioning,* the trunk, arms, and legs are aligned in a symmetrical posture. *Abduction* is lateral movement of the limbs away from the midline of the body. *Adduction* is lateral movement of the limbs toward the midline.

Many individuals with severe or profound handicaps exhibit *primitive reflexes.* In individuals who develop normally these reflexes appear early in life and then are integrated into normal movement patterns. Many techniques that are used to assist a student with severe or profound handicaps in instructional settings (such as positioning and handling) must be designed so that these primitive reflexes are inhibited and other normal movement patterns are facilitated. Following is a brief description of some of these primitive reflexes.

- *Asymmetrical Tonic Neck Reflex (ATNR).* Sometimes referred to as the "fencing" posture, the reflex is observed when the individual is supine. If lateral movement (i.e., to the right or left side) of the head occurs, the extremities on the face side extend, while the extremities on the skull side flex. The ATNR is most commonly observed in only one direction and varies in severity. In students with an extreme form of the reflex, the typical posture may also be observed in sitting. The reflex is *obligatory* if the student is unable to return to midline posture independently.
- *Symmetrical Tonic Neck Reflex (STNR).* The STNR is present if: (1) flexion of the chin to the chest results in flexion of the upper extremities and extension of the lower extremities, and (2) extension of the head/neck results in extension of the upper extremities and flexion of the lower extremities. The STNR can be observed with prone, supine, or sitting positions.
- *Tonic Labyrinthine Reflex.* When the individual is supine, the arms and legs show extensor tone. When the individual is prone, flexor tone of the extremities dominates.

- *Positive Supporting Reaction.* When held in a vertical position, placed on the balls of the feet on a hard surface and bounced, the individual exhibits increased extensor tone in the legs.

- *Moro Reflex.* There are two phases to this reflex. In phase 1, sudden extension of the individual's head results in extension and abduction of the arms. In phase 2, the arms flex and adduct.

Handling Techniques

Physical management of students with neuromuscular involvement requires a set of skills that are difficult to teach through written materials alone. The physical "give and take" necessary to control excessive and/or fluctuating muscle tone requires sensitivity to minor tonal changes as well as the confidence to use firm support when necessary to "break up" abnormal patterns (as in hyperextension, where the student displays extension beyond that necessary merely to straighten a part of the body). Because of the difficulty in applying these principles, it is recommended that persons completely unfamiliar with tone normalization activities avail themselves of the guidance of a therapist or skilled teacher/trainer until mastery of these techniques is obtained.

Rotation can be either a handling technique to be used during lifts and carries, an antecedent condition to maximize performance in an instructional program, or a separate target behavior. It should be used for all students. *Rotation* is movement around the body axis. The objective of rotation is to decrease tightness throughout the trunk. This in turn may make breathing easier, normalize tone, and increase voluntary movement. Rotation can be facilitated at the hips and/or shoulders.

Rotation can be either a target behavior or a relaxation technique. The student is positioned on the back on either a partially deflated ball or a mat. A small pillow may be placed behind the neck to bring the chin slightly forward to the chest and limit the amount of extension induced by the supine position. The teacher flexes the student's hips and knees so an angle of approximately 45 degrees (or less) is formed at the hips. The teacher then grasps the student's legs above the knees in one of two ways. For the student with too much external rotation at the hips, the teacher's forearms should be outside the student's thighs with the teacher's fingers over the top of the student's thighs. A maximum separation of two to three inches between the thighs should be allowed (see Figure 9-1). For students whose legs pull tightly together (too much adduction), the opposite arm position should be used with the teacher's forearms inserted between the

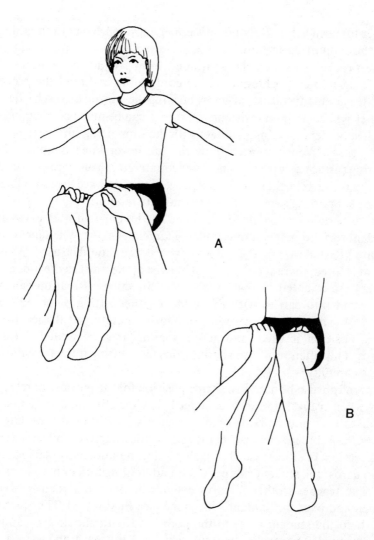

Figure 9-1 Positions for Rotation. **A**, for students with too much external rotation at the hips; **B**, for students with too much adduction (the legs pull tightly together).

student's legs to provide more separation between the knees. After positioning the hands, the teacher should gently move the child's hips together in a swivel motion in as wide an arc as the child's range of motion will allow. If the student's upper trunk moves with the swivel motion, the teacher can reduce the distance of the arc or, if the student is small, the teacher can attempt to control both legs with one hand and arm and place the other forearm across the student's upper chest to keep both shoulders flat on the supporting surface.

These procedures should be continued from five to ten minutes. A simple measurement technique can be used before and after the procedures. Measurement consists of gently pushing the legs once to each side as far as they will go without resistance. A record can be made of whether or not both shoulders remain in contact with the supporting surface (a positive response). Approximately how far the lower knee is above the supporting surface before resistance is encountered can also be measured. If rotation is a target behavior, the objective may be to have the lower knee touch the supporting surface after a ten-minute session.

Rotation should be used during lifts and carries of small students as an antecedent relaxation technique, and as a target behavior. When incorporated into lifts and carries, the following procedure should be used. When a student is lifted, there should be a slight twist at the waist so the hips and shoulders are oriented in slightly opposite directions. Rotation can be incorporated into carries with the student either sitting or prone (see Figure 9-2). The twist at the waist should be maintained if the prone carrying position is used, and gentle shaking may be added if tone increases. This often results in spontaneous head lifting if the transitions are done carefully.

Rotation can also be used in a sitting position for the purpose of relaxation or when trunk rotation is a target behavior. For small students, a position astride one or both of the teacher's legs is used. For larger students, both student and teacher may sit astride a barrel or roll facing the same direction. In either case, the teacher holds the student by placing one forearm across the student's upper chest and holding him or her near the axilla. The teacher's other forearm extends across the student's lower abdomen and over the student's hip bone (see Figure 9-3). The teacher should hold the student close to the body, and both should be leaning slightly forward. The teacher then twists his or her body at the waist and provides a push in opposite directions at the student's hips and upper body. The direction of the push should alternate every 10 to 15 seconds or after resistance to the movement ceases. The following record can be made if a measurement system is desired. Before and after the session the teacher should provide the push at the shoulders only. A crease or "wrinkle" in the trunk at or slightly above the waist is considered a positive response, as the hips must remain oriented in a forward direction for the crease to appear. This measurement requires that the student's shirt be lifted slightly for ease of observation.

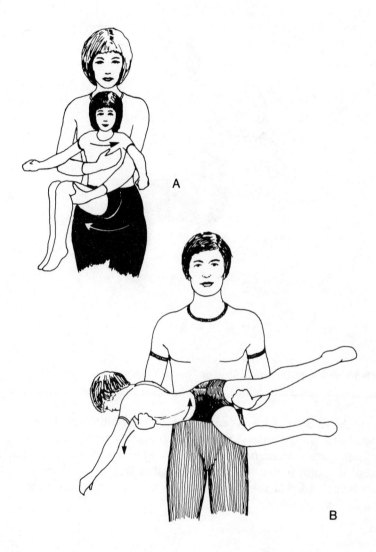

Figure 9-2 Trunk Rotation in Carrying. **A**, in a sitting position; **B**, in the prone position.

The final use of rotation as a handling technique is in a side-lying position for students who are too large to be easily accommodated in a sitting position. The student should be positioned in side-lying with good body alignment (see the following section). The teacher usually kneels behind the student's back and places one hand on the student's shoulders and the

Figure 9-3 Trunk Rotation with Student on Teacher's Leg.

other on the student's hips. A gentle pushing and pulling movement is then provided with the shoulders and hips alternating in forward and backward directions. A measurement procedure similar to the one just described can be used to monitor the effectiveness of this technique. A push or pull should be provided at the shoulders only with concomitant observation for a crease at the waist.

Positioning

Positioning, like handling, should be used as an antecedent event in programming for students with neuromuscular involvement. Too many classrooms are conducted according to a schedule that requires only that students be positioned with an attractive toy or mobile within reach. Although there are limited times during the school day when this arrangement is necessary (such as during staff lunch breaks), therapeutic positioning without systematic instruction is insufficient to meet the educational needs of these students. Positioning should be viewed instead as a facilitator to maximum participation in educational tasks. For organizational reasons, however, the remainder of this section describes general principles of positioning followed by specific suggestions for each of the most common positions. Specific examples of positioning as an antecedent event are included in the next section.

The goals of therapeutic positioning are good body alignment and normalization of muscle tone. Correct body alignment helps lessen the devastating effects seen when certain muscle groups exert disproportionate force on the student's body. This results in spinal curvature and/or deformities at the joints. Normalization of muscle tone permits freedom from tightness (or stability for students with fluctuating tone) and the possibility for more normal movement.

The first step in achieving these goals is to observe each student in his or her typical position. The following abnormal patterns are commonly seen: In supine, the student's head and shoulders are pushed back into the supporting surface and the hips are extended. The legs are stiff and straight and held tightly together (so tightly they may cross in a "scissor" pattern). Variations in this pattern may include emergence of an ATNR. Also possible is a position where the arms are extended with the shoulders rolled forward and hands tightly fisted. Another common deviation is seen in the hip position of some students. These students show flexion at the hips and knees with external rotation at the hips. These abnormal patterns are illustrated in Figure 9-4.

After observing each student's typical posture, more normal tone can usually be encouraged by *reversing* the student's abnormal patterns and/or movement. Students with extreme deviations in tone (very high or very low) will show little spontaneous movement. The goal for students with excessive tone is positioning that provides relaxation so more normal movement can be initiated. For students with low tone, stability and support should be provided at the shoulders, hips, and throughout the trunk as needed to give a secure base for spontaneous movement. For students who show almost continuous movement (often from one abnormal reflex to another), support and stability at the key points of head/neck, shoulders, and hips are required.

The final general consideration in therapeutic positioning is an analysis of the effects of gravity on a student's body. Despite the resistance encountered in handling students with abnormal tone, they are weak rather than strong in their ability to move against the force of gravity. Gravity, however, can be used to advantage through good positioning. Examples of how these general guidelines operate in various positions follow.

Prone positioning is beneficial for some students as it may encourage development of strength in the shoulder area and spontaneous head lifting. Proper prone positioning requires the following:

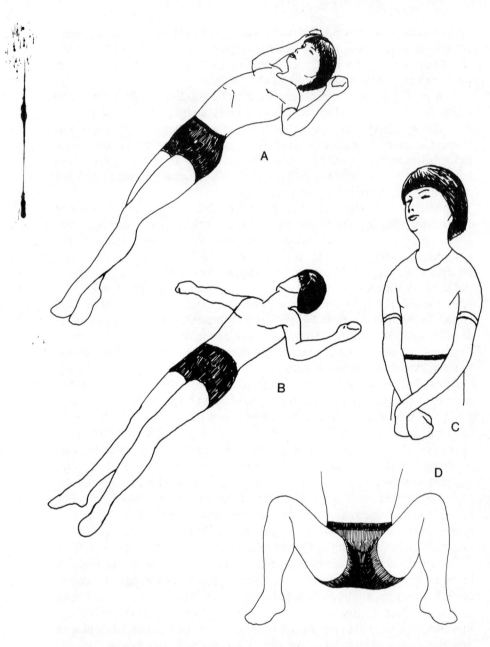

Figure 9-4 Common Abnormal Patterns. **A**, Head and shoulders pushed back into the supporting surface with extended hips and "scissored" legs; **B**, ATNR; **C**, Rounded shoulders with extended arms and fisted hands; **D**, Externally rotated hips with flexion at hips and knees.

- The supporting surface must be of appropriate height. The student should be able to bear weight on either elbows or open hands.

- The student should be placed far enough forward on the supporting surface to allow for weight bearing on the upper extremities. The edge of the supporting surface should be at the student's axilla.

- Good body alignment can be promoted through placing long sandbags on both sides of the trunk. Sandbags may also help prevent the student from rolling off the wedge or roll if tone increases.

- Many students show extreme extension in the prone position. This can be alleviated somewhat by correct positioning of the feet. A small roll or sandbag can be placed under the student's ankles to provide

Figure 9-5 Positioning in Prone. **A,** Typical use of a wedge; **B,** Wedge reversed to promote postural drainage, head lifting, and slight weight bearing on lower extremities.

slight flexion at the knees. In addition to reducing extension, the roll allows the force of gravity to pull the student's feet into a more normal position and puts a slight and beneficial stretch on the heel chords. See Figure 9-5 for an illustration of prone positioning.

- For students who show extension in the prone position, the typical use of a wedge can be reversed. The student can be placed to bear weight on the elbows at the low end of the wedge. The student's hips are flexed at an angle less than 90 degrees so weight is also borne on the knees (refer to Figure 9-5 for an illustration). In addition to controlling extension, this use of a wedge may increase head lifting because of the inverted position and aid in postural drainage (drainage of congestion from throat and chest).

- Gradual transition into the prone position may reduce extension. It is often helpful to place the student on the wedge or roll in a side-lying position first. Relaxation is then induced by gentle shaking and trunk rotation. The arms are gradually extended over the edge of the wedge as the body is rolled slowly over into prone.

Supine positioning is the least desirable for therapeutic purposes as it is a typical position for many students and one in which little freedom of movement is possible. Supine positioning puts pressure on the back of the skull and may increase extension. The head may also deviate easily from midline, resulting in an ATNR. Supine positioning can be used for short periods of the day, however, if the following precautions are taken:

- Flexion of the chin to the chest should be provided to lessen pressure of the skull against the supporting surface and increase the student's visual field.

- Small pillows can be placed under the student's shoulders if they are retracted (pushed back). The pillows increase the possibility for movement of the upper extremities and hand-to-hand contact.

- Flexion should be provided at the hips and knees, and the feet should be as flat as possible on the supporting surface. This adaptation can be provided by placing large sandbags along the student's hips and ankles. Correct supine positioning is shown in Figure 9-6.

Positioning in side-lying is one of the most beneficial positions, especially for students who exhibit an ATNR or have flat chests. In side-lying, gravity prevents deviation of the head from midline (and subsequent emergence of the ATNR) and provides a pull to bring the rib cage into its more normal rounded position. The side-lying position promotes relaxa-

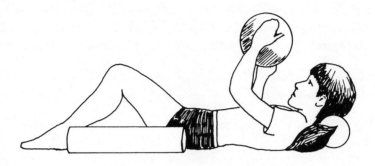

Figure 9-6 Positioning in Supine.

tion for students with high tone, allows eye-hand activities, and provides good alignment of the spine. The elements of good side-lying positioning are as follows:

- The student's head should be in alignment with the spine. This can be accomplished by use of a small pillow under the head if necessary. The head should also be flexed slightly forward to assist in maintaining this position and promoting visually directed upper extremity movement.

- The lower shoulder should be brought far enough forward to free the elbow from being trapped under the trunk. This allows better alignment of the spine, helps decrease rolling out of the position, and allows two-handed activities.

- The hips, knees, and ankles should form 90-degree angles to promote relaxation and maintenance of the position.

- A small pillow should be placed between the knees and ankles if they are extremely bony. If the student exhibits adductor spasticity (the legs pull tightly together), experimentation with the use of a cushion between the knees may be required. A soft pillow *may* stimulate more adduction and a harder substance (such as Styrofoam covered with cloth) may be used.

- As in prone positioning, the transition into side-lying should be gradual. Intermittent rotation will promote relaxation and prolong the time the position is maintained.

The *sitting position* is beneficial for performance of preacademic, fine motor, and communication programming as it helps provide free movement of the upper extremities. The availability of adapted wheelchairs has increased significantly in the past few years, but certain guidelines remain regarding a correct sitting position. The most important are:

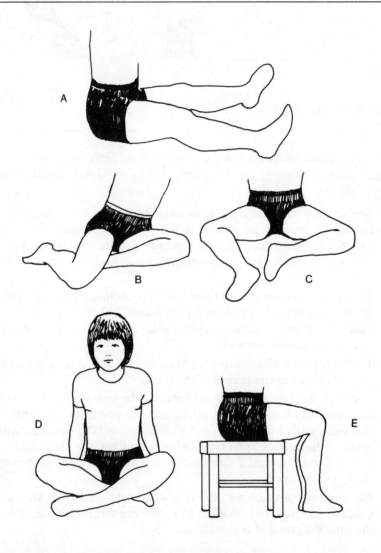

Figure 9-7 Positioning in Sitting. **A**, Long sitting; **B**, Side sitting; **C**, Ring (circle) sitting; **D**, Tailor (Indian style) sitting; **E**, Sitting on a low stool.

- The depth of the chair seat should be modified to ensure that the student is sitting well up on the buttocks rather than on the lumbar vertebrae. The knees and hips should form 90-degree angles, and the feet should rest firmly on the floor or a footrest.
- For students with extreme extension, an angle of less than 90 degrees at the hips is sometimes recommended, especially during feeding. With some students, however, the decreased angle allows the student enough leverage to push into extension with foot pressure on the supporting surface.
- A vest or harness may be necessary for students with inadequate trunk stability. If a chest support is used, an attempt should be made to loosen the straps gradually over time to increase trunk strength.
- The recommended sitting positions for students with too much external rotation at the hips are long-sitting and side-sitting to alternate sides (see Figure 9-7).
- The recommended sitting positions for students with too much internal rotation at the hips and adductor spasticity are ring sitting, tailor (or Indian style) sitting, and side-sitting (see Figure 9-7).
- For students with low tone, sitting on a wooden box or stool of appropriate height (feet flat on the floor) is recommended to increase trunk control (see Figure 9-7). Any other sitting position is also appropriate for these students unless there is too much external rotation at the hips, in which case long-sitting and side-sitting to alternate sides are preferred.
- For students positioned in a corner chair, the same guidelines apply regarding seat depth and vests. An additional suggestion is the use of dowel rods to assist in proper alignment of the hips and legs. For students with too much external rotation at the hips, padded dowel rods can be placed on the outside of the legs to encourage long-sitting and extension at both knees and hips. For students with adductor spasticity, the dowel rods should be placed between the legs to encourage more abduction (see Figure 9-8).

The availability of prone boards has greatly simplified and increased the use of the *standing position.* The benefits of standing are many, including improved bowel and bladder function, decreased flexion contractures (permanent shortening of a muscle-tendon unit) at the hips, knees, and ankles, and prevention of brittle long leg bones. Its most important benefit is a possible decrease in the incidence of hip dislocation. Measurement and fitting for a prone board are usually completed by a

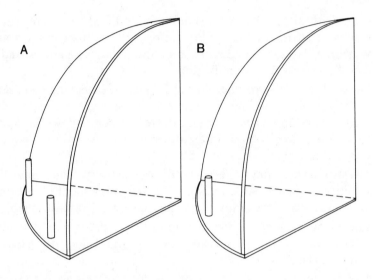

Figure 9-8 Use of Dowel Rods in a Corner Chair. **A,** Dowels outside the legs to encourage long sitting (for students with too much external rotation at the hips); **B,** Dowel between the legs to separate legs held tightly together.

therapist or an adaptive equipment salesperson. The following are some guidelines that govern positioning in standing.

- The legs should be separated slightly with the hips in alignment (as indicated by both feet pointing straight ahead).
- The knees should be flexed slightly.
- Both feet should be flat and parallel.

These positioning guidelines are meant to be applied in a trial and error fashion. The distribution of tone and combination of abnormal reflex activity vary tremendously from student to student. Many of the techniques must be combined to meet the varied needs of this population. The presence of good body alignment and normalized muscle tone should be the final factor in determining whether a particular position or handling technique is appropriate for an individual student.

There are three other physical management skills that are extremely valuable in providing quality services to students with severe or profound handicaps. The first two are co-contraction and joint approximation. The appropriate use of these techniques requires well-developed judgment regarding good body alignment. Refer to Buttram and Brown (1977) for information on these techniques as well as to a therapist for supervised practice in their application. The third physical management skill is the development of equilibrium and righting reactions. Refer to Bobath and Bobath (1972), Buttram and Brown (1977), and Johnson (1978) for theoretical information and illustrated instructions on the appropriate use of these techniques.

Motor Programming

This section includes strategies that may be used to program for development of gross and fine motor skills. The selection of a particular strategy should be done in conjunction with a therapist as the type and distribution of abnormal tone vary from one student to another. Implementation of each strategy should be measured, and decisions regarding continued use of a strategy should be made on the basis of student performance data.

Assessment

Assessment is one of the basics of program development. At this time, however, there are no completely satisfactory assessment models in the area of motor development for this population. Individual patterns of neuromuscular involvement and the presence of sensory deficits make reliance on a single assessment instrument unlikely. The conflict between the developmental and functional/remedial models has not yet been clearly resolved. This is due, at least in part, to individual factors such as the student's age and present and future home and school environments, all of which should contribute to the selection of priority skills for assessment and intervention. The presence of noncompliant behavior also complicates assessment because of the difficulty in discriminating which skills a student *will not* do from those he or she *cannot* do. The solution to this dilemma lies in synthesizing portions of a number of assessment models into one in which the following factors are considered:

- the student's age
- the student's present and future school and home environments
- parental priorities
- noncompliance and/or other behavior problems
- gross developmental level in all areas

- the presence of a functional operant response to be used in language/cognitive programming

Refer to Bricker and Campbell (1980); Brown (1987); and Gaylord-Ross and Holvoet (1985) for information that should contribute to the development of a functional, highly individualized assessment model.

Teaching Strategies

A number of systematic instructional strategies are available to teachers of students with severe or profound handicaps. Many of these are described in Falvey, Brown, Lyon, Baumgart, and Schroeder (1980); Liberty, Haring, and Martin (1981); and Snell and Zirpoli (1987). There is, however, an additional strategy of particular use in programming skill acquisition for this population. The strategy requires development of a well-defined shaping procedure. There are two applications of systematic shaping. The first is used for training active motor responses (such as reaching). The motor response is task analyzed until the smallest final component of the behavior is determined. The student is then put through all earlier steps in the task analysis and only the final segment is required. An example is a program to teach the response of reaching toward and touching a toy. The student is positioned to promote maximum freedom of movement. The teacher grasps the student's dominant arm and provides upward support against gravity. The arm is then extended until contact with the toy is made. This is reinforced enthusiastically. The teacher then extends the arm to the toy a second time but stops within one-half to one inch of contact. The student is required to extend the arm slightly to touch the toy in order to receive reinforcement. If a correct response is not made, the distance is shortened even further until an active correct response is made. The amount of prompting decreases in one-half- to one-inch increments over a series of training sessions as the student improves.

There are two differences between systematic shaping and what is more commonly done. Shaping requires that each trial end with an active response on the part of the student rather than the student being put through the correct response as a consequence for failure to perform correctly. The latter may result in the student receiving gradually increasing amounts of reinforcement for passive performance.

The second difference between shaping and more typical programming is that the student has an opportunity to experience the correct response before any effort is required. For students with little voluntary movement, motivation, or contingency awareness, this practice trial may clarify the contingent relationship necessary for reinforcement to be forthcoming.

The second application of systematic shaping is in training behaviors that are static (require the student to maintain a position). An example is in training balance in standing. If the goal is ten seconds of independent standing, the first step in the program is positioning the student in standing and providing support (downward pressure at the hips or shoulders) for nine to nine and one-half seconds. Support is then lessened, and a record is made of whether the student maintains independent standing for one-half to one second. As that criterion is reached, support is provided less and less over a series of sessions (decreasing in one-second increments).

This strategy has been effective with a number of students who are passive during instruction. It requires careful measurement of student performance, however, so that appropriate decisions regarding when a change in the level of physical prompting can be made.

Measurement

Precise, daily measurement should accompany systematic instruction to give direction to the teacher regarding the success/failure of the procedures, for accountability reasons, and to reinforce the teacher by providing evidence of small improvements in behavior.

Two types of measurement are possible. The first is *direct* measurement of the behavior as it is occurring. Examples include *percentage correct* or number correct *(frequency)* out of a set number of opportunities to respond, *duration,* counting the *number of prompts,* and recording the *levels of assistance* (verbal cue, gesture, etc.) required before the student makes a correct response. *Indirect* measurement is used when a particular technique is conducted for a specified time and a record is made as to whether or not the technique produced the desired result (as with determining the presence or absence of a "crease" at the waist after rotation). Examples of both types of measurement accompany the suggested gross and fine motor training strategies that follow.

Gross Motor: Head Control

Initial head control is typically taught in either (or both) the prone or supine position. In the prone position, the student is placed over a wedge or roll, and a noisemaker or attractive toy is used to encourage head lifting. In the supine position, the child is pulled to a sitting position, and the presence or absence of head "lag" (failure of the head to remain in alignment with the spine as the trunk is raised) is noted. Both procedures have some merit, but more systematic instruction is needed for many students to acquire this skill. The following strategies may be effective in the development of head control.

>*Head Control Strategy 1.* The student is placed in a prone position over a wedge or roll. The head is lifted gently into alignment with the spine with the teacher's less dominant hand. Control of the head is lessened gradually and replaced by gentle tapping of the student's forehead if the head begins to fall forward. Reinforcement in the form of verbal praise and/or a more tangible reward such as music (e.g., a radio with the volume preset and controlled with an on/off switch) is used *only* for those segments of time during which the student exerts effort to maintain head erect behavior.

This strategy differs from more traditional methods because verbal encouragement and tangible items (potential reinforcers) are used only as consequent rather than as antecedent events (the student receives attention when performing the behavior *not* before performing it). Another difference is that the student is provided with an opportunity to experience the "feel" of a correct response rather than having to experiment with other responses (such as head turning) that may be undesirable. Finally, it is easier to maintain a head lift than it is to lift the head from a lower position. The latter often results only in extension without true head lifting.

An appropriate measurement technique for this strategy is to count the number of times (out of ten, for example) that head lifting is maintained for more than three seconds after removal of support. As duration of head lifting consistently exceeds three seconds, another measure, such as mean duration of head lifting across ten opportunities, can be used.

>*Head Control Strategy 2.* This strategy requires use of trunk rotation and side-sitting (see Figure 9-9). The height of the teacher's knee may be modified during this procedure as needed. If the student's head and neck hyperextend (fall or extend backward to rest on the back), the teacher's knee should be lowered. If the student's head falls forward, the knee should be elevated slightly. If extreme extension occurs, the trainer's leg can be gently bounced to provide relaxation.

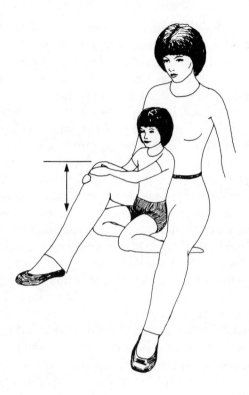

Figure 9-9 Position for Head Control Strategy 2—Trunk Rotation and Side-sitting. Teacher should modify height of knee (indicated by arrow) to control position of the student's head.

An appropriate measurement technique for this strategy is to measure total duration out of a ten-minute period in which head erect behavior occurred.

Gross Motor: Sitting

Traditional training in many gross motor milestones consists of placing the student in position (side-sitting, for example), withdrawing support, and measuring the duration of independent performance. It is not uncommon for the student to end a trial by falling over when his or her limit is reached; nor is it uncommon for reinforcement to be delivered after the student ceases independent performance. To correct this misapplication of behavioral principles, a *changing criterion design* (Hartman & Hall, 1976) should be used. Its use first requires baseline measurement of the behavior until stable performance is documented. The mean performance should be determined, and a level slightly above the mean should be the goal for the initial step of training. For example, if mean duration levels of sitting behavior across four days of baseline are 6, 5, 7, and 5 seconds, respectively, the mean is 4.6 seconds and an appropriate goal for training is 6 seconds. Each training trial for this step would consist of placing the child in the appropriate position, withdrawing support, and starting the stopwatch. Verbal and/or tangible reinforcement would be provided during the time the behavior is performed and cease if the student stops performing. When the goal of 6 seconds is reached, the trial would be *interrupted* by the teacher by reintroducing support and/or hugging the student. After an interval of rest, the student would be repositioned, and another trial would begin. As soon as the goal is met (80% or more of the trials in three of five sessions), the next training step with a slightly higher criterion would begin.

Programming according to a changing criterion design prevents accidental reinforcement of the termination of the behavior and the punishing consequence of having the student fall when he or she tires. Collection of baseline data is critical to the success of this procedure as the training goals (especially the initial one) must be within the student's capability. The design can be applied to training any motor milestone in which increased duration is the goal. This approach forms the basis for Sitting Strategy 1.

Sitting Strategy 1. The student is placed in a side-sitting position with some trunk rotation provided by a slight twist at the waist. His or her arms should be extended, and weight should be borne on open hands. Placement of the hands in relation to the body should be adjusted until sitting balance is obtained in as upright a position as possible. The legs should be semiflexed at the hips and knees. When secure sitting balance is obtained, support is gradually withdrawn, and timing of independent performance is begun. Reinforcement should accompany correct sitting behavior. When the goal is reached, the student's body should be supported, a brief rest period should be provided, and the trial should be repeated to the opposite side.

Measurement during the changing criterion design differs from baseline to training conditions. Baseline data are used to establish initial training goals and consist of mean duration of target behavior per session. Training steps consist of a preset goal, and a running record of each trial is made.

Exhibit 9-1 Partially Completed Data Sheet Showing Progression of Data for Changing Criterion Design

| Student: | D. Miller | | | Program: Side-sitting (Propped both arms) |
| Teacher: | K. Ferrel | | | Next Program: Side-sitting (Propped one arm) |

	Baseline				Training Step 1 Goal 6 Secs.					Training Step 2 Goal 8 Secs.					
Date:	8/24	8/25	8/26	8/28	8/31	9/1	9/2	9/3	9/4	9/7	9/8	9/10	9/11	9/14	9/15
Trial 1	7	5	7	4	5	5	6	6	6	6	9	5	8	8	10
Trial 2	5	4	8	6	6	4	5	5	6	8	10	9	8	7	9
Trial 3	6	6	5	4	7	7	5	7	7	9	8	10	11	10	8
Trial 4	5	4	7	6	8	6	7	8	8	8	8	8	6	9	11
Trial 5	7	6	8	5	6	7	6	6	7	6	6	6	7	8	9
x	6	5	7	5	80%	60%	60%	80%	100%	60%	80%	60%	60%	80%	100%

The percentage of trials that meet or exceed the goal is computed. Changes in the criterion are made based on these data. A partially complete data sheet showing this progression is presented in Exhibit 9-1.

In programming for sitting or any other "static" motor milestone (kneeling, standing, etc.), it is important to program two other skills concurrently. The first is the set of *transition behaviors* that surround the milestone. In this case the transition behaviors are assuming side-sitting from side-lying positions and moving from side-sitting to side-lying positions. Increasing duration of a behavior without training in transitional skills does little to increase the student's overall motor development and independence. The second related skill is *protective reactions* (the ability to "catch" oneself if balance is lost) in that position. Protective reactions would be taught concurrently with the example outlined in Strategy 1 because they develop normally in conjunction with or just after propping in that position.

The training of transition behaviors and protective reactions in conjunction with motor milestones can be done in a common-sense sequence. The transition is trained first, followed by a trial on the static milestone. Several opportunities for protective reactions to be demonstrated are then provided. Additional trials on the static milestone are followed by training on the transition out of the position. This sequence represents one application of the Individualized Curriculum Sequencing

(ICS) model. See Gaylord-Ross and Holvoet (1985) for additional information on the use of this model in the motor domain.

> *Sitting Strategy 2.* The student is placed in a sitting position facing away from the teacher with legs abducted over one or both of the trainer's thighs. The student's back should be within two to three inches of the teacher's trunk. The student's hips and knees should be flexed at angles of 90 degrees or less, and the feet should rest firmly on the floor. Support (downward pressure) is initially given at the shoulders with the shoulders rounded slightly forward. When balance is obtained and the head is in alignment with the spine, support is moved (one hand at a time) from the shoulders down to the hip bones, where downward pressure is again applied. The teacher should gently bounce the student on his or her legs if extension begins. If extension is severe, the teacher should lean forward and push the student's trunk forward with his or her trunk (providing flexion at the hips) until extension subsides.

Gross Motor: Hands and Knees Position (All Fours)

The hands and knees position is beneficial for development of arm and shoulder strength and is necessary for the development of creeping.

> *All Fours Strategy 1.* The procedure described below can be used to train the transition from side-sitting to the all fours position. The procedure begins with the student in side-sitting with arms extended and weight bearing on open hands. The hand position should be at approximately a 45-degree angle to the student's midline. When the student is stable in this position, the following instructional/task analysis is performed.
>
> 1. Gently move the student's hands two to three inches from their initial position, away from the student.
> 2. Slide the underneath leg slightly back and away from the hands and move the top leg slightly forward.
> 3. Slip one hand under the student's lower hip and elevate the hips three to four inches.
> 4. Continue upward support of the hips but add a tapping movement, which is repeated two or three times.

5. Slide the underneath leg back and away from the hands and move the top leg slightly forward again, making sure the hips and knees remain flexed at approximately 90 degrees.
6. Continue tapping the hips in an upward direction until weight is borne on the knees.
7. Make adjustments of body alignment until the legs are parallel and weight is borne on all four extremities.
8. Maintain this position for 20 to 30 seconds. Reinforce with music or an active toy.
9. Repeat the steps in reverse order to return the student to the side-sitting position.

Measurement of this skill can consist of counting the number of voluntary adjustments the student makes to bear weight during performance of the analysis. The number of taps required before the student assumes the all fours position can also be counted.

All Fours Strategy 2. This strategy requires an inflatable cylinder. The cylinder should be wide enough in diameter to fit underneath the student's trunk and provide slight support in the all fours position. The procedure begins with the cylinder in place on the mat or floor and the student tall-kneeling (trunk extended vertically) next to it with the teacher behind. The teacher grasps the student's arms just below the shoulders and extends them (by shaking them gently if necessary) at an angle of approximately 45 degrees above shoulder level. The teacher then brings the student forward and down until weight is borne on open hands and the student is supported throughout the trunk by the cylinder. The position should be maintained for 20 to 30 seconds with reinforcement provided by music or an active toy. During this interval the teacher should produce downward pressure, alternating between pressure at the shoulders and hips.

Measurement should consist of recording whether or not the student maintains the position for the desired length of time. Phases of the program should be outlined, and inflation of the cylinder and downward pressure should both be faded over time.

Gross Motor: The Progression to Upright Posture

The following may be used to train a student to adopt upright posture. Before this progression is begun, the student should be able to tall-kneel for short periods and have adequate protective reactions.

> *Strategy.* The student should be in the all fours position with the teacher behind. When stability is obtained on all fours (by providing short episodes of downward pressure at the shoulders and hips if necessary), the pelvis should be shifted slightly to the right side so weight is borne on the right knee. The left leg is placed in a squat position so that the left foot is flat on the floor. The teacher's left leg should be placed outside the student's leg to provide support. The pelvis should be shifted to the left so weight is borne on that leg. A one- to two-second pause should occur to see if the right leg spontaneously adopts the squat position. If not, the right leg should be prompted into that position. Another pause of a few seconds should occur for balance to be obtained in the full squat position. To facilitate this, the student's weight should be forward of the body axis. The teacher then either offers a hand for support at the upper extremities if the student has good voluntary grasp or provides support at the trunk just below the axilla. A slight lift is provided, and the student should rise to standing.

Gross Motor: Simulated Standing

Many students are too involved to bear weight in the normal fashion. Limited benefits of weight bearing (particularly proper hip formation) can be provided by a simulated standing program.

> *Strategy.* A large, heavy barrel is needed. The barrel is preferable to a therapy ball because only front/back movement is needed. The student should be placed in a prone position over the top of the barrel with arms extended or flexed so weight is borne on the elbows. The teacher kneels behind the student and separates the student's legs slightly (abduction) with external rotation at the hips. The feet are supported at the arches by having them rest in the palms of the teacher's hands. A 90-degree angle should be formed at the ankles. Relaxation is produced by slowly rolling the barrel forward and back. When the student is relaxed, he or she is rolled back toward the teacher until some of the student's body weight is borne on the teacher's hands. This position should be

maintained for 20 to 30 seconds or until tone increases, in which case the barrel is rolled forward again, and relaxation is provided. The barrel can be rolled far enough back to allow the student to bear weight on the floor if capable. If the latter adaptation is used, the student's weight should be shifted gradually from the teacher's hands to the floor.

This procedure should be carried out for an eight- to ten-minute period. The total length of time the student bears weight should be recorded.

Gross Motor: Walking

Some students with severe or profound handicaps can walk with support but lose their balance easily because of instability in the trunk. The following procedures are designed to increase trunk strength and balance but are carried out just before the time walking will be required.

Strategy. Place the student on a barrel so that the legs straddle it. The teacher straddles the barrel behind the student and places his or her hands on the student's hips to provide support. The barrel is rolled to the left six to eight inches. The student should arch the trunk so that the shoulders move to the right. The arch should occur within five to ten seconds. The barrel is returned to its original position, and upright alignment of the trunk should follow. The barrel is then rolled to the right six to eight inches, and the student should arch the trunk again but with the shoulders moving to the left. The barrel is returned to its original position, and the entire sequence is repeated five times.

Two measures of the effectiveness of this procedure are possible. The first is a record of whether the student arches within five to ten seconds of each shift in space. The second is a count of the number of times the student loses balance while walking a certain distance (such as 30 feet) immediately after the procedures.

Fine Motor Development

Adequate fine motor performance requires that the student be positioned well to normalize tone as much as possible and to control reflex activity. Control of the hands is dependent on stability and control in the upper extremity joints close to the trunk of the body (the elbow and shoulder joints). Training fine motor behavior, therefore, should begin with gross arm movements and gradually progress to more refined responses.

Fine Motor: Reaching

The student should be positioned with a table or wheelchair tray placed slightly above waist level. The teacher should face the student and cup a hand around the shoulder joint of the student's preferred upper extremity to provide stability and direct the arm toward midline. The hand should also provide a slight lift to offset the force of gravity and make arm movements easier. The teacher then positions the other hand (or toy, functional object, etc.) within one to two inches of the student's hand. The teacher cues the student to touch the stimulus, and pauses. If the student touches the stimulus within five to ten seconds, he or she is reinforced. If he or she fails to respond correctly, the teacher should move the student's arm (at the shoulder) through the correct response, back to its original position, and then present the cue again. The student must then make some small movement toward the stimulus to be reinforced.

Measurement should be divided into phases according to the distance the student must move. A weighted scoring system can be used that gives the student two points for touching after the initial cue, one point after the prompt and cue have been presented again, and zero points if the student fails to respond. As the number of points earned is equal to or above 80% of the total points possible, the required distance should increase.

Fine Motor: Grasping

The same position described in the previous strategy is used. The student's preferred upper extremity should be flexed at the elbow and rest on the wheelchair tray or table. If the student has high tone, a crayon, pencil, or something similar should be inserted into a cone-shaped cylinder. This will assist in normalizing tone in the hand and arm. If the student has low tone, a soft material such as foam should cover the object to be held. The object is then inserted into the student's hand, and the teacher holds the student's hand around it for four to four-and-one-half seconds. The teacher's grasp loosens, and the student should maintain the grasp for one-half to one second. The teacher should offer support again and put the student through a scribbling response as a consequence for grasping. The amount of teacher prompting should be systematically faded over time.

Measurement is again divided into phases dependent on the amount of teacher prompting. The level of prompting decreases in one-half- to one-second increments over time as an 80% criterion at each level is reached.

Fine Motor: Release

The procedures to promote release occur in two stages. The first is slight extension at the elbow with simultaneous cueing to release. A pause of a few seconds is given. If extension at the elbow does not produce release, a second procedure should follow. This procedure requires gentle bending of the hand downward at the wrist joint to produce extension of the fingers and release.

Release can also be measured with a weighted scoring system. The student can be given two points for releasing the object after extension at the elbow, one point after bending at the wrist, and zero points if the object must be removed manually.

Feeding Techniques

The poor coordination seen in students with neuromuscular involvement is not restricted to overall body patterns but is also seen in the oral musculature. Abnormal or primitive oral patterns necessitate systematic feeding techniques to ensure adequate intake of nutrients (both liquid and solid) during the six-hour school day.

The responsibilities an individual teacher has for feeding depend on the service delivery model in operation. A basic understanding of feeding and eating, however, is necessary for all professionals who serve this population.

Assessment

The expertise of an occupational or speech therapist is critically important during feeding assessment. This is due to the many factors that need to be considered, including assessment of oral reflexes, oral hypersensitivity, and responses to texture. The staffing available for services to students with physical handicaps varies from program to program, but almost all programs have access to therapists for initial assessment. In those rare instances where consultant services are not available, the teacher should contact the nearest university medical center (or similar agency) so that a comprehensive feeding evaluation can be completed for all students in need of such services.

Although feeding assessment should be completed by a therapist, teachers should know the areas to be assessed and be able to assist in the process (and periodic re-evaluation) if necessary. Refer to Campbell (1979) and Morris (1982a & 1982b) for assessment guidelines. In general, the following areas should be evaluated:

- overall muscle tone
- abnormal or primitive total body reflexes
- gross motor developmental level
- abnormal or primitive oral reflexes
- feeding patterns (such as tongue movements)

Positioning for Feeding

During the feeding process, the student should be seated upright with hips and knees at 90-degree angles and the feet flat. The head position is important in all therapeutic positioning because of the role it has in controlling extensor tone and abnormal reflex activity. The head position becomes even more important during the feeding process because of the danger of choking and aspirating food. The head must be in midline with slight flexion of the chin to the chest to promote an active swallow. For students who lack even minimal head control, the correct head position should be provided by adaptations of the seating equipment.

In some instances (e.g., a very large student with a heavy head), positioning in a fully upright position can be difficult. A slight backward tilt of the supportive equipment may help stabilize the head. If the tilted position is used, a small roll must be placed behind the student's neck to provide slight flexion of the chin to the chest. This is necessary to avoid the hazards of "bird feeding."

Position of the Feeder

Two feeding positions are commonly seen. The first and most common is face-to-face with the student. In the face-to-face position, jaw control (and/or manipulation of the oral musculature) is provided from the front (see Figure 9-10). This position is beneficial for feeding students who tend to show extensor tone. In this case, the face-to-face position permits the feeder to rest the side of the wrist and forearm of the hand, providing jaw control on the student's sternum at midline. If extension begins, the feeder can put firm pressure on the sternum with the forearm in combination with gentle shaking from side to side to normalize tone. Pressure on the sternum tends to bring the student's chin down to the chest, thereby interrupting the extension pattern. The face-to-face position also permits eye contact and is conducive to speech-building activities. The feeder should

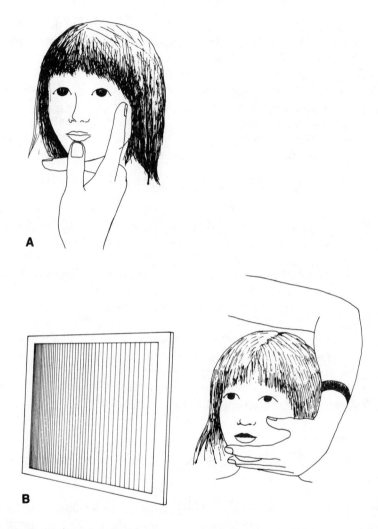

Figure 9-10 Positions for Providing Jaw Control. **A**, Jaw control from the front; **B**, Jaw control from the side and back with both teacher and student facing a mirror.

sit very close to the student, however, and maintain the student's upright sitting position to minimize strain on the lower back.

The second possible position for the feeder is next to the student, with jaw control provided from around the back and side of the student (see Figure 9-10). This position is *not* recommended for students with an ATNR unless the feeder's hand preference and student's ATNR side are such that the feeder can be positioned on the opposite side of the student's predominant head turn. The side-by-side position is less conducive to social interaction during the feeding process, and the feeder may have difficulty seeing during use of the intervention strategies. For this reason, both the student and teacher may face a mirror. It is, however, the preferred position for presenting liquids from a cup.

The position of the food should also be considered. It should be placed within easy reach of the feeder so the spoon can be refilled without interruption of jaw control.

Intervention Strategies for Feeding Problems

This section describes specific intervention strategies for several of the most common feeding problems. Refer also to Campbell (1979); Connor, Williamson, and Siepp (1978); and Morris (1982a & 1982b) for additional information regarding intervention strategies.

The importance of team service delivery cannot be overemphasized. Selection of priority target behaviors and appropriate intervention strategies should be a team process with input from a variety of professionals as well as parents.

Most students will present only a portion of the problems these strategies are designed to remediate. Also, some of the strategies (such as correct spoon presentation) are appropriate interventions for a variety of feeding difficulties. Therefore, a combination of strategies appropriate for the problems presented by each student must be selected.

Precautions

A number of precautions should be considered before and during the feeding process.

- The medical information available on each student should be scrutinized. Look for information regarding food allergies and any mention of anatomical deformities in the respiratory or digestive systems that could interfere with the feeding process.
- Each student should be assessed for the ability to breathe through the nose before implementation of intervention. This is done by holding a small mirror directly beneath the student's nostrils to see if two distinct "clouds" appear during exhalation of air. Jaw control should be used during this procedure if the student has a habitually open mouth. If clouding fails to occur, the student should be examined by a physician to see if mouth breathing is a habit or whether there are anatomical reasons for failure to breathe through the nose.

For students who are habitual mouth breathers and for those with obvious colds and congestion, jaw control and other procedures that interfere with mouth breathing should be used for only 15 to 20 seconds.

- Many students respond to ingestion of dairy products with additional mucous production. For this reason, end each meal with a glass of water or tart juice to rinse milky residue remaining in the mouth.

- Students with inadequate lip closure and/or tongue thrust are messy to feed. Food is often expelled from the mouth and runs down the chin. Care must be taken to *blot* rather than wipe the facial area every three or four bites. A soft absorbent terry cloth material should be used. Wiping the facial area or scraping the chin with the spoon to collect (and reintroduce) expelled food should be avoided. Both practices may elicit oral reflex activity and mouth opening.

- Most students with feeding problems are given a diet of pureed foods. There is little support for this practice as most students can tolerate soft lumpy foods. Increasing texture may in fact result in development of more mature feeding patterns. Another practice is combining all foods of a meal in a blender and mixing milk into all pureed foods. Both practices should be eliminated; the first because it is dehumanizing to eliminate variety from the student's diet, and the second because all foods become mucous producing after the addition of milk.

- In addition to increasing texture, an attempt should be made to control food temperature. Extremes in temperature should be avoided, but warming bowls should be used when appropriate to maintain food at a palatable temperature during lengthy feeding sessions.

- Verbal instructions should be avoided during the initial stages of intervention in the feeding process. Some students respond to verbal instructions with increased tone as a side effect of goal-directed behavior. For example, refrain from saying "Open your mouth" to a student with clenched teeth. Instead, use one of the intervention strategies to open clenched teeth in conjunction with a description of the student's response to that strategy (such as "Good, your mouth is open now"). As the student gains voluntary control over oral musculature and becomes familiar with the sensations associated with the verbal labels, verbal instructions can be introduced.

The following description is of two strategies that produce *mouth opening* in students with clenched teeth. Both use upward pressure on the lower jaw. Before their use, however, close observation is necessary to determine if the jaws are aligned correctly. If the jaws are not aligned (if the teeth do not meet evenly and/or the lower jaw protrudes forward, to either side, or is retracted), the lower jaw should be gently manipulated to bring about proper alignment before either strategy is used. When proper alignment is observed, firm pressure upward is applied for 15 to 20 consecutive seconds; *or,* a series of three or four firm upward movements separated by a few seconds each should be used. The position described earlier for jaw control is used to provide upward pressure. This procedure is also helpful for releasing teeth clamped on a utensil because of a hyperactive bite reflex.

The spoon should be filled so the food is heaped in the first third of the bowl of the spoon. This will allow easy removal of food from the spoon. The filled spoon should be placed on the first third of the tongue. This is especially important for students with a hyperactive gag reflex. As the spoon is placed on the tongue, firm downward pressure is applied and maintained for two or three seconds to control tongue thrust and encourage lip closure around the spoon for removal of the food.

The spoon should be removed horizontally *without* upward movement of the handle (this will prevent removal of food from the spoon by the student's teeth). If the student's lips do not spontaneously assist in food removal, a series of exercises should be completed before each of the first

Figure 9-11 Use of the Teacher's Index Finger To Pull Upper Lip Down over Spoon To Remove Food.

ten bites of every meal. These prefeeding exercises are outlined in the section on lip closure. For the remainder of the meal (and for older students whose upper lip may be permanently retracted) the index finger of the hand providing jaw control can be used to pull the lip down over the spoon to remove the food (see Figure 9-11).

After spoon removal, the mouth should close and remain closed until swallowing occurs. If the mouth does not close spontaneously (or if a tongue thrust is present), jaw control to close the mouth manually may be required. Mouth closure and swallowing should be an active process. The appropriate use of jaw control requires a sensitive give-and-take to allow maximum independent mouth movement in combination with quick closure to control tongue thrusting if necessary.

A technique that puts a stretch on the circular muscle around the mouth is sometimes effective for students with inadequate *lip closure*. The tech-

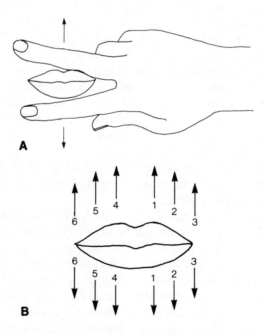

Figure 9-12 Placement of the Teacher's Fingers To Promote Lip Closure. **A,** Index and middle fingers extended above and below the mouth with firm stretch applied in the directions indicated by the arrows; **B,** Numbered points indicate positions where firm stretch is applied in the direction of arrows with fingertips of teacher's index and middle fingers.

nique can be performed in one of two ways. The first requires use of the feeder's index and middle fingers, as shown in Figure 9-12A. The second uses the fingertips of the feeder's index and middle fingers (see Figure 9-12B). In both cases the feeder should apply enough pressure to feel the student's gums and/or teeth through the student's face.

After placement of the feeder's fingers in one of the two positions, a quick firm stretch is applied. For the first position, the direction of the stretch is indicated by the arrows in the figure. The firm quick stretch should be repeated three or four times in succession. For the second position, one quick stretch outward at each of the numbered points should be applied. The feeder should start at the midline of the lips and move first to one corner of the mouth and then to the other corner (stretch at points 1, 2, and 3; then at points 4, 5, and 6). The entire sequence should be repeated three times.

One of the two applications of this technique should be used before *each* of the first ten bites of every meal to improve lip closure and active removal of food from the spoon. The procedure can also be used at various times throughout the school day to promote a more normal mouth position and control drooling.

The following procedure is recommended after removal of the spoon and mouth closure for students without an active swallow. The feeder's index finger should be placed midway between the upper lip and nose (see Figure 9-13). Pressure should be applied in this position for up to 30 seconds or until a swallow occurs. The pressure should be firm enough for the feeder to feel the jaw and/or teeth through the student's face. This procedure should be used in conjunction with jaw control and is most effective if the chin is flexed to the chest.

Many students lack free *movement of the tongue* in all directions (up, down, in, out, and to both sides). Two strategies may be effective in promoting tongue movement.

The first requires the use of a thick sticky substance, such as peanut butter, which should be placed at a number of locations in the mouth to encourage tongue movement. Placement should occur once at each of the following locations in succession: the roof of the mouth (just behind the upper front teeth), lower front teeth, and the left and right lower molars. Approximately one minute should be allowed for the student to retrieve the substance at each location and coordinate a swallow.

The second procedure requires a tongue blade covered with tape to prevent splintering. The tip of the tongue blade should be used to push the tongue gently to both sides, and back into the mouth. The tongue will move in the direction *opposite* the direction of the push after removal of the blade. The gentle push should be maintained for two to three seconds

Figure 9-13 Placement of the Teacher's Fingers To Encourage Swallowing. Inward pressure is applied with the index finger.

in each direction in succession. The sequence should be repeated three times and may be a beneficial prefeeding exercise.

Many students with neuromuscular involvement exhibit abnormal tongue movements. The presence of these movements may cause extreme feeding difficulties and deformities in the teeth. Firm downward pressure on the tongue during presentation of the spoon is helpful in controlling abnormal tongue movements in many students. In extreme cases, it may be necessary to replace use of a spoon with a taped tongue blade. The tongue blade is used to place food on the lower molars on either side. Manual rapid mouth closure should follow presentation of each bite and horizontal removal of the tongue blade.

A beneficial prefeeding exercise to aid in control of abnormal tongue movements is tongue walking (tongue walking may also help reduce hyperactive bite and gag reflexes). Tongue walking requires firm pressure down on the midline of the tongue with a taped tongue blade or swizzle stick. Downward pressure begins at the front of the tongue and moves in a series of one-half inch increments toward the back of the tongue. The tongue should be resting behind the lower teeth when the procedure is begun. Backward movement should cease either two-thirds of the way back on the tongue or as soon as the tongue begins to "hump," indicating elicitation of the gag reflex. Each series of movements should be accompanied by jaw control and end with mouth closure to promote an active swallow of the saliva produced by this procedure. Tongue walking should be repeated no more than two or three times in succession, as it is generally unpleasant for the student.

In terms of *normalization of oral sensitivity,* some students show extreme sensitivity to touch around the facial area. For these students it may be beneficial to carry out prefeeding exercises. These procedures require firm jaw control from beginning to end to prevent avoidance of the procedures and to provide assistance in mouth closure and swallowing of accumulated saliva. The jaws are held closed and in symmetry with the feeder's less-preferred hand. The index finger of the other hand is inserted into the student's mouth, and the outer surface of the upper gums is stroked firmly two or three times from the molars forward to midline, first on one side and then on the other. Each sequence should be followed by removal of the feeder's finger and mouth closure to promote swallowing. The same steps should be followed with the outside surface of the lower gums. For students who have unrestricted hand-to-mouth movement, the student's index finger can be used for the stimulation (the adult physically assists the student to complete the movements.) A second desensitization procedure is to brush the student's teeth gently with a soft toothbrush. This is also important for students who receive anticonvulsant medications (e.g., Dilantin) that cause excessive gum growth.

Many of these intervention strategies require manipulation of the student's oral musculature. The oral desensitization and tongue-walking procedures can be unpleasant because of their invasiveness. For this reason, the procedures should be implemented with concern and sensitivity for the student's reactions, and use of these procedures should be introduced gradually.

Chewing has as prerequisites the inhibition of abnormal tongue movements and the development of tongue lateralization (side-to-side movements). The development of chewing can be encouraged through the use of two strategies that should be implemented in combination.

The first strategy is to increase texture with the hope that chewing will develop spontaneously. The second strategy requires strips of firm bread crusts, licorice whips, or any four- to six-inch strip of food that will provide resistance. One end of the food strip is inserted between the molars on either side of the student's mouth. Jaw control is used to produce firm mouth closure. A quick firm stretch is applied to the other end of the food strip. Jaw control should then lessen slightly to allow spontaneous chewing.

This procedure is remarkably effective in producing short periods of chewing behavior. There is, however, little generalization seen from the use of this procedure to spontaneous chewing of lumpy foods. For this reason, the procedure should be used every few bites throughout each meal to increase carryover. Manipulation of the lower jaw in an up-and-down or rotary pattern is generally ineffective for producing chewing.

Proper presentation of liquids requires the following procedures: The student should be seated and fully upright. The feeder should sit or stand next to the student and provide jaw control from the side. The feeder's elbow and forearm should support the back of the student's neck to help ensure a good head position by providing some flexion of the student's chin to the chest.

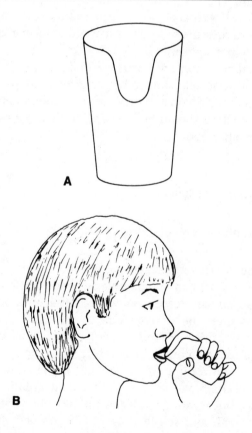

A

B

Figure 9-14 Cup Drinking. **A,** Cut out cup; **B,** Placement of the cup on the lower lip outside the teeth.

The cup should be cut out and be presented so the edge rests gently on the student's lower lip (see Figure 9-14). The cup should *never* be presented so that it touches the student's teeth. Enough jaw control should be provided to almost completely close the student's mouth around the edge of the cup. The cup is then tipped slowly until a swallow of liquid runs into the student's mouth. The mouth is then closed completely (although the cup is *not* removed from between the student's lips), and a pause for swallowing is allowed. A second and third swallow of liquid are presented in this manner before the cup is removed. The procedure is repeated several times in succession until adequate liquid is provided.

For students with poor lip closure, the stretching exercises around the mouth described earlier can be used before presentation of the cup. For an older student with a permanently retracted upper lip, the index finger of the hand providing jaw control should be placed above the student's upper lip, and downward pressure should be provided to form a seal around the edge of the cup to prevent spillage.

Four important behaviors are necessary for successful *self-feeding*. It is not necessary for these behaviors to be performed independently before the development of self-feeding. If they are not in the student's repertoire, however, their function should be replaced through the use of adaptive equipment. These behaviors are

- head control
- trunk control/sitting balance
- grasping
- hand-to-mouth movement

There is some controversy regarding when a student with severe or profound handicaps with an oral pathologic condition should begin self-feeding. This is an issue because many students show a deterioration in feeding patterns after the development of self-feeding. A number of factors should be considered in this decision, of which the most important are the student's age and motivation to self-feed. A compromise may be to begin training in self-feeding (if the student is motivated) in the later preschool years in combination with continued intervention on abnormal feeding patterns. Intervention strategies can be used during the first ten bites of every meal, and self-feeding can be trained throughout the remainder of the meal. Refer to Banerdt and Bricker (1978) for an example of a self-feeding program, and to Barnes, Murphy, Waldo, and

Sailor (1979) and Campbell (1979 & 1987b) for additional information on feeding equipment.

CONCLUSION

More than ten years have passed since the passage of P.L. 94-142. As a profession, we continue to struggle to resolve issues surrounding service delivery for students with severe or profound handicaps. Two primary issues are the role of related services personnel, and the skills and knowledge required of teachers to meet the multiple needs of their students. It is this author's interpretation of the law that related services are provided to maximize students' participation in special education. The continued practice of isolated therapy (therapy conducted in a therapy room separate from the classroom and without explicit transfer of knowledge and skills from the therapist to the teacher) is *not* supported by this interpretation. Instead, a model of the teacher as *educational synthesizer* is needed. In this model, teachers acquire *basic* knowledge and skills from a variety of disciplines (e.g., speech, occupational therapy, nutrition, etc.). Only specialized strategies are reserved for medical professionals. In exchange for knowledge and skills from the various disciplines, teachers share their expertise in applied behavior analysis, systematic instruction, and measurement across traditional team boundaries. What can result from such collaboration is a cohesive model of service delivery in which students receive consistent education and treatment throughout the school day. It is only through such a model that the spirit of P.L. 94-142 can be realized.

REFERENCES

Banerdt, B., & Bricker, D. (1978). A training program for selected self-feeding skills for the motorically impaired. *AAESPH Review, 3,* 222-230.

Barnes, K.J., Murphy, M., Waldo, L., & Sailor, W. (1979). Adaptive equipment for the severely multiply handicapped child. In R.L. York & E. Edgar (Eds.), *Teaching the severely handicapped* (Vol. IV) (pp. 108-152). Columbus, OH: Special Press.

Bobath, K., & Bobath, B. (1972). Cerebral palsy. In P.H. Pearson and C.E. Williams (Eds.), *Physical therapy services in the developmental disabilities* (pp. 31-185). Springfield, IL: Charles C Thomas.

Bricker, W.A., & Campbell, P.H. (1980). Interdisciplinary assessment and programming for multihandicapped students. In W. Sailor, B. Wilcox, & L. Brown (Eds.), *Methods of instruction for severely handicapped persons* (pp. 3-46). Baltimore: Paul H. Brookes.

Brown, F. (1987). Meaningful assessment of people with severe and profound handicaps. In M.E. Snell (Ed.), *Systematic instruction of persons with severe handicaps* (pp. 39-63). Columbus, OH: Charles E. Merrill.

Buttram, B., & Brown, G. (1977). *Developmental physical management of the multidisabled child.* Tuscaloosa: The University of Alabama, Area of Special Education.

Campbell, P.H. (1979). Assessing oral-motor skills in severely handicapped persons: An analysis of normal and abnormal patterns of movement. In R.L. York and E. Edgar (Eds.), *Teaching the severely handicapped* (Vol. IV) (pp. 39-63). Columbus, OH: Special Press.

Campbell, P.H. (1987a). Programming for students with dysfunction in posture and movement. In M.E. Snell (Ed.), *Systematic instruction of persons with severe handicaps* (pp. 188-211). Columbus, OH: Charles E. Merrill.

Campbell, P.H. (1987b). Physical management and handling procedures with students with movement dysfunction. In M.E. Snell (Ed.), *Systematic instruction of persons with severe handicaps* (pp. 174-187). Columbus, OH: Charles E. Merrill.

Campbell, P.H., & Stewart, B. (1986). Measuring changes in movement skills with infants and young children with handicaps. *Journal of the Association for Persons with Severe Handicaps, 11,* 153-161.

Connor, F.P., Williamson, G.G., & Siepp, J.M. (1978). *Program guide for infants and toddlers with neuromuscular and other developmental disabilities.* New York: Teachers College Press.

Falvey, M., Brown, L., Lyon, S., Baumgart, D., & Schroeder, J. (1980). Strategies for using cues and correction procedures. In W. Sailor, B. Wilcox & L. Brown (Eds.), *Methods of instruction for severely handicapped persons.* (pp. 109-143). Baltimore: Paul H. Brookes.

Finnie, N. (1975). *Handling the young cerebral palsied child at home.* New York: E.P. Dutton.

Fraser, B.A., & Hensinger, R.H. (1983). *Managing physical handicaps. A practical guide for parents, care providers, and educators.* Baltimore: Paul H. Brookes.

Gaylord-Ross, R.J., & Holvoet, J.F. (1985). *Strategies for educating students with severe handicaps.* Boston: Little, Brown and Company.

Hartman, D.P., & Hall, R.V. (1976). The changing criterion design. *Journal of Applied Behavior Analysis, 9,* 527-532.

Johnson, J.L. (1978). Programming for early motor responses within the classroom. *AAESPH Review, 3,* 4-15.

Kuharski, T., Rues, J., Cook, D., & Guess, D. (1985). Effects of vestibular stimulation on sitting behaviors among preschoolers with severe handicaps. *The Journal of the Association for Persons with Severe Handicaps, 10,* 137-145.

Liberty, K., Haring, N.G., & Martin, M.M. (1981). Teaching skills to the severely handicapped. *Journal of the Association for the Severely Handicapped, 6,* 5-14.

Morris, S.E. (1982a). *The normal acquisition of oral feeding skills: Implications for assessment and treatment.* New York: Therapeutic Media.

Morris, S.E. (1982b). *Pre-speech assessment scale.* Clifton, NJ: J.A. Preston.

Noonan, M.J. (1984). Teaching postural reactions to students with severe cerebral palsy: An evaluation of theory and technique. *The Journal of the Association for Persons with Severe Handicaps, 9,* 111-122.

Norton, Y. (1975). Neurodevelopment and sensory integration. *American Journal of Occupational Therapy, 29,* 93-100.

Scherzer, A.L., Mike, V., & Wilson, J. (1976). Physical therapy as a determinant of change in the cerebral palsied infant. *Pediatrics, 58,* 47-52.

Snell, M.E., & Zirpoli, T.J. (1987). Intervention strategies. In M.E. Snell (Ed.), *Systematic instruction of persons with severe handicaps* (pp. 110-150). Columbus, OH: Charles E. Merrill.

Sobsey, R., & Orelove, F. (1984). Neurophysiological facilitation of eating skills in severely handicapped children. *The Journal of the Association for Persons with Severe Handicaps, 9,* 98-110.

Tyler, N.B., & Kahn, N. (1976). A home treatment program for the cerebral palsied child. *American Journal of Occupational Therapy, 30,* 437-440.

Chapter 10

Prelanguage Communication Instruction

Les Sternberg and Colleen D. McNerney

PROBLEM

Although much has been written about language development theory (Chomsky, 1969; McNeill, 1970), assessment of language (MacDonald, 1978; Kirk, McCarthy, & Kirk, 1968; Lee, 1971), and language intervention programs and techniques (Gray & Ryan, 1973; Horstmeier & MacDonald, 1978; Guess, Sailor, & Baer, 1974, 1976; Warren & Rogers-Warren, 1985), until recently there has been little theoretical, assessment, and intervention information pertaining to *prelanguage* communication skills. In the past, literature focused narrowly on the area of communication/language, with the tendency to equate communicative ability with only one's skills at acquiring and using formal language structures (Rowland, 1985). This was appropriate only if the human subjects under investigation could understand and use such formalized languages (e.g., words, signs, gestures, etc.). For many individuals with severe or profound handicaps, the synonymity of "communication" and "language" is certainly not warranted. Educational foci on this population have forced us to conceive of communication as separate from, yet related to, language. Communication becomes a process through which individuals exchange information. Language is only one structure through which they may communicate.

PAST PRACTICES

To put prelanguage communication interventions into perspective, it is important to understand basic concepts of communication development. For an individual to communicate, he or she must have some connection with the social world. It is probable that the asocial student can never fully participate in or appreciate communication, since communication is a social act. To interface the social aspects with communicative behaviors, the student must realize a number of prelanguage communication accomplishments and concepts. The first is the awareness that he or she is separate from the environment. The individual must know the boundaries of self as well as the interfacing boundaries of the environment. We can often recognize whether an individual has such knowledge by observing the way in which the individual manipulates objects. For example, if a student with severe or profound handicaps immediately mouths objects, always manipulates objects close to the body, or never varies the manner of playing with the objects, then we may hypothesize that the student does not comprehend that the object is separate from himself or herself.

This perception of separation is necessary for the individual to acquire and display two prelanguage accomplishments: (1) that he or she can communicate, and (2) that there are things around him or her to communicate about and people with whom to communicate. Actively interacting with people and objects helps the student learn specific aspects related to the people and familiar events that characterize routine day-to-day experiences. Then as the student develops, he or she may learn that an aspect of an object, person, or event can represent that object, person, or event. Once the student knows that he or she can communicate, that there are things to communicate about, and that those things can be represented using body movements, the student may begin using idiosyncratic representations to think and to communicate. These representations are very student-specific and may be understood by only a select few. Eventually, they may be replaced by conventional representations or language.

Past investigative work in the areas of communication and language has produced significant dividends in terms of how we have come to view communication development. Bates (1976) provided a developmental model that focuses on normal child communication. It has come to represent both a theoretical and methodological foundation for many past and present intervention efforts. In her view, communication develops through various phases, but individuals do not merely acquire one phase before they begin another. Instead, the phases appear to meld as one phase naturally leads to the next.

The earliest phase of communication, termed *perlocutionary*, does not really appear to be communicative in the typical sense. Here, the individual exhibits various behaviors that are viewed and reacted to by others as communicative. For example, the child may gurgle for apparently no reason, yet an attending adult may talk back to the child as if the child were communicating. In the early stages of this phase, it would not be uncommon for a child to exhibit only primitive reflexes in reaction to various stimuli. Toward the middle of this stage, a child might exhibit a movement after an enjoyable interplay has taken place. It would appear to an observer that the child was moving because he or she wanted the interplay to continue. However, in both of these cases, direct communicative intent or meaning by the child cannot be inferred but rather is generated by one who is attending to the child. Toward the latter part of the perlocutionary stage, intent begins to develop.

During the second phase, termed *illocutionary,* communicative intent is generated by the child. During the early stages of this phase, the child might make very general types of requests. For example, the child might grasp a toy and wave it in front of an individual. The intent is to get assistance, but the specific type of assistance is not clear. Therefore, at this level, *clear* intent is still generated by another. During the latter stages of this phase, more refinement of specific communicative intent takes place. Pointing and other gestures begin to develop. The child might display the object to an adult *and* point to a part of the object with which he or she needs assistance. Regardless of the stage in this phase, most of the child's communication is tied to whether the objects or desired events are present in the immediate environment; if not present, the child will most likely not communicate about them.

The last communication phase, termed *locutionary,* involves formal language accomplishments. It is during this phase that the child begins to use conventional words and/or signs. These words or signs are truly representational or symbolic in nature in that the objects, people, or events being referred to do not have to be present in the immediate environment.

Using this phase-to-phase scenario of communication development, it becomes obvious that various interrelated factors may either account for or provide impetus to skill acquisition and demonstration. One of these factors is the interplay between communication and social-interactive behaviors. The social interaction bases for communication development are rather well founded (Bates, 1979; Bricker & Schiefelbusch, 1984; Dunst, 1978; McLean & Snyder-McLean, 1978; MacDonald, 1986; MacDonald & Gillette, 1986b; Rogers-Warren & Warren, 1984). Specific social-interactive skills, including attention to aspects of one's environment and the ability to interact and respond to another individual, appear as crucial correlates to communication development.

A second factor is cognitive competence (Bates, Benigni, Bretherton, Camaioni, & Volterra, 1977; Lobato, Barrera, & Feldman, 1981). The ability to process information (cognitive competence) has been viewed as directly associated with whether an individual can develop specific communication skills. Although there is more agreement as to the *general* level of cognitive competence that might be necessary for various communication skills, such is not the case for the specific *types of cognitive behavior* that might be crucial. For example, there seems to be a consensus that a base level of sensorimotor cognitive functioning (as described in the work of Jean Piaget) correlates with success in different phases of communication skill development. One must remember, however, that sensorimotor functioning is comprised of a number of interrelated types of behaviors (e.g., object permanence, means-end relations, imitation, causality; Robinson & Robinson, 1983). It is when one tries to correlate these specific behaviors to success at demonstrating different communicative abilities that disagreements arise (Bates, 1979; Cromer, 1981; Frye, 1981; Leonard, 1978; Reichle & Karlan, 1985).

As was alluded to previously, past communication training instructional practices for students with severe handicaps have focused rather narrowly on the development of language as *the* ultimate criterion of success. With the presence of students with profound handicaps in the public education arena, the instructional focus has shifted to the development of prelanguage communication skills. The effect of these communication skills on further language development remains a prominent research topic (Sugarman, 1981). As with language development, the concept of the interplay among communication, social, and cognitive skills development still seems to be at the forefront of any designed intervention effort.

SUGGESTED METHODS

Students with severe or profound handicaps typically present a myriad of instructional problems to teachers. This is especially the case in the area of communication. Communication development is perhaps the one area in which almost all students with severe or profound handicaps exhibit difficulties. This is most probably due to the extent and degree of their impairments and how those impairments affect both social-communicative input and output possibilities (Bryen & Joyce, 1985). If a student wishes to communicate but has difficulty in exhibiting communicative behaviors, and if the student's caregivers cannot interpret any of the student's communicative "messages," both parties may give up the task, and skill development may ultimately cease.

A number of communication training models and programs were developed to meet the expressed communication needs of students with severe or profound handicaps. Almost all of these programs have as their desired end the development of a generative language system; that is, a system comprised of a finite number of words, symbols, signs, or gestures that can be used to make an infinite number of statements. Each of these models or programs places different emphases on prelanguage communication skill development, although considerable similarities can be seen in their theoretical and methodological foundations.

The Transactional Approach

McLean and Snyder-McLean (1978) adopted as the cornerstones of their approach many of the tenets espoused by Bates (1976). Aside from what they see as a phase-to-phase development of communication skills (e.g., perlocutionary to illocutionary), they emphasize again and again the social-interactive qualities of communication. Also important is their contention that what a child or student will eventually communicate about is based, for the most part, on his or her cognitive competence (level and type of cognitive functioning). *Transaction* involves how the child or student can develop control over the environment (people, objects, and events) using communicative, social-interactive, and cognitive skills.

In terms of prelanguage skill development, McLean and Snyder-McLean systematically refined and behaviorized the phases of early communication development. In the perlocutionary phase, they see a *reactive stage* leading to a *proactive stage*. In the former, the individual merely responds (reacts) to environmental stimuli using both voluntary (e.g., crying) and involuntary (e.g., reflex) behaviors. These reactions can "force" others to attend. However, the individual never actually intends for this to happen. In the proactive stage the individual more directly wants to achieve a goal, but the intent does not seem to be planned. For example, the individual might be involved in a motor activity with another person (e.g., rocking together). Once the activity stops, the individual might begin a component of that activity. The other person may ascribe intent to the movement and begin the motor activity again. In this case, the actual motor activity had to be presented before the "intentional" response was generated.

In the illocutionary phase, a *primitive stage* is seen as progressing toward a *conventional stage*. In the primitive stage, the individual displays self-initiated communicative intent: The individual wants and does begin to communicate about something in particular. Unfortunately, there may still be a problem with how clear the intent is. For example, the individual may purposefully reach or cry out for another person. The person will definitely know that he or she is wanted, but will have to discover the specific thing that he or she is to provide or do. This situation is not the case during the conventional stage. Here, not only is purposeful communicative intent displayed, but the individual is much clearer concerning what he or she wants. For example, the individual might not only reach for the other person but might also display a gesture or pointing motion to indicate exactly what he or she wants.

In terms of the cognitive components of prelanguage communication, McLean and Snyder-McLean view sensorimotor cognitive development as crucial to social-communicative development. Especially important are the areas of means-end behavior, object interaction (referred to as schemes relating to objects), and causality. For example, an individual may reach out for something in view (means-end behavior), demonstrate an understanding of the object by using it in a functional manner (object interaction), or exhibit communicative intent by purposefully handing the object to another so that the object can be activated (causality).

The transactional approach provides a framework for viewing the development of communication skills. By referring to behavioral exemplars that represent the interplay among social-interactive, communication, and cognitive skills development, the practitioner can not only understand an individual's current type of communication functioning but can also outline a methodological approach for effecting communication skill change.

The Ecological Communication (ECO) Systems Approach

MacDonald and Gillette (1984a,b; 1986a,b) provide an approach for communication development whose components, in many respects, resemble those of McLean and Snyder-McLean (1978). The basic premise of this approach is that communication develops as a result of social-interactive interchanges in the natural environment. It is these interchanges that are emphasized in the ECO systems approach (MacDonald & Gillette, 1986b). In terms of prelanguage communication skill development, these interchanges begin as *noninteractive* (e.g., "solo play" where there are only generalized reactions or responses to social contact) and then become *interactive* (e.g., "social play" where the child exhibits give-and-take play skills). However, very little if any communicative intent is exhibited during these interchanges. This general level of social interchange, therefore, corresponds to perlocutionary stage developments described by others. Communicative intent is later acquired from interactive exchanges using sound, movement, and/or gestural expressions (*nonlinguistic* or "communications," which correspond to illocutionary stage developments).

The ECO system can be viewed as addressing four questions concerning communication: What is the basic foundation for communication skill development? How can an individual communicate? What can the individual communicate about? Why should the individual communicate?

The answer to the first question is found in the idea that communication is based on, first and foremost, interactions with another. In the ECO system, therefore, emphasis is placed on providing highly structured interactive activities for the individual. Initial activities will typically take the form of the individual moving together with another person. In the ECO system, these movements are referred to as *joint action routines.* They are followed by *reciprocal turntaking* experiences, a major methodologic aspect of social-communicative interactions. Early types of turntaking will involve the individual producing an action or component of an action, followed by another either mimicking the action or providing another component of the action. Although at this stage no communicative intent would be obvious (MacDonald & Gillette, 1984a; 1985), this give-and-take type of interaction can provide the impetus for helping the individual understand how he or she can communicate. If a turntaking activity is desired by the individual, intentional pauses in that activity can be used as a facilitative method to cue the individual to produce an intentional signal to continue the activity. Of paramount importance, however, is the concept that the "how" of communication must first come from the individual's own behavior, rather than from another forcing a signal system on that person. And if interaction development is to be successful, it must follow the rules of *progressively matched turntaking (PMTT;* MacDonald & Gillette, 1986b), where the adult continues to perform like the child but *gradually* changes his or her imitative model.

In terms of what to communicate about and why communicate at all, again the answer is found in the social interplays in the natural environment. Exposure to many different aspects of the environment in the social context of communication can effectively afford the individual the opportunity for communication and the necessity to communicate. The availability of extensive social interplay (people) and environmental interactions (objects and events) can effectively increase the scope and need for "vocabulary."

One of the most noteworthy aspects of the ECO system are descriptions and examples of how caregivers can *impede* communication development (MacDonald & Gillette, 1986b). For example, adults often provide "communicative mismatches" for students with severe handicaps. This occurs when an adult expects a student to perform a communicative skill that is considerably above his or her current communication developmental level. Also, adults often participate in turntaking with students for only a brief period ("dead-end contacts"), so the students never really have the time to learn the targeted skill. Some of these turntaking episodes are completely controlled by the adult ("turn dominance"), which will likely interfere with the development of appropriate student participation.

The Developmental/Social Interaction Approach

Dunst and Lowe (1986) proposed another systems approach to communication development. Their system has a major component emphasis that is also found in the transactional and ecological systems approaches: the importance of an individual's communicative competence in a social/interactive context. Their approach is also based on the premise that development occurs in a fixed stage-to-stage hierarchical pattern (one stage builds upon another). Two interrelated concepts flow through their approach. The first is *predictable responses.* This refers to the idea that an individual must display a certain communication response repertoire that is highly predictable. If not, others to whom he or she is communicating will be unable to read responses as communicative. Response *readability* then, is the second concept imbedded in their approach.

The developmental/social interaction approach has a number of levels. In terms of prelanguage communication, the first is *behavior state communication* and is seen when changes in an individual's nonverbal behavior are given communicative intent by another. The second level is *recognitory communication.* At this stage, the individual shows nonverbal behaviors that indicate that he or she recognizes familiar objects, persons, and events. The third stage, *contingency communication,* is made up of nonverbal behaviors that are used to gain and maintain the attention of another individual. The behaviors are often idiosyncratic in that they are understood only by a select few. However, during the fourth stage (*instrumental communication*), more conventional nonverbal behaviors are used to achieve a desired goal (e.g., pointing to obtain some object). During the fifth stage, *triadic communication,* the individual uses intentional nonverbal communicative behaviors either to get an adult to obtain a desired object or to gain and maintain an adult's attention while displaying an object. The important accomplishment during this stage is the ability of the individual to use objects and persons simultaneously.

Dunst and Lowe (1986) outlined a number of strategies for increasing communicative competence. The first category is *conditional strategies.* Their basic purpose is to increase social-communicative interactions by systematically reinforcing such events (Dunst, 1981). Also included are suggestions for increasing the individual's understanding of response-contingent relations with inanimate objects (e.g., turning the head will produce a toy-produced aural or visual effect).

A second category is *interactive coaching*. Strategies, such as imitation and turntaking, are suggested to help one initiate and sustain communicative interactions with another.

The third category, *incidental teaching,* builds on the previous strategies. A number of instructional steps are outlined, proceeding from helping the individual attend to environmental events (*attention-getting* and *attention-holding*); to determining the specific aspects that are maintaining that attention so they can be used as reinforcers; to helping the individual develop more conventional ways in which to communicate.

The Van Dijk Approach

The Van Dijk communication program (Van Dijk, 1965a,b; 1967, 1969) was originally designed for use with individuals who are deaf and blind. It is applicable to other severe and profound handicapping conditions, however, especially those accompanied by cognitive deficits (Sternberg, Battle, & Hill, 1980). It is interesting that, although recently much has been written about the Van Dijk approach, individuals still are interpreting its methodological foundations and principles (Stillman & Battle, 1984).

The goal of the Van Dijk program is to develop communicative intentions and communication procedures through conversation using movement, signals, gestures, objects, pictures, signs, or speech. The major mission of the program is to help the prelanguage, noncommunicative individual develop communication and eventually language. This is accomplished by using a stage-to-stage procedure that employs movement by the student and the teacher to foster communication awareness.

Siegel-Causey and Guess (1985) presented an overview of the theoretical concepts imbedded in the Van Dijk approach. In that students with severe or profound handicaps often exhibit isolated and "inward" types of behaviors, they see the Van Dijk program as being used to assist the individual in directing communication outward to another. Four overlapping levels of program implementation are seen. In the first level (*ego consciousness*), a primary nurturing relationship is developed between the student and his or her caregiver(s). This relationship can often be seen in the extremely close (i.e., body-to-body) movements the student shares with the caregiver. These relationships are also used to help the student tolerate such contact and to comprehend the concept of separation of one's body from one's environment. This concept, as described earlier, is crucial to later communication development.

In the second level (*resonance motor patterns*), shared and in-physical-contact movement patterns are again the principal interventions.

Whereas tolerance for contact was a major purpose of this type of move-ment during the previous level, at this level the major purposes are increased student participation and anticipation of single movements and movements conducted in fixed sequences.

In the third level (*development of body schema*), interventions are directed toward assisting the student develop improved body and body parts awareness. A number of substages are evident. In the coactive substage, the student is required first to display parallel movement sequences while in physical contact with another. Later, these movements are made without physical contact. In the imitation substage, the student is required to make simultaneous imitations of limb movements demon-strated by another. Also, nonrepresentational reference behaviors (e.g., pointing gestures) are developed.

In the final level, *natural gestures,* the student begins to display his or her own signals or gestures to communicate. They are initially idiosyn-cratic and represent what a particular student might do with a certain object or in a certain activity. Later, they will become *denaturalized* (less idiosyncratic and more "normal") and *decontextualized* (not tied to an observable object, activity, or person).

Modified Van Dijk Approach

We took some of Van Dijk's theoretical underpinnings and created what is, for many, a modified Van Dijk approach to prelanguage communica-tion development. The modifications involve three instructional elements. The first is a systematic attempt at controlling the distance (in-contact and no contact) between the student and his or her care-giver(s). The second is controlling the time in instructional interchanges: both individuals are involved in interchanges simultaneously (no break in time), or the interchanges require a delay (a break in time). The third instructional element is the breaking down of many of the conceptual components into more refined and simplified instructional procedures. This modified approach also tends to emphasize, perhaps to a greater degree than most other programs, the various skill developments imbedded in very early prelanguage communication.

The first procedural stage of the program is *resonance*. At this stage the student learns that his or her movements can be used to affect another's behavior. Here, one responds to the student's movements as if they were communicative, thereby helping the student learn that his or her move-ments can effect change. Emphasis is placed on the development of a primary relationship between the teacher and student to provide the student with a connection to the outside world. The teacher's behavior is contingent on the student's behavior. Initially, one starts with basic movement patterns of the student (such as rocking). If the student shows no consistent movement patterns, the teacher must help the student develop movements that can be used in a movement program. Such movements can usually be promoted through the use of shaping and the application of other behavioral principles as a part of the student's regular physical education or physical therapy training. Starting with these nonthreatening movement patterns will help make the necessary later transition to altered body movements easier.

In the resonance stage it is mandatory that the teacher be in the same physical plane with the student (body-to-body). For example, if the student has been observed to rock, the teacher would rock with the student with the student's back against the teacher's chest. Later, after the student demonstrated success in the body-to-body plane, the teacher would proceed to the opposition plane (the teacher facing the student), but physical contact would still be necessary.

In resonance, there is no separation in time or space. Receptive resonance skills are evident when the student demonstrates awareness of the mutual movement (e.g., by smiling or cooing). As the teacher and student move together, the teacher should stop and wait to see if the student provides a cue to initiate the movement again. The teacher can develop these expressive resonance cues (such as an intentional push backward against the teacher's chest or patting the teacher's leg) initially by physical guidance and by always following the cue with the desired movement.

Once the student operationalizes this signal-to-movement connection, the teacher may begin to create a more complete *movement dialogue.* Here, additional movements and cues are added, and an order of movements is established to help the student build anticipation and memory. Generally, no extrinsic reinforcement is necessary, for movement itself is intrinsically reinforcing. Again, the purpose of this procedural stage is not to teach movements but to use movement to communicate.

The second stage is *coactive movement.* At this level, the teacher and the student are separated in space but not in time. For example, the teacher may sit beside the student, remaining in close proximity. The teacher may initiate a familiar movement (with or without a corresponding cue) to determine the student's receptive coactive movement (awareness of the mutual movement), or the student may use a signal to initiate a mutual movement (an expressive coactive movement). The movement dialogue continues, but because of the separation in space, the student must observe the teacher as the teacher proceeds from one movement to another. Again, sequence and anticipation are developed by gradually building up sequences the student can perform with the teacher. Typically, gross motor movements are pursued before fine motor movements. Symmetric movements (such as both limbs moving in one directional plane at the same time) seem to be easier to duplicate than asymmetric movements. Once the student can move through a variety of sequences with the adult, objects can be introduced into the movement sequences. For example, teacher and student might coactively get farm animals from a toy box, carry them to the play area, and place the animals in a toy barn. Through this type of activity, the constructive use of objects and interactive play are stimulated. The student learns about objects in relation to his or her body and movements, thus helping the student use the body as a tool for exploring the world.

When the student can follow a series of coactive symmetric and asymmetric movements, *nonrepresentational reference* activities are initiated. The purposes of these activities are first to build body image and to teach the student that the body can be represented. As an extension of the activities, a direct approach is used to help the student understand that objects, events, and people can be referred to without formal labels (e.g., by pointing gestures). Initially, the teacher points out parts of his or her own body and encourages the student to duplicate the pointing being modeled. Once the student displays consistent nonrepresentational reference movements with the teacher as a model, the teacher may introduce a doll as a model. The doll-as-teacher model then shifts to a clay figure–as–doll model and finally to a paper and pencil or chalkboard stick figure representation of the body. Again, each model and the student are separated in space, but the model remains for the student to duplicate. Again, the purposes of these activities are to develop body image, to help the student become aware that the body can be represented, and to teach pointing.

The third stage is *deferred imitation*. Here, there is separation in both time and space. The teacher may display a certain movement pattern, stop the movement, and wait for the student to duplicate the pattern (receptive deferred imitation), or the student may imitate the same activity, providing the expressive cue (expressive deferred imitation). The key difference between coactive movement and deferred imitation, then, is that in deferred imitation whatever model is used is no longer available for the student to duplicate. For example, if one were using a chalkboard stick figure as representation, the teacher would draw the stick figure model, ask the student to look at it, erase the model, and ask the student to duplicate what he or she saw. In this situation, the student must defer the movement until the model is no longer available.

A communication device suggested for use throughout the coactive movement and deferred imitation stages is *anticipation shelves.* Typically, these are a series of connected cubicles, each representing a different activity during the school day. In each cubicle will be placed an object the student will associate with the specific activity (a cup, for example, representing lunch). Just before each activity, the student is requested to get the appropriate object signal (initially this will be done through physical guidance), and then proceed with the object to the related activity area. When the student is finished with this activity, he or she is directed toward putting the object back into a separate "finished box." The finished box is used as a preliminary indicator that the activity is over. Once this understanding is displayed by the student, he or she might be encouraged merely to place the object back into its appropriate shelf. During coactive movements, the major purpose of the shelf is to have the student associate the object with the physical movement toward the corresponding activity area; in deferred imitation, the purpose is to have the student associate the object with the actual activity.

The pattern of using the anticipation shelves is consistently repeated, and the procedure helps the student structure the day, teaches the function of objects, and helps the student make transitions from one activity to another. Concrete to abstract representation is used with the anticipation shelves. One initially starts with object signals, then proceeds to predrawn pictures or photographs of the objects, and finally arrives at graphic or line drawings of the objects. Again, before the student can use an abstract representational system (language), he or she must become aware that things can be represented.

Resonance, coactive movement, and deferred imitation should not be looked upon as procedures to be used in an isolated activity approach; they must be infused into a student's total program. For example, if the student is basically in the coactive level for communication instruction, everything that happens during the day should be done coactively (washing hands, emptying wastebaskets, etc.). Given the supraordinate nature of communication, its relation to other ecological events must be stressed.

As a result of a student's progression through deferred imitation, *natural gesture construction* will become evident. This phase serves as the transition from reference to representation. Here, the student learns that refined body movements can be used to communicate. This realization is necessary for the student to move from the concrete to the abstract, and to understand the future use of symbols and language. Natural gestures are, by definition, those that are self-developed. As such, they are not really amenable to procedural development. Initially, the gestures will represent what the student typically does with the object (performative function; e.g., a tearing motion for paper, a throwing motion for a ball) and proceed to what the object looks like (referential function, e.g; a spherical hand shape for a ball). Again, it is extremely important that whatever natural gestures are constructed reflect a motor behavior the student has consistently exhibited. In the beginning of the natural gesture phase, the gestures are truly unique to the student and do not have meaning to anyone else. Therefore, the purpose of the initial natural gestures may be self-communication (receptive and expressive communication within the individual). Later, these gestures will be based on request, and then for the purpose of expressive (to other) communication.

Assessing the Student for Communication Programming. Acquiring communication assessment information for students with severe or profound handicaps is, at best, problematic. Rowland (1985) described assessment concerns and problems in relation to students with both deafness and blindness. Some of these concerns relate directly to the students' handicapping conditions (e.g., the effect of the handicaps on one's ability to display communicative behaviors, and the extreme heterogeneity of handicaps associated with the population). Other concerns relate to assessment instruments, including their nonavailability and/or inadequacies. Although many problems are apparent, Rowland still sees a consensus in the field regarding what appropriate communication assessment procedures to follow. Among these are the necessity for obtaining measures of cognitive, social, and communication skills; the present and potential interplay of these skills; and a determination of the purposes and forms that communication behaviors may take (McLean, Snyder-McLean, Rowland, Jacobs, & Sack, 1981; Stremel-Campbell, 1984).

In relation to the modified Van Dijk program, it is necessary to determine where an individual falls in the sequence before any formal instruction is given. Given the assessment directions described by Rowland (1985), it would seem appropriate to obtain general assessment information that might be used for initial program placement. Given the posited relations among cognition, social indices, and communication/language (Bretherton, Bates, Benigni, Camaioni, & Volterra, 1979; Cromer, 1974; Finch-Williams, 1984; Furth, 1970, 1971; Kahn, 1975; Moorehead & Ingram, 1973), developmental assessment information pertaining to these areas would prove beneficial in determining in which programming stage an individual primarily belongs. To this end, the *Communication Programming Inventory* (see Appendix 10-A) was developed to give an indication to the teacher (or other communication facilitator) of the developmental level of functioning of a student in various areas. It samples behaviors in the areas of cognition, receptive communication, expressive communication, and social-affect. Selected behaviors in each area were gleaned from a number of sources concerning

Table 10-1 Translating Assessed Levels into Procedural Levels

	Critical Developmental Levels (Months)			
	Cognition	*Receptive communication*	Expressive communication	*Social affect*
Preresonance Tolerance	0-1	0-1	0-1	0-1
Initial resonance Receptive: awareness Expressive: participation	0-1	1-4	1-4	1-4
Final resonance Receptive: anticipation Expressive: motor/vocal signals	1-4	4-8	4-8	4-8

Initial coactive movement
Receptive: gross-motor
    imitation
Expressive: fine-motor
    signals
	4-8	4-8	4-8	4-8

Final coactive movement Receptive: fine-motor imitation Expressive: object signals	8-12	8-12	8-12	8-12

Initial deferred imitation
Receptive: body/movements
    imitation, nonrepre-
    sentational
    referencing
Expressive: Abstract
    signals, starting
    gestures
	8-12	12-18	12-18	12-18

Final deferred imitation
Receptive: abstract model
    referencing
Expressive: natural
    gesture
    construction
	12-18	12-18	12-18	12-18

developmental behaviors (*Callier-Azuza Scale,* Stillman, 1978; *Developmental Pinpoints,* Cohen, Gross & Haring, 1976). These behaviors were separated by area and developmental age ranges. An attempt was made to avoid duplication of behaviors across different areas (e.g., cognition and receptive communication), although it would not be unexpected to find these behaviors listed under different areas in other developmental scales or inventories.

Interpreting Results from the Communication Programming Inventory. After levels of functioning are established in all areas, one can refer to Table 10-1. Here, critical developmental levels are associated with specific communication programming procedural levels. For example, if a student is functioning in cognition from 1–4 months, in receptive communication from 4–8 months, in expressive communication from 4–8 months, and in social-affect from 4–8 months, the student is probably ready for communication training at the final resonance level. As a rule of thumb, however, the student's obtained cognitive level ought to be used as the key indicator for initiation into any programming level.

Although the results from the *Communication Programming Inventory* can be used to identify a starting level of prelanguage communication programming, it is important to remember that many students with severe or profound handicaps may be ready for instruction in more than one level at a time. Much will depend on the student's total behavioral repertoire. For example, even though the results from the inventory may indicate preferred initial program placement at a resonance level step, it might be appropriate to attempt certain programming at a higher (coactive) level if the student exhibits certain behavioral exemplars indicating readiness for that level.

Given the many problems inherent in obtaining communication assessment information for students with severe or profound handicaps (Rowland, 1985), a word of caution is in order. The *Communication Programming Inventory* was developed to provide *rough* estimates of functioning levels. Its intended use is for initial instructional program placement and, as such, should not be considered an instrument appropriate for either in-depth assessment or as a post-test for instructional gain.

Operationalizing Communication Programming. The following are programming strategies presented in relation to the procedural levels specified in Table 10-1. Use of many of the strategies with students with profound handicaps has received preliminary research support, although the longitudinal nature of skills development has not been validated (McNerney, Sternberg, & Kowsakowski, 1987; Sternberg, McNerney, & Pegnatore, 1985; Sternberg, McNerney, & Pegnatore, 1987; Sternberg, Pegnatore, & Hill, 1983).

All strategies are written from the perspective that the reader is the communication facilitator. Again, given the heterogeneity both between and within students with severe or profound handicaps, it might be appropriate to attempt programming endeavors at more than one level.

Procedural Level: Preresonance
Area: Tolerance
Objective: To accept (tolerate) resonance level physical contact
Strategy: This strategy is used with students who are eligible for resonance level communication programming but who cannot tolerate or accept any body-to-body or tactual types of input. First determine a preferable resonance level position in which you intend to conduct communication training (e.g., a body-to-body rocking position). Align the student and yourself close to this position, making sure that no direct body-to-body contact is evident. Slowly, assume the resonance level position in contact with the student. If the student shows displeasure with the contact (e.g., cries, attempts to scoot away, etc.), immediately discontinue the resonance level contact. Wait a brief period, and reinstitute the resonance level contact. Attempt to determine the average amount of time between the initiation of the resonance level contact and the beginning of displeasure.

During subsequent training sessions, the intent is to increase gradually the amount of time the student will tolerate or accept the resonance level contact. When one resonance level position is tolerated, proceed to other resonance positions. If the student has the potential for an extremely limited behavioral repertoire (a student who is, for example, bedridden and quadriplegic), you may attempt to accomplish the same tolerance development on a water bed or by using tactual stimuli other than body-to-body contact (e.g., applying different-textured objects against the body, applying a warm electric blanket on the body, tickling, etc.).

Procedural Level: Initial Resonance
Area: Receptive Communication
Objective: To produce a motor or vocal response that indicates awareness of resonance movement
Strategy: Place yourself in a position in close physical contact with the student (e.g., sitting on a mat with the student's back against your chest). If the position prevents you from observing the student's face, it is probably best to place a full-length mirror in front of the student. Begin to move with the student, following the student's lead. Make sure to employ a movement the student has in his or her behavioral repertoire (such as rocking). While

moving, observe whether the student exhibits a behavior (smiling, furrowing the brow, cooing, etc.) that indicates he or she is aware of the movement. Stop the movement to determine whether the student's awareness behavior changes to indicate that he or she realizes the movement has terminated.

Feel free to modify the rate and intensity of the movement during any intervention session. Also, it is appropriate to experiment with other types of resonance level movements that are in the behavioral repertoire of the student (e.g., swaying, swinging on a swing) to see if they lead to the display of communication awareness behaviors.

If the student can move but does not consistently display either a preference for a certain movement or any independent movement you can easily target for intervention, select a movement you feel is appropriate and nonthreatening. For example, you may bounce with a student on a trampoline in a resonance position. Then proceed with the strategy.

If the student's behavioral repertoire is extremely limited (as with a bedridden student who is quadriplegic), but some movement can be initiated, move the student carefully in a repetitious manner (e.g., rolling back and forth on the side using a vestibular board or water bed). If you are moving the student by pushing with your hands on his or her back, place a mirror so that you can observe facial reactions (awareness). Stop the movement to determine if the awareness behavior changes.

If the student's behavioral repertoire is so limited as to preclude the possibility of movement, provide alternative resonance level stimuli, such as tickling the face or torso, a heat lamp, rubbing a wet washcloth or cream on the face or torso, or other types of tactual stimuli. The on-again, off-again strategy described above should be employed. Any awareness behavior should be monitored, including nonvocal and nonvoluntary motor behaviors (e.g., primitive reflex patterns or changes in postural tone). It would also be appropriate to provide gustatory, olfactory, or vestibular stimuli if tactual stimuli do not produce any effect.

Procedural Level: Initial Resonance
Area: Expressive Communication
Objective: To demonstrate more active participation movements during resonance communication
Strategy: Place yourself in a position in close physical contact with the student (e.g., sitting on a mat with the student facing you with upper legs draped over your upper legs). Begin to move with the student, employing a movement the student has in his or her behavioral repertoire (such as swaying). While moving, observe

whether there is a noticeable change in the level of participation of the student.

Initial participation may be only a voluntary acceptance by the student of your guiding him or her into the movement. More active participation might be an increase in the rate of movement of the student, an introductory attempt at expressing his or her desire to continue. Use different types of resonance level movements during intervention sessions.

For students with extremely limited behavioral repertoires, consistent duration decreases between the termination of a resonance level stimuli (e.g., tickling) and the exhibition of a response (e.g., a vocalization) may be taken as an indication of more active participation.

Procedural Level: Final Resonance
Area: Receptive Communication
Objective: To make anticipatory responses during resonance communication
Strategy: Place yourself in a position in close physical contact with the student (e.g., sitting on a mat with the student's back against your chest). Begin to move with the student, employing a movement the student has in his or her behavioral repertoire (such as rocking). Once the student stops the movement (you may wish to stop the movement yourself if the student continues the movement for a prolonged time), see whether the student, of his or her volition, begins a component of the movement (e.g., a slight movement forward). If the component is begun by the student, follow it immediately with the entire resonance movement. It is also possible that the student will begin an anticipatory movement once the position for resonance movement is assumed (e.g., once both of you are sitting on the mat in close physical contact). In this case, make sure the total resonance level movement follows his or her movement immediately.

It is appropriate, at this time, to use *fixed* sequences of resonance level movements in each training session (e.g., rocking and then swaying). Again, if the student displays a partial anticipatory movement during a pause in movement (e.g., a partial rock forward for rocking *or* a slight lean to the left or right for swaying), follow the anticipatory behavior with the corresponding resonance level movement.

In the case of a student with an extremely limited behavioral repertoire, anticipatory responses may be extremely difficult to observe. However, be aware of any behavior the student may begin to employ for both communication and anticipation (e.g., a reflex movement exhibited just before the application of tactile stimuli or as a result of merely being positioned for resonance level training).

Procedural Level: Final Resonance
Area: Expressive Communication
Objective: To produce gross to fine motor initiation signals (and/or vocalizations) during resonance communication
Strategy: Place yourself in a position in close physical contact with the student (e.g., sitting on a mat with the student facing you, on your lap, with upper legs draped over your upper legs). If your position prevents you from observing the student's face, it is probably best to place a full-length mirror in front of the student. If you are using only one resonance level movement, begin the movement with the student. This should be a movement the student has in his or her behavioral repertoire and one for which the student has shown preference. Do not wait for the student to stop the movement, rather stop the movement yourself after a short duration. If the student makes a very defined gross body movement (such as a *full* rock forward), follow this immediately with the corresponding movement (rocking). Stop the movement after a short duration. Wait for the *same* full gross body movement and follow this *signal* immediately with the corresponding movement. In the event the student makes some other movement (a rock backwards, swaying), do *not* follow with the movement. Rather, physically guide the student's body through the appropriate signal response (pushing the student fully forward), and follow the signal immediately with the corresponding movement. Any appropriate vocalization (non–self-stimulatory sound) or attempt at vocalization (such as mouth opening) can also be used as a signal for the movement. If, however, a body movement signal is used, it should represent a portion of the resonance activity.

If you are using more than one type of resonance level movement with the student during an intervention session, you should use them in a *fixed* sequence (e.g., rocking and then swaying). The same strategy is used, with one difference. If the student displays a signal for a movement different from the one just terminated, *do* follow that signal with the requested movement. This signal may not only indicate a desire to initiate the movement but a *choice* by the student (preference for one movement over another).

Once the student shows a consistent full gross body signal to start a movement, begin to shape a fine motor signal. For example, if a full, forward rocking movement is the signal, each time the signal is given make sure the student at the same time produces a fine motor signal (such as grabbing your hand or patting the mat). This can be accomplished by physically guiding the student's hand to produce the intended fine motor signal. The fine motor signal selected should be one the student is capable of exhibiting and that preferably has no self-stimulatory qualities associated with it. After a period of time, begin to fade out the physical guidance. It will also be necessary to fade out the gross body signal and, finally, to use only the fine motor signal as a cue for movement. Be extremely aware of the student's voluntary use of the signal as opposed to your continued cueing of the signal.

It is necessary to develop a number of signal-to-movement matches. If you are operating with a fixed sequence of movements, it would not be unusual to find that a fine motor signal developed with one movement will be used by the student to attempt to initiate another movement. This is probably due to the fact that the fine motor signal is more abstract than the gross motor signal, and that the student understands the signal as only a "start" or "go" signal for any movement. Therefore, *in fixed sequence training,* it is important to delay the resonance level movement briefly after a fine motor signal is displayed. During the delay, see which movement (or, perhaps, gross motor signal) the student begins to initiate. If it is the "correct" movement (the one associated with the signal), proceed with the movement. If it is not, begin shaping for a new fine motor signal to be associated with the movement. If vocalization or attempts at vocalization are used as signals, make sure discrete signals are used (distinctly different vocalizations for different movements).

In the case of a student with an extremely limited behavioral repertoire but whose body can be moved (e.g., by rocking on the side on a vestibular board, by rocking on your lap in a rocking chair), you may begin to shape the student's facial movements or postural tone as discrete signals for movements you initiate and terminate with the student's body.

If no movement is possible, very basic responses (e.g., stimulated reflex patterns, increased or decreased respiration levels, eye blinks) should be monitored as possible signals.

Procedural Level: Initial Coactive Movement
Area: Receptive Communication

Objective: To imitate gross motor symmetric movements or
positions during coactive movement sequences
Strategy: Place yourself in a position so that the student can
observe your movements. Body-to-body physical contact is not
necessary. Begin to exhibit gross motor movements or positions
that are symmetric (e.g., both arms moving up and down, both
arms extended to the side and held there). If the student is accustomed to resonance activities, you may wish to use movements
that were used during that level. Indicate to the student that you
want him or her to exhibit the same gross motor movement or
positions *while* you are exhibiting the movement or position.
This can be accomplished by showing the movement or position,
and then, as he or she exhibits the movement or position, duplicating with your body. Focus should be on the student's voluntary imitation of gross motor symmetric movements or positions
while the student observes a model performing the movement or
assuming a position.

If the student is blind, make sure that as you perform a movement or
assume a position you allow the student to touch your body (tactile
receptive communication) to indicate what to imitate. Follow the
procedure, allowing the student to break during his or her imitation to
touch your body continually to provide the model cue for his or her
movement or position.

For sighted students with limited motor repertoires, major adaptations
in acceptable responses will be necessary. If any student gross motor
movements or positions are possible, use them as either coactive models
or as acceptable approximations of other more in-depth movements or
positions you assume.

It is important to select the activities, if possible, in the framework of
functional imitation. That is, attempts should be made to develop imitation of purposeful movements/positions rather than imitation skills in
and of themselves.

Procedural Level: Initial Coactive Movement
Area: Expressive Communication
Objective: To produce fine motor signals (and/or vocalizations)
to initiate coactive movement exercises
Strategy: Place yourself in a position so that the student can
observe your movements. Body-to-body physical contact is not
necessary. It is assumed that the student has already shown the
capability of coactively imitating the movement you have

selected, and that the movement is typically preferred by the student. Initially, you may display the coactive model and allow the student to imitate the movement. However, before you display the movement again, request that the student exhibit a fine motor signal (such as grasping your hand) or vocalization (or vocalization attempt). The fine motor signal or vocalization selected should be one the student is capable of displaying and that does not have any self-stimulatory qualities associated with it. The request for the signal can be initiated by shaping the signal and must be followed immediately by a movement. It is imperative that once the movement is stopped, the signal is terminated. This will aid the student in understanding that the signal is used to *start* the movement, not to stop it.

If the student has been involved in resonance activities, you may wish to use movements and signals that were used in that level. It is also appropriate to allow the student to exhibit the movement while you exhibit the movement, provided that the signal is employed each time to initiate the activity.

If the student is blind, make sure that as you perform a movement you allow the student to touch your body (tactile receptive communication) to indicate that his or her signal is being followed by your movement.

In the case of a sighted student with an extremely limited behavioral repertoire, major adaptations will be necessary. You may have to follow shaped or programmed signals (on the part of the student) with your movements. For example, if the student has a certain facial twitch as a signal for rocking, you should wait for that signal (physical guidance will be necessary at first), and then rock with your body so the student may observe your rocking. The student might not be able to exhibit the movement coactively, but the assumption is that, if possible, such coactive imitation would be accomplished. Again, the observed coactive model should be preferred by the student (e.g., in the past, the student smiled whenever you made the movement or assumed the position in front of him or her).

Procedural Level: Final Coactive Movement
Area: Receptive Communication
Objective: To imitate fine motor asymmetric movements or positions during coactive movement sequences
Strategy: Place yourself in a position so that the student can observe you. Body-to-body physical contact is not necessary. Begin to exhibit fine motor movements or positions that are asymmetric (e.g., extending and contracting the fingers on one

hand, a finger point). Indicate to the student that you want him or her to exhibit the same fine motor movement or position (*while* you exhibit it. This can be accomplished by showing the movement or position to the student, physically guiding him or her into the same movement or position, and then, as he or she exhibits the movement or position, duplicating it with your body. Focus should be on the student's voluntary imitation of fine motor asymmetric movements or positions *while* he or she observes a model performing the movement or assuming the position.

If the student is blind, make sure that as you perform a movement or assume a position you allow the student to touch your body (tactile receptive communication) to indicate what he or she is to imitate. Follow the procedure, allowing the student to break to touch your body continually to provide the model cue for the movement or position.

For sighted students with limited motor repertoires, major adaptations in acceptable responses will be necessary. If any student fine motor movements or positions are possible, use them as either coactive models or as acceptable approximations of other more in-depth movements or positions you assume.

Procedural Level: Final Coactive Movement
Area: Expressive Communication
Objective: To use objects to signal forthcoming activities
Strategy: Place, within reaching distance of the student, a set of horizontally connected cubicles (*anticipation shelves*), each large enough to hold objects that may be associated with a fixed sequence of activities conducted during the day (washcloth for washing, cup for mealtime, etc.). There should be enough cubicles to represent the major discrete activities of the day. Place in each cubicle an exact replica of a three-dimensional object that will be used routinely during a specific activity. Before that activity is to be conducted, take the student to the shelf to obtain the object signal. With the object in the student's hand, take the student to the activity area. The object is then placed aside. Once the activity is terminated, have the student pick up the object signal and return it to the shelf or (preferably) to a separate drop-off container (a "finished box" near the shelf). Every other activity in sequence should follow this pattern, with different objects associated with the remaining activities. Be aware of any anticipation responses on the part of the student (e.g., if he or she

begins to go to the shelf to obtain the object or to the appropriate activity area once the object is obtained). These anticipation responses should be developed by slowly fading out your physical guidance or assistance in using the shelf.

The composition and length of the shelf should be adjusted to meet the sensory and physical needs of the student. Attending to color contrast variables will assist students with visual difficulties. The actual size and number of cubicles should be reduced if the student has limited range of the upper extremities. For example, presenting a shelf with three cubicles to a student with limited reaching skills would mean the shelf would need to be "refilled" more than once a day.

Cue redundancy can also be used with the shelves. For example, each shelf can be lined with different textured or colored paper to provide additional separation cues. These additional cues can be faded once the student displays successful shelf behaviors.

If there are many occurrences of the same activity during the day (e.g., a number of toileting times), each of the occurrences should have its own cubicle in sequence; the same object should be used in each of the cubicles. That means that at any point in the day, there might be two or more identical object signals in different cubicles.

In the event the student has difficulty operating with more than one cubicle at a time (e.g., he or she tends to go after the closest object), it is appropriate to start with only one cubicle and one object. Once success has been achieved in using the cubicle, another cubicle and corresponding object can be added to its right. If the student then "regresses" to reaching for either object haphazardly, it is wise to stay with the two cubicles, but have only one object at a time placed in its appropriate cubicle (the remaining cubicle is left empty). Slowly expand the number of cubicles to represent all activities during the day.

If a student has an extremely limited behavioral repertoire, it will probably be necessary to shape an eye-attending or head-pointing response to the object on the shelf. The movement of the object to the activity area will be your responsibility. However, anticipatory eye-attending or head-pointing responses should be encouraged while en route to or upon arrival at the designated activity area.

Although these procedures can be used to teach the student to use the shelf mechanically, the ability of the student to represent the activity with the object is the desired end. Two teaching strategies can be used to help determine if activity representation is taking place. First, once the student has successfully displayed the mechanics, you can "mistakenly" switch the object placement in the shelf (e.g., put cubicle 3's object into cubicle 1). If the student takes the object and goes to the incorrect activity area (but the right one in sequence), he or she is only displaying knowledge of the correct activity sequence. However, if the student takes the object to the activity area the object represents (even though it's not the time to go to that activity), he or she is displaying initial representation. Second, you can leave all the objects in their correct cubicles. However, after the student acquires an object and begins to proceed to the correct activity area, you can attempt to redirect him or her to another ("wrong") activity. If activity representation is present, you would expect the student to indicate to you that he or she should be going to the "correct" activity (e.g., by holding out the object to you as if saying "No. This is where I'm supposed to be.").

Anticipation shelf procedures can also be used to develop choice behaviors. In this case, it is important to determine what activities the student prefers. One adaptation involves placing objects that represent those activities in cubicles in an anticipation shelf separate from the one used for the regular school-day schedule. During the day, the student can be taken to this shelf. The student is expected to select the shelf object. In this case, no right or wrong object is evident. Whichever object the student selects dictates which corresponding activity will then occur.

Procedural Level: Initial Deferred Imitation
Area: Receptive Communication
Objective: To imitate body movements and sequences of body movements after a model has been given
Strategy: Place yourself in a position so that the student may observe you. Tactile receptive communication may be necessary if the student is blind. Body-to-body physical contact is not necessary. Demonstrate any bodily movement or position to the student. Stop the demonstration, and request the student to do what you did. Begin to build up to sequences of bodily movements and positions (e.g., walking to crawling to sitting). Here, you model the entire sequence of movements or positions and then request the student to duplicate the sequence. Be extremely aware of any difficulty the student may encounter in remembering too many components of a sequence.

It may be appropriate to conduct some sequences on a long narrow bench. Aside from the flexibility afforded a teacher in terms of the many different movements and positions that can be conducted on a bench, a bench also has more obvious starting and stopping points (each end of the bench).

For students with extremely limited motor behaviors, it is important to use as models *any* behaviors the student can voluntarily exhibit provided they are not self-stimulatory in nature.

Procedural Level: Initial Deferred Imitation
Area: Receptive Communication
Objective: To point to various parts of his or her body and objects after a model has been given
Strategy: Place yourself in a position so that the student may observe you. Body-to-body physical contact is not necessary. Begin to point to parts of your body (e.g., nose, ear, mouth, arm, leg). Request the student to point to the same body part on his or her body. Initially, you may have to keep your model present while physically guiding the student to make the reference point on his or her body. As the student shows consistent success, fade out the physical guidance, and begin to ask the student to point to a specific body part *after* you have modeled the reference. For example, you should point to your foot, stop pointing, and ask the student to point to his or her foot (that is, do what I *did*). Emphasis should be placed on delaying (deferring) the student's imitation of *nonrepresentational reference* gestures. Although understanding verbal labels is important, the major purpose of this procedure is to help the student develop an understanding that he or she *can* reference his or her body through a pointing gesture.

If the student is blind, allow him or her to touch your body (tactile receptive communication) to indicate what to imitate. Emphasis should still be on the development of the reference gesture (point).

Once success is obtained using your own body as a model, provide a more abstract model (e.g., pointing to parts of a doll figure or to parts of the body on a picture of a person). As before, you may have to keep your model present while physically guiding the student to make the correct reference with his or her body. As the student shows consistent success, fade out the physical guidance, and begin to ask the student to duplicate the reference made on the abstract model *after* you have provided the model.

If the student is blind, and you are using a three-dimensional abstract model (e.g., a doll), allow the student to touch the doll (tactile receptive communication) to indicate what to imitate.

Once preliminary success has been seen with pointing to body parts, the pointing gesture should quickly be directed toward objects in the student's environment. Start with preferred and familiar objects, and then proceed to objects that are unfamiliar. As with the body parts reference, the major purpose of these procedures is to teach the student that he or she *can* reference objects in the environment.

Procedural Level: Initial Deferred Imitation
Area: Expressive Communication
Objective: To use abstract items to signal forthcoming activities
Strategy: Place, within reaching distance of the student, a set of horizontally connected cubicles (*anticipation shelves*), each large enough to hold pictures that may be associated with a fixed sequence of activities conducted during the day (a picture of a washcloth for washing, a picture of a cup for mealtime, etc.). There should be enough cubicles to represent the major discrete activities of the day. Place in each cubicle a picture that will be used in association with a specific activity. Selection may be based on objects used during an earlier use of anticipation shelves (final coactive movement level), and the shelf used may be identical. Before the activity is to be conducted, the student must obtain the corresponding picture and take it to the activity. Once the activity is completed, the student must return the picture to the empty cubicle or put it in a finished box or finished area. Every other activity in sequence should follow this pattern, with different pictures associated with the remaining activities.

Follow the use of pictures with line drawings, and eventually large print cards, each card containing a word associated with the picture and/or activity (thus, in place of a picture of a washcloth is a *WASH* word card). Initially, these cards should display both the line drawing and the word. Slowly fade out the use of the line drawing so that the student begins to rely increasingly on the more abstract representation.

As the shelves are used more often, begin to delay the onset of each activity until the student voluntarily obtains the abstract item and uses it to indicate to you that an activity should be forthcoming. For example, the student may obtain the picture or word card, come to you, and lead you to the activity area.

If the student has an extremely limited behavioral repertoire, it will probably be necessary for the student to use an eye-attending or head-pointing response to the abstract item as a signal. When returning the picture to the finished box, the student should use the same head or eye response to signal where he or she wants the picture placed.

Procedural Level: Initial Deferred Imitation
Area: Expressive Communication
Objective: To develop natural gestures as a form of self-communication
Strategy: Observe the student's interaction with objects, people, and events. Pay close attention to any fine motor behavior that he or she exhibits whenever an interaction takes place. A student playing with a favorite toy may initially touch or grasp it in a certain way (e.g., using a pincer grasp and rubbing the fingers together on a part of the toy). A student may rub his or her cheek each time feeding is to occur or shake the arms each time a certain person is present. These *natural gestures* are to be encouraged. Each time an object, person, or event that has an associated natural gesture is exposed to the student, the student should be requested to use the gesture. Encouragement can initially take the form of physical guidance and modeling of the gesture. For example, the student may exhibit a gesture when confronted with a favorite toy. You might then briefly remove the toy, grasp the student's hands and/or fingers to recreate that gesture, model the exact gesture with your hands and/or fingers in front of the student, and finally give the toy back to the student.

At this level one should not automatically expect that the student will use natural gestures expressively. That is, the student will not necessarily exhibit them to you to obtain an object, person, or event. Rather, the student will exhibit them when you request the student to do so.

Be keenly aware of situations where the student begins to use a gesture before playing with an object, interacting with a person, or participating in an activity, apparently for the purpose of self-communication. Also, at this level do not request that the student use a conventional word, sign, or symbol in association with natural gestures. You may wish to use these formal language signals with his or her gestures while you "converse" with the student, but it is only appropriate to request that the student use natural gestures.

Procedural Level: Final Deferred Imitation
Area: Receptive Communication
Objective: To reference people, objects, and activities after corresponding abstract representations have been provided
Strategy: Starting with persons, objects, and activities that are familiar and preferred by the student, create an abstract representation for each. It is appropriate to start with actual photo-

graphs of each referent. Begin to associate each representation with the corresponding person, object, or event. For example, you might point to a photograph of the student's favorite toy and ask him or her to point to the actual toy. Physical guidance or modeling of the correct response might be necessary, and initially you may have to keep the abstract representation present as the student points to the actual referent. Later, you should display the representation to the student, and then remove it. At this point, indicate to the student that you want him or her to then point to the corresponding referent that he or she just *saw*.

Once successful pointing performance has been accomplished using the actual photographs, you may proceed to use other pictures or line drawings that correspond to the person, object, or activity. The same strategies can then be extended to the new representations. You may have to pair the actual photograph with the more abstract representation initially, and then gradually fade the use of the photograph. Again, physical guidance or modeling of the response may be necessary.

Once you have successfully moved from actual photographs as representations, an alternative approach might be used. If the student can draw, allow him or her to draw his or her own representations of people, objects, and activities. These can then be associated with the corresponding referent.

If a student's motor difficulties preclude the possibility of exhibiting a pointing gesture, accept a head point or eye point as the appropriate gesture.

Procedural Level: Final Deferred Imitation
Area: Expressive Communication
Objective: To use natural gestures as a form of communication
Strategy: Request that the student use all of his or her natural gestures when such use is appropriate (when beginning to interact with objects, people, or events). Begin to interrupt such interaction (well after it has started) by requesting that the student exhibit the natural gesture associated with it. This interruption is done to show the student that the natural gesture can stand on its own as a sign for the object, person, or activity and is not merely a signal for the beginning of an interaction activity. Continue this procedure until the student begins to use the natural gestures expressively. This will typically take the form of natural gesture requests on the part of the student (without cueing from you) to obtain specific objects, people, or activities.

Once these requests become consistent, it is appropriate to pair each of the student's gestures with a formal language model (a word, sign, or symbol). In this case, each time the student exhibits an expressive natural gesture, duplicate it, and then model the formal language cue for that gesture. Then, encourage the student to imitate the formal language cue.

CONCLUSION

One might assume that the relative recency of programming efforts for students with severe or profound handicaps might produce a void in suggested interventions for communication skill development. Fortunately, this is not the case. Options are available, and it is up to professionals in the field not only to determine their utility but to develop further alternatives when necessary.

As previously discussed, once the student with handicaps has demonstrated the ability to use his or her own natural gestures expressively, formal language cues should be associated with them. The purpose is to aid the student in making the transition from "self-developed" communication symbols to "society-developed" language forms. The next chapter summarizes the major models of formal language instruction for students with severe handicaps, and outlines the various adaptations that might prove beneficial to formal language skills development.

REFERENCES

Bates, E. (1976). *Language and context: The acquisition of pragmatics.* New York: Academic Press.

Bates, E. (1979). *The emergence of symbols: Cognition and communication in infancy.* New York: Academic Press.

Bates, E., Benigni, L., Bretherton, I., Camaioni, L., & Volterra, V. (1977). From gesture to the first word: On cognitive and social prerequisites. In M. Lewis and L. Rosenblum (Eds.), *Interaction, conversation, and the development of language* (pp. 247-307). New York: John Wiley.

Bretherton, I., Bates, E., Benigni, L., Camaioni, L., & Volterra, V. (1979). Relationships between cognition, communication, and quality of attachment. In E. Bates (Ed.), *The emergence of symbols* (pp. 223-269). New York: Academic Press.

Bricker, D., & Schiefelbusch, R. (1984). Infants at risk. In L. McCormick & R. Schiefelbusch (Eds.), *Early language intervention* (pp. 243-266). Columbus, OH: Charles E. Merrill.

Bryen, D.N., & Joyce, D.G. (1985). Language intervention with the severely handicapped: A decade of research. *The Journal of Special Education, 19,* 1-39.

Chomsky, C. (1969). *The acquisition of syntax in children from five to ten.* Cambridge, MA: M.I.T. Press.

Cohen, M., Gross, P., & Haring, N. (1976). Developmental pinpoints. In N.G. Haring & L.J. Brown (Eds.), *Teaching the severely handicappe Vol. 1*, (pp. 35-110). New York: Grune & Stratton.

Cromer, R.F. (1974). Receptive language in the mentally retarded: Processes and diagnostic distinctions. In R.L. Schiefelbusch & L.L. Lloyd (Eds.), *Language perspectives: Acquisition, retardation, and intervention* (pp. 237-267). Baltimore: University Park Press.

Cromer, R. (1981). Reconceptualizing language acquisition and cognitive development. In R. Schiefelbusch & D.D. Bricker (Eds.), *Early language: Acquisition and intervention* (pp. 51-137). Baltimore: University Park Press.

Dunst, C.J. (1978). A cognitive-social approach for assessment of early nonverbal communication behavior. *Journal of Childhood Communication Disorders, 2*, 110-123.

Dunst, C.J. (1981). *Infant learning: A cognitive-linguistic intervention strategy.* Hingham, MA: Teaching Resources Corporation.

Dunst, C.J., & Lowe, L.W. (1986). From reflex to symbol: Describing, explaining, and fostering communicative competence. *Augmentative and Alternative Communication, 2* (1), 11-18.

Finch-Williams, A. (1984). The developmental relationship between cognition and communication: Implications for assessment. *Topics in Language Disorders, 5*, 1-13.

Frye, D. (1981). Developmental changes in strategies of social interaction. In M. E. Lamb & L. R. Sherrod (Eds.), *Infant social cognition: Empirical and theoretical considerations* (pp. 315-331). Hillsdale, NJ: Lawrence Erlbaum Associates.

Furth, H. (1970). On language and knowing in Piaget's developmental theory. *Human Development, 13*, 241-257.

Furth, H. (1971). Linguistic deficiency and thinking: Research with deaf subjects, 1964-1969. *Psychological Bulletin, 71*, 83.

Gray, B., & Ryan, B. (1973). *A language program for the nonlanguage child.* Champaign, IL: Research Press.

Guess, D., Sailor, W., & Baer, D. (1974). To teach language to retarded children. In R. L. Schiefelbusch & L. L. Lloyd (Eds.), *Language perspectives: Acquisition, retardation, and intervention* (pp. 529-563). Baltimore: University Park Press.

Guess, D., Sailor, W., & Baer, D. (1976). *Functional speech and language training for the severely handicapped.* Lawrence, KS: H & H Enterprises.

Horstmeier, D., & MacDonald, J. (1978). *Ready, set, go—Talk to me.* Columbus, OH: Charles E. Merrill.

Kahn, J. (1975). Relationship of Piaget's sensorimotor period to language acquisition of profoundly retarded children. *American Journal of Mental Deficiency, 79*, 640-643.

Kirk, S., McCarthy, J., & Kirk, W. (1968). *Illinois test of psycholinguistic abilities.* Urbana, IL: University of Illinois Press.

Lee, L. (1971). *Northwestern syntax screening test.* Evanston, IL: Northwestern University Press.

Leonard, L. (1978). Cognitive factors in early linguistic development. In R. Schiefelbusch (Ed.), *Bases of language intervention* (pp. 67-96). Baltimore: University Park Press.

Lobato, D., Barrera, R.D., & Feldman, R.S. (1981). Sensorimotor functioning and prelinguistic communication of severely and profoundly retarded individuals. *American Journal of Mental Deficiency, 85* (5), 489-496.

MacDonald, J.D. (1978). *Environmental language inventory.* Columbus, OH: Charles E. Merrill.

MacDonald, J.D. (1986). *ECO II: Interactional assessment of social play, communication, language and conversation.* Columbus, OH: Nisonger Center, Ohio State University.

MacDonald, J.D., & Gillette, Y. (1984a). Conversation engineering: A pragmatic approach to early social competence. *Seminars in Speech and Language, 5* (3), 171-183.

MacDonald, J.D., & Gillette, Y. (1984b). *ECOMAPS: A manual for assessing language through conversation and glossary for ECO intervention program.* Columbus, OH: Nisonger Center, Ohio State University.

MacDonald, J.D., & Gillette, Y. (1985). Taking turns: Teaching communication to your child. *The Exceptional Parent, 15,* 49-52.

MacDonald, J.D., & Gillette, Y. (1986a). *ECO-MATCH: Assessing communication development of delayed persons with their significant others.* Columbus, OH: Nisonger Center, Ohio State University.

MacDonald, J.D., & Gillette, Y. (1986b). Communicating with persons with severe handicaps. Role of parents and professionals. *Journal of the Association for Persons with Severe Handicaps, 11*(4), 255-265.

McLean, J.E., & Snyder-McLean, L. (1978). *A transactional approach to early language training.* Columbus, OH: Charles E. Merrill.

McLean, J.E., Snyder-McLean, L., Rowland, C., Jacobs, P., & Sack S. (1981). *Generic skills assessment inventory.* Lawrence, KS: Bureau of Child Research, University of Kansas.

McNeill, D. (1970). The development of language. In P. Mussen (Ed.), *Carmichael's manual of child psychology* (pp. 1061-1161). New York: John Wiley.

McNerney, C., Sternberg, L., & Kowsakowski, D. (1987). *The use of objects as communication signals with students with profound handicaps.* Geneseo, NY: State University College at Geneseo. Unpublished manuscript.

Moorehead, D., & Ingram, C. (1973). The development of base syntax in normal and deviant children. *Journal of Speech and Hearing Research, 16,* 330-352.

Reichle, J., & Karlan, G. (1985). The selection of an augmentative system in communication intervention: A critique of decision rules. *The Journal of the Association for Persons with Severe Handicaps, 10*(3), 146-156.

Robinson, C.C., & Robinson, J.H. (1983). Sensorimotor functions and cognitive development. In M.E. Snell (Ed.), *Systematic instruction of the moderately and severely handicapped* (2nd ed., pp. 227-266). Columbus, OH: Charles E. Merrill.

Rogers-Warren, A.V., & Warren, S.F. (1984). The social basis of language and communication in severely handicapped preschoolers. *Topics in Early Childhood Special Education, 4,* 57-72.

Rowland, C.M. (1985). Perspectives on communication assessment. In M. Bullis (Ed.), *Communication development in young children with deaf-blindness: Literature review I* (pp. 1-19). Monmouth, OR: Deaf-Blind Communication Skills Center, Teaching Research Division, Oregon State System of Higher Education.

Siegel-Causey, E., & Guess, D. (1985). Early development of prelinguistic communication. In M. Bullis (Ed.), *Communication development in young children with deaf-blindness: Literature review I* (pp. 61-77). Monmouth, OR: Deaf-Blind Communication Skills Center, Teaching Research Division, Oregon State System of Higher Education.

Sternberg, L., Battle, C., & Hill, J. (1980). Prelanguage communication programming for the severely and profoundly handicapped. *Journal of the Association for the Severely Handicapped, 5,* 224-233.

Sternberg, L., McNerney, C., & Pegnatore, L. (1985). Developing co-active imitative behaviors with profoundly mentally handicapped students. *Education and Training of the Mentally Retarded, 20*(4), 260-267.

Sternberg, L., McNerney, C., & Pegnatore, L. (1987). Developing primitive signalling behavior with profoundly mentally handicapped students. *Mental Retardation, 25* (1), 13-20.

Sternberg, L., Pegnatore, L., & Hill, C. (1983). Establishing interactive communication behaviors with profoundly handicapped students. *Journal of the Association for the Severely Handicapped, 8*(2), 39-46.

Stillman, R. (Ed.). (1978). *The Callier-Azusa scale.* Dallas: University of Texas at Dallas, Callier Center for Communication Disorders.

Stillman, R.D., & Battle, C.W. (1984). Developing communication in the severely handicapped: An interpretation of the Van Dijk method. *Seminars in Speech and Language, 5* (3), 159-169.

Stremel-Campbell, K. (1984). *The Communication Placement Assessment.* Monmouth, OR: Teaching Research Division, Oregon State System of Higher Education.

Sugarman, S. (1981). The development of preverbal communication: Its contribution and limits in promoting the development of language. In R. Schiefelbusch & D.D. Bricker (Eds.), *Early language: Acquisition and intervention* (pp. 26-67). Baltimore: University Park Press.

Van Dijk, J. (1965a). The first steps of the deaf-blind child towards language. *Proceedings of the conference on the deaf-blind, Refsnes, Denmark.* Boston: Perkins School for the Blind.

Van Dijk, J. (1965b). Motor development in the education of deaf-blind children. *Proceedings of the conference on the deaf/blind, Refsnes, Denmark.* Boston: Perkins School for the Blind.

Van Dijk, J. (1967). The nonverbal deaf-blind child and his world: His outgrowth towards the world of symbols. *Verramelde Studies* (pp. 73-110). I. St. Michielsgestel, The Netherlands: Instituut voor Doven.

Van Dijk, J. (1969). Educational approaches to abnormal development: Deaf-blind children and their education. *Proceedings of the international conference on the education of deaf-blind children at St. Michielsgestel, The Netherlands.* Rotterdam, The Netherlands: Rotterdam University Press.

Warren, S. & Rogers-Warren, A., (Eds.). (1985). *Teaching functional language.* Baltimore: University Park Press.

Appendix 10-A

COMMUNICATION PROGRAMMING INVENTORY

DIRECTIONS FOR COMPLETING AND SCORING THE INVENTORY

To assess a student for communication programming, it is necessary that one who is familiar with the student provide the assessment information. However, it is not recommended that this information be based on material obtained from an interview. Rather, careful observation is required with the addition of anecdotal records (if appropriate). The following is a list of preferred strategies for conducting an assessment with this inventory:

- Become familiar with the selected behaviors sampled. This will require becoming aware of slight differences between similar behaviors at different developmental levels. Numbers preceding behaviors indicate the relative ordinal position of the behavior in that level. Letters indicate different behaviors at the same basic position and do not presuppose any order of development.
- Observe the student, preferably in different situations with different people. This observation should be conducted for no less than one week. This will give the opportunity for enough behaviors to be sampled and observed.
- Determine if behaviors observed are either person-specific or situation-specific. If the student exhibits an observed behavior only with a certain person present or only within a certain situation, do *not* conclude that that behavior is within the student's repertoire.

345

- Determine if behaviors observed occur only when certain artificial cues are given. For example, if the student exhibits a behavior only when a physical prompt is administered, do *not* conclude that the behavior is in the student's repertoire. *Remember, however, that an artificial cue to one individual might be a natural cue to another* (e.g., a student who is deaf and blind might need a tactual cue to respond; this may very well be that student's natural cue).

Once the observation is concluded, the inventory should be completed. Each behavior listed in the *Communication Programming Inventory* can be rated in one of four ways. A *Yes* check indicates the behavior is in the student's repertoire (it occurs without artificial prompts and occurs across different people and different situations). A *Pos* check indicates the behavior is present but either occurs with the use of artificial prompts or is person- or situation-specific. A *No* check indicates the student does not exhibit the behavior at the present time, but may in the future. A *NA* check indicates the student's handicapping condition precludes present *and* future exhibition of the behavior (a student who is born without eyes, for example, will not be able to track a moving object visually. *All behaviors on the inventory should be rated.*

It is important to note that items that can be adapted ought to be adapted to the student's handicapping condition. For example, an item that stresses a visual cue may be changed for a student who is blind. If the item were "recognizes the object as same whether he or she sees part or all" (Cognition: 4-8 months), it would be appropriate to allow a student who is blind to touch only a part of a familiar toy and see whether he or she discards the toy or attempts to play with it without further tactual investigation. This type of adaptation is necessary for students with auditory and/or motor impairments as well. For each adaptation the communication facilitator feels is justified, a notation of the type of adaptation should be made to the side of the item.

To score the responses on the *Communication Programming Inventory,* complete the following steps:

1. Add up the number of *Yes, Pos,* and *No* responses per level (such as Cognition: 0-1 month) to obtain the *Total # Score.*
2. Divide the *# Yes Score* by the *Total # Score* and multiply by 100. This produces the *% Yes Score.*
3. Locate the *% Yes Score* that is at least 50% and that has the highest position in the developmental sequence. This score is used to determine the *functioning level in each area.* For example, if one obtained in the area of receptive communication a 0-1 month *% Yes Score* of

100%, a 1-4 month *% Yes Score* of 80%, and all following level *% Yes Scores* below 50%, the functional level in the area of receptive communication would be designated as 1-4 months.

4. If two sequential levels have *% Yes Scores* above and very close to 50% (and the following level *% Yes Scores* are below 50%), it would probably be wise to designate the lower level as the functioning level.

Obviously, there may be students who do not exhibit behaviors that follow a simple or consistent sequence. It is advised that, if possible, another individual should conduct an independent observation of the student; later, both observations should be compared for consensus. If questions still exist, communication facilitator judgment should be used as the deciding factor.

Communication Programming Inventory

AREA: COGNITION

Level	Behaviors	Rating

Rating columns: Y E S / P O S / N O / N A

0 – 1 Month

1a. Reflexive behavior predominates (e.g., sucking, grasping, crying, body and head movements). ____ ____ ____ ____

  b. Movement present but not in response to external stimulation. ____ ____ ____ ____

  c. Not responsive to the environment. ____ ____ ____ ____

*2a. Objects evoke undifferentiated reflexive responses. ____ ____ ____ ____

*b. Behavior changes when stimulated (aurally, visually, or tactually). ____ ____ ____ ____

Total # Score + + / = ___
% Yes Score = ___

1 – 4 Months

1a. Repeats bodily movements; self-stimulation of body. ____ ____ ____ ____

  b. Anticipates familiar event when body placed in certain position (e.g., placement in slight reclining position for feeding leads consistently to an increase in movement). ____ ____ ____ ____

  c. Looks at spot where moving object or person last seen. ____ ____ ____ ____

  d. Moves head and eyes toward a sound in front of him/her that is coming from left or right (eye-ear coordination). ____ ____ ____ ____

  e. Eyes follow moving objects. ____ ____ ____ ____

  f. Sucks thumb (hand-mouth coordination). ____ ____ ____ ____

2a. Recognizes a familiar object or the beginning of a familiar activity (e.g., student produces the same type of sound or movement when confronted with familiar object or activity). ____ ____ ____ ____

  b. Shows preliminary object discrimination (e.g., quiets when given certain blanket but not when other objects are given). ____ ____ ____ ____

3. Unintentionally commits behavior(s) with object(s) and then repeats the behavior(s) on the object(s) (e.g., accidentally pushes object off table, continues to push other objects off table). ____ ____ ____ ____

Total # Score + + / = ___
% Yes Score = ___

*If *YES*, credit previous 1a, 1b, and 1c as *YES*.

AREA: COGNITION

Level	Behaviors	Rating
		Y P N N E O O A S S

4 – 8 Months

1a. Reaches persistently for objects or persons.   — — — —

  b. Grasps and manipulates all objects s/he can reach.   — — — —

  2. Performs one and then another behavior with objects, chaining these behaviors in a similar sequence with all objects (e.g., shakes and then mouths objects).   — — — —

3a. Turns back to where an object is after losing contact to attend to another object or activity.   — — — —

  b. Recognizes object as same whether s/he sees part or all (e.g., grabs partially hidden toy).   — — — —

  c. Explores new objects by visual, aural, and/or tactual means. — — — —

  d. Performs specific actions on specific familiar objects (e.g., squeaky toy is squeaked).   — — — —

  e. Anticipates positions objects will pass through while they are moving (e.g., looks for objects in places where s/he predicts they have fallen).   — — — —

Total # Score +   +   / = __
% Yes Score   = __

8 – 12 Months

1a. Searches for objects that disappear but not always in places where they are viewed to disappear; no comprehension of visible sequential displacement (e.g., s/he may look for an object that was hidden in the first hiding place although s/he saw that it was moved from that place to a second hiding place).   — — — —

  b. Uses two typical behaviors in sequence to obtain an object intentionally or achieve a goal (e.g., pushing aside one object to pick up another object).   — — — —

  c. Realizes that objects can cause action (e.g., another person shakes toy, the student grabs that person's hand to lead it to the toy to reproduce the action).   — — — —

AREA: COGNITION

Level	Behaviors	Rating
		Y P N N E O O A S S

8 – 12 Months

2a. Recognizes size differences of objects (e.g., handing the student a large object produces a wide arm grasp; a smaller object, vice versa). — — — —

b. Has preliminary shape constancy (e.g., given round blocks and shape formboard with only round holes, student places round blocks into the round holes). — — — —

Total # Score + + /

= __

% Yes Score = __

12 – 18 Months

1a. Looks for object in the place where s/he saw it disappear; comprehension of visible sequential displacement (e.g., after seeing an object hidden in one place and then another, the student searches for the object in the last hiding place). — — — —

b. Plays with objects in new ways, emphasizing the special visual, auditory, and/or tactual characteristics of the objects (e.g., rubs a rubber doll against his/her cheek). — — — —

2a. Spontaneously scribbles with pencils, pens, crayons, etc. — — — —

b. Shows, without a request, clothing and/or toys to familiar person. — — — —

3a. Functionally uses a variety of common objects other than those customarily used for feeding and dressing (e.g., uses a comb to comb his/her hair). — — — —

b. Locates objects in the place where they are customarily stored. — — — —

c. Experiments through trial-and-error to find new ways to solve problems (e.g., tries to reach toy on shelf by jumping up and down). — — — —

d. Places round and square blocks in formboard (given a formboard with round and square holes). — — — —

e. Begins to understand the use of household objects. — — — —

f. Engages in imaginary play using objects in their customary fashion (e.g., uses a spoon to feed a doll). — — — —

Total # Score + + / = __
% Yes Score = __

AREA: COGNITION

Level		Behaviors	YES	POS	NO	NA
18 – 24 Months	1a.	Solves practical problems without first engaging in trial-and-error behaviors (e.g., reaches toy on shelf by immediately getting a chair on which s/he can stand).	___	___	___	___
	b.	Plays by using objects to represent other objects (e.g., uses a bowl as a steering wheel).	___	___	___	___
	c.	Reproduces activities that normally occur in a different situation (e.g., pretends to make a bed in an area that is not for sleeping).	___	___	___	___
	d.	Understands that a picture can represent a real object if the picture is the same size and color as the object.	___	___	___	___
	2a.	Locates object where s/he left it after a protracted period of time (object is not customarily kept in that place).	___	___	___	___
	b.	Knows that a picture represents a real object even though the picture is a different size and/or color than the real object.	___	___	___	___
	c.	Recognizes differences in sizes of a set of objects (color and shape are the same) with which s/he plays frequently (e.g., stacking rings done correctly).	___	___	___	___
	d.	Finds objects that are hidden by invisible displacement; has object permanence (e.g., teacher's hand closed around thimble; hand under blanket; thimble released; hand withdrawn; student locates thimble under blanket).	___	___	___	___
	e.	Finds objects that are hidden by invisible sequential displacement (same as above, but sequential hiding places where the student first searches for the object in the last hiding place).	___	___	___	___

Total # Score + + / = ___

% Yes Score = ___

AREA: RECEPTIVE COMMUNICATION

Level	Behaviors	Rating
		Y P N N E O O A S S

0 – 1 Month

1a. Shows startle response to loud, sudden noises. — — — —

b. Stops movement in response to emitted noise (bell, rattle, noisemaker). — — — —

2a. Responds to tactile or kinesthetic stimulation. — — — —

b. Stops movement in response to voice. — — — —

c. Stops whimpering in response to friendly voice. — — — —

Total # Score + + / = __
% Yes Score = __

1 – 4 Months

1a. Exhibits gross body movement as attention to voices. — — — —

b. Looks toward speaker (head movement and/or eye movement) and responds by smiling. — — — —

c. Moves eyes toward source of noise. — — — —

d. Participates in *familiar* motion or movement after another has started the motion; physical contact necessary (e.g., student usually sways; teacher sways with student while in close physical contact; student freely participates in movement). — — — —

2a. Participates in another's *modification* of his/her movement after another provides physical cue (e.g., using physical guidance to assist the student through a new movement, the student more actively cooperates and participates). — — — —

b. Localizes speaker with eyes. — — — —

c. Watches lips and mouth of speaker. — — — —

3a. Searches for speaker. — — — —

b. Responds to angry voice by furrowing the brow or frowning. — — — —

c. Raises arm to be picked up in response to outreached arms of another. — — — —

Total # Score + + / = __
% Yes Score = __

AREA: RECEPTIVE COMMUNICATION

Level	Behaviors	Rating

Rating columns: Y E S / P O S / N O / N A

4 – 8 Months

1a. Responds to own name. ___ ___ ___ ___

b. Stops crying when someone talks to him/her. ___ ___ ___ ___

2a. Exhibits appropriate behavior to one or more tactile signals (e.g., tugging the student's arm leads to approach behavior). ___ ___ ___ ___

b. Begins the next movement in a routine sequence of movements (e.g., when accustomed to rocking and then swaying, student begins to sway after rocking stopped). ___ ___ ___ ___

c. Briefly continues new movement when another changes one of his/her habitual movements; physical contact is necessary (e.g., student waves arms horizontally; teacher physically guides student to wave arms vertically; student continues to wave arms vertically). ___ ___ ___ ___

d. Responds with appropriate bodily movements to "come," "up," "bye-bye," etc. ___ ___ ___ ___

e. Imitates familiar movements and/or sounds being produced by another (must see movement or hear sounds s/he is producing). ___ ___ ___ ___

f. Responds to angry tone by crying. ___ ___ ___ ___

3a. Turns head to familiar word. ___ ___ ___ ___

b. Stops activity when name is called. ___ ___ ___ ___

c. Responds to gestural games (e.g., peek-a-boo produces smile). ___ ___ ___ ___

d. Stops movement to the word *no*. ___ ___ ___ ___

Total # Score + + / = ___
% Yes Score = ___

8 – 12 Months

1a. Exhibits appropriate behaviors when commanded by gesture (e.g., teacher motions through gesture for student to sit down, student sits down). ___ ___ ___ ___

b. Imitates speech noises (e.g., smacking lips). ___ ___ ___ ___

2a. Anticipates a routine event from cues (e.g., shown an object that is being associated with an activity, the student goes to the activity). ___ ___ ___ ___

AREA: RECEPTIVE COMMUNICATION

Level	Behaviors	Rating

Rating columns:
Y P N N
E O O A
S S

8 – 12 Months

b. Gives toys or other objects on verbal request. ___ ___ ___ ___

c. While another is moving or vocalizing, student copies the different movements or vocalizations; physical contact is not necessary (movements or vocalizations must be in student's behavioral repertoire). ___ ___ ___ ___

3a. Interacts with an appropriate object when a gesture is made by another indicating how the student uses the object; the object must be present (e.g., making comb motion through hair, student touches comb that is present). ___ ___ ___ ___

b. Attends to object, person, or event being pointed to. ___ ___ ___ ___

c. Responds to rhythmic music by body or hand movements. ___ ___ ___ ___

d. After another completes simple movement, student imitates movement; position cue must be given; movement must be in student's behavioral repertoire. ___ ___ ___ ___

e. Enjoys rhymes and simple songs. ___ ___ ___ ___

f. Complies with certain actions to verbal requests (e.g., opens mouth when asked). ___ ___ ___ ___

Total # Score + + / = ___
% Yes Score = ___

12 – 18 Months

1a. Interacts with an appropriate object when a gesture is made by another indicating how the student uses the object; the object is not present (e.g., making a writing motion, student goes and obtains a crayon). ___ ___ ___ ___

b. After another has finished performing a simple movement, gesture, or vocalization, the student imitates; movement, gesture or vocalization is in student's repertoire; no position cue is necessary. ___ ___ ___ ___

2a. Exhibits appropriate behaviors to a few simple one-word commands communicated in formal language (e.g., "come," "sit," "eat"). ___ ___ ___ ___

b. Identifies familiar objects when those objects are referred to by the use of formal language (e.g., "cup," "shoe"). ___ ___ ___ ___

c. Responds to inhibitory words communicated in formal language (e.g., "stop," "wait"). ___ ___ ___ ___

AREA: RECEPTIVE COMMUNICATION

Level	Behaviors	Rating
		Y P N N E O O A S S

12 – 18 Months

d. After another has finished performing *new* (to the student) simple movements, gestures, or vocalizations, the student imitates. — — — —

3a. Exhibits appropriate behavior to two- or three-word commands or requests; action-object variety (e.g., "give shirt"). — — — —

b. Points to familiar persons, animals, toys on request. — — — —

c. Understands correspondence between parts of a three-dimensional model and parts of his/her body (e.g., points to his/her body parts that are being pointed to on a doll). — — — —

4a. Recognizes names of various parts of the body. — — — —

b. Imitates a *new sequence* of behaviors when each behavior within the sequence is part of the student's repertoire. — — — —

5a. Identifies any one object from a picture. — — — —

b. Carries out two-step directions with familiar object (e.g., "put the ball in the can and in the box"). — — — —

Total # Score + + / = __
% Yes Score = __

18 – 24 Months

1a. Carries out two-stage related commands stated in formal language (e.g., "get the ball and go out the door"). — — — —

b. Responds appropriately to "what" and "where" questions. — — — —

c. Demonstrates understanding of distinction in pronouns (e.g., "give it to her" versus "give it to me"). — — — —

2a. Carries out three-step directions with familiar object (e.g., "put the crayon on the table, in the drawer, and on the chair"). — — — —

b. Imitates activity or behavior sequence after a considerable amount of time. — — — —

c. Imitates two- and three-word sentences. — — — —

3a. Points to two objects given three choices. — — — —

b. Matches familiar objects. — — — —

c. Understands concept of "more." — — — —

Total # Score + + / = __
% Yes Score = __

AREA: EXPRESSIVE COMMUNICATION

Level	Behaviors	Rating

Rating columns: Y E S / P O S / N O / N A

0 – 1 Month

1a. Turns eyes to person's face (not prompted).   — — — —

b. Displays frequent crying.   — — — —

*2a. Vocalizes (other than crying).   — — — —

*b. Cries when hungry or uncomfortable.   — — — —

Total # Score + + / = ___
% Yes Score = ___

1 – 4 Months

1a. Smiles as familiar person talks.   — — — —

b. Smiles spontaneously.   — — — —

c. Makes single vowel-like sounds (e.g., "an," "en," "un").   — — — —

d. Vocalizes when spoken to (non-speech vocal noises resembling speech sounds).   — — — —

2. Cries with changes in pitch.   — — — —

3a. Signals by movement or vocalization to continue an activity; physical contact is necessary (e.g., student rocks with teacher in close physical contact; teacher stops movement; student signals to start movement again).   — — — —

b. Laughs during play with objects.   — — — —

c. Babbles using a series of syllables.   — — — —

Total # Score + + / = ___
% Yes Score = ___

*If *YES*, credit previous lb, as *YES*.

AREA: EXPRESSIVE COMMUNICATION

Level	Behaviors	Rating

Rating columns:
Y E S (YES), P O S (POS), N O (NO), N A (NA)

4 – 8 Months

1a. Uses movement or vocal signals in *several* activities to indicate to another to continue the activity (e.g., student may use multiple oral and/or motor signals to continue a movement). — — — —

b. Laughs aloud spontaneously. — — — —

2. Makes spontaneous vocal sounds for socialization purposes (e.g., growls, grunts). — — — —

3. Vocalizes single syllable (e.g., "da," "ba"). — — — —

4a. Makes polysyllabic vowel sounds (e.g., "ga-ma"). — — — —

b. Vocalizes with intonational pattern changes (pitch changes.) — — — —

c. Uses some gestural language (e.g., shaking head appropriately for "no"). — — — —

Total # Score + + / = ___
% Yes Score = ___

8 – 12 Months

1a. Uses simple gestures or vocalizations (not crying) to express wants or needs; the gestures or vocalizations are started by the student (e.g., although the request "what do you want?" is *not* given, student pulls another to door to leave the room). — — — —

b. Seizes noisemaker in hand and imitates noisemaker's action. — — — —

c. Babbles repeating syllables in a string (e.g., "ma-ma-ma"). — — — —

2a. Says first words often (e.g., "da-da"). — — — —

b. Uses echolalic *syllable* speech. — — — —

3a. Says one word (or short syllable) consistently to designate an object. — — — —

b. Initiates speech-gesture games like "pat-a-cake" or "peek-a-boo." — — — —

Total # Score + + / = ___
% Yes Score = ___

AREA: EXPRESSIVE COMMUNICATION

Level	Behaviors	Rating

		Y P N N
		E O O A
		S S

12 – 18 Months

1a. Has one or more gestures or vocalizations meaningful to him/her and others but only used in specific context (e.g., uses a bathroom gesture only at home). ___ ___ ___ ___

b. Offers objects to another. ___ ___ ___ ___

2a. Uses gestures when asking for or identifying objects; the gesture indicates how the student *uses* the object (e.g., sticks two fingers in mouth indicating that s/he wants a "security" blanket). ___ ___ ___ ___

b. Points to make another attend to something. ___ ___ ___ ___

3a. Spontaneously uses one or two words that stand for a variety of related objects, activities, and feelings; used in new and appropriate situations (e.g., uses a word for bathroom when s/he uses the bathroom, when s/he sees another using the bathroom, when s/he visits a new bathroom area.) ___ ___ ___ ___

b. Uses gesture, word, sign, or point to request aid in getting something. ___ ___ ___ ___

c. Uses gesture, specific vocalizations, or signs to represent objects or activities (object must be within student's perceptual field). ___ ___ ___ ___

d. Uses gesture, word, sign, or point to obtain interaction with another person. ___ ___ ___ ___

4a. Has vocabulary of at least four to six spontaneously used words (often indicating immediate wants and needs). ___ ___ ___ ___

b. Vocalizes in protest. ___ ___ ___ ___

Total # Score + + / = ___
% Yes Score = ___

18 – 24 Months

1a. Has vocabulary of at least ten spontaneously and appropriately used words. ___ ___ ___ ___

b. Begins using words rather than gestures to express wants and needs. ___ ___ ___ ___

c. Makes one word responses using initial consonant with vowel but not final consonant. ___ ___ ___ ___

AREA: EXPRESSIVE COMMUNICATION

Level	Behaviors	Rating
		Y P N N E O O A S S

18 – 24 Months

2. Uses gestures, vocalizations, or signs to represent objects or activities (object need not be within student's perceptual field). — — — —

3a. Uses successive single words or signs to describe the same object or event (e.g., "ball" then "red"). — — — —

b. Shows interest in learning new words. — — — —

c. Combines two different words in speech to form short phrase/sentence (e.g., "go bye-bye"). — — — —

4. Uses expressive vocabulary of at least 15 words. — — — —

5a. Uses "me," "you," refers to self by name. — — — —

b. Asks for water when thirsty (formal language). — — — —

c. Asks for food when hungry (formal language). — — — —

6a. Has oral language of 50 spontaneously and appropriately used words. — — — —

b. Combines two words in form: modifier-object (e.g., "pretty ball"), object-modifier (e.g., "ball pretty"), action-object (e.g., "go car"), object-object (e.g., "Tommy bike"). — — — —

c. Uses "no" to indicate refusal. — — — —

d. Begins to use "no," "not" in combination with other words (e.g., "no milk"). — — — —

e. Names familiar picture cards. — — — —

Total # Score +   +   /   =   __
% Yes Score   =   __

AREA: SOCIAL/AFFECTIVE BEHAVIORS

Level		Behaviors	Rating

			Y E S	P O S	N O	N A

0 – 1 Month

			Y E S	P O S	N O	N A
1.	Reacts positively to comfort or pleasant stimuli.		—	—	—	—
2.	Reacts negatively to unpleasant stimuli.		—	—	—	—
3a.	Reacts to people in immediate environment.		—	—	—	—
b.	Fixes eyes on person's face (not prompted).		—	—	—	—
4a.	Looks at (fixates on) an interesting object (8-12″ away).		—	—	—	—
b.	Maintains gaze as an object is slowly moved side to side.		—	—	—	—

Total # Score + + / = __
% Yes Score = __

1 – 4 Months

1a.	Regards people alertly.		—	—	—	—
b.	Shows emerging interest in environment.		—	—	—	—
c.	Inspects environment visually.		—	—	—	—
d.	Increases/decreases activity level upon seeing an interesting object.		—	—	—	—
2.	Reacts to direct attention by moving, vocalizing, or smiling.		—	—	—	—
3.	Shows emerging recognition of a few familiar people.		—	—	—	—
b.	Responds in a specific way to a person, sound, or object in a familiar routine or activity.		—	—	—	—
4.	Enjoys attention from familiar others.		—	—	—	—

Total # Score + + / = __
% Yes Score = __

4 – 8 Months

1a.	Exhibits sustained interest in objects.		—	—	—	—
b.	Demonstrates specific desires through facial movements, vocalizations, muscle tone, etc.		—	—	—	—
c.	Displays active interest in environment.		—	—	—	—
2a.	Responds to social approach and continues interest in persons present.		—	—	—	—
b.	Responds consistently in at least two various ways when adult is stimulus.		—	—	—	—

AREA: SOCIAL/AFFECTIVE BEHAVIORS

Level	Behaviors	Rating

Rating columns: **YES PNO NOS NA**

4 – 8 Months

3a. Recognizes familiar people (e.g., produces the same type of sound or movement when confronted with a familiar person).   — — — —

b. Shows some kind of discrimination toward strangers (e.g., crying, staring).   — — — —

c. Recognizes self in mirror.   — — — —

4a. Demonstrates awareness of strange situation.   — — — —

b. Expresses protest through body movements, sounds, or mood changes.   — — — —

c. Will resist adult who attempts to take toy away.   — — — —

5. Attempts to solicit adult attention through eye contact, vocalizing, smiling.   — — — —

Total # Score +   +   /   =   __
% Yes Score   =   __

8 – 12 Months

1. Displays curiosity, yet is overtly cautious.   — — — —

2a. Demonstrates affection or extreme contentment in specific familiar situations.   — — — —

b. Overtly seeks reactions from others.   — — — —

3a. Responds consistently to name with smile, eye contact, head turn, etc.   — — — —

b. Demonstrates beginning awareness of the meaning of "no."   — — — —

c. Shows understanding of difference between 'good' and 'bad' (e.g., naughty).   — — — —

4a. Repeats a performance that elicits laughter from others (i.e., demonstrates awareness of social approval).   — — — —

b. Solicits familiar persons through reaching or shouting.   — — — —

Total # Score +   +   /   =   __
% Yes Score   =   __

AREA: SOCIAL/AFFECTIVE BEHAVIORS

Level	Behaviors	Rating

Rating columns: Y E S (Yes), P O S (Pos), N O O (Noo), N A (Na)

12 – 18 Months

1. Cooperates in social interaction when initiated by others (e.g., simple games, self-care routines, etc.) _ _ _ _

2a. Will surrender toy to an adult upon request. _ _ _ _

b. Shows preference for completing tasks on own. _ _ _ _

3a. Will initiate interaction with familiar people by offering an object, imitating an action, or initiating a play routine. _ _ _ _

b. Interacts with groups of children in a parallel fashion when common toys or objects are present. _ _ _ _

c. Expresses compassion for other children. _ _ _ _

d. Will put own toys away in imitation of adult doing same. _ _ _ _

Total # Score + + / = __
% Yes Score = __

18 – 24 Months

1a. Demonstrates refusal to comply (which may take form of a temper tantrum) as adult demands are made. _ _ _ _

b. Shows beginning use of objects to establish social relations with people. _ _ _ _

c. Imitates others in play. _ _ _ _

2a. Will direct an adult to continue a preferred activity. _ _ _ _

b. Demonstrates self-identification (e.g., can call self by name, or refer to objects as 'mine'). _ _ _ _

c. Begins to claim and defend ownership of personal things. _ _ _ _

3a. Will actively seek out friend or familiar other, avoiding strangers in a social setting. _ _ _ _

b. Enjoys role playing, particularly when adult activities are being modelled. _ _ _ _

c. Will occupy self at play either on own initiative or at adult's suggestion. _ _ _ _

Total # Score + + / = __
% Yes Score = __

Chapter 11

Language Instruction

Lawrence F. Molt and Kay Younginger

PROBLEM AND PAST PRACTICES

Even as prelanguage instruction for the student with severe or profound handicaps is beginning, consideration of all probable future modes of primary language communication should be initiated. Although different concepts and definitions of language have been tendered, in the context of this chapter language is conceived of as a formal structure of communication in which output is generative and spontaneous. *Generative* means that a finite number of responses (e.g., words, signs, symbols, or gestures) can serve to communicate an infinite number of messages. *Spontaneous* means that output occurs in the presence of naturally occurring cues (situations).

Factors that shape prelanguage instruction, and additional factors affecting communication that are often discovered during prelanguage preparation, are also critical in shaping the selection of future modes of language instruction and usage for an individual. Discussing the options and issues relating to language instruction and relating and recommending methodology for language instruction for students with severe or profound handicaps in a single chapter is no easy matter. The difficulty rests not only with the heterogeneity of the population but with the preponderance of instructional options. The advocacy of a single instructional model is inappropriate for such a diverse population. The communication impairment of a student with severe or profound handicaps may be the manifestation of any number of etiologic, physical, neurologic, or emotional factors appearing in isolation, or, as is more often observed in the population, in combination. Each factor will have its unique influence on communication development and performance, and the nature of this influence will vary widely among factors. Determining the influence of any single factor often may be further confounded by the interaction of factors.

Historically, past practices in language training for these students often emphasized the use of a number of methodological formats (Bryen & Joyce, 1985). Primarily, targeted language skills were often viewed in the same context as any other skill. For example, efforts to assist students acquire language skills were often very similar to those used to help them perform various other tasks or activities of daily living. It was not uncommon to see language programs conducted as one-to-one isolated attempts, in artificial environments, and without thoughts of integrating the language skills into other appropriate situations or skills development. Often, language responses were developed under stimulus control procedures (Halle, 1987) such that responses were trained to questions (e.g., "What do you want?"), commands (e.g., "Tell me what you want."), or verbal labels as models (e.g., "plate"). Aside from the on-request nature of these prompts, they often reflected the highly restrictive nature of the training environment (Carr & Kologinsky, 1983). These past practices, although partially effective at developing certain language skills, often proved fruitless in relation to developing a language system that would be generalizable.

To fully comprehend the facets of effective language instruction, a number of concerns and issues should be discussed. Overall, the selection of the appropriate primary language mode, such as vocal, manual/gestural, or instrumentally assisted, is the focal point in discussing language instruction for students with severe or profound handicaps. The purpose of this chapter is twofold: to examine the decision-making process in selecting the optimum language mode, and to explore some of the various options currently available. It is important to note, however, that deciding what form language instruction should take is difficult and complex. Such decisions should be made by qualified individuals after extensive and appropriate assessment. The role of the speech-language pathologist in this process should not be underestimated.

SUGGESTED METHODS

Selecting the Optimum Language Mode

A multitude of primary language mode options are available that reflect the diverse needs of students with severe or profound handicaps. They vary from normal vocal language formats to those adapted for use with the population (including assistive adaptions to vocal communication, as with alphabet or symbol boards to augment and enhance distorted or limited vocal output), and extend to purely gesturally or symbolically based nonvocal language. The recent revolution in microelectronic computer technology greatly expanded the electronically produced symbol and synthesized speech communication system options for the nonvocal communicator. Determining the appropriateness of a mode for an individual student, however, is a major task.

Musselwhite and St. Louis (1982) proposed a four-stage decision process model for developing and implementing a language program for students with severe or profound handicaps. The first stage is deciding *how much emphasis to place on vocal or nonvocal language.* If the decision is to use a primarily vocal mode, the second stage is *selecting an appropriate language instructional method.* If a nonvocal mode, either as primary or augmentative (assistive), is determined appropriate, the second stage is *selecting either a gestural or symbolic language mode.*

Stages 3 and 4 are to be used for individuals with whom a gestural or symbolic nonvocal system will be used. Gestural systems use limb movements (typically arm and hand) to communicate a message without the assistance of equipment or devices separate from the body. Symbol systems use symbols external to the body, located on a communication device. The third stage is *selecting the specific system for primary emphasis,* such as total communication (sign language combined with vocal), Blissymbols communication board, electronically synthesized speech, or American Sign Language. The fourth stage is *selecting the appropriate method of instruction using the selected system.*

The first stage (determining the individual's optimum language mode) is obviously critical for instructional and communicative success. Musselwhite and St. Louis feel that, since students with severe or profound handicaps may use some components of both vocal and nonvocal language modes successfully, the question is which communication mode should receive primary emphasis, not exclusive emphasis. They suggest viewing language modes on a continuum, with completely nonvocal at one end and completely vocal language at the other end. Then one determines where on the continuum an individual would be placed: How much can be achieved through the vocal mode and how much augmentation would be required from gestural or symbolic systems to maximize the individual's language output?

The authors provide specific options or areas to consider at each stage, arranged in hierarchial order. For example, if at stage 2 the decision is made that a symbolic system, as either a primary or augmentative mode, will provide the optimum language strategy for the client, one then selects the most appropriate category of symbolic system (e.g., representational, abstract, or symbolic language code). Once the category is selected, one then selects the most appropriate specific system, based on the individual's abilities and disabilities. If the selection is a representational symbol system, the specific suggested methods include options, such as Blissymbolics, Rebuses, photographs, pictures, or line drawings (these options are described later).

Other authors have also discussed the decision process in determining optimum language mode. Chapman and Miller (1980) compared the individual's chronological age with five areas of behavior in making the vocal/nonvocal mode choice:

1. cognitive ability
2. language comprehension level, involving syntax (word order) and vocabulary
3. language production ability, which involves syntax, semantics (meaning of words and phrases), and phonology (sounds)
4. overall communication function
5. motor skills (gross, fine, and visual-motor)

Shane and Bashir (1980) provided a ten-level branching decision matrix, intended primarily for use with individuals with congenital disorders. Their ten levels are:

1. cognitive factors (e.g., intelligence and mental age)
2. oral reflex factors (e.g., presence of both normal and abnormal reflexes)
3. language and motor speech production factors (in general)
4. motor speech—specific contributing factors (e.g., eating problems)
5. communication production—specific factors (characteristics of current communication attempts)
6. emotional factors (e.g., refusal to communicate)
7. chronological age factors that may change methods or expectations
8. previous therapy factors (including type and progress)
9. previous therapy—specific contributing factors
10. implementation factors—environment (e.g., family participation)

The branching nature of the system provides a hierarchical framework for the decision process. For example, at level 3, if the individual has a discrepancy between receptive and expressive language skills, an attempt is made to account for it on the basis of motor speech disorders or expressive language disorders. If the underlying problem is motor speech–based, the examiner proceeds to level 4; if the problem is with expressive language skills, the examiner proceeds to level 7.

These decision-making models are provided only as examples. Interested readers are referred to additional models, such as those provided by

Harris and Vanderheiden, 1980; Harris-Vanderheiden and Vander-heiden, 1977; Murdock and Hartmann, 1985; Sailor and Guess, 1983; and Silverman, 1980. Detailed decision-making models for determining a specific mode for individuals who seem to benefit from a primarily nonverbal language approach include those of Goossens' and Crain (1986a) and Reichle and Karlan (1985). Musselwhite and St. Louis (1982), however, stressed that the decision on optimum mode is a continuing process, subject to alterations in selected mode as the individual matures or experiences changes in any of the critical factor areas.

Aside from determining an optimum present or potential future language mode for students with severe or profound handicaps, one must also be knowledgeable of available language instruction methods.

Characteristics of Language Instruction Programs

Once the primary language mode has been decided, the next step is to choose or develop the language instruction program. Usually one will either select a published or commercially marketed program, or, in the case of a clinician- or teacher-designed program, select the sequence and strategies for teaching. There are several areas to consider with choosing either, including the theoretical language model behind the program; the method and environment used for training; and the specific items, concepts, and skills to be trained.

Theoretical Language Model

Language instruction programs generally follow either a developmental or remedial approach to language training. Those based on the *developmental model* use the same sequence of language structure targets that are reported as steps of normal language acquisition. They generally include components of both receptive and expressive language. The advantage of such an approach is that the model provides a logical and established sequence for language acquisition with monitorable and measurable steps. Knowledge of normal language development allows the teacher to determine specifically where the individual student is experiencing difficulty. It also provides a definitive starting place for instruction, and insures that all important areas of language acquisition are trained.

There are, however, drawbacks to this type of model. While such models are based on observation of language development, the selection of specific language acts and their sequencing is often theoretically based and may lack empirical support. The normal developmental models also are based on acquisition of milestones by normally functioning children. Therefore, they may not be appropriate for individuals experiencing various intellectual, physical, and emotional disabilities, or for those living or being trained in "abnormal" environments. Finally, many students with severe or profound handicaps already have some communicative strategies in place before the clinician or teacher is asked to assess and provide services. These existing strategies and experiences may interfere with training systems based on a developmental model. While recognizing these drawbacks, the majority of current vocal language programs do use many components of the developmental model.

Remedial language instruction models may center more on the characteristics of the handicapping condition(s), the individual's current abilities and limitations, and the ways in which he or she copes with current functioning levels and demands in reaching a more normal functioning status. The remedial programs may be based on developmental sequences in specific populations, such as those who are intellectually handicapped, rather than on the normal developmental sequence. They may still be heavily data-based, as are the normal sequence models, but the observations are based on students with handicaps. Other types of remedial models rely on the teacher's intuition or analysis of the individual or environment rather than on comparison with a similar population.

Drawbacks of the remedial models include difficulty in fully evaluating the individual's abilities and disabilities to provide appropriate starting places, and recognition that the diversity of handicapping conditions and environments limits the effectiveness of establishing normative data for the disabled and applying it to individuals. While the remedial model is less frequently used in vocal language programs, it seems to be the predominant instructional model for primary and augmentative nonvocal communication.

Methods and Environments for Training

The actual methodological approach to instruction is another area in which instructional programs may differ. Methodological differences among programs include the use of operant versus cognitive training approaches, whether content of language should be emphasized over context of language in training, and whether it is necessary to train comprehension of a concept before training production of it.

The two predominant approaches to training seem to be operant/ behavior management methods and a more naturalistic, cognitive "discovery" model. Both have advocates. Operant approaches are highly structured, often training language responses in an artificial setting, such as repetitive presentations of a single word or concept in an individual training session in a therapy room (Gray & Ryan, 1973). Success on a task and progress in a session are determined by preset criteria, such as correct repetition or use of the target in 80% of attempts. Those advocating a naturalistic, cognitive approach attempt to control or structure the individual's environment so that an opportunity to experience ("discover") the target word or concept occurs. While proponents of this approach (e.g., Hart & Rogers-Warren, 1978; McLean & Snyder-McLean, 1978) point out that this is how much of language develops in the individual without handicaps, proponents for behavioral management methods (e.g., Gray & Ryan, 1973) support their technique on the basis of efficiency and the fact that many individuals with handicaps have already demonstrated that learning has not taken place through natural opportunities.

Some programs blend the two methodologies. For example, a number of researchers advocate using the natural environment or natural situations for language training and specific behavioral techniques within those environments. Goetz, Gee, and Sailor (1985) and Hunt, Goetz, Alwell, and Sailor (1986) suggested the use of behavior chain interruption, whereby a particular trained chain of responses is purposely interrupted to determine if the student will communicate a response to continue or a request for assistance. A delay procedure was also recommended. In this case, a preferred object has been continually paired with a verbal label given by the teacher. During probe situations, the object is displayed to the student but no verbal label is given. The delay in giving the label is used to determine if the student will then self-initiate the verbal label (Charlop, Schreibman, & Thibodeau, 1985).

Related to the operant versus cognitive issue is the content and context of instruction. Some authors suggest that primary emphasis be placed on training a multitude of words and concepts so that the individual has a sufficient vocabulary to control the environment (Gray & Ryan, 1973). This emphasis on content is often observed in operant-based programs. Others stress that training words and concepts in an artificial setting is inadequate (Horner, Sprague, & Wilcox, 1982). Rather than the amount of language content being critical, they see the actual usage of words and concepts in the environment as the important issue. The cognitive-based approaches often advocate the training of language in context on the basis that actual use of language, even if limited in scope, is more important than knowledge and production of a large vocabulary that goes unused (McLean & Snyder-McLean, 1978).

Stremel-Campbell, Clark-Guida, and Johnson-Dorn (1984) not only advocated the use of the natural environment in basic language instruction but emphasized its utility in assessing and training the social functions of language. They outlined 14 social functions expressed by prelanguage and language behavior and provided observations, based on longitudinal data, on acquisition of these functions by students with severe or profound handicaps. Examples include protest/rejection of activities, requesting continuation of an activity, requesting attention to self, and providing an answer to a question. For a more complete description of this approach, the reader is referred to Gaylord-Ross, Stremel-Campbell, and Storey (1986).

The third issue in methodology of training is the sequencing of targets during instruction. Normal developmental models traditionally separate skills into receptive and expressive areas, and much of the research in language development indicates that comprehension of a word or concept generally precedes production of it (Bloom & Lahey, 1978). Training programs based on the developmental model (e.g., Reike, Lynch, & Soltman, 1977) generally train comprehension first. While training receptive language skills first will not adversely affect the learning of production skills (Schumaker & Sherman, 1978), some authors indicated that such sequencing may not be necessary, and in fact may slow the rate of instruction and acquisition. Bloom and Lahey (1978) and Guess, Sailor, and Baer (1978) advocated training production before comprehension on the basis that such a pattern enhances comprehension without directly working on it. It also provides more immediate reinforcement for learning the task, as it allows for control of the environment.

Specific Items, Concepts, and Skills To Be Trained

There are large differences among instructional programs and individually developed plans in the specific content that is trained. Issues are selection of vocabulary for instruction, and whether such skills as generalization, self-initiation, self-monitoring, self-evaluation, and self-correction must be trained.

As indicated, the nature of the initial lexicon (vocabulary) is an issue in language instruction. Virtually all programs advocate the selection of an initial lexicon for training that is functional and appropriate for the individual's immediate needs and environment. Musselwhite and St. Louis (1982) suggested several factors to consider in selecting the initial vocabulary, whether it be for vocal, assisted, or aided language modes. These factors include client preference, frequency of occurrence of the word or concept in the individual's environment, success of the word in directly meeting communicative needs, versatility of the word in meeting a variety of communicative functions, ease with which the word or concept can be demonstrated in context, the ease of discrimination and production of the word or concept (for both sender and receiver), and the efficiency of a word or concept (e.g., its ability to meet both current and future communicative needs).

The second issue affecting content is the abilities the individual possesses that affect the nature of instruction. These specifically involve the individual's ability to generalize words, concepts, rules, and strategies learned in training to other language areas and environmental settings, and the individual's ability to self-initiate and self-regulate language usage.

Brown, Nietupski, and Hamre-Nietupski (1976) questioned the ability of some individuals with severe or profound handicaps to generalize. They suggested that many such individuals, particularly those with severe mental retardation, are unable to infer from one situation to another, or from one response to another. Instruction of such students would require the use of one of two options: Either all desired behaviors must be directly trained in each and every situation in which it is desired that the behaviors occur, or a global generalization ability (strategy) must be trained. Training generalization ability would seem to be the more efficient, and has generally taken the form of either direct training of such skills as instruction-following (e.g., Striefel, Wetherby, & Karlan, 1978) or structuring the training environment to facilitate the development of generalization skills.

Stokes and Baer (1977) identified nine strategies reported by various authors to facilitate generalization of learned behaviors. They cited training the behavior to sufficient examplars (e.g., systematically training the action with several people, objects, activities, and settings; see Stremel-Campbell & Campbell, 1985) as the most commonly used technique. Other procedures included introducing the behavior in naturally maintaining conditions; "train and hope," in which the behavior is taught by several people in the hope that the effect will more easily generalize to others; and the use of sequential modification, in which the action is trained in one setting and tested in another. In this last type of generalization training, if the action is not performed in the second setting, it is trained there and tested in a third, and continues until generalized to an untrained setting.

Brown, Nietupski, and Hamre-Nietupski (1976) also questioned the ability of many individuals with severe handicaps to self-initiate, self-monitor, self-assess, and self-correct their language attempts. Williams, Brown, and Certo (1975) suggested that many rely instead on the cues, prompts, and gestures of others as the primary motivator to use language (as these are often used in the instructional environment to indicate when to use a language structure that is being trained).

Halle (1987) indicated that practitioners should become much more aware of the different types of cues or prompts they use to assist a student to develop language, for it is the level of the cue that may determine whether or not the individual is using more or less spontaneous language. Halle places prompts on a continuum that describes their controlling effect on spontaneity. For example, he sees physical guidance and modeling cues as producing the least amount of spontaneous language. Questions, commands, and the necessity for the presence of objects or events are cues that lead to intermediate spontaneity. Finally, if the presence of a listener or some internal or situational motivational state leads to language production, this is considered the most spontaneous.

Many language instruction programs that emphasize training in the natural environment (or milieu training), such as Halle (1982); Hart (1985); and Kaiser, Alpert, and Warren (1987), attempt to create situations in which the individual spontaneously attempts communication, thus training self-initiation. As self-initiation proceeds, Reike, Lynch, and Soltman (1977) recommended that the trainers limit their roles to the "3Rs": responding, reiterating, and reinforcing the clients self-initiated attempts. Gradually removing reinforcement from distorted or incorrect attempts sometimes brings some of the self-regulation skills into play, and reinforcement is provided when self-correction is attempted.

The preceding is by no means an exhaustive list of issues. The next section is a brief description of some commercially available vocal language instruction programs. The following definitions are provided for classification of the primary nature of the instructional program (from Sternberg, 1982).

- In a syntactic based program, the word form and sequence of words (symbols) used to create complete thoughts (sentences) takes precedence. The general purpose of training is to teach the student the basic rules of correct word usage (such as plurality) and combining words to form sentences.
- In a semantic based program, the emphasis is on the meaning of the word or sequence of words rather than on the correct word form or order.
- In a developmentally based program, the student's cognitive functioning level is used as a major index of what language programming techniques to employ.
- In a behaviorally based program, the presence or absence of a language behavior, rather than the cognitive readiness of the individual to understand the language behavior, dictates what is to be taught and how it is to be taught.

- In an isolated training program, the student is instructed in language for a specified (usually fixed) amount of time or number of trials per day.
- In an integrated (or ecological) training program, all natural environmental opportunities for language usage are employed (social interactions, activities of daily living, etc.).

Descriptions of Specific Vocal Language Instructional Programs

Steps to Independence: Speech and Language—Levels I and II

This behaviorally based program uses operant conditioning to train skills. The sequencing of the language targets follows the normal developmental language acquisition model (Baker, Brightman, Carroll, Heifetz, & Hinshaw, 1978). Unlike the majority of the other programs described in this chapter, this program is specifically designed for use by parents in the home. As such, steps are clearly laid out, and all content is specified in the program (e.g., rather than tailoring the vocabulary to the individual's needs and environment, word lists are provided and the parent uses them to target what words to teach). Prompts to elicit the desired response are provided in the manuals, and real life examples are provided of how specific skills would be taught by the parent. The program can be adapted for use with individuals with essentially no current language usage or individuals with language skills. An appendix is provided with strategies for training a total communication mode using sign language and fingerspelling to augment vocal communication.

The program begins with training receptive language skills. The sequence moves from attending behaviors; to identifying people, places, and objects; following directions; and discriminating between two directions. Expressive language skills begin with identification of sounds the student can produce to aid in selection of words from the word list that can be produced intelligibly (to ensure early success and reinforcement). Expressive skills move through imitating actions, words, vocabulary expansion, and multiword utterances (phrases and short sentences). The relation of actions and words is taught through pictures.

Each of the two manuals for the program, Level I and Level II, contains a question and answer section where questions commonly asked by parents are addressed. The program ends at an approximate four-year-old language level. No mention of future training or more advanced training is made.

Early Communication Development and Training

This developmentally based program (Bricker, 1983) was designed to be used with infants and young children experiencing difficulty with normal communication development and for older children with severe to profound communication impairments. The program is based on four assumptions: (1) early communication should focus on sensorimotor and social communication processes; (2) the normal communication acquisition sequence should guide the instructor in what to teach; (3) operant training methods should be employed to teach objectives; and (4) all training should be functional for the student and used in the context of the individual's environment. While the ultimate goal of the program is vocal communication, it is vocal communication trained through, and integrating, a multimodality approach, with gestures and vocal tones accompanying the words to enhance meaning.

As the title implies, the program begins with training behavioral requirements seen as prerequisites for language instruction (e.g., visual and auditory attention). As attending behaviors increase, the program goals move to training reciprocal interaction between the student and the instructor. Imitation is used to a large extent during this sequence.

The characteristics of objects, and the actions that can be performed upon them, are emphasized and used in training basic language and cognitive concepts. For example, words are trained through pairing vocal productions with gestures accentuating characteristics of the object, and vocal tones indicating wants and needs. The lexicon is selected on the basis of its functional usage in the environment and its features that would facilitate acquisition (such as the extent that gestures can identify the word). As the vocabulary expands, multiword comprehension is taught in the same manner (vocal productions accompanied by characteristic gestures for the combined words). This is followed by multiword production, and is the level at which the program ends, leaving the individual at an approximate three- to four-year-old child language level. The content of the child's attempts at language is more important than the form of the language, yielding a program that is more semantic than syntactic oriented.

*The Teaching Research Curriculum for Moderately and
Severely Handicapped*

This is a comprehensive training program (Fredericks, Riggs, Furey, Grove, Moore, McDonnell, Jordan, Hanson, Baldwin, & Wadlow, 1976) based on normal developmental sequences, moving from muscle tone normalization and fine and gross motor skills, through receptive and expressive language training, and concluding with reading and writing skills. It was developed for use by classroom teachers. The authors indicate it should be successful in its published form for approximately 75% of students classified as moderately or severely retarded, and can be adapted to other populations with severe handicaps. Only the receptive and expressive language sections of the curriculum are reviewed in this chapter.

Receptive language training is the first stage of the program, and begins with skill training in attending to auditory cues. Development in this area is considered prerequisite to formal language training as are others (e.g., maintenance of eye contact). Students progress through skill areas in phases, with closely monitored teacher-directed activity in the first phase in each area, and each succeeding phase moving toward greater independence for the student in the activity. The terminal goal in each area is stated as a behavioral objective, and the phases form the task analysis to reach that objective. Students may work on more than one phase at a time in a given skill area. The 4 receptive skill areas encompass 21 phases.

The expressive language training portion is based on steps from the *Teaching Research Initial Expressive Language Program* (TRIELP; McDonnell, Fredericks, & Grove, 1975) and from the *Distar Language Program* (DLP; Engelmann & Osborn, 1976). The first program (TRIELP) provides instructional suggestions for training motor vocal actions, sounds, chaining sounds to make words, and chaining words together. The second program (DLP) provides guidance for training more advanced language skills, such as pluralization, pronoun usage, categorization, and order. There are 39 phases in 8 areas in the TRIELP section, followed by 43 phases in 11 areas in the DLP section. With the addition of the DLP component, this program is predominantly syntactic based. The expressive language program ends at a language level of approximately a six- to seven-year-old child, with the curriculum then moving into writing skills and cognitive areas such as numbers, monetary, and time-telling skills.

Functional Speech and Language Training for the Severely Handicapped

This is a behaviorally based program, and training is done in an isolated framework (Guess, Sailor, & Baer, 1978). The authors indicate the program can be used with virtually any person with handicaps, and in any setting, as long as the instructor understands behavior management techniques. Directions are given regarding materials to be used, specific training instructions, expected and acceptable student responses, and methods to facilitate generalization.

A detailed step-by-step training sequence is used to assist the individual in developing five primary language concepts in relation to six content areas. Concepts include reference (the linking of specific sounds to objects), control (use of the sounds to obtain objects), and reception (the understanding of questions asked and statements heard). These concepts are developed as the student moves through the six content areas, including persons and things (identification of label with objects and people); actions with persons and things (label for verb action); possession (use of possessive pronouns "my" and "your"); color, size, relation, and location ("on," "under," "inside," and "outside"). Training in expressive use precedes instruction in receptive identification in the content areas. Skill tests are given preceding each step as baseline measures, and movement from one step to the next is based on a pre-established criterion of either 80% correct responses or 12 consecutive correct responses in a training session. Individuals who do not achieve criterion within 40 sessions are allowed to proceed to the next step. Training sessions generally last 30 minutes and occur twice daily.

Those successfully completing the program would emerge with a language level of four to five years of age. While initial stages allow for correctness to be judged on semantic factors, the later stages of the program are syntactic based.

Environmental Language Intervention Program

This is a cognitively oriented and thus developmentally based program that stresses interaction between the individual and the natural environment for language development training, (Horstmeier & MacDonald, 1978a,b). It can be used with students with handicaps who have little or no language in place. There are four portions to this program, three of which are assessment instruments used to determine the individual's communicative function at various language levels, the ability of the student to learn a new response, the optimum cues and prompts for eliciting responses, and the level of competence for specific communication behaviors.

The three assessment devices are designed to examine developmental functioning and provide information from the parents' observations. The assessment instruments are the *Environmental Prelanguage Battery* (EPB), *Environmental Language Inventory* (ELI), and the Communication Inventory (referred to as *Oliver*). The EPB and the ELI are prelanguage and language assessment batteries administered by the teacher or instructor, and the parent-administered *Oliver* presents questions on the student's ability to communicate, *Oliver* also provides assessment tasks for the parent to administer to determine more fully the individual's communication performance level. The EPB is used to examine prelinguistic skills necessary for the development of spoken language, such as attending behaviors, receptive language, and motor and verbal imitation. The ELI assesses eight semantic-grammatical rules (e.g., ordering of words to convey a generalized meaning such as agent + action, as in the phrase "boy run"). Both the EPB and ELI employ cues and prompts to elicit and examine each behavior, and attempts are made to train the language behaviors if they are not in the student's repertoire. The success of using the various cues or prompts provides vital information for training procedures.

Information from the EPB, ELI, and *Oliver* are used to place the student at the appropriate starting level of the instructional part of the program, the *Ready, Get Set, Go; Talk To Me* program. As the title of the program suggests, major emphasis is placed on applying the instructional techniques to multiple environmental sites, facilitating integration and control of the learned behaviors in the student's natural environment. The instructional program is comprehensively designed, providing instructional cues, training probes to determine improvement, carryover probes to assess generalization to untrained situations and objects, and structured play situations to assess and facilitate spontaneous language usage.

Some programs provide training on a limited and specific lexicon and communication pattern. The Environmental Language Intervention Program is designed to foster the development of semantic-grammatical language rules that will allow for an infinite number of language attempts.

*Teaching Functional Language: Strategies for
Language Intervention*

This is an integrated program with both semantic and developmental bases (Kaiser et al., 1987). The program uses the naturalistic milieu teaching technique to train functional language emphasizing specific intent in communication and interactional language strategies. Specific intent is trained by teaching the target language form in a functional manner. The teacher uses the environment to elicit responses from the student by presenting stimulating material to which the student is attracted. The student's attempts to gain the material, accompanied by teacher models and mands (requests), yield intentional language usage that is systematically generalized to other materials and situations. Interactional strategies are classes of behaviors that (1) provide support for the student in practicing language, (2) improve interaction with others so that there is an increased opportunity for language use, and (3) are useful in soliciting new linguistic or conceptual information.

Four procedures are used in the milieu teaching technique. The first stage, child-directed modeling, establishes the joint attention of the instructor and student on a topic (e.g., an object in the environment) by using stimulating material that attracts the student's interest. Once joint attention is established, the instructor provides a model to imitate that is related to the topic (e.g., verbally naming the object). If the student imitates the model, the instructor expands the student's response (providing a new model) and presents the topic material to the student. If the student fails to imitate, the model is presented again.

These imitative responses are expanded in the second stage, the mand-model procedure. When the student approaches topic material, the instructor mands a response related to the topic (e.g., a request for a descriptor for the topic). If no response is given, the instructor provides a model.

The third stage, the time-delay procedure, involves changing the environmental cues for language use. The instructor delays the response to the student's communicative intent (e.g., delays giving the student the material). The student must then respond to this change in pattern, rather than responding only to the topic material.

Incidental teaching procedures, the fourth stage, is designed to require further categories of language forms in the student's response. For example, stimulating materials are placed out of the student's reach, so that the student must use mands to satisfy intent.

In a milieu approach, all persons in the student's environment become instructors. This results in communicative opportunities and a stimulating language environment throughout the individual's day. The program provides suggestions on structuring the environment and prerequisite teaching skills. Assessment instruments are described for exploring communicative opportunities in the child's environment (ecological inventories) and the student's cognitive, social, motor, and language skills (student skill assessments). Detailed generalization procedures are also presented. While the program is primarily designed to produce vocal language, the authors indicate it is easily adaptable to gestural or symbolic language modes.

Language Acquisition Program for the Retarded or Multiply Impaired

This behaviorally based program is conducted in an isolated fashion (Kent, 1974). The program is primarily designed to teach oral language to the population with severe retardation. It is adaptable with modified materials, however, for teaching language to individuals with other sensory, motor, or emotional disorders. The program includes an assessment instrument to determine entry level. The author, however, indicates that simply starting the student at the initial section of the program is acceptable as it provides immediate success and reinforcement. In the initial prelanguage training section, edible reinforcers are used, then are gradually faded for a token system. This is gradually faded into a delayed reinforcement system with a reinforcement menu to approximate reinforcement in the natural environment more closely.

The program is divided into three sections: preverbal, verbal-receptive, and verbal-expressive. The preverbal section trains primarily prelanguage skills such as attending behaviors and motor imitation. The verbal-receptive portion is divided into six phases, beginning with the Basic Receptive Phase. This phase pairs verbal labels with objects, room parts, and body parts, and also pairs initial action requests to the stimuli (e.g., "close your eyes"). This is followed by Receptive Expansion Phases I through V, which expand the initial receptive lexicon and train receptive skills relative to prepositional relationships, colors, sorting by size, and following multistep commands.

The program then moves into the five phases of the Verbal-Expressive Section. The Vocal Imitation Phase begins the section with training vocal imitation of at least 10 of the 20 vocabulary words used in the Basic Receptive Phase. Training then moves to production of vocabulary words in response to simple questions (Basic Expressive Phase), and then to complex questions involving concepts such as possession, prepositional relations, missing objects, and relationships (Expressive Expansion Phase I). Expressive Expansion Phases II and III are used to train word sequencing for short noun phrases (e.g., color + noun, number + noun) to expand the verb vocabulary and train counting.

While the final sections do train some word-ordering aspects, the primary emphasis in the program is transmitting semantic intent. The student exits the program with language approximately at the level of a four-year-old.

Communication and Language Intervention Program

This program was designed for individuals with moderate or severe handicaps, and can be used for vocal, augmentative, or nonvocal modes

(Murdock & Hartmann, 1985). Rather than providing a set of procedures to be followed sequentially, Murdock and Hartmann provide guidelines and suggestions for each type of activity found in communication and language training programs. Major category areas include instructional settings; establishing attending behaviors; eliminating interfering behaviors; establishing communication; reinforcement types, techniques, and schedules; recording data for accountability; establishing specific language structures; use of the natural environment; and generalization. The instructor uses procedures from each area as needed to design an individualized program for each student based on weaknesses discovered in a preliminary communication and language assessment.

A considerable amount of information is provided by the authors. Techniques discussed in the area of establishing communication, for example, include specific suggestions and examples on using discriminative stimuli, modeling, imitation, prompting, fading, chaining, and shaping. In the area of specific language structures, suggestions are provided for sequencing training of specific phonologic (sound order), syntactic (word order), and morphologic (word form) structures.

The very diverse nature of the program and its varying design based on individual needs do not fit in any one program classification. The sequences used in language training follow developmental models; behavior management techniques are used to train behaviors; procedures can be used in isolated or integrated environments; cognitive function has a role in selecting areas and tasks for instruction; and the breadth of the options allow expansion from semantic to syntactic based instruction. It would seem to be best used by an experienced clinician or teacher who has the background necessary for comprehensive assessment, task selection, and integration of components. The breadth of the program allows instruction to proceed to high levels of language function for those students who possess the capability.

West Virginia System: Receptive Language Curriculum for the Moderately, Severely, and Profoundly Handicapped and Expressive Language Curriculum for the Moderately, Severely, and Profoundly Handicapped

The West Virginia System (St. Louis, Mattingly, Esposito, & Cone, 1980; St. Louis, Rejzer, & Cone, 1980) has separate programs for training adaptive skills (e.g., gross motor, feeding, recreation, toileting), receptive language, and expressive language. While receptive and expressive language are presented as separate programs, the two can be combined for concurrent training. The two language programs are applicable to students with all degrees and types of handicapping conditions, and instruction is provided for adapting the programs for use with manual communication or communication boards. The program is designed for use by classroom teachers and paraprofessionals who have access to consultation from a speech-language pathologist.

The Receptive Language Curriculum has 25 subareas. Method cards are provided for objectives in each, with detailed descriptions for teaching specific receptive language behaviors. Each method card lists general prerequisites needed for each objective, and objectives are sequenced so that earlier tasks may become prerequisites for tasks that follow. Method card objectives are written in behavioral terms, provide mastery criterion for movement to the next objective, and specify materials needed for instruction. The initial objectives concern general awareness of auditory and/or gestural cues. The final two subareas require the ability to follow multiconcept directions and understand stories.

The Expressive Language Curriculum is set up in a similar manner. There are 25 subareas, with a total of 350 expressive language objectives (method cards). The initial objectives concern determining whether vocal or nonvocal modes should receive primary emphasis. They include attempts at producing sounds and gestures. While early objectives emphasize the semantic content of communicative attempts, the overall expressive program trains the ability to produce complete sentences that are syntactically correct. One to three generalization method cards are included in each subarea to facilitate expansion and maintenance of the skill in other environments. The individual exits the program at approximately the language level of a five-year-old.

Instructional Issues Unique to Nonvocal Language Modes

Issues relating to the instructional model and nature and content of the instructional program, as previously described, are essentially the same for vocal and nonvocal modes. There are additional issues relating to the selection of a nonvocal language mode that need to be addressed. Goosens' and Crain (1986a), Murdock and Hartmann (1985), Musselwhite and St. Louis (1982), and Reichle and Karlan (1985) provided insight into some of these concerns.

One concern is cost of implementing the nonvocal system. While gestural systems such as sign language may require little or no equipment besides training manuals and glossaries, it may be necessary to provide special training to teachers and others in the individual's environment in comprehension and production of sign language. Similarly, symbol systems such as Blissymbols or Rhebus may also require special training in interpretation for others in the environment. If more elaborate electronic communication boards or computerized speech synthesis units are used, equipment costs may be several thousands of dollars, may still require specialized training, and may have significant associated maintenance expenses.

Another concern is the mobility of the system. Communication boards may be awkward to transport, require a power source, and, depending on the user's physical disabilities, may require additional equipment such as head pointers, electronic switches, or mounting systems that further impede mobility. Some systems that employ personal computers may not be transportable. The individual's own mobility problems, such as the use of walkers or crutches, may also hamper transporting the symbol system. Gesture systems, being considerably less bound to equipment, hold the advantage in terms of mobility.

Often, commercially available nonvocal systems do not perfectly match the user's needs or limitations. A third concern, therefore, is the adaptability of the system to the individual. There are readily available modified gestural systems (e.g., one-handed sign language systems) that require less fine motor control. Also, both depth and breadth of content and abstractness of gestures can be controlled for use with individuals with cognitive impairments.

The majority of electronic symbol systems offer a variety of controlling mechanisms to match the user's physical limitations. These include "sip or puff" switches operated by blowing or sucking, large paddle switches operated by head or gross limb movements, and scanning modes (automatic sequential presentation of all vocabulary items, halted by the user when the desired item is reached) if the individual's motor abilities do not allow direct selection from a board or panel. Similarly, nonelectronic communication boards also may need to be specifically designed to accommodate the individual's physical or cognitive limitations. Simply providing more space between items or providing an elevated border between items on the board can benefit users with fine motor control problems, and the amount, type, and abstractness of printed words, symbols, or pictures can be adjusted to meet cognitive limitations.

The nature of the nonvocal message must be considered. Many gestural systems (e.g., American Sign Language and American Indian Sign Language) and symbol systems (e.g., Blissymbols and Rhebus symbols) allow communication only with others skilled in their use. This is obviously a very limited portion of the general population and a problem for individuals being provided instruction in the least restrictive environment, or those employed or operating in nonsheltered environments. The latest generation of computerized speech synthesis communication boards overcome some of these problems, providing an understandable verbal output and storage of messages. Some even provide a printed output, yielding a permanent record of the individual's responses.

The message is also affected by the nature of language in the individual communication system. Many gestural and symbolic systems may be inefficient in getting the speaker's intended message across and may limit the communication that can be carried on. The individual's cognitive or physical limitations may slow the speed or accuracy of the message, turning communication into a tiring and frustrating experience for both sender and receiver.

A tangential issue related to message type is the amount of social interaction that the system allows. Those communicating with a student using a symbolic message board often must concentrate on the board, rather than maintaining eye contact. Gestural systems often allow greater contact with the message sender; however, the type and location of gestures also may limit many of the pragmatic aspects of communication.

Yet another major concern is the flexibility of the system to meet changing needs and increasing performance levels for individuals in language instruction programs. While the vocabulary in gestural systems, such as sign language, can be constantly and easily enlarged as the student's language skills increase, many communication boards are limited in space, thus limiting vocabulary expansion. While some electronic symbol boards may be limited in content, the latest generation of computer-based systems often provide extensive memory and expansion capabilities. By providing the capability to select speech sounds and combine them to produce words, which in many cases can be stored in the unit's permanent memory, such units allow essentially an unlimited vocabulary.

The demands that a specific nonvocal system places on the individual user also affect flexibility. Since space on communication boards is at a premium, some electronic units use numeric codes (rather than pictorial or printed symbols) to call up specific phonemes (individual speech sounds), words, or phrases. While this allows a much larger vocabulary as it is not limited to space for physical representation on the board, the user must have the necessary memory and cognitive capabilities to use such a system. Similarly, the gestural user must have sufficient long-term visual and motor memory to store and retrieve their own vocabulary, as well as visual and/or auditory memory and language processing capabilities to receive and decode messages sent to them.

A final concern is how language can be trained in a specific nonvocal system. Many gestural sign language systems and symbol systems do not use grammatical structure parallel with English. This may require the person to be essentially "bilingual" if the primary reason for nonvocal system usage is physical limitations on language output and their primary receptive mode is spoken English. For those limited both receptively and expressively to nonvocal systems, and therefore receiving all language training through the gestural or symbolic mode, the nature and require- ments of the language used in the system may affect the individual's learning strategies. These in turn, as they are deviant from standard strate- gies, may affect or limit learning in other areas of instruction, not only in language skills but also in other educational tasks.

Nonvocal Communication System Options

Silverman, in a 1980 report, estimated that at that time there were more than 100 nonvocal system options available for the student whose severe or profound handicaps made vocal language production impractical or unusable. The number of nonvocal language and communication system options currently available for persons with severe or profound handicaps is so extensive that entire books are devoted to exploring and describing the choices. For example, Bengston, Brandenberg, and Vanderheiden (1985) provide a sourcebook on commercially marketed electronic communication, training, and signalling aids; nonelectronic signalling aids; pointing devices; and controlling mechanism options for various systems. Goossens' and Crain (1986a) provide information on various augmentative system options and assessment procedures for system selec- tion. They also wrote a second volume (1986b) detailing intervention strategies for the implementation of augmentative systems.

For the purposes of this chapter, nonvocal language system options are described in two categories of systems: gesture systems and symbol systems. As stated previously, Musselwhite and St. Louis (1982) defined gesture systems as those that necessitate movement of the body, typically the arms and hands, to produce the message but do not require access to equipment or devices separate from the body. They defined symbolic systems as those involving the use of symbols external to the body, located on a communication device.

Gesture Systems

There are many gesture systems to choose from. Categorical types include (1) sign language systems, (2) gestural language codes, and (3) illustrative gesture systems.

Sign language systems are symbolic and rule-based. Some sign languages, such as American Sign Language (ASL or Ameslan) and British Sign Language (BSL) are not manual forms of English, but rather separate, self-contained languages that differ from English and other languages in several ways. Miller and Allaire (1987) reported that in ASL these differences include (1) English word order is not used; (2) it has no form of the verb "to be"; (3) it has no passive voice; (4) it uses no articles; (5) it marks verb tense for an entire conversation or conversational segment, not for individual verbs; (6) it does not have signs for pronouns but rather establishes the intended referent(s) in space; and (7) it can use movement in space to convey in a single sign a subject + object + verb statement that would require three words in English.

Musselwhite and St. Louis (1982) indicated that candidates for ASL should possess the following skills: (1) good motor control of both hands (19 basic hand configurations are used); (2) good range of motion with both arms (because movement patterns and positions impart meaning); (3) good control over facial musculature (some nuances of meaning are passed through facial expressions); (4) good visual acuity and visual discrimination; and (5) sensorimotor stage 5 or 6 intelligence (see Chapman & Miller, 1980). One difficulty with ASL and many of the other sign languages is that the majority of signs are not transparent (i.e., the sign's meaning cannot be understood from its form alone; Klima & Bellugi, 1979). This lack of transparency limits communication to only those trained in the system.

Several language training programs, (e.g., Kent, 1974; St. Louis, Rejzer, & Cone, 1980; Murdock & Hartmann, 1985) were adapted for teaching ASL signs to students with various handicapping conditions. While ASL and other sign languages are generally "taught" rather than learned as a natural language when used by students with severe handicaps, Musselwhite and St. Louis (1982) suggested that the nature of ASL would lend itself well to environmental or naturalistic program settings.

Other sign language systems, such as Signed English (Bornstein, Saulnier, & Hamilton, 1983) and Signing Exact English (Gustason, Pfetzing, & Zawolkow, 1980) were designed to parallel English grammar and syntax specifically. These systems draw their basic signs from ASL, but incorporate signs for grammatical features such as suffixes (e.g., "-s" for pluralization and "-ed" for past tense), pronouns, and articles. The various systems differ in the rules used to reflect English structure and morphology. Musselwhite and St. Louis (1982) indicated that Signed English seems to be the simplest and might be most appropriate for individuals with severe handicaps. They recommend that candidates have the same abilities required for ASL, except that facial musculature control is not so important.

A second category of gestural systems is *gestural language codes*. These systems allow the user to code a specific language, such as English. Gestures are used to represent segments of a spoken language (e.g., sounds or syllables) or written language (e.g., letters of the alphabet). Rather than serving as an independent language, gestural code systems use the structure of the language, such as English, in which they are employed. Fingerspelling and Cued Speech are examples of gestural language codes.

When used with English, fingerspelling gestures are 26 distinct hand configurations that represent the 26 letters of the Roman alphabet. Twenty-four letters are identified by the specific handshape; the letters "j" and "z" also require hand motion during production. As each word must be spelled (e.g., "word" would require the sequenced production of four handshapes), fingerspelling is slow in comparison with signing or speech (Wilbur, 1979).

To use fingerspelling in language successfully, Musselwhite and St. Louis (1982) recommended that the user possess good fine motor control of one hand (to produce the small rapid movements necessary for handshape configuration); a high level of cognitive development, including the ability to spell; and good visual discrimination skills. While fingerspelling could be used to provide the language output to any of the language instruction systems previously discussed, it adds complexity to the tasks by requiring the retention and production of multiple gestures to represent a single word, rather than a single sign. Additionally, fingerspelling slows communicative rate considerably. Musselwhite and St. Louis suggested it may be more beneficial in augmenting speech in a person with limited intelligibility. Simply fingerspelling the initial letter of a word aids the listener by limiting possible interpretations of a distorted word, yet should not slow rate appreciably.

Cued Speech (Cornett, 1967) is a gestural language code that may be used as an augmentative device by individuals with limited speech intelligibility. It was originally developed for use with individuals with impaired hearing to provide additional cues when speech reading (lip reading), as many of the phonemes (speech sounds) cannot be differentiated solely by the visual cues of lip position and movement. The gestural symbols are produced in synchronization with speech and, when combined with lip position and movement cues, provide information as to the sound being produced. Information on consonants is provided via handshape, and information on the following vowel is conveyed by the position the hand-shape is produced on the body (relative to the mouth). There are eight handshapes, each of which represents two or three consonants that would look different from each other on the lips. The handshapes are produced in four positions relative to the mouth, with each position representing a group of vowels for which each member would use a different lip position in production. A single gesture (handshape and position) would therefore identify a limited group of phonemes (speech sounds) from which a conso-nant and the following vowel could be selected based on accompanying lip position and movement. Musselwhite and St. Louis (1982) indicated such a system could be used to augment speech for a student having difficulty producing audible or intelligible output as long as the lip movements for speech were normal. User requirements are similar to those for finger-spelling, except that less fine motor control is required.

The third category of gestural systems, *illustrative gesture systems*, lacks the formal structure of a language and cannot be used to code an existing language. They are instead systems of highly transparent gestures, many of which can be understood by untrained persons, used to communicate intent of the speaker. Examples of illustrative gesture systems are natural gestures and Amer-Ind.

Hamre-Nietupski, Stoll, Holtz, Fullerton, Ryan-Flottum, and Brown (1977) compiled a list of more than 160 natural gestures that have a high level of transparency and are understandable to untrained persons. The majority are commonly occurring body movements used by individuals without handicaps in everyday communicative interactions; e.g., shaking the head from side-to-side to indicate "no," shaking a fist to indicate anger, shivering and rubbing crossed arms to indicate being cold, or simply pointing to an object to indicate interest in it or a need for it.

The use of natural gestures does not restrict the communicative audi-ence to those trained in the system, a limiting factor previously noted for sign language systems. An additional advantage over sign language systems is that natural gesture systems generally involve gross motor rather than fine motor movements in producing the gesture. Communica-tion with natural gestures, however, is primarily limited to concepts that are highly concrete (Lloyd, 1985). This may be a disadvantage, for it limits vocabulary in the system and the number of messages that can be expressed (Miller & Allaire, 1987).

Amer-Ind reflects the modernization and adaptation of many of the gestures of American Indian Hand Language, a centuries-old gestural communication system developed and used by a variety of Indian tribes to circumvent problems created by each tribe's use of an independent language. The gestures in Amer-Ind represent concepts, rather than words, and each concept embraces several English words. For example, the gesture for the concept "quiet" is the index finger held in front of the lips, and encompasses such words (English concepts) as calm, hush, dormant, mute, noiseless, silence, serene, still, and tranquil (Skelly & Schinsky, 1979). There are approximately 250 concept labels in the Amer-Ind repertoire, expressing approximately 2,500 English words, and through the process of agglutination (combining a string of gestures to communicate concepts for which there are no signs) additional English words can be expressed. Skelly and Schinsky provided the example of "teacher," for which there is no direct concept or gesture, and which can be indicated by sequencing the gestures for the concepts "person" + "gives" + "knowledge." They also indicated that 80% of the concepts are expressed through one-handed gestures, and the majority of those remaining can be adapted to one-hand usage.

Amer-Ind is an action-oriented, reality-based code system that relies heavily on context for communication effectiveness. As such, it would seem to be adaptable for use with natural language instructional programs. Skelly and Schinsky (1979), however, did not recommend using it in such programs, and instead developed treatment programs for three categories of individuals (see Skelly & Schinsky, 1979, for detailed information). Musselwhite and St. Louis (1982) suggested that due to the high transparency of the gestures, Amer-Ind would be beneficial as an augmentative language source.

Symbol Systems

A 1981 position statement on nonspeech communication by the American Speech-Language-Hearing Association (American Speech-Language-Hearing Association Ad Hoc Committee, 1981) recommended the use of the term aided communication techniques to describe the systems encompassed by the Musselwhite and St. Louis (1982) symbol systems category. There are three categories of components to consider in the selection of an aided communication system: (1) the specific type of physical aid or device, such as communication boards, electronic communication devices, or physical supports for the body; (2) the nature of the response required of the student in using the device, such as pointing, gazing, or touching a switch; and (3) the type of symbol system used on the device, such as orthographic words, representational symbols, or line drawings. There are tremendous numbers of options available for each component, allowing tailoring of the system to meet each student's strengths, limitations, and needs. Some possible options are described below (see

Silverman, 1980; Musselwhite & St. Louis, 1982; Bengston et al., 1985; or Goossens' & Crain, 1986a,b for more detailed descriptions).

Individuals with limited ability to produce vocal language but with the ability to point often use communication boards. These boards take many forms. Vicker (1974) indicated that single sheet displays (symbols on a single page, plate, card, or board) are the easiest for the student to use, as the limited display space limits vocabulary and complexity of response. Such displays are located where they can be easily accessed by the student, such as on a wheelchair tray (Silverman, 1980), on a card carried by the student (to be used for specific situations or environments; Bottorf & DePape, 1982), or simply kept in strategic locations in the environment. Students with greater physical skills, such as those needed for equipment operation or page-turning, or with greater cognitive abilities, such as needed for using large vocabularies or operating sound-blending devices, may use multiple sheet displays. Examples of multiple displays include notebooks (often color-coded or tabbed by category to facilitate locating symbols; Vicker, 1974; Dettamore & Lippke, 1980), flip-charts (e.g., a series of cards where symbols are arranged in sequential order appropriate to language structure; Vicker, 1974), and individual cards on a chain or metal ring (Silverman, (1980).

Both single and multiple sheet displays also can be used on electronic communication devices. These are discussed relative to the second component, the response required from the student to indicate the selected symbol.

Some students with severe or profound handicaps have physical limitations that affect the ability to point to a symbol on a communication board. They may require either a gaze board or electronic devices to indicate the choice of symbol. *Gaze boards* use symbols on a transparent board, usually made of clear plastic. The board is held between the message "sender" and the message "receiver." The receiver watches the student's eyes through the board to determine at which symbol the sender is gazing. Electronic devices include communication boards that illuminate the desired symbol and computer-based systems that produce recorded or synthesized (electronically produced) speech.

Response options are chosen based on the student's response capability, and include the use of direct selection of symbols, scanning systems, and encoded messages. *Direct selection,* as the title implies, involves direct indication of the symbol via pointing or touching. If paralysis or weakness of the limbs limits or excludes pointing with the fingers, options include head-pointing devices, such as a stick or light worn on a headpiece fastened around the forehead. The stick would be used to touch the target symbol, or a beam of light would be used to illuminate the desired symbol.

Other light systems use infra-red beams, invisible to the naked eye, that trigger an indicator next to the desired symbol.

For the individual incapable of pointing, as may happen when paralysis, tremor, or muscular incoordination is present, electronic systems can be set to present all symbols sequentially in a *scanning mode*. Commonly encountered communication board scanning systems often indicate the symbol being presented by a light located next to the symbol. Other systems, using recorded or synthesized speech output, electronically "vocalize" each item sequentially.

No matter what type of symbol indicator is used, the student indicates when the appropriate item has been reached by halting the scanning. This is accomplished by activating a switch. For those with severely limited physical mobility, switch options include pressing a limb or the head against a large paddle connected to the switch, or using a sip (sucking) or puff (blowing) activated switch, with a sensor triggered by air movement placed in or near the mouth. A second movement of the switch reactivates the scanning sequence so that the student can move to the next desired symbol if a multiunit message is being produced. If a multiple sheet (or level) display device is used, the scanner can be set first to move among levels, and when the appropriate level is reached, switch activation would begin sequential movement through all items on that level. Scanning speed, the rate the system sequentially moves between items, can be adjusted to allow appropriate response time for each individual.

Another response category option is *encoded messages*. Rather than using an individual symbol for each word or concept (limiting vocabulary to the space available on the board), the student with good cognitive skills may use a code system. Each item in the vocabulary would be represented by a numeric, color, or graphic code. For example, if a numeric code were used, the word "eat" might be assigned the code number 10, with 25 for "fly," and 100 for "blue." A board with the numbers 0 through 9 could be used to produce all possible code sequences. The student would indicate the numeric code for the desired word, using any of the aforementioned direct or scanning modes, and the receiver would look up the sequence on the student's vocabulary card to determine what word was indicated.

The advantage of encoded systems is that they permit the use of a much larger vocabulary than is available in many direct representation systems. They do, however, use a multistep representational and sequencing process for production, and this limits applicability to students functioning at a high cognitive level.

The third component of an aided communication system is the type of symbol used in the system. A number of options are available. Musselwhite and St. Louis (1982) categorized symbol systems into three types: representational symbol systems (the meaning is suggested by the symbol's appearance), abstract symbol systems (the meaning is not suggested by appearance), and symbolic language codes (codes representing the letters or sounds of a language).

Representational symbol systems include the use of actual objects, photographs, pictures, or line drawings to represent a referent pictographically (e.g., an outline of a person in a dress for "woman") or ideographically (e.g., an outline of a circle on top of a box for "on"). Similar to the concept of transparency for gestures is iconicity for symbols. The closer a symbol resembles its referent, the higher is its iconicity (Miller & Allaire, 1987), and the easier it is for someone untrained in the system to recognize. Photographs, pictures, and line drawings generally are highly iconic and easily trained and understood. Highly iconic systems, however, may work best with concrete rather than abstract concepts. Representational symbol systems that are somewhat lower in iconicity include Blissymbolics and Rebus symbols.

Blissymbolics is a visual, semantically based system developed by Bliss (1965) to serve as an international nonalphabet communication system. While receiving limited acceptance for its original purpose, it was first used as an alternative communication system for children with communication handicaps in 1971 (Kates & McNauton, 1975). While some symbols in the system are highly iconic, using line drawings of common objects, many can only be understood and remembered once the meaning has been given, and others bear no resemblance to their referent. This limits the use of Blissymbols to those trained in the system, although it has been recommended that labels be placed above the symbols to facilitate communication with those not trained in the system. Some concepts are expressed by combining symbols to form compound symbols, and where there is no standard symbol, users can create their own, referred to as combined symbols. Bliss provided a syntax for Blissymbols, or they can be adapted to use with English syntax.

Rebus symbols are used to represent words or parts of words. While a standard glossary has been published for Rebus (Clark, Davies, & Woodcock, 1974), it is not a closed system, and anyone may design symbols. As with Blissymbolics, some symbols are highly concrete and iconic (e.g., a drawing of a face with arrows extending from the eyes for "see"), and others are highly abstract (e.g., a diamond shape for "could"). Rebus symbols can be combined with printed letters to provide plurals, prefixes, suffixes, or to create new words (e.g., "s" + symbol for "on" creates "son").

Abstract symbol systems are limited in number. Musselwhite and St. Louis (1982) provided information on two systems, both developed for work with primates. Carrier (1976) used one of the systems, Premack-type tokens, in the *Non-Speech Language Initiation Program* for children with severe to profound mental retardation. Premack-type tokens are color-coded plastic or masonite symbols with a unique shape for each word or concept represented. The English words they represent are printed on them.

Romski, Sevcik, and Rumbaugh (1985) used Yerkish lexigrams in a communication skills program for students with severe mental retardation. Yerkish is a synthetic language devised for use in an ape-language program, and uses lexigrams (distinctive geometric figures used to represent words) as symbols. The symbols are highly abstract, making their use difficult for some individuals. As both Premack-type tokens and Yerkish lexigrams have low iconicity, users can only communicate with others trained in the system.

Symbolic language codes represent a spoken or written language. The alphabet, Morse code, and Braille are common examples, with a symbol representing a letter in the written language. If a student can read, traditional orthography (the written alphabet) is the most useful symbol system, as it can be understood by all other readers in the user's environment and provides an unlimited vocabulary. It is also commonly used in conjunction with other symbol systems, through the use of labels, to provide a bridge between the system and the common language. Traditional orthography linked to a computer system has been used to teach children with severe physical disabilities to read as part of the language training program (Coon & Lambert, 1985).

Phonemic alphabets (each symbol corresponds to a sound in the language) have been incorporated in electronic communication devices that combine electronically produced phonemes (sounds) to produce synthesized speech. Such devices provide the user with an unlimited vocabulary as long as the student knows how to select the sounds that comprise the word. This can be a problem in English, for the written alphabet does not correspond to the phonemic alphabet, and simply spelling the word may not result in the desired vocal production. For example, the words "bite," "byte," and "bight" are spelled differently but pronounced the same, while the single alphabetic representation of "read" has two pronunciations. Use of the International Phonetic Alphabet (IPA) or International Teaching Alphabet (i.t.a.) on the device's keyboard can overcome the problem. IPA uses some Roman alphabet symbols to represent sounds, but unlike the orthographic system, each symbol is a referent for a single sound. Phonetic alphabets also have potential use as augmentative systems, such as providing initial letter phonemic cues when the speaker has limited intelligibility.

Many of these vocal language instructional programs can be adapted for use with nonvocal gesture and symbol systems. These include Kent (1974); St. Louis, Rejzer, and Cone (1980); Murdock and Hartmann (1985); and Kaiser et al. (1987). Silverman (1980) and Goossens' and Crain (1986b) provide language instructional programs designed specifically for use with nonvocal communication modes. The options available for nonvocal communication are extensive and allow individualization of a system to meet each student's abilities and limitations.

CONCLUSION

The number of vocal language training programs and the number of nonvocal language options described in this chapter are indicative of the abundance of information, material, and techniques available for practitioners attempting to provide successful language facilitation for students with severe or profound handicaps. As the number of language instruction issues explored in this chapter and the diversity of methods used across various systems indicate, clear-cut choices of best practices are not readily apparent, and as Halle (1987) pointed out, many questions still remain regarding if and how language can become more naturalized for students with severe or profound handicaps.

Determining the appropriate language instructional approach for each student is a very dynamic and demanding process. Successful implementation of language instruction is a goal that requires collaborative efforts from a variety of persons and disciplines. The task may be long and arduous, but the reward is great.

REFERENCES

American Speech-Language-Hearing Association Ad Hoc Committee (1981). Position statement on non-speech communication. *Journal of the American Speech and Hearing Association, 23,* 577-581.

Baker, B.L., Brightman, A.J., Carroll, N.B., Heifetz, B.B., & Hinshaw, S. (1978). *Speech and language: Level 1 and 2.* Champaign, IL: Research Press.

Bengston, D., Brandenberg, S., & Vanderheiden, G.C. (1985). *Non-vocal communication resource book.* Madison, WI: Trace Research and Development Center, University of Wisconsin-Madison.

Bliss, C.K. (1965). *Semantography—Blissymbolics.* Sydney, Australia: Semantography Publications.

Bloom, L., & Lahey, M. (1978). *Language development and language disorders.* New York: John Wiley.

Bornstein, H., Saulnier, K.L., & Hamilton, L.B. (1983). *The comprehensive signed English dictionary.* Washington, DC: Gallaudet College Press.

Bottorf, L., & DePape, D. (1982). Initiating communication systems for severely speech-impaired persons. *Topics in Language Disorders, 2,* 55-71.

Bricker, D. (1983). Early communication: Development and training. In M.E. Snell (Ed.), *Systematic instruction of the moderately and severely handicapped (2nd ed.,* pp. 269-288). Columbus, OH: Charles E. Merrill.

Brown, L., Nietupski, J., & Hamre-Nietupski, S. (1976). Criterion of ultimate functioning. In M.A. Thomas (Ed.), *Hey, don't forget about me.* Reston, VA: The Council for Exceptional Children.

Bryen, D.N., & Joyce, D.G. (1985). Language intervention with the severely handicapped: A decade of research. *Journal of Special Education, 19,* 7-39.

Carr, E.G., & Kologinsky, E. (1983). Acquisition of sign language by autistic children II. Spontaneity and generalization effects. *Journal of Applied Behavior Analysis, 16,* 297-314.

Carrier, J.K. (1976). Application of a nonspeech language system with the severely language handicapped. In L.L. Lloyd (Ed.), *Communication assessment and intervention strategies* (pp. 523-547). Baltimore: University Park Press.

Chapman, R.R., & Miller, J.F. (1980). Analyzing language and communication in the child. In R.L. Schiefelbush (Ed.), *Nonspeech language and communication: Analysis and intervention* (pp. 159-196). Baltimore: University Park Press.

Charlop, M.H., Schriebman, L., & Thibodeau, M.G. (1985). Increasing spontaneous verbal responding in autistic children using a time delay procedure. *Journal of Applied Behavior Analysis, 18,* 155-166.

Clark, C.R., Davies, C.O., & Woodcock, R.W. (1974). *Standard rebus glossary.* Circle Pines, MN: American Guidance Service.

Coon, C., & Lambert, H. (1985). A communication skills learning and improvement program. *Communication Outlook, 7 (II),* 5-6.

Cornett, R.O. (1967). Cued speech. *American Annals of the Deaf, 112,* 3-13.

Dettamore, K., & Lippke, B. (1980). Handicapped students learn language skills with communication boards. *Teaching Exceptional Children, 2,* 104-106.

Engelmann, S., & Osborn, J. (1976). *Distar language I.* Chicago: Science Research Associates, Inc.

Fredericks, H.D.B., Riggs, C., Furey, T., Grove, D., Moore, W., McDonnell, J., Jordan, E., Hanson, W., Baldwin, Y., & Wadlow, M. (1976). *The teaching research curriculum for moderately and severely retarded.* Springfield, IL: Charles C Thomas.

Gaylord-Ross, R., Stremel-Campbell, K., & Storey, K. (1986). Social skill training in natural contexts. In R.H. Horner, L.H. Meyer, & H.D.B. Fredericks (Eds.), *Education of learners with severe handicaps: Exemplary service strategies* (pp. 161-187). Baltimore: Paul H. Brookes.

Goetz, L., Gee, K., & Sailor, W. (1985). Using a behavior chain interruption strategy to teach communication skills to students with severe disabilities. *Journal of the Association for Persons with Severe Handicaps, 10(1),* 21-31.

Goossens', C., & Crain, S. (1986a). *Augmentative communciation assessment resource.* Lake Zurich, IL: Don Johnston Developmental Equipment, Inc.

Goossens', C., & Crain, S. (1986b). *Augmentative communication intervention resource.* Lake Zurich, IL: Don Johnston Developmental Equipment, Inc.

Gray, B., & Ryan, B. (1973). *A language program for the non-language child.* Champaign, IL: Research Press.

Guess, D., Sailor, W., & Baer, D. (1978). Children with limited language. In R.L. Schiefelbusch (Ed.), *Language intervention strategies* (pp. 101-143). Baltimore: University Park Press.

Gustason, G., Pfetzing, D., & Zawolkow, E. (1980). *Signing exact English.* Silver Springs, MD: Modern Signs Press.

Halle, J.W. (1982). Teaching functional language to the handicapped: Using the natural environment as the context for teaching. *Journal of the Association for the Severely Handicapped, 7,* 29-37.

Halle, J.W. (1987). Teaching language in the natural enviroment: An analysis of spontaneity. *Journal of the Association for Persons with Severe Handicaps, 12*(1), 28-37.

Hamre-Nietupski, S., Stoll, A., Holtz, K., Fullerton, P., Ryan-Flottum, M., & Brown, L. (1977). Curricular strategies for teaching selected nonverbal communication skills to nonverbal and verbal severely handicapped students. In L. Brown, J. Nietupski, S. Lyon, S. Hamre-Nietupski, T. Crowner, & L. Greunewald (Eds.), *Curricular strategies for teaching functional object use, nonverbal communication, problem solving and meal time skills to severely handicapped students* (pp. 94-250). Madison, WI: Department of Specialized Educational Services, Madison Metropolitan School District.

Harris, D., & Vanderheiden, G.C. (1980). Enhancing the development of communicative interaction. In R.L. Schiefelbusch (Ed.), *Nonspeech language and communication: Analysis and intervention* (pp. 227-257). Baltimore: University Park Press.

Harris-Vanderheiden, D., & Vanderheiden, G.C. (1977). Basic considerations in development of communicative and interactive skills for non-vocal severely handicapped children. In E. Sontag (Ed.), *Educational programming for severely and profoundly handicapped* (pp. 323-334). Reston, VA: Division on Mentally Retarded, The Council for Exceptional Children.

Hart, B. (1985). Environmental techniques that may facilitate generalization and acquisition. In S.F. Warren & A.K. Rogers-Warren (Eds.), *Teaching functional language.* Baltimore: University Park Press.

Hart, B., & Rogers-Warren, A. (1978). A milieu approach to teaching language. In R.L. Schiefelbusch (Ed.), *Language intervention strategies* (pp. 193-235). Baltimore: University Park Press.

Horner, R.H., Sprague, J., & Wilcox, B. (1982). General case programming for community activities. In B. Wilcox & G.T. Bellamy (Eds.), *Design of high school programs for severely handicapped students* (pp. 61-98). Baltimore: Paul H. Brookes.

Horstmeier, D., & MacDonald, J. (1978a). *Environmental prelanguage battery.* Columbus, OH: Charles E. Merrill.

Horstmeier, D., & MacDonald, J. (1978b). *Ready, set, go; talk to me.* Columbus, OH: Charles E. Merrill.

Hunt, P., Goetz, L., Allwell, M., & Sailor, W. (1986). Using an interrupted behavior chain strategy to teach generalized communication responses to students with severe disabilities. *Journal of the Association for Persons with Severe Handicaps, 10 (3),* 196-204.

Kaiser, A.P., Alpert, C.L., & Warren, S.F. (1987). Teaching functional language: Strategies for language intervention. In M.E. Snell (Ed.), *Systematic instruction of persons with severe handicaps* (pp. 247-272). Columbus, OH: Charles E. Merrill.

Kates, B., & McNauton, S. (1975). *The first application of Blissymbolics as a communication medium for non-speaking children: History and development, 1971-1974.* Toronto, Canada: Blissymbolics Communication Institute.

Kent, L.R. (1974). *Language intervention program for the retarded and multiply impaired.* Champaign, IL: Research Press.

Klima, E.S., & Bellugi, U. (1979). *The signs of language.* Cambridge, MA: Harvard University Press.

Lloyd, L.L. (1985). Comments on terminology. *Augmentative and Alternative Communication, I,* 95-97.

McDonnell, J.J., Fredericks, H.D.B., & Grove, D.N. (1975). *The teaching research initial expressive language program.* Monmouth, OR: Teaching Research Publications.

McLean, J.E., & Snyder-McLean, L. (1978). *A transactional approach to early language training.* Columbus, OH: Charles E. Merrill.

Miller, J., & Allaire, J. (1987). Augmentative communication. In M.E. Snell (Ed.), *Systematic instruction of persons with severe handicaps* (pp. 273-297). Columbus, OH: Charles E. Merrill.

Murdock, J.Y., & Hartmann, B.V. (1985). *Communication and language intervention program.* Springfield, IL: Charles C Thomas.

Musselwhite, C.R., & St. Louis, K.W. (1982). *Communication programming for the severely handicapped: Vocal and non-vocal strategies.* San Diego: College-Hill Press.

Reichle, J., & Karlan, G. (1985). The selection of an augmentative system in communication intervention: A critique of decision rules. *Journal of the Association for Persons with Severe Handicaps, 10,* 146-156.

Reike, J.A., Lynch, L.L., & Soltman, S.F. (1977). *Teaching strategies for language development.* New York: Grune & Stratton.

Romski, M.A., Sevcik, R.A., & Rumbaugh, D.M. (1985). Retention of symbolic communication skills by severely mentally retarded persons. *American Journal of Mental Deficiency, 89,* 441-444.

Sailor, W., & Guess, D. (1983). *Severely handicapped students: An instructional design.* Boston: Houghton-Mifflin.

St. Louis, K.W., Mattingly, S., Esposito, A., & Cone, J.D. (1980). *Receptive language curriculum for the moderately, severely and profoundly handicapped.* Morgantown, WV: The West Virginia System, West Virginia University.

St. Louis, K.W., Rejzer, R., & Cone, J.D. (1980). *Expressive language curriculum for the moderately, severely and profoundly handicapped.* Morgantown, WV: The West Virginia System, West Virginia University.

Schumaker, J.B., & Sherman, J.A. (1978). Parent as intervention agent: From birth onward. In R.L. Schiefelbusch (Ed.), *Language intervention strategies* (pp. 237-315). Baltimore: University Park Press.

Shane, H.C., & Bashir, A.S. (1980). Election criteria for the adoption of an augmentative communication system: Preliminary considerations. *Journal of Speech and Hearing Disorders, 45,* 408-414.

Silverman, F.H. (1980). *Communication for the speechless.* Englewood Cliffs, NJ: Prentice-Hall.

Skelly, M., & Schinsky, L. (1979). *Amer-Ind gestural code based on universal American Indian Hand Talk.* New York: Elsevier North Holland.

Sternberg, L. (1982). Communication instruction. In L. Sternberg and G.L. Adams (Eds.), *Educating severely and profoundly handicapped students* (pp. 209-241). Rockville, MD: Aspen Systems Corp.

Stokes, T., & Baer, D. (1977). An implicit technology of generalization. *Journal of Applied Behavioral Analysis, 10,* 349-367.

Striefel, S., Wetherby, B., & Karlan, G.R. (1978). Developing generalized instruction-following behavior in the severely retarded. In C.E. Meyers (Ed.), *Quality of life in severely and profoundly mentally retarded people: Research foundation for improvement.* Monograph No. 3. Washington, D.C.: American Association of Mental Deficiency.

Stremel-Campbell, K., & Campbell, C.R. (1985). Training techniques that may facilitate generalization. In S.F. Warren & A.K. Rogers-Warren (Eds.), *Teaching functional language.* Austin, TX: PRO-ED.

Stremel-Campbell, K., Clark-Guida, J., & Johnson-Dorn, N. (1984). *Pre-language and language communication curriculum for children/youth with severe handicaps.* Monmouth, OR: Teaching Research.

Vicker, B. (Ed.). (1974). *Nonoral communication system project, 1966/1973.* Iowa City, IA: Campus Stores, Publishers, The University of Iowa.

Wilbur, R.B. (1979). *American sign language and sign systems.* Baltimore: University Park Press.

Williams, W., Brown, L., & Certo, N. (1975). Basic components of instructional programs for severely handicapped students. *Theory Into Practice, 14,* 123-136.

Chapter 12

Transition Programming: Independent Living Skills Development

William Sharpton and Paul A. Alberto

PROBLEM AND PAST PRACTICES

One of the emerging issues in the field of education for students with severe or profound handicaps is transition programming. In the past, due to the preponderance of restrictive training efforts and placement options, it was not very important to consider movement of students with severe or profound handicaps from one social environment or services delivery system to another. The fact was that such movement was not often encouraged. And, if movement was possible, the flexibility in the new system was highly controlled.

Transition programming has been defined in a number of ways. Often, the definitions are tied to the age of the individual (e.g., Will, 1984). Ianacone and Stodden (1987) view transition programming from a more global perspective. They see transitions as occurring on an ongoing basis throughout one's life, with types and levels of educational efforts geared toward one's movement from one type of environment to another. Throughout all transitions, individuals would be required to develop crucial behaviors in relation to all new environments, including *increased awareness* and *exploratory skills* as well as the *application* and *integration* of information and skills necessary for success in those environments. The transition service providers are seen as individuals responsible for preparing the individual for making a transition; establishing a preparatory environment before final placement; and providing the final placement environment with full access and participation options. The ultimate goal of such efforts remains the achievement, by the individual, of *independence* in these environments. However, *participation, contribution,* and *satisfaction* are also considered noteworthy outcomes.

Although transition programming concerns should obviously be addressed throughout the entire lifespan of all students with severe or profound handicaps, the majority of recent attempts in this area have focused on transitions from school to work and postschool adult options. In this case, transition programming efforts refer to the coordination of school and adult education services to allow for a smooth movement from school to the least restrictive and most productive adult options. This issue has received increased attention as the first wave of graduates who has had the benefit of a publicly sponsored education under P.L. 94-142 leaves the schools. Most reports in the literature describe the process of transition as one relevant to vocational needs and options after school (Rusch & Phelps, 1987). This view should be expanded to encompass the four domains of one's life style as an adult: work, domestic, community access, and leisure.

This chapter focuses on the content of instruction for domestic and community activities that will promote independence and maximal participation for students with severe or profound handicaps.

SUGGESTED METHODS

The activities targeted for instruction in a school program are critical to the postschool status of students with severe or profound handicaps. Appropriate educational objectives and preparation will allow them a greater number of life style options than previously experienced by members of this population. The degree to which they can participate in life style options, with or without support, depends on the functional skills selected for instruction and their incorporation into functional activities (Wilcox & Bellamy, 1982).

The 1960s and 1970s were known for adopting normalization as the guiding principle for designing programs to support this population. The 1970s and 1980s are associated with developing appropriate teaching technology that allows concepts of normalization to be placed into practice. The 1980s and 1990s will be associated with implementing community-based programs that allow the opportunity for an individual with severe or profound handicaps to be a community participant, thus allowing access to community services, resources, and facilities.

Determining the Content of Instruction

The selection of appropriate activities and skills for instruction to these students should be based on a number of assumptions. One is *partial participation,* which establishes the value of allowing individuals to at least partially engage in an activity rather than denying or delaying involvement because a number of assumed prerequisite skills have not been learned (Baumgart, Brown, Pumpian, Nisbet, Ford, Sweet, Messina, & Schroeder, 1982).

The second is that the skills selected must be *socially valid,* or have relevance to the social situation or environment. The number and types of community and domestic activities that may be selected for instruction are diverse. In fact they may vary not only from community to community but within families of a given community. For that reason, it is important that skills selected for instruction be validated in terms of their utility in various school and nonschool environments. Kazdin (1980) stated that the social validation of skills can be determined based on their functionality, frequency of use, and perceived importance.

The third assumption is that domestic and community skills training should take place in *natural settings.* This is a clear departure from the traditional school-based model. Instruction in natural settings requires creative use of staff and material resources as well as flexibility in scheduling.

A fourth assumption is that all individuals must be allowed to experience reasonable risk under varying degrees of supervision. Perske (1972) described this concept as the *dignity of risk.*

Finally, education is a *future-oriented* process. The purpose of education is to prepare a student for maximal participation in real world options that he or she would not have been able to access without the benefit of a quality education. Therefore, it is important that teachers consider not only the demands of the current environments but those where participation in the future is desired. The educational system carries a clear responsibility to equip students with severe or profound handicaps with skills that will allow the most productive life style, just as the system performs this function for students without handicaps.

Curriculum Design

Teachers often assume that a curriculum is a commercially prepared manual from which they select goals and objectives. This implies that universally appropriate curricula are available for purchase from a variety of educational vendors. Unfortunately, such packaged curricula often do not meet the individualized domestic and community living skills needs of students with severe or profound handicaps who live in a variety of locations across the country. Meeting the needs of such students requires that curriculum be individually developed. Therefore, teachers of students with severe or profound handicaps must be knowledgeable not only in the use of instructional technology but in the development of an appropriate curriculum for their particular students.

Selecting Objectives

Designing an appropriate curriculum requires selecting functionally useful activities and skills for instruction. This process involves a functional analysis of both the environment in which instruction is to take place and the student's existing skills. Two tools were developed to assist in this process: the *ecological inventory* and the *student repertoire inventory.* The ecological inventory (Brown, Branston, Hamre-Nietupski, Pumpian, Certo, & Gruenewald, 1979) is an analysis of the actual setting in which the activity is to be performed to determine the activities and skills needed to successfully participate in it. It is important to note that the ecological inventory is based on the performance of people without handicaps. A comparison of the behavior of the individual with disabilities in terms of performing the identified competencies in the targeted setting yields the student repertoire inventory.

Performing an ecological inventory requires six steps. First, *select the domain of instruction.* Typically, community-based instruction is structured around four curriculum domains: domestic, community access, vocational, and leisure. Second, *identify the potential environments for instruction.* Environments are the settings in which instruction will take place, and are those places in which a related group of activities and skills will be used, such as in the bathroom at home, at a fast-food restaurant, on a bus in the community, or in the school setting. The third step is *divide the environment into its subenvironments.* In the case of a fast-food restaurant, the subenvironments would include the entry area, the service counter area, the eating area, and the restrooms. These are identified as subenvironments because they are all areas associated with a cluster of related activities performed in geographically distinct areas. The fourth step is *define, specific to each subenvironment, the activities people perform in that area.* For example, at the service counter of the fast-food restaurant, the primary activity is ordering. Finally, *divide each activity into the skills necessary for successful performance.* Ordering requires the individual to wait appropriately in line, decide what he or she wishes to eat, communicate effectively with the counter person, pay the correct amount, ask for any necessary items (e.g., ketchup), possibly receive change, and

Exhibit 12-1 Sample Ecological Inventory

Domain: Community
Environment: Popeye's Chicken
  Subenvironment: Parking lot
    Activity: Enter store
    Skills: Exit car
        Locate entry
        Go to entry
        Enter doorway
  Subenvironment: Order area
    Activity: Wait in line
    Skills: Locate order area
        Take place in line
        Move up appropriately
    Activity: Order meal
    Skills: Determine desired food/beverage
        Communicate choice
        Respond to questions
        Wait for food/beverage
  Subenvironment: Dining area
    Activity: Locate a seat
    Skills: Carry tray
        Obtain napkins, etc.
        Identify empty table
        Go to table
        Sit down at table
    Activity: Eat meal
    Skills: Open cartons, etc.
        Eat appropriately
        Converse (if in group situations)
  Subenvironment: Entry/exit area
    Activity: Leave restaurant
    Skills: Carry tray
        Locate trash recepticle
        Dispose of trash/stack tray
        Exit doorway

carry the tray of food without droppage or spillage. Exhibit 12-1 illustrates the organization of an ecological inventory completed for such a subenvironment and its activities.

The information resulting from an ecological inventory is a listing of functionally necessary skills. A model for assembling such activities and skills was developed for organizing the selection and prioritization of activities. Known as an *activities catalogue,* it provides a brief description of a number of functional activities specific to each domain of instruction, thus creating a menu of instructional options (Wilcox & Bellamy, 1987). It lists more skills and objectives than can be taught in one year; therefore, objectives must be ranked according to priority. A variety of individuals should be involved in selecting and prioritizing activities for instruction.

The importance of values negotiation in the design of an individualized education program was presented by Brown, Falvey, Vincent, Kaye, Johnson, Ferrara-Parrish, and Gruenewald (1980) and Vogelsberg, Williams, and Bellamy (1982). This process allows parents and a variety of professionals to discuss the value each places on potential activities and skills included in a student's curriculum. Exhibit 12-2 presents an adaptation of checklists and an evaluation system for prioritizing activities for instruction (Falvey, 1986). It provides a framework for considering a number of variables that should be taken in to account by the team.

The information resulting from an ecological inventory can be used as a criterion-referenced assessment instrument. It serves as a framework for documenting the various skills the student is able to perform in the natural environment as well as those incorrectly performed or not performed at all. These items can then be targeted for instruction. The teacher can be assisted in identifying and analyzing the discrepancy between current performance capability and the performance required in the target setting through the use of a student repertoire inventory strategy (Falvey, Brown, Lyon, Baumgart, & Schroeder, 1980). Falvey (1986) provided the following steps for completing a student repertoire inventory:

1. Delineate the skill performed by nonhandicapped age peers for a given activity as outlined in the ecological inventory;
2. Observe and record whether the student is able to perform the skills performed by nonhandicapped age peers for a given activity;
3. Conduct a discrepancy analysis of the student's performance against his or her nonhandicapped peers' performance. The specific aspects of the skill which cause difficulty for the student should be noted (e.g., materials, natural cues, rate of performance);
4. Design an instructional program to teach the needed skill, provide an adaptation to facilitate successful performance, provide support (e.g., peer assistance) during the activity, or teach a different but related skill (pp. 21-22).

Exhibit 12-2 Domestic Skills Priority Checklist

Student name:_____ Date: _____

Activity: _____

	No	Somewhat	Average	Very much
1. Family input:				
Is this a skill the student routinely needs at home?	1	2	3	4
Is this a skill the family considers critical?	1	2	3	4
Will this skill increase the student's participation in family routines?	1	2	3	4
Is this skill relevant to the student's home culture?	1	2	3	4
Average score for this item: _____				
2. Functional nature:				
Is this a skill that someone else must now perform for the student?	1	2	3	4
Is this a skill the student must use often?	1	2	3	4
Is this a skill that will continue to be useful in later domestic environments?	1	2	3	4
Average score for this item: _____				
3. Current and subsequent environments:				
Is this a skill that can be used in a number of environments other than the present home environment?				
For example: Vocational	1	2	3	4
Community	1	2	3	4
Other domestic environments	1	2	3	4
Later domestic environments	1	2	3	4
Average score for this item: _____				
4. Number of uses:				
Is this a frequently occurring activity?	1	2	3	4
Average score for this item: _____				
5. Social significance:				
Will performing this skill increase the student's social acceptance?	1	2	3	4
Will this skill enhance the student's interpersonal skills?	1	2	3	4
Average score for this item: _____				
6. Physical harm:				
Will learning this skill increase the student's personal safety?	1	2	3	4
Is the skill itself safe to perform, even when done inappropriately?	1	2	3	4
Can the skill be performed without adult supervision?	1	2	3	4
Average score for this item: _____				
7. Logistics:				
Can this skill be taught or practiced in other environments?	1	2	3	4
Is this a skill that will increase the student's independent participation in domestic and other environments?	1	2	3	4
Average score for this item: _____				
8. Age appropriateness:				
Is this a domestic skill a nonhandicapped peer is likely to perform?	1	2	3	4
Is this a skill preferred by nonhandicapped peers?	1	2	3	4
Is this a skill expected of siblings in the home?	1	2	3	4
Average score for this item: _____				

Total skill score (add average scores): _____

Developing Skills in the Domestic Domain

Targeted student behaviors in the domestic domain typically include activities and skills that will increase the degree of independent performance of the student in a range of residential options. Although these activities are numerous, they can generally be grouped into *personal care* activities and *home living* activities.

Personal Care

The goal in this curriculum area is to increase student independence both in the current home setting and in future group living settings. Corollaries to such student independence are (1) greater freedom for family members, by releasing them from the need to perform such tasks for the student; and (2) meeting entry requirements for various residential settings targeted for future entry. These activities are central to good hygiene, and therefore are necessary regardless of how disabled an individual may appear. At a minimum, personal care and maintenance activities include grooming, toilet training, menstrual care, and dressing.

Grooming focuses on the ability to perform the components of a personal grooming routine. Such a routine typically includes activities in the same environment: the bathroom. In this environment are two subenvironments: the sink and the tub/shower area. In the sink area, minimally necessary activities include the same activities engaged in each morning (and evening) by individuals without handicaps of comparable age: washing hands, washing face, brushing teeth, shaving for males, and brushing hair. In the tub/shower area activities include either showering or bathing, toweling dry, and applying deodorant.

The basic instructional approach to each of these activities and their required skills is to treat each as a performance chain, and to use a task analysis as a planning format. Examples of such task analyses are presented in Table 12-1.

Actual instruction based on the task analysis involves the use of both response prompting and antecedent prompting. *Response prompting* teaches the actual motor patterns and sequence required for each activity through use of levels of physical and/or verbal assistance. To further independence in activity initiation and continuing performance of a sequence of activities, an *antecedent prompt,* such as a pictorial sequence of activities attached to the mirror above the sink, may be used. It is important for the teacher to remember that a full sequenced routine of these various

Table 12-1 Sample Task Analysis for Applying Deodorant

Full Participation	*Partial Participation*
Pick up deodorant from storage area (with nondominant hand)	Student indicates where deodorant is stored Teacher retrieves deodorant
Remove cap (with dominant hand)	Student holds deodorant
Check to see if deodorant stick is visible	Teacher removes cap
Turn dial (if needed, until deodorant stick appears)	Student places one hand on deodorant stick
Raise opposite arm	Student raises arm
Apply deodorant (2 strokes)	Teacher assists in application of deodorant
Transfer deodorant stick to other hand	Student places other hand on deodorant stick
Raise opposite arm	Student raises other arm
Apply deodorant (2 strokes)	Teacher assists in application of deodorant
Replace cap	Teacher places cap in front of student
Return deodorant to storage area	Student places hand on cap
	Teacher places cap on deodorant stick
	Student indicates where deodorant is stored
	Teacher returns deodorant stick to storage area

activities is the goal. While it is probably easier from a perspective of instructional management to teach each activity separately (e.g., face washing and shaving), individual activities must be sequenced into a larger chain of activities to form a total grooming routine to be followed in the morning (Freagon, Wheeler, Hill, Brankin, Costello, & Peters, 1983; Jarman, Iwata, & Lorentzson, 1983; Sharpton & Alberto, 1985).

In the initial daily scheduling of instruction, activities should be scheduled at the most natural times of occurrence. For example, hand washing instruction should take place before snack and lunch, as well as after play activities; brushing teeth could logically follow lunch; and brushing hair could be taught in preparation to leave for community instruction.

Instruction of showering or bathing requires attention to the privacy rights of the student, and to gaining parental consent. Matson, DiLorenzo, & Esveldt-Dawson (1981) analyzed showering, drying, and applying deodorant into a 27-step chain. The prompts used included the instructor modeling all steps, although the water was not turned on, and the teacher remained dressed. Verbal cues were used for continued student performance. These researchers taught the skill to groups of students in a state institution. In a public school setting, individual training should be considered because of concern for student privacy and dignity.

Toilet training should be included as a critical objective in personal care. In addition to the concern for increased independence, there are the concerns of increasing the personal dignity of the student to be able to manage such private bodily functions; health factors related to the ability to eliminate in a hygienic manner; increasing the efficient scheduling of classroom activities; and relieving parents of this physical management requirement.

Two methods of toilet training, which have been variously adapted, are reported in the literature to have high success rates. The first focuses on *trip* or *schedule training* (Fredericks, Baldwin, Grove, & Moore, 1975; Giles & Wolf, 1966, Hundziak, Maurer, & Watson, 1965; Kimbell, Luckey, Barberto, & Love, 1967; Linford, Hipsher, & Silikovitz, 1972). Trip training involves routinizing the student's elimination such that there results a predictable schedule of regularly occurring trips to the restroom. The term "elimination" is used to refer to both urination and voiding because formal training in school usually approaches both at the same time even though bowel movements are generally regulated before urination.

For students with severe handicaps the goal is for eventual independence in the toileting process. For students with profound and significant multiple handicaps, the goal may be adjusted to toileting on a regular schedule so the teacher and caregiver can predict the need for elimination and plan accordingly to create a hygienic schedule. These students will also have greater access to community options if their toileting needs can be handled in a routine manner.

The basic steps in such a toilet training program seem to be the following:

1. Determine the most frequent times of accidents by collecting baseline data for three (Foxx & Azrin, 1973) to 30 days, depending on how long it takes to recognize an elimination pattern (Fredericks et al., 1975; Giles & Wolf, 1966). If a natural pattern cannot be determined, the teacher may want to consider the alternative "rapid training approach." Baseline data may be collected as a simple event record of accidents. A more descriptive data collection system can be designed in which data are coded in a way so as to provide whatever information the teacher feels is functionally important. For example, the teacher may want to code the nature of the elimination (e.g., urine or bowel) and note antecedents such as snack, liquid intake, lunch, or medication.
2. Based on patterns affirmed in the baseline data, one can set up a schedule such that the student is taken to the bathroom approximately ten minutes before the time of expected elimination. This should be scheduled not every hour on the hour but to the elimination needs and pattern of the individual student. Once on the commode, toileting time should not be perceived by the student as a play time. The act of elimination should be heavily reinforced. It is

also suggested that the student be on the commode for no more than ten minutes in the event no elimination takes place.

The second approach to toilet training is used when the student is not adhering to a schedule, or a consistent time of accidents cannot be predicted from the baseline data. This procedure is known as *rapid toilet training* (Azrin & Foxx, 1971; Foxx & Azrin, 1973). It includes preset scheduling, "dry pants inspection," and the use of signaling devices. A modification of this procedure involves collecting baseline data according to prescheduled inspection for accidents approximately every half hour. Liquids are given to the student to increase the likelihood of elimination. The additional liquids increase the frequency of elimination, which helps establish a pattern of elimination. On the half hour, a dry pants inspection is conducted in which the student is questioned about his or her dryness, prompted to look at and feel the crotch area of the pants, and if the pants are dry, reinforced for dryness with praise and a primary reinforcer. If pants are wet, the student is verbally reprimanded and the primary reinforcers withheld.

Some students may be more difficult to toilet train and may, therefore, require instruction through use of the full procedure outlined by Azrin and Foxx (1971). The procedure is a process in which sessions last a minimum of four hours per day, with training sessions initially scheduled at half-hour intervals.

Two signaling devices are used in this program. As can be seen in Figure 12-1, one device is connected to snaps placed on the student's underwear; the other is connected to an insert placed on the toilet bowl. When the area between the snaps is moistened, a tone is produced. The teacher and student sit near the commode. The teacher gives the student liquids, and the student is reinforced for eliminating in the bowl. The teacher can tell that the student has eliminated because of the tone from the bowl-signaling device. If the student wets his or her clothing, the signaling device connected to the student's underwear is activated, and the teacher initiates an accident correction procedure.

In such a case, the student must go through an overcorrection procedure by cleaning up the mess, and then practicing the correct toileting behavior six times including going to the bathroom, pulling down pants and underwear, sitting on the commode, pulling up underwear and pants, and returning to the place where he or she wet. When the student begins to self-initiate toileting, the teacher begins to gradually fade the intensity of this process. The student's chair is moved further away from the toilet, longer

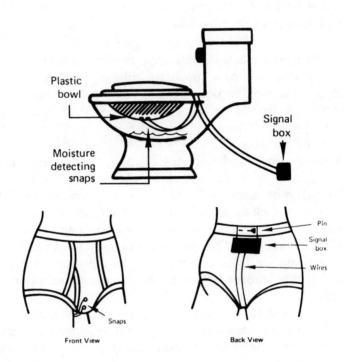

Figure 12-1 Signaling Devices for Toilet Training. *Source:* From *Toilet Training the Retarded: A Rapid Program for Day and Nighttime Independent Toileting* (p. 30) by R.M. Foxx and N.H. Azrin, 1973, Champaign, Ill.: Research Press Company. Copyright 1973 by Research Press Company. Reprinted by permission.

time periods are scheduled between pants checks, the signaling devices are removed, and the student must find the bathroom from various locations.

Toileting accidents will likely occur, and varying degrees of consequences (from less to more restrictive) can result. Extinction can be employed by the teacher by silently taking the student to change his or her clothing. Verbal reprimands can be used, followed by having the student sit in wet clothing for a few minutes, and then by use of the extinction strategy. An overcorrection strategy can be employed in which the student must dress in clean clothing, wash out the soiled clothing, and clean the area in which the accident occurred. This can be expanded to include positive practice of all the steps involved in the appropriate toileting procedure (Azrin & Foxx, 1971; Foxx & Azrin, 1973).

The teacher must determine at which point to instruct a full toileting activity sequence. Such a sequence is essential for generalized use in nonschool settings. A complete toileting skill sequence includes the additional behaviors of:

1. *Signaling the need to use the restroom.* One approach to teaching a student to signal is to guide him or her to ring a bell when on the commode as he or she begins to eliminate. This is done to teach an association between this signal and the act of elimination. Over time, one can set the bell next to the student in the classroom so it may be used as a signal before elimination, thereby pretraining accident avoidance.
2. *Going to the restroom.* When generalizing to various restrooms, this should include the ability to identify the correct room by gender.
3. *Identification of facility.* In the restrooms, the student must have the ability to differentiate the appropriate urinals and commodes. With some students, it may be most efficient just to teach commode use, which includes closing the stall door to assure privacy.
4. *Pulling down pants and underwear.* Care should be taken in the differential clothing management required for standing at a urinal and in using a commode.
5. *Sitting on commode or standing at urinal.*
6. *Elimination.* With some students with physical handicaps this may include instruction in use of adaptive equipment such as a hospital bottle or stabilization bars; how to transfer from wheelchairs, crutches, or a walker; and/or how to perform self-catherization.
7. *Wiping and appropriate disposal of toilet tissue, including flushing.*
8. *Readjustment of clothing.*
9. *Washing hands.* Instruction will be required in generalized knowledge of various types of faucets and hand drying operations.
10. *Exiting of restroom without lingering.*

Appropriate feminine hygiene, especially *menstrual care,* is also crucial to effective transitions. Richman, Reiss, Bauman, and Bailey (1984) taught five women residing in institutions three tasks associated with menstrual care. The women were taught first to recognize and change artificially stained underwear, then to change stained sanitary napkins, and finally to change both.

While the natural cue for this process is a blood stain, food coloring was used to increase the number of training opportunities. A forward chaining procedure was used in which the women repeated the sequence when an error occurred. It is noteworthy that time for skill mastery decreased after the first task was learned, since there was great overlap in the steps associated with the three targeted steps of the sequence. One possible alternative for students with profound and multiple handicaps, if instruction has proven unsuccessful, is to teach them to use and change sanitary napkins on a daily basis. This procedure could be used indefinitely, or on a temporary basis until other menstrual management skills have been learned.

The instruction of *dressing skills* should also be approached as a performance chain, employing the task analysis content planning format. The literature suggests that the procedures of shaping and backward chaining, with appropriate use of response prompts, have most often proven successful (Baldwin, Fredericks, & Brodsky, 1973; Ball, Seric, & Payne, 1971; Colwell, Richards, McCarver, & Ellis, 1973; Martin, Kehoe, Bird, Jensen, & Darbyshire, 1971; Minge & Ball, 1967). The total task or whole task approach to chained instruction of dressing has also been successful (Young, West, Howard, & Whitney, 1986).

Once the instructional strategy is selected, seven guidelines will make instruction, and the student's ability to learn, more efficient.

1. Teach one piece of clothing at a time. The motor requirements for dressing are complex. The instruction of more than one item at a time is likely to cause undue confusion of motor patterns.
2. The use of large, loose fitting clothing will assist initial learning (Kramer & Whitehurst, 1981; Minge & Ball, 1967) as the motor movements required are larger and therefore easier for the student to perform and for the teacher to correct. Caution should be exercised when moving from easier motor patterns to more complex ones as the actual response being requested may be different and student responding may become inconsistent.
3. Undressing is motorically an easier process and should be taught first. When undressing, the body provides a stable "mannequin" for the clothing; therefore, there is a built-in environmental cue. Also, the student does not have to attend to the task of positioning clothing. For example, he or she does not have to discriminate the front and back of a piece of clothing when undressing. The operation of fasteners is also easier during the process of undressing (e.g., unbuttoning is easier than buttoning, unsnapping is easier than snapping, and untying is easier than tying; Minge & Ball, 1967).
4. It is most efficient for maintenance and generalization of learning to teach with natural clothing, in natural settings, and at natural times (Freagon & Rotatori, 1982). Rather than teaching dressing in sets of isolated trials from 9:00 to 9:30 AM, instruction should be provided in relation to naturally occurring demands of scheduled daily activi-

ties. Instruction can begin in conjunction with toileting where a certain amount of clothing manipulation is required. Additionally, the student can be taught putting on and taking off coats and sweaters at school arrival and departure, as well as in conjunction with community instruction. It should be noted, however, that Azrin, Schaeffer, & Wesolowski (1976) used a rapid training model for teaching dressing in which three-hour instructional sessions were conducted.

5. Clothing should be chosen wisely to make the skills less frustrating for the student and care providers. Selected clothing should require minimal manipulation (e.g., pullover shirts and sweaters; elasticized waistband pants instead of pants that have fasteners, zippers, and belts; velcro fasteners in place of buttons and snaps whenever possible (Finnie, 1975).)

6. While there is literature about teaching how to tie shoes (Baldwin et al., 1973; Martin, Kehoe, Bird, Jensen, & Darbyshire, 1971), the use of loafers or shoes and sneakers with velcro eliminates skills difficult to learn by students with physical handicaps.

7. Clothes should not only be selected to accommodate the physical limitations of the student but to insure age appropriateness.

Some of these suggestions may affect styles of clothing, and potentially produce undesirable side effects. For example, to reduce negative attention to adolescents and adults as a result of their possibly more limited clothing selection, Nutter and Reid (1978) taught individuals to coordinate their clothing "choices" more effectively (e.g., by assisting individuals match solid color clothing by more carefully controlling the stocking of their closets with more limited choices). This procedure not only helped eliminate the need to teach the difficult skill of clothing coordination but likely helped in making the overall clothing look "less noticeable."

Home Living Activities

As with personal care, the goal of instruction in the home is not necessarily independence but maximal participation. In the case of *home maintenance,* it may be viable for certain tasks to be completed by a small group of individuals rather than by one person. This arrangement is well suited to the concept of partial participation and allows for people with severe or profound disabilities to be included in home-related activities.

Home living activities also include food preparation, housekeeping, telephone use, and acquisition of safety behaviors. In the process of designing instruction for any of these home living activity areas, consideration should be given to the following points:

- *Site selection.* Opportunity must be provided for students to perform the target activity in natural environments, and in response to the natural cues and materials associated with that setting. Teaching home skills in natural sites is an issue that has been addressed by few school districts. Certainly, instruction of food preparation in the home economics room is more desirable than using makeshift supplies and equipment in the classroom; however, two creative alternatives have been presented.

  A school district can lease a home in a local neighborhood for the express purpose of providing domestic instruction in a natural setting. Freagon et al. (1983) described such a program where students of all ages received domestic instruction during the day and older students (aged 18 to 21 years) participated in overnight sessions to ensure that skills were used at natural times. If leasing is not a viable option, a cooperative agreement with a community group home can be arranged such that when the residents are at their vocational placements during the day, school personnel can use the home for instruction of school age students.

  A second alternative for domestic activities training in real homes is using a number of homes. In this model, parents, school staff, and interested neighbors volunteer their home on a scheduled basis for domestic instruction. Students are taught in small groups and rotate to different homes to ensure that a range of stimuli and responses associated with activity performance is sampled. This model allows not only for generalization training but for students to be periodically taught in their own home, provided their home is included in the training site pool.

- *Grouping.* Students should be grouped in such a way as to insure heterogeneity. This allows students with less severe handicaps to be taught in a smaller group and individuals with profound disabilities to participate partially in activities. The size of the group should be defined by the environment in which one is teaching. For example, in teaching cooking, the group is limited to the number who can reasonably and safely engage in activities in a kitchen. Grouping for domestic activities instruction should also assure that both sexes have equal opportunity to engage in the activities.

- *Content selection.* Content must be based on the results of an ecological inventory specific to the targeted individual and to his or her needs in current and potential environments.
- *Environmental structuring.* The important perspective for teachers to keep is that it is impossible to predict the exact domestic environment a given student will subsequently enter. Therefore, it is the responsibility of educators to teach maximal participation in the greatest number of activities associated with a residence. While it is the primary responsibility of the receiving adult program to arrange the environment to accommodate the skill level of the individual, teachers should also structure environments to support optimal student performance and instructional efficiency. Two ways to arrange the environment are selecting products and materials that are easier to use and exaggerating stimulus features associated with household items.

When selecting products for use during instruction, premeasured products or those packaged in individual units can bypass inconsistent or missing measuring skills and increase the speed of student performance. Accidents can be eliminated by using plastic containers. Certain types of products eliminate steps or help in their performance. For example, most garbage bags require that a tie be twisted around the top to prevent spillage. Certain brands are made so that handles can be pulled to close the bag automatically. Fewer operations are required with this product; therefore, student performance is enhanced.

Exaggerating stimulus features is accomplished through use of antecedent prompts. For example, model paint can be used to provide cues to the operation of appliances. Two dots can be painted on the toaster to indicate where to put the bread. The lever that controls the timing can be painted with lines of the same color. When making beds, tape can be placed on the perimeter of the spread so the edges line up with the bed. Dial adaptations that indicate the exact positions for operation can be added to washing machines and dryers. A template for a microwave control panel will allow the student to gauge timing with numbers or colors.

Food preparation can be complex because of the number of embedded skills such as measuring, counting, and using various kitchen utensils and appliances. Fortunately, the advent of packaged and convenience foods has made it possible for individuals with severe or profound handicaps to participate to an increasing extent in the preparation of food if instructional programming is well designed.

Design of the instructional program must include what to teach in a food preparation sequence. It is important to consider the various activities that can be performed in a kitchen, including using a range, conventional oven, and/or a microwave; using a refrigerator and storage cabinets; setting a table; and washing dishes. The ecological inventory process can identify the subenvironments that most often occur across kitchens and to target the activities and skills they require (c.g., oven, refrigerator, sink, cabinets).

While reports of teaching students with mild or moderate handicaps to prepare complex meals are found in the literature, few studies successfully report traditional meal preparation by individuals with severe or profound handicaps. Adaptations in task performance should seriously be considered, especially for students with severe cognitive disabilities. Use of a microwave oven for hot meal preparation or consumption of a prepackaged snack are the best options for the most independent performance.

Three noteworthy methods of teaching food preparation are found in the literature. Schleien, Ash, Kiernan, and Wehman (1981) used a system of least intrusive prompts to teach a woman with profound mental retardation to cook three items. This study lends support to the value of systematic instruction in teaching a functional activity. A second technique is using pictorial cues. Pictorial recipe cards were used to teach food preparation skills effectively (Johnson & Cuvo, 1981; Martin, Rusch, James, Decker, & Trytol, 1982; Spellman, DeBriere, Jarboe, Campbell, & Harris, 1978) as were line drawings or photographs as recipe directions. In their study, Johnson and Cuvo (1981) also reported that maintenance of acquired skills can be supported by providing confirmation of the next step and giving nonspecific prompts ("What's next?" versus "Now, get the salt."). A third approach is to use recorded auditory prompts to support a student's performance in the absence of a teacher. Alberto, Sharpton, Briggs and Stright (1986) successfully used auditory prompts via a "Walkman" recorder to teach three students, two with severe handicaps, to prepare a sandwich and a cup of soup. Eight-month follow-up data documented long-term maintenance of learned skills.

It is important to note that the goal of instruction need not be total removal of a prompting system. Provided that the prompts are readily available, provide choices, and can be self-managed, student independence can still be maximized.

Housekeeping skills are important to an independent or cooperative residential option for individuals with severe or profound handicaps. At home with their family, or in a future group living arrangement, house-keeping chores such as vacuuming, dusting, floor mopping, bed making, and bathroom cleaning are shared through individual assignment. While few students are likely to be completely independent in the performance of all housekeeping activities, acquisition of some skills in this area will allow the individual to be more independent in a present environment and to access a wider variety of options in adulthood. To determine which activities to target for instruction, the individual education program (IEP) team should focus on housekeeping tasks performed by age peers or those deemed especially important by the family, and/or those skills needed for access to future residential environments.

The instruction of housekeeping skills requires selecting an instructional procedure, including designing an appropriate performance strategy for each student, selecting or designing any adaptive equipment needed by a student, and designing a scheduling system to prompt the student when to perform activities. Teaching procedures may range from using a least intrusive prompt system (Cronin & Cuvo, 1979) to using intensive assistance in the initial phase of instruction, which allows for a reduction in assistance over time (Snell, 1982). A combination of teaching strategies may also be used. Cuvo, Leaf, and Borakove (1978) used two instructional strategies to teach students with moderate mental retardation to clean a school restroom. A most-to-least intrusive system of prompts was used for 20 steps identified as being more difficult. For the remaining steps, a least-to-most intrusive system of prompts was used.

Housekeeping activities are rarely performed in isolation: They occur in a sequence, which will vary from one home to another. Student self-sequencing of housekeeping tasks may be structured through the use of a coded calendar that has a different task pictured for each day; or a sequence booklet in which each page pictures the student performing a task. Completion of the entire booklet results in completion of all tasks in proper sequence.

Housekeeping activities may also be performed in response to naturally occurring conditions such as wiping the counter after spilling water when filling a glass. In such cases, students must be taught to recognize the naturally occurring prompts associated with incidents that call for the performance of a housekeeping activity.

Using a telephone is a skill that allows people to maintain communication with others, summon assistance in emergency situations, and request services (e.g., order a taxi). In considering target objectives for students with severe handicaps, teachers and others should not confine the options to traditional use of the telephone. As with other activities discussed in this chapter, alternate performance strategies can be designed to meet specific needs.

Consider a student who lacks a verbal form of communication but has learned to shop, eat, and play video games at the local shopping mall. His mother and teacher have arranged a communication system that meets his needs. He is dropped off at the mall by his mother, who then returns home. When ready to leave, he calls home, vocalizes when his mother answers, and then waits at a prearranged location for her to pick him up. While the form of his behavior differs significantly from other teen-agers who depend on their family for transportation, its function certainly does not.

Telephone instruction can be divided into home use, community use, and emergency use. Home use centers on calling significant others or perhaps ordering services. Community use involves the use of a pay phone. Emergency use includes calling specific individuals when in need of assistance or using the 911 emergency service available in many communities.

Instruction of telephone use requires designing appropriate perform-ance strategies and using systematic instruction. Students will need two performance strategies: one to determine the number to call, and one to operate the telephone. Individual cards can be prepared for important numbers with pictorial cues to indicate their purpose. Snell and Browder (1987) suggested using a personal telephone book for easy access to desired numbers. A flip chart that allows a student to see only one number at a time may assist in dialing. It is important that the booklet have a clear beginning and ending so that the student always begins dialing the correct number.

Instruction of dialing is best approached as a matching task. The student is taught to match each number on the telephone number card to the numbers on the telephone button as a seven-step matching process. The speed dialing feature offered by many telephone companies is an example of a commercially available option that reduces the complexity of the required behavior to operate a telephone.

Many students can learn to use the telephone in emergency situations. In such cases, the student must recognize that an emergency exists, dial the appropriate number, and state the nature of the problem. Risley and Cuvo (1980) reported the successful instruction of three individuals with moderate handicaps to make emergency calls to specific numbers. Photographs of emergency situations and nonfunctional telephones were used to provide instruction. Sharpton and Alberto (1985) listed a procedure for teaching a student to use a pay telephone in a community setting when lost.

The student

a) identifies and locates a pay phone with a printed telephone number on the dial or under the pushbuttons.
b) identifies and retrieves appropriate coins to operate the phone.
c) uses an emergency telephone number card in his wallet to locate an appropriate telephone number (for example, that of the teacher, parent, employer, house-parent).
d) dials the phone.
e) says: "My name is _____. I am lost. The number of this phone is _____ (reads number from telephone).
f) waits for a person at the telephone location. Upon receiving the call, the teacher, house-parent, etc. calls the operator, explains the emergency, and gives the telephone number of the pay phone at which the student is located (p. 181).

With this information the operator can cross-reference the number and give the exact location of the pay telephone at which the student is waiting.

The issue of *safety training* has received increased attention as individuals with severe or profound handicaps have moved into community residences in greater numbers. Self-preservation skills, including the ability to evacuate in response to a fire alarm, often are needed for an individual to be accepted in the least restrictive community residence.

Rae and Roll (1985) used daily fire drills to teach ten adults with profound mental retardation to exit an apartment building. Drills began at least disruptive times and gradually were scheduled during times at which it was more difficult to evacuate. Six months of training were required before the first notable increase in rate of performance. More expedient results were reported by Jones, Sisson, and Van Hasselt (1984) who used a packaged approach that combined instructions, rehearsal, corrective feedback, social reinforcement, tokens, and review.

The importance of fire safety skills for admittance to postschool residential programs calls for school programs for students with severe or profound handicaps to address this behavior. Fire escape skills have been taught to school-age individuals with severe handicaps using an area for training that was altered with props to look more realistic (Haney & Jones, 1982). This type of training could easily be incorporated into one of the domestic training models that uses realistic settings.

Developing Skills in the Community Domain

Community activities are a broad area of an instructional curriculum for students with severe or profound handicaps. It would be impossible to

Table 12-2 Potential Instructional Sites for Community Activities

Activity Clusters	Instructional Sites
Uses public services	Post Office
	Clinic
	Library
	Human services office
	Recreation center
Uses commercial services	Bank
	Restaurant (e.g., fast-food, "menu", cafeteria)
	Laundromat
	Recreation sites (e.g., bowling alley, video arcade)
Purchases goods/services	Convenience store
	Grocery store
	Shopping center
	Discount/variety store
	Shopping mall
Moves about in community	Local neighborhood
	Shopping areas
	Other community settings
	Transit routes

provide a detailed description of all instructional opportunities associated with the array of environments found in community settings. Table 12-2 presents an overview of potential instructional sites for several activities.

Due to the complexity of moving instruction out to community settings, a number of programmatic variables must be considered. These issues can generally be grouped under instructional practices and administrative support.

Instructional Practices

As with instruction in the domestic domain, it is important for students to learn activities related to community competence in the actual settings where they will be used. The first step in the design of a community-referenced curriculum is to *select the areas of instruction*. This process can be assisted through the use of an activities catalog (Wilcox & Bellamy, 1987), as described earlier in the chapter.

It is important to consider how often an activity will be used by a student. Consider the example of identifying coin values in counting appropriate amounts. Typically, coin counting begins with pennies since they are members of the smallest unit and the easiest to count. In reality, most people have devised informal mechanisms to prevent the routine handling of pennies. Many people carry four pennies in "self-defense" so that they can give a cashier the correct number of pennies to prevent getting more in change. It is not at all rare for people to keep a jar for pennies they collect over time. In fact, many individuals only deal with pennies on an annual basis when they roll the accumulated coins to exchange them for paper bills at the bank. It would be a waste of valuable instructional time to concentrate on a skill that may be useful only once a year. Therefore, it is important to use probability as a guide in the selection of skills for instruction. Activities the student and/or the family currently perform on a more regular basis or that are likely to be performed in future settings with reasonable frequency should be prioritized for instruction.

After targeting community activities for instruction, it is necessary to select the locations in the community where instruction will take place. As described in the earlier chapter on instructional technology, *general case programming* (Horner, Sprague, & Wilcox, 1982) is a procedure by which specific settings for community instruction are selected according to variations in characteristics of each site (stimuli) and in the specific behavior required for correct performances (responses). This process allows students to learn a range of variations associated with a given community activity concurrently. General case programming also calls for selecting two sets of sites for each targeted activity that are functionally equivalent in the range of variables sampled. One set should be used for instruction until the student reaches the established criterion for mastery. Then, the other set is used to probe or test for skill integrity.

If each student is to participate maximally in the targeted activity, it is important for the teacher to *design a performance strategy* that "works." Successful instruction of students with severe or profound handicaps in natural settings is in large part dependent on the ability of the teacher to design a strategy the student can use to perform a skill despite deficits or characteristics that cannot currently be overcome. This premise is based on the notion that the presenting needs of these students are extremely broad. Therefore, it is unlikely that all students can use the same strategy to accomplish the targeted activity. Wilcox and Bellamy (1982) defined this concept as an *alternate performance strategy,* and Exhibit 12-3 illustrates various strategies for the behavior of ordering at a bakery counter in the grocery.

Often individual performance strategies will require an adaptive piece of equipment, which is usually teacher made. These prostheses should be

Exhibit 12-3 Sample Alternate Performance Strategies

Task: Ordering at a grocery bakery counter

Alternate performance strategies

- Student verbally orders item presented in display case or from memory
- Student verbally orders using picture card as prompt
- Student points to item desired
- Student points to photo of desired item in picture booklet
- Student activates recorded audiotape to place order
- Teacher/peer gives order card to wait person when student touches card (partial participation)

---

designed to enhance and facilitate a person's independence in the natural setting. For example, a student may not be able to give an order at the counter of the fast-food restaurant. It would be appropriate for the teacher to design a strategy in which the student makes selections from a choice board in the classroom, places them on an order card to take to the restaurant, and hands the card to the counter person to make the request known. Another example of a teacher-made device is a laminated cardboard coin board that provides an opportunity to match coins so that the student will leave with the appropriate amounts for bus fare in both directions and for a vending machine while at work.

In designing these devices, three factors should be used to judge whether the prosthesis is appropriate for use with a given student. First, the device must be effective. If it does not produce the required outcome, it will be of no use to the student. The device should be durable so it can be used over time and is not in constant need of replacement or repair. Second, the device should be age appropriate and as inconspicuous as possible so that it does not draw negative attention or sacrifice the individual's dignity. Finally, the device should be portable so that it can be easily used in a number of settings. While this is an individualized procedure, the teacher can design a range of performance strategies that will accommodate the presenting skill levels and/or limitations of a variety of students.

The next step of instructional design is to *develop a task analysis* that incorporates the selected performance strategy. It can also be devised so that it can function as the mechanism by which performance data are routinely collected. Exhibit 12-4 presents a sample task analysis for a community activity.

Another important instructional decision is the number of opportunities earmarked for each targeted activity on a weekly basis. This is

Exhibit 12-4 Sample Individualized Task Analysis

Task: Shopping at neighborhood drug store

At home, student:
- Determines items needed (student selects photos from file of photos representing items most often used)
- Calculates money needed (prompt board assists student in taking sufficient number of one-dollar bills)

In store, student:
- Enters store
- Picks up basket, if needed
- Locates first item
- Places item in basket (or hand)
- Locates second item
- Places item in basket (or hand)
- Continues locating and placing until all items are obtained
- Moves to checkout area
- Enters checkout lane
- Places basket (items) on counter
- Gets money ready
- Listens for cashier's response
- Looks for first number on register or listens for first number stated by cashier
- Counts out corresponding number of dollars plus one more
- Holds out hand for change and receipt
- Picks up bag
- Thanks cashier
- Exits store

---

extremely individualized and should be based on the degree of importance assigned to the activity by the IEP team and the logistics of addressing training and probe sites. This concern can best be reduced by carefully selecting sites that offer a variety of training situations associated with a number of community activities (e.g., shopping centers).

At this point, the teacher is ready to design a master *schedule of instruction.* This schedule should be comprehensive; therefore, community activities should be integrated with the instructional activities associated with the leisure, vocational, and domestic domains. Wilcox and Bellamy (1982) suggested that the following variables be considered when designing a schedule of instruction: the range of IEP objectives, individual student instructional priorities, instructional skills of staff, resource availability, and possible student groupings. The percentage of instructional time that should be spent in nonschool settings has not been determined at this time. As seen in Figure 12-2, Sailor, Halvorsen, Anderson, Goetz, Gee, Doering, and Hunt (1986) recommended times for different chronological age groups.

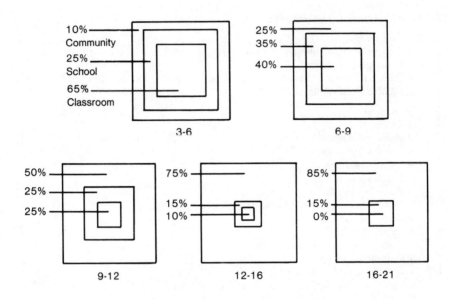

Figure 12-2 Percentages of optimal educational time spent in these areas: classroom, other school, and nonschool community, all as a function of chronological age grouping regardless of severity of handicapping conditions. *Source:* From "Community Intensive Instruction" by W. Sailor et al. in *Education of Learners with Severe Handicaps: Exemplary Service Strategies* (p. 253) by R. Horner, L. Meyer, and H.D. Fredericks (Eds.), 1986, Baltimore, Md.: Paul H. Brookes Publishers. Copyright 1986 by Paul H. Brookes Publishers. Reprinted by permission.

The following scheduling guidelines are offered by Ford, Dempsey, Black, Davern, Schnorr, and Meyer (1986):

- Schedule a predictable flow of activities.
- Take advantage of the natural times to teach skills.
- Take advantage of integration opportunities.
- Schedule enough time for each activity.
- Use small group instruction rather than one-to-one instruction.
- Strive for heterogeneous student groupings.
- Make predictable staff-to-student assignments.

Wilcox and Bellamy (1982) offered additional guidelines:

- Schedule weekly time for teachers to train and supervise classroom staff (e.g., tutors, aides, related service personnel).
- Schedule inflexible activities first.
- Schedule community training experiences before in-class or in-school activities.

With the completion of the planning steps previously discussed, *instruction in the community* may begin. It is important for all instructional staff, administrators, and parents associated with the program to understand that a community intensive program must be systematically implemented and is not a series of field trips. The same instructional procedures discussed in Chapter 7 must be used in community settings.

The teacher should catalog the naturally occurring cues in each setting and work toward student reliance on those natural cues rather than on those provided by instructional staff (Ford & Miranda, 1984). Where additional support is necessary to ensure success, it should be provided in the following order: by an alternate performance strategy, by employees in the community site, or by others.

Data collected during community instruction will provide valuable feedback as to the quality of the educational program. The teacher should monitor these data carefully to determine if and when program alterations are needed.

Students must perform the targeted activities under conditions typically found in the setting identified for instruction. While it may be impossible at first for the student to rely totally on naturally occurring cues, the teacher should carefully consider how he or she designs and delivers prompts when teaching in the community. As much as possible, performance strategies should allow for self-managed prompts that focus attention on the relevant cues in the setting.

Ford and Miranda (1984) described a model for making decisions related to the use of natural cues and corrections in community instruction. Their model includes five phases:

1. identifying errors made in a community environment that might be attributed to a failure to respond to natural cues
2. deciding whether to allow a natural correction to occur
3. selecting relevant natural cues and their salient features
4. determining the types of teaching and reinforcement procedures to use in a community environment
5. fading instructional cues

The use of *simulation* has been proposed as a solution to the difficulty of scheduling all instruction in natural settings. Simulation involves designing instructional sequences in school or other controlled settings that approximate performance conditions in natural settings under natural conditions. It is important for instructional staff to consider seriously how simulation will likely result in accurate performance. As the time in actual community settings is limited, it is important that the student's instructional time in those settings be optimally used.

Quality of performance in actual settings where the activity is performed is the only variable ultimately of concern. Still, simulation may have a valuable role in the instruction of critical community activities if it positively affects performance. Vogelsberg et al. (1982) suggested the following reasons for using simulation: (1) to facilitate the acquisition of difficult-to-learn skills, (2) to minimize risk, (3) to decrease cost, (4) to provide remedial trials and repeated practice, and (5) to reduce fears of embarrassment.

Nietupski, Hamre-Nietupski, Clancy, and Veerhusen (1986) offered the following guidelines to using simulation as an adjunct to community instruction:

- Inventory community settings to determine the range of stimulus and response variations potentially facing students.
- Systematically vary simulations to provide a sufficient range of training exemplars.
- Use community performance data to modify simulations.
- Use simulations to provide intensified practice in problem areas.
- Schedule simulations to allow for sufficient in vivo instruction and to provide simulations in close temporal proximity to in vivo instruction.

The decision to use simulation should be specific to individual student needs. If used, simulation should not be used in isolation, or as a prerequisite to involvement in community settings. Finally, instructional staff should monitor performance data from natural settings to determine whether to continue the use of simulation or to adapt or refine a simulated activity.

Consider the case of teaching a student when to signal the driver that he or she wishes to exit a bus. Repeated practice would require a good deal of money and time as the student could only identify the targeted stop when traveling in the correct direction. A videotape of the route could be used in school to offer opportunities for the student to identify the stop. Obviously, this instructional strategy would not be used in isolation. Rather, the student would also be involved in opportunities in the community. The use of simulation in this case may well decrease the cost of instruction, provide for greater efficiency of instruction, and allow greater control over variables in the setting (e.g., time elapsed before presentation of "target stop" could be varied until it approximated the bus ride).

The *materials of instruction* should be those that are naturally found at the site the activity is to be performed. The student should display competence in handling the materials associated with a given setting. For example, the student uses realistic materials when he or she places coins in a vending machine and operates the controls, uses a cart in the grocery store, or operates a microwave oven.

A traditional administrative pattern for instruction calls for one teacher to work with a given group of students, usually with the assistance of a paraprofessional. Often these students are grouped according to a diagnostic label (e.g., autism), or by level of functioning (e.g., severe retardation). A practice that is receiving increased support, particularly for programs that promote community-intensive instruction, is *heterogeneous grouping*. The grouping of students by various levels of ability and physical needs insures that students can receive small group instruction and also promotes the concept of partial participation. A compromise administrative pattern for districts that do not yet allow heterogeneous grouping pairs two teachers of different categories of students so that they can co-schedule instructional activities using both class members as a common pool.

Baumgart and VanWalleghem (1986) offered the following alternative staffing strategies to implement community intensive instruction: (1) the consultant model, (2) staggered implementation of community-based instruction, (3) use of heterogeneous grouping of students, (4) restructuring of related services instructional time intervals, (5) procurement of temporary paraprofessional assistance, (6) team teaching, (7) use of computer-managed and computer-assisted instruction, and (8) use of volunteers and peer tutors.

Examples of Comprehensive Instructional Practices

A number of examples of community-intensive educational programs are reported in the literature. In many cases, individuals with mild to moderate handicaps are the focus, although an increasing number include students with severe handicaps. Following is a discussion of concerns related to specific instructional programs that not only adhere to a community-referenced model of educational delivery but have varied literature support.

Community mobility is a critical skill if students with severe or profound handicaps are to use community services and settings. Mobility includes two areas of skill clusters: pedestrian skills and skills related to the use of public transit systems or alternative transportation options.

In teaching pedestrian skills, the first decision facing a teacher is the types of streets the student will learn to cross. This decision requires input from family members as well as instructional personnel. Factors that should be considered include the types of community environments likely to be accessed and the level of supervision needed by the individual. For example, some individuals using wheelchairs may find it easier to use shopping malls and areas with accessible sidewalks for the majority of their community activities.

In designing the instructional program, the variables associated with different community settings need to be considered. The major variables by which streets vary include whether an intersection is controlled (e.g., a traffic light), is partially controlled (e.g., a yield sign), or is uncontrolled (e.g., no sign). Other factors include the volume of traffic and the number of lanes.

Additional questions that must be addressed involve the relative merits of in vivo and classroom training. Findings of Matson (1980) and Vogelsberg and Rusch (1979) support the use of in vivo instruction. Another question relates to the manner by which the level of difficulty of the streets and intersections can be controlled within the instructional program. As students gain mastery, supervision may be reduced by fading the proximity of the teacher or by pairing students so that one relies on the other for assistance (e.g., determining the appropriate time to cross).

Later in the instructional program, exceptions to common situations may be presented systematically. These circumstances vary from one setting to another and may include such situations as traffic lights that are out of order or cars turning right on a red light. Mobility training also provides opportunities for teaching other behaviors. Reid and Hurlbut (1977) described a program in which students using wheelchairs had to indicate, by pointing on a choice board, where they wanted to go before assistance was provided by peers. Integrated programming efforts such as this provide optimum circumstances for both instruction and demonstration of functional use of skills.

An important setting for the use of pedestrian skills is the parking lot in small and large shopping centers. For many youngsters and adults with severe or profound disabilities, the majority of the time they will require appropriate walking skills will be in these settings as they move from the parking lot to the shopping center, and from one shop to another.

Individuals with severe handicaps have also learned to ride public transit independently (Sowers, Rusch, & Hudson, 1979). Again, instruction must be systematic and should include features such as selecting a destination, finding the bus stop, waiting for the bus, signaling the bus to stop, entering the bus, paying the fare, finding a seat, watching for and determining where to exit, signaling the driver of intention to exit, and exiting the bus. Performance strategies may include using tokens or a bus pass, carrying a photograph of the destination, or providing the driver with the destination when entering the bus. Simulation and in vivo training strategies have been used effectively in combination to teach bus riding skills to individuals with mild and moderate handicaps (Neff, Iwata, & Page, 1978; Robinson, Griffith, McComish, & Swasbrook, 1984); however, the role of simulation in teaching this activity to individuals with severe handicaps remains unclear.

Alternative transportation modes will vary from one community to another. One likely strategy is learning to take a taxi. While some students may be taught to order a taxi by telephone, others may use one ordered for them, or one that is routinely scheduled.

Shopping is a complex set of activities that may take place in department, grocery, or convenience stores. As with other community skills, it is important for the instructional staff to equip the student with viable performance strategies. In general, two strategies must be developed; one for item selection, and another for paying the cashier.

Gaule, Nietupski, and Certo (1985) described the use of a prosthetic shopping aid in which the student was prompted as to what to buy and how much it cost. Squares, each representing 50 cents, were printed on the shopping aid to help the student add the total. Some individuals have also learned to use a pocket calculator while shopping (Nietupski, Welch, & Wacker, 1983). A well-structured training program that included simulation and in vivo instruction was used by McDonald and Horner (1985) to teach eight young adults with moderate to severe handicaps to locate 15 specific grocery items. Slides were used in the classroom to demonstrate the various locations of the selected items in different stores. The results indicated that such simulation in combination with actual in-store training results in greater generalized ability of the shopping skills.

Operation of a vending machine is a useful activity in vocational, community, and leisure settings. Sprague and Horner (1984) supported the use of a general case program to teach individuals with moderate to severe handicaps to use untrained machines. They described a performance strategy in which students used only quarters to activate a machine.

Other options may be developed to meet an individual's needs. A cardboard counting card with recesses for appropriate coins and the amount it totals printed on it allows the student to match the card to the amount listed on the machine, find the appropriate coins, and then use the machine without "counting" the coins.

Restaurant skills are important to individuals with severe handicaps both in terms of a leisure activity and opportunities to interact with persons who are not handicapped and family members. Evidence to support the ability of individuals with severe or profound handicaps to learn to eat in a restaurant is presented by Marholin, O'Toole, Touchette, Berger, and Doyle (1979), and Storey, Bates, and Hanson (1984). Of interest in the study by Storey et al. was the assessment of skill generalization to other restaurants.

In general, restaurants may be grouped into fast-food, cafeteria, and "menu." As with all activities, performance strategies using adaptive materials have been developed for students with severe or profound handicaps to promote success in restaurant settings. Students who are unable to order verbally may use a written order card or manipulate a choice board to make their requests known. Students who are unable to perform the complete activity may use a partial participation strategy.

Administrative Support

To ensure that teachers of students with severe or profound handicaps can provide quality instruction in community settings, school administrators must address problems commonly encountered by school districts. The problems and possible solutions presented in Table 12-3 have been reported by Falvey (1986), and Hamre-Nietupski, Nietupski, Bates, and Maurer (1982).

CONCLUSION

This chapter dealt with the independent living skill needs of students with severe or profound handicaps with a special focus on issues and concerns related to effective transitions to postschool adult environments. Although transition has been interpreted by some to mean preparation in more restrictive environments *before* placement in less restrictive environments, a major message of this chapter is that such delay is not warranted. Rather, community-referenced instruction can be used to dictate *immediate* community placement as a part of preferred instructional practice. The next chapter focuses on effectively extending this point of view toward vocational programming.

Table 12-3 Administrative Problems of and Solution to Providing Community-Based Instruction

Administrative Problem	Possible Solution
Limited staff	Team teaching
	Use of support personnel
	Use of volunteers, peer tutors
Transportation	Careful selection of training sites
	Use of volunteer staff
	Regularly scheduled bus runs
	Use of public transit
	Reimbursement for use of private vehicles, including liability insurance
	Drop off to training sites by regular school bus
Cost	Realign purchase priorities
	Cooperate with other agencies (e.g., use of group home for training)
	Allow students to shop for others
	Transfer monies from school lunch
	Hold fundraiser
Negative reaction to change in curriculum emphasis	Demonstrate that academic skills can be taught in context of community
	Monitor positive reactions from community members as a result of consistent training in natural sites
Perception that community intensive instruction is not applicable to students with multiple handicaps	Partial participation
	Heterogeneous grouping

REFERENCES

Alberto, P.A., Sharpton, W., Briggs, A., & Stright, M.H. (1986). Facilitating task acquisition through the use of a self-operated auditory prompting system. *Journal of the Association for Persons with Severe Handicaps, 11,* 85-91.

Azrin, N.H., & Foxx, R.M. (1971). A rapid method of toilet training the institutionalized retarded. *Journal of Applied Behavior Analysis, 4,* 89-99.

Azrin, N.H., Schaeffer, R.M., & Wesolowski, M.D. (1976). A rapid method of teaching profoundly retarded persons to dress by a reinforcement-guidance method. *Mental Retardation, 14*(6), 29-33.

Baldwin, V.L., Fredericks, H.D.B., & Brodsky, G. (1973). *Isn't it time he outgrew this? or, A training program for parents of retarded children.* Springfield, IL: Charles C Thomas.

Ball, T.S., Seric, K., & Payne, L.E. (1971). Long-term retention of self-help skill training in the profoundly retarded. *American Journal of Mental Deficiency, 76,* 378-382.

Baumgart, D., Brown, L., Pumpian, I., Nisbet, J., Ford, A., Sweet, M., Messina, R., & Schroeder, J. (1982). Principle of partial participation and individualized adaptations in educational programs for severely handicapped students. *Journal of the Association for the Severely Handicapped, 7,* 17-27.

Baumgart, D., & VanWalleghem, J. (1986). Staffing strategies for implementing community-based instruction. *Journal of the Association for Persons with Severe Handicaps, 11,* 92-102.

Brown, L., Branston, M.B., Hamre-Nietupski, S., Pumpian, I., Certo, N., & Gruenewald, L. (1979). A strategy for developing chronological age appropriate and functional curricular content for severely handicapped adolescents and young adults. *Journal of Special Education, 13,*(1), 81-90.

Brown, L., Falvey, M., Vincent, B., Kaye, N., Johnson, F., Ferrara-Parrish, P., & Gruenewald, L. (1980). Strategies for generating comprehensive longitudinal and chronological age-appropriate individual educational plans for adolescent and young adult severely handicapped students. *Journal of Special Education, 14,* 199-216.

Colwell, C.N., Richards, E., McCarver, R.B., & Ellis, N.R. (1973). Evaluation of self-help habit training of the profoundly retarded. *Mental Retardation, 11*(3), 14-18.

Cronin, K.A., & Cuvo, A.J. (1979). Teaching mending skills to retarded adolescents. *Journal of Applied Behavior Analysis, 12,* 401-406.

Cuvo, A.J., Leaf, R.B., & Borakove, L.S. (1978). Teaching janitorial skills to the mentally retarded: Acquisition, generalization, and maintenance. *Journal of Applied Behavior Analysis, 11,* 345-355.

Falvey, M.A. (1986). *Community-based curriculum: Instructional strategies for students with severe handicaps.* Baltimore: Paul H. Brookes.

Falvey, M., Brown, L., Lyon, S., Baumgart, D., & Schroeder, J. (1980). Strategies for using cues and correction procedures. In W. Sailor, B. Wilcox, & L. Brown (Eds.), *Methods of instruction for severely handicapped students* (pp. 109-133). Baltimore: Paul H. Brookes.

Finnie, N.R. (1975). *Handling the young cerebral palsied child at home* (2nd ed.). New York: E.P. Dutton.

Ford, A., Dempsey, P., Black, J., Davern, L., Schnorr, R., & Meyer, L. (1986). *The Syracuse community-referenced curriculum guide for students with moderate and severe handicaps.* Syracuse, NY: Syracuse City School District.

Ford, A., & Miranda, P. (1984). Community instruction: A natural cues and correction model. *Journal of the Association for Persons with Severe Handicaps, 9,* 79-88.

Foxx, R.M., & Azrin, N.H. (1973). *Toilet training the retarded: A rapid program for day and nighttime independent toileting.* Champaign, IL: Research Press.

Freagon, S., & Rotatori, A.F. (1982). Comparing natural and artificial environments in training self-care skills to group home residents. *Journal of the Association for the Severely Handicapped, 7,* 73-86.

Freagon, S., Wheeler, J., Hill, L., Brankin, G., Costello, D., & Peters, W.M. (1983). A domestic training environment for students who are severely handicapped. *Journal of the Association for Persons with Severe Handicaps, 8,* 49-61.

Fredericks, H.D.B., Baldwin, V.L., Grove, D.N., & Moore, W.G. (1975). *Toilet training the handicapped child.* Monmouth, OR: Instructional Development Corporation.

Gaule, K., Nietupski, J., & Certo, N. (1985). Teaching supermarket skills using an adaptive shopping list. *Education and Training of the Mentally Retarded, 20,* 53-59.

Giles, D.K., & Wolf, M.M. (1966). Toilet training institutionalized severe retardates: An application of operant behavior modification techniques. *American Journal of Mental Deficiency, 70,* 766-780.

Hamre-Nietupski, S., Nietupski, J., Bates, P., & Maurer, S. (1982). Implementing a community-based educational model for moderately/severely handicapped students: Common problems and suggested solutions. *Journal of the Association for the Severely Handicapped, 7,* 38-43.

Haney, J.I., & Jones, R.T. (1982). Programming maintenance as a major component of a community-centered preventive effort: Escape from fire. *Behavior Therapy, 13,* 47-62.

Hundziak, M., Maurer, R.A., & Watson, L.S. (1965). Operant conditioning in toilet training of severely retarded boys. *American Journal of Mental Deficiency, 70,* 120-124.

Horner, R.H., Sprague, J., & Wilcox, B. (1982). General case programming for community activities. In B. Wilcox & G.T. Bellamy (Eds.), *Design of high school programs for severely handicapped students* (pp. 61-98). Baltimore: Paul H. Brookes.

Ianacone, R.N., & Stodden, R.A. (1987). Transition issues and directions for individuals who are mentally retarded. In R.N. Ianacone & R.A. Stodden (Eds.), *Transition issues and directions* (pp. 1-7). Reston, VA: The Council for Exceptional Children, Division on Mental Retardation.

Jarman, P.H., Iwata, B.A., & Lorentzson, A.M. (1983). Development of morning self-care routines in multiple handicapped persons. *Applied Research in Mental Retardation, 4,* 113-122.

Johnson, B.F., & Cuvo, A.J. (1981). Teaching mentally retarded adults to cook. *Behavior Modification, 5,* 187-202.

Jones, R.T., Sisson, L.A., & Van Hasselt, V.B. (1984). Emergency fire-safety skills: A study with blind adolescents. *Behavior Modification, 1,* 59-78.

Kazdin, A.E. (1980). *Behavior modification in applied settings* (2nd ed.). Homewood, IL: Dorsey Press.

Kimbell, D.L., Luckey, R.E., Barberto, P.F., & Love, J.G. (1967). Operation dry pants: An intensive habit-training program for the severely and profoundly retarded. *Mental Retardation, 5,* 32-36.

Kramer, L., & Whitehurst, C. (1981). Effects of button features on self dressing in young retarded children. *Education and Training of the Mentally Retarded, 16,* 277-283.

Linford, M.D., Hipsher, L.W., & Silikovitz, R.G. (1972). *Systematic instruction for retarded children: The Illinois program, Part III: Self-help instruction.* Danville, IL: Interstate.

Marholin, II, D., O'Toole, K.M., Touchette, P.E., Berger, P.L., & Doyle, D.A. (1979). "I'll have a Big Mac, large fries, large coke, and apple pie" . . . or teaching adaptive community skills. *Behavior Therapy, 10,* 236-248.

Martin, G.L., Kehoe, B., Bird, E., Jensen, V., & Darbyshire, M. (1971). Operant conditioning in dressing behavior of severely retarded girls. *Mental Retardation, 9* (3), 27-30.

Martin, J.E., Rusch, F.R., James, V.L., Decker, P.J., & Trytol, K.A. (1982). The use of picture cues to establish self-control in the preparation of complex meals by mentally retarded adults. *Applied Research in Mental Retardation, 3,* 105-119.

Matson, J.L. (1980). A controlled group study of pedestrian-skill training for the mentally retarded. *Behaviour Research and Therapy, 18,* 99-106.

Matson, J.L., DiLorenzo, T.M., & Esveldt-Dawson, K. (1981). Independence training as a method of enhancing self-help skills acquisition of the mentally retarded. *Behaviour Research and Therapy, 19,* 399-405.

McDonald, J.J., & Horner, R.H. (1985). Effects of in vivo versus simulation–plus–in vivo training on the acquisition and generalization of grocery item selection by high school students with severe handicaps. *Analysis and Intervention in Developmental Disabilities, 5,* 323-343.

Minge, M.R., & Ball, T.S. (1967). Teaching of self-help skills to profoundly retarded patients. *American Journal of Mental Deficiency, 71,* 864-868.

Neff, N.A., Iwata, B.A., & Page, T.A. (1978). Public transportation training: In vivo versus classroom instruction. *Journal of Applied Behavior Analysis, 11,* 331-344.

Nietupski, J., Hamre-Nietupski, S., Clancy, P., & Veerhusen, K. (1986). Guidelines for making simulation an effective adjunct to in vivo community instruction. *Journal of the Association for Persons with Severe Handicaps, 11,* 12-18.

Nietupski, J., Welch, J., & Wacker, D. (1983). Acquisition, maintenance and transfer of grocery item purchasing by moderately and severely handicapped students. *Education and Training of the Mentally Retarded, 18,* 279-286.

Nutter, D., & Reid, D.H. (1978). Teaching retarded women a clothing selection skill using community norms. *Journal of Applied Behavior Analysis, 5,* 475-487.

Perske, R. (1972). The dignity of risk. In W. Wolfensberger (Ed.), *The principle of normalization in human services.* Toronto: National Institute on Mental Retardation.

Rae, R., & Roll, D. (1985). Fire safety training with adults who are profoundly mentally retarded. *Mental Retardation, 23,* 26-30.

Reid, D.H., & Hurlbut, B. (1977). Teaching nonvocal communication skills to multihandicapped retarded adults. *Journal of Applied Behavior Analysis, 10,* 591-603.

Richman, G.S., Reiss, M.L., Bauman, K.E., & Bailey, J.S. (1984). Teaching menstrual care to mentally retarded women: Acquisition, generalization, and maintenance. *Journal of Applied Behavior Analysis, 17,* 441-451.

Risley, R., & Cuvo, A. (1980). Training mentally retarded adults to make emergency telephone calls. *Behavior Modification, 4,* 513-525.

Robinson, D., Griffith, J., McComish, L., Swasbrook, K. (1984). Bus training for developmentally disabled adults. *American Journal of Mental Deficiency, 89,* 37-43.

Rusch, F.R., & Phelps, L.A. (1987). Secondary special education and transition from school to work: A national priority. *Exceptional Children, 53,* 487-492.

Sailor, W., Halvorsen, A., Anderson, J., Goetz, L., Gee, K., Doering, K., & Hunt, P. (1986). Community intensive instruction. In R.H. Horner, L.H. Meyer, & H.D.B. Fredericks (Eds.), *Education of learners with severe handicaps: Exemplary service strategies* (pp. 251-288). Baltimore: Paul H. Brookes.

Schleien, S.J., Ash, T., Kiernan, J., & Wehman, P. (1981). Developing independent cooking skills in a profoundly retarded woman. *Journal of the Association for the Severely Handicapped, 6,* 23-29.

Sharpton, W.R., & Alberto, P.A. (1985). Behavior analytic strategies in community settings: Problems and solutions. In M.P. Brady & P.L. Gunter (Eds.), *Integrating moderately and severely handicapped learners: Strategies that work* (pp. 169-184). Springfield, IL: Charles C Thomas.

Snell, M.E. (1982). Teaching bedmaking to severely retarded adults through time delay. *Analysis and Intervention in Developmental Disabilities, 2,* 139-155.

Snell, M.E., & Browder, D.M. (1987). Domestic and community skills. In M.E. Snell (Ed.), *Systematic instruction of persons with severe handicaps (3rd ed.)*, (pp. 390-434). Columbus, OH: Charles E. Merrill.

Sowers, J., Rusch, F.R., & Hudson, C. (1979). Training a severely retarded young adult to ride the city bus to and from work. *AAESPH Review, 4,* 15-23.

Spellman, C., DeBriere, T., Jarboe, D., Campbell, S., & Harris, C. (1978). Pictorial instruction: Training daily living skills. In M.E. Snell (Ed.), *Systematic instruction of the moderately and severely handicapped* (pp. 391-411). Columbus, OH: Charles E. Merrill.

Sprague, J.R., & Horner, R.H. (1984). The effects of single instance, multiple instance, and general case training on a generalized vending machine use by moderately and severely handicapped students. *Journal of Applied Behavior Analysis, 17,* 273-278.

Storey, K., Bates, P., & Hanson, H.B. (1984). Acquisition and generalization of coffee purchase skills by adults with severe disabilities. *Journal of the Association for Persons with Severe Handicaps, 9,* 178-185.

Vogelsberg, R.T., & Rusch, F.R. (1979). Training severely handicapped students to cross partially controlled intersections. *AAESPH Review, 4,* 264-273.

Vogelsberg, R.T., Williams, W., & Bellamy, G.T. (1982). Preparation for independent living. In B. Wilcox & G.T. Bellamy (Eds.), *Design of high school programs for severely handicapped students* (pp. 153-174). Baltimore: Paul H. Brookes.

Wilcox, B., & Bellamy, G.T. (1982). *Design of high school programs for severely handicapped students.* Baltimore: Paul H. Brookes.

Wilcox, B. & Bellamy G.T. (1987). *The activities catalog: An alternative curriculum for youth and adults with severe disabilities.* Baltimore: Paul H. Brookes.

Will, M. (1984). *OSERS programming for the transition of youth with disabilities: Bridges from school to working life.* Washington, DC: Office of Special Education and Rehabilitative Services.

Young, K.R., West, R.P., Howard, V.F., & Whitney, R. (1986). Acquisition, fluency training, generalization, and maintenance of dressing skills of two developmentally disabled children. *Education and Treatment of Children, 9,* 16-29.

Chapter 13

Transition Programming: Improving Vocational Outcomes

Janet W. Hill and M.V. Morton

PROBLEM AND PAST PRACTICES

The appropriateness of systematic longitudinal vocational training for the population of students with severe or profound handicaps addressed in this text is still seriously questioned by many educators and parents. Even now, a vocational program may simply not exist in the education plan for many students with more severe handicaps, nor are special educators prepared for the vocational needs of these students (Snell, 1987). The vocational training that does exist primarily focuses on training students with severe or profound handicaps for sheltered segregated employment (Falvey, 1986). This situation exists even though there appears to be a preponderance of evidence that vocational training for more competitive types of employment can prove to be of significant benefit to individuals with severe handicaps (Gersten, Crowell, & Bellamy, 1986; Hill, Banks, Handrich, Wehman, Hill, & Shafer, 1987).

It is ironic that with the current emphasis on transition, and in our struggle to provide appropriate educational services to all students with handicaps, that the vocational expectations for this group of students are so low that vocational training is considered questionable. Although curriculum development has surged in nearly all other areas, there remains a paucity of information on basic vocational directions for individuals who are the most significantly handicapped. It is these individuals who undoubtedly most need early and sustained vocational training if they are to become vocationally integrated in their community (Snell, 1987).

Low expectations of vocational potential for persons with severe handicaps have not been formed from demonstrations that have proved it is impossible to train this population. On the contrary, it has been repeatedly demonstrated that this population can achieve successful performance levels in the acquisition of complex tasks (Bellamy, Horner, & Inman

439

1979; Moss, Dineen, & Ford, 1986). From a practitioner's point of reference, there exist two concrete problems of application that have contributed to the proliferation of ideas of low expectation and lack of growth in the field of vocational education for these students. The first is the basic inadequacy of our vocational service delivery system for persons with severe handicaps. Each year, between 250,000 and 300,000 students graduate from special education programs, and approximately 90% of these young adults are not placed in employment (Stark, Kiernan, Goldsburg, & McGee, 1986). Follow-up studies have also noted the problems with the transition from school to work regarding unemployment (Hasazi, Gordon, & Roe, 1985; Schalock, 1984; Wehman, Kregel, & Seyfarth, 1985) and low parental expectations (Hill, Seyfarth, Banks, Wehman, & Orelove, 1985).

The inadequacy of our service delivery system is shown by the lack of transition possible through an intended continuum of services. This continuum includes day activity centers, work activity centers, sheltered workshops, and eventually competitive employment. Today, however, stilted upward movement is often the reality (Bellamy, Rhodes, Bourbeau, & Mank, 1986). The work activities centers are often a terminal placement for many persons who are handicapped. Surveys show that activities centers, often not geared toward preparation for eventual employment, have grown at remarkable rates over the last 20 years, as have sheltered workshops. Bellamy et al. (1986) reported that 9,997 people were served in work activity centers in 1968. By 1976 that number rose to 63,917. Only 3% of these people annually move to more independent vocational placements (Bellamy, Rhodes, Bourbeau, & Mank, 1982). Ultimately, people with severe handicaps are trapped at the lower end of the continuum.

The second problem is that people without handicaps in general have definite preconceived notions regarding skill levels required in a remunerative situation. Individuals with severe handicaps are viewed as so different from the norm or from the average paid worker that functioning in the world of work seems implausible. Therefore, students with more severe handicaps often lack vocational credibility, and because their potential contributions are viewed as inconsequential, many educators and rehabilitators believe training emphasis should be placed elsewhere. Parental attitudes regarding the employment potential of their sons or daughters are highly influenced by the developmental level (IQ) of the child (Hill, Seyfarth, Banks, Wehman, & Orelove, 1985).

Although a great many policy changes are needed at the state and federal levels to support the development of adult programs aimed at enabling persons the greatest amount of vocational independence possible (Bellamy et al., 1982; Hagner, Nisbet, Callahan, & Moseley, 1987), educators of students with severe handicaps can and must exert pressure for change. Special educators are perhaps best equipped to design, develop, and implement exemplary programs demonstrating the vocational potential of these students. Such programs would effectively apply upward pressure for transition on the community-based programs and, hopefully, help to create improved vocational options.

Recent Innovations Improving Service Provision

The mid-1980s have brought about a revolution in the field of vocational and employment services for persons with severe disabilities, guiding a major redirection of efforts away from job readiness training toward the provision of actual employment opportunities in integrated work settings (Will, 1984). This restructuring of our service system is referred to as the provision of supported employment, and it represents a massive federal initiative toward improved employment opportunities for persons who traditionally would be served in day activity centers or sheltered workshops. "Supported employment" means competitive or paid work in integrated work settings (Report 99-995, Sec. 103 Definitions, House of Representatives).

Supported employment has brought with it creative programming alternatives that effectively work around a sluggish service delivery system (Flippo & McDaniel, 1986). Obviously, the most important of these are efforts to place people with severe handicaps directly in integrated paid employment opportunities without preplacement in day activity programs or workshops. Many investigators around the country have found that by using appropriate behavioral technologies and a direct on-the-job training approach many persons previously thought to have little vocational potential can be employed and maintain a job (Hill, Hill, Wehman, Banks, Pendleton, & Britt, 1985; Moon, Goodall, Barcus, & Brooke, 1986; Pietruski, Everson, Goodwyn, & Wehman, 1985; Rusch & Mithaug, 1980; Vogelsberg, Ashe, & Williams, 1986; Wehman, Hill, Wood, & Parent, 1987). Individuals placed in integrated employment in this manner often require a network of support services (Belmore & Brown, 1978) as well as an initially high expenditure of staff time. However, a supported employment model has repeatedly proven successful and cost-effective (Hill, Hill, & Wehman, in press; Hill & Wehman, 1983; Hill et al., 1987).

Although in the near future a more comprehensive range of adult vocational services may be available to persons with severe handicaps, the quality of these services will need much improvement over services now provided in day and work activity programs. The models that have developed to serve adults with more severe handicaps have included an essential and previously missing ingredient for improved services: integration of workers with and without handicaps. Hill, Hill, Wehman, Banks, Pendleton, & Britt (1985) found that previous integrated work experience significantly improved later job retention capabilities of persons with severe disabilities. These improved employment alternatives, which will be discussed later in the chapter, experimented with using workers without handicaps as models, placing enclaves of workers with severe handicaps in industry, placing workers without handicaps in enclaves in sheltered workshops, and developing integrated community work crews.

It should be apparent to the teacher, however, that we cannot simply wait for these models to be developed in the community adult services network. Instead, work should begin in middle and secondary education to provide vocational training for students with severe handicaps in integrated community-based training settings. The impending transition of students who are well prepared for integrated paid employment opportunities will serve as additional pressure on the adult service system to decrease the exclusive emphasis of a center-based or workshop approach.

Lack of Vocational Credibility

The second problem, already mentioned, that has hampered greater vocational development for people with more severe handicaps is the commonly held attitude that these individuals are so vastly deficient compared with the average paid worker that it would be literally impossible to prepare them for any type of consequential work (Hansen, 1980). This attitude is reinforced by the fact that the more handicapped an individual is, the greater is the requirement for increased staff, materials, financial expenditure, and elaborate interventions to effect behavioral change (Bellamy et al., 1982). In the past ". . . it was easier, and still is, to discount the severely handicapped person's chances of learning anything useful and to move on to the lower risk client" (Flexer & Martin, 1978, p. 422). Financial reasons, as well as taking the easiest options first, have compelled educators, rehabilitators, and even researchers to expend their energies with individuals who are less handicapped.

Changing Attitudes

As previously mentioned, the prevalence of negative assessments of vocational potential is still quite evident in schools, adult services, and with parents. However, several positive arguments are currently being put forth by innovators, and these will, hopefully, assist in changing the vocational image of persons who have severe or profound handicaps.

Demonstrations of Success

The strongest argument for improving vocational outcomes is based on the many successful demonstrations of training of these persons. The training of persons with severe or profound handicaps has truly seen a turnabout in this century from bedlam to bicycle brake assembly. The last decade was a period of experimentation and application with greatly encouraging results. Investigators consistently found that, given adherence to systematic training procedures, individuals with severe handicaps show the ability to learn complex vocational tasks (Bellamy et al., 1979; Brooke, Hill, & Ponder, 1985; Gold, 1976; Shafer, Brooke, & Wehman, 1985; Wehman, 1981; Wehman, Hill, Wood, & Parent, 1987). In view of the short history of education of people with severe handicaps, these demonstrations of vocational potential are quite remarkable. They should also be a source of optimism for those involved in training the next generation of students who will receive early and continued education. Only ten years ago, it was highly unlikely that persons with mild to moderate handicaps would work in the community; now these outcomes are becoming commonplace (Wehman & Hill, 1985; Rusch, 1986).

Individuals' Rights

Even in view of these demonstrations, many skeptics maintain that vocational training for people with severe handicaps is inappropriate because these persons will never achieve complete vocational independence. However, given this country's commitment to the work ethic and our society's stress of the value and desirability of working, the advocate for vocational services can clearly argue that every individual, no matter how handicapped, has the right to the option of work (Bellamy et al., 1982). Total independence in employment is not necessary as long as appropriate supports exist in the community (Hill, Hill, & Wehman, in press). In addition, legislation in the form of the Rehabilitation Act of 1973, especially Section 504, legally validates these arguments. Eventually, programs will be confronted with the *illegality* of withholding vocational services from people with severe handicaps (Laski, 1979).

To implement fully and provide these withheld services, our preconceived definitions of what constitutes consequential work, how and where it is performed, and what degree and type of support can be supplied must be adjusted. If success is to be attained, it is certain that creatively different and nontraditional work alternatives will be needed for this group of people.

Socially Valued Roles in the Community

Some may still argue that it is unethical to force persons with the most severe handicaps to perform work. Is this itself ethical? The affirmative answer to a question such as this must be based on the acceptance of the concept of normalization and social role valorization (Wolfensberger, 1972; 1983). Many innovators believe employment assists in normalization by the community seeing the individual performing a socially valued role in their community (Wehman, 1981). Through participation in employment we clearly increase the likelihood of acceptance of people with handicaps by the community (Falvey, 1986). The goal of work ultimately becomes a vehicle by which the opportunity to live as normal a life as possible is increased.

Finally, skeptics further insist that students with severe handicaps more critically need training in other areas such as self-help, language, and motor development, and think vocational training should be considered secondary. This argument reflects a developmental readiness approach to teaching often used by educators of students with more severe handicaps. For them, each curricular area must have a separate practice time period if learning is to occur. It is such an approach that has contributed to the artificiality in training and lack of generalization in learning (Falvey, 1986). Bellamy et al. (1982) noted that this problem continues also into adult services, where there is a lack of clearly specified program models that combine work training concurrently with other needed services.

Because of the magnitude and diversity of student needs, more complex training approaches aimed at simultaneous skill development in more than one area must be established. Fortunately, the vocational area provides an excellent arena in which to establish such procedures, since to demonstrate even partial vocational proficiency, the student must practice and apply skills from nearly all other curricular areas. For example, to function successfully in a community-based vocational training setting, the student must acquire certain communication, motor, self-help, and social skills, as well as necessary vocational skills.

Past Failures

A considerable body of evidence regarding the potential and the rights of students with severe handicaps to improved vocational outcomes has accumulated. Demonstrations of successful systemwide programs are reported (Bellamy et al., 1979; Bellamy, Peterson, & Close, 1975; Gold, 1973; Karan, Wehman, Renzaglia, & Schultz, 1976; Larson & Edwards, 1980; Lynch & Singer, 1980). The following questions then arise: Why can't the average school or community service system take such information and implement appropriate programs? Why have many community vocational programs for individuals with mild disabilities failed in the past to bring about appropriate employment outcomes?

Failures in the practical application of vocational training stem from many of the problems already discussed, especially those involving lack of administrative commitment because of estimates of high risk, low return (Gold, 1973), and other general low expectations for skill development in handicapped populations. In addition, Whitehead (1979) pointed out that innovators involved in exemplary programs must devise better methods of helping to replicate these successful programs under normal staffing and funding conditions.

Two other past practices led to low vocational outcomes. They must be mentioned because they have strong implications for future directions in constructing vocational services for persons with severe disabilities. First, in the past and unfortunately still today, many school or community-based vocational programs for people with handicaps have been conducted in settings isolated from the real world. This practice has led to teaching skills that are so artificial that they have little relevance in the world of work. Therefore, generalization of learning and later transition to less restrictive vocational situations are unlikely. Second, it is apparent that the key to effective behavior change with people with severe handicaps is largely dependent on staff skill (Wehman, 1981). Unfortunately, until only recently, the multidisciplinary skill requirements of the trainer or habilitator were neither well defined nor attainable given the focus of current personnel preparation programs. In the past, the teacher charged with vocational training had little knowledge or experience in training vocational behaviors in real employment settings; therefore, he or she could not respond appropriately to the vocational needs of individuals with severe handicaps (Moon et al., 1986).

Often, programs develop without input or focus from already existing community programs or local private industry (Hill, Wehman, & Pietruski, 1982). Neither educators nor participants were exposed to realistic expectations found in the real world in the community; thus student objectives were developed arbitrarily, based on developmental assessments, or perhaps selected from outdated career education curriculum guides. This type of training conducted in isolation from the community work world does a disservice not only to the trainees but to the community itself, which will one day be charged with responsibility for these persons. Repeatedly, it has been found that without transitional planning for students with handicaps and direct communication among community agencies, vocational failure is the result (Hill, Banks, Wehman, & Hill, in press; Hill, Hill, Wehman, Banks, Pendleton & Britt, 1985; Wehman, Kregel, Barcus, & Schalock, 1986; Wehman, Moon, & McCarthy, 1986).

The failures of the past lend support to current trends of early and sustained generalization training in a variety of community settings (Falvey, Brown, Lyon, Baumgart, & Schroeder, 1980) and a community integrative approach (Wehman & Hill, 1980) allowing for skill development directly in community settings. Among the many important advantages of training in real settings for the vocational educators is the assurance that student objectives will reflect realistic community work expectations. Clearly, if the vocational outcomes are to be improved, ". . . educators must move out from the confines of the school building and open lines of communications with those who recruit, employ, and train workers" (Gold & Pomerantz, 1978, p. 434).

Educator and Habilitator Skills

It was not until the results of recent innovative programs were gathered that the degree of skill required for a successful trainer was realized (Renzaglia, 1986). Clearly the special educator involved in transitional vocational training for students with more severe handicaps must be equipped with some sophisticated skills in some rather distinct areas. Some of these are systematic assessment and training, applied behavior analysis, and public relations with business, service agencies, and parents. Teacher training must include field-based practicum experience as well (Renzaglia, 1986; Umbreit, Karlan, York, & Haring, 1980). We know that the teacher must carefully arrange the learning environment if behavior change is to occur. Finally, this person needs a great deal of common sense and a keen awareness of the production realities and worker expectations in business and industry. Although such an array of skills appears overwhelming for one person, given the development of good personnel preparation programs and the use of resource persons within a transdisciplinary approach, this teacher can and does exist.

However, there is a severe shortage of teachers with the dual emphasis needed: special education and vocational education. Lack of staff trained in these areas is also a result of an influx of students with severe handicaps who are beginning vocational training programs (McAlees, 1984). Hopefully, with increased practical information on program development, improved personnel preparation programs will emerge.

SUGGESTED METHODS

The curriculum guidelines presented below describe methods of early and sustained vocational training for persons with severe or profound handicaps. Vocational training is advocated for all persons regardless of the severity of their handicap.

General Program Development

The acceptance of the principle that all individuals, no matter how handicapped, deserve the opportunity to work leads educators to some heretofore unresolved problems. These include the very basic issues of what, when, and how to teach these persons vocational skills and how to assist them to access the opportunities of our society. These opportunities, as they relate to employment, include factors such as decent pay, meaningful work, and community integration. A sequence of necessary factors that may assist the reader in conceptualizing the large picture of systems change is given in Exhibit 13-1.

Exhibit 13-1 General Program Development

Define a vocational commitment

Assess community employment needs and resources

Determine model of transitional services

Design and implement program phases

Use community-based instruction

Evaluate student progress and vocational outcomes

Modify program based on evaluation data

Define a Vocational Commitment

Program development must begin with a statement or commitment articulating that the mission of the program is to prepare all students for the least restrictive vocational environment. This goal also assumes the philosophy that a transition process, resulting in paid employment opportunities, should occur for *all* students. It does not ensure that all related persons and agencies will be convinced that the students in question have vocational potential. It simply means that the program mission is clearly identified and should be apparent to all others dealing with the program (other agencies, parents, administrators, teachers, more advanced programs, etc.). Identifying program commitment and conveying it to others sets the goal or vision for the program and helps others interpret policies based on that goal. Reaching the goal may then be approached through the remaining steps in the program sequence.

Assess Community Employment Needs and Resources

With the conceptual shift from a developmental to a functional program paradigm, greater emphasis has been placed on assessment of the requirements and resources specific to a community before program development in most curricular areas. For example, before developing a vocational training program, the teacher must closely examine the employment needs and resources of a given community in order that the students may actually get the opportunity to use the skills they are being taught. This type of planning is especially critical in vocational program development because the outcome of a successful transition from school to work should result in paid employment opportunities.

Public program resources available in most communities include the following: state vocational rehabilitation services, mental health/mental retardation services, vocational education, the National Association for Retarded Citizens (NARC), state employment commissions, the National Alliance of Business, and local business advisory councils. The resources they may offer as well as specific information regarding entry requirements for their services should be determined early in program development. In addition, communication with these public agencies is essential to ease the transition in the future.

The community job market is a major program determinant for several reasons. First, assessment of the job market defines the type of non-sheltered jobs the program should be emphasizing in training, because of job availability. Second, a community job may serve as a less restrictive nonpaid or paid training environment for students who are still in school.

Examination of the job market shows the type of specific work and employment available in a given community. For instance, it would be inappropriate to stress horticultural training in an urban area that cannot accommodate a greater number of greenhouse workers. This would seem to be a most obvious consideration in program development. However, many schools or service agencies overlook this point and determine arbitrarily what the content of the program will include without an examination of the community job market.

If a community is rich in certain types of jobs or industry, creativity must be exercised to determine how such jobs or parts of jobs can be completed by persons who have more severe handicaps. Prosthetic aids or adaptive equipment could change a seemingly impossible job into one that could be easily accomplished by a person with severe handicaps. Rehabilitation engineers and occupational therapists can provide the technical assistance needed to adapt vocational training settings in the community and make them accessible.

Once community resources are identified and coordination has taken place, one must give some thought as to how these resources can be used by the program for a variety of purposes, such as generalization environments, additional funds, staff in-service, interaction with the work world, etc.

Determine Model of Transitional Services

After a realistic examination of community resources, the programmer then has the rare opportunity to be idealistic by conceiving the program's theoretical model of transition services. This model should be based on current community resources and optimistic projections for services in the future. We should not develop programs based on what is actually available at present for adults who have severe or profound handicaps (Bellamy et al., 1982) because, as noted earlier, very little is currently available. Thus, we should begin with an ideal plan of vocational transition from which to direct realistic efforts.

An impetus for innovations in regard to vocational training for students with severe handicaps has been the federal initiatives regarding transition. Since 1984, both OSERS and the Administration on Developmental Disabilities have made transition a national priority (Will, 1984). Transition is defined as a "carefully planned process, which may be initiated either by school personnel or adult service providers, to establish and implement a plan for either employment or additional vocational training of handicapped students who will graduate or leave school in three to five years. Such a process must include special educators, vocational educators, parents, and/or the student, an adult service system representative, vocational rehabilitators, and possibly an employer" (Wehman, Kregel, & Barcus, 1985, p. 26).

The amendments to the Education for all Handicapped Children Act (P.L. 98-199) states: ". . . The subcommittee [on the Handicapped] recognizes the overwhelming paucity of effective programming for unnecessarily large numbers of handicapped adults who become unemployed and therefore dependent on society. These youth have not been adequately prepared for the changes and demands of life after high school" (Section 626, P.L. 98-199).

Vocational transition was described as a three-stage model by Wehman et al., (1985). Their model requires community-based service delivery through a functional curriculum and an integrated school setting. This service is provided through an individualized transition plan that requires input from the parents, the student, and the school, and interagency cooperation through a variety of adult service providers. The third stage results in vocational outcomes in a variety of employment settings. Follow-up demonstrates the long-term effectiveness of the model.

Design and Implement Program Phases

The next step in program development is always the most difficult. Given staff, funding, and time constraints, program design and actual implementation can be extremely complicated. Designs of effective vocational programs vary greatly from program to program, as do the training content, training approach, task selection, and other elements. There are, however, certain characteristics of appropriate vocational programming that can be delineated.

Although not necessarily in priority order, critical vocational program characteristics to consider when designing and implementing programs include the following:

- transition planning
- use of systematic training procedures
- generalization training
- parental involvement
- more complex program models combining work training concurrently with other needed training
- age-appropriate handling of the following variables: physical environment, training content, task selection, staff and student attitudes, and daily time commitment to training

Transitional planning, as described earlier, must form the basis of a vocational program. This means that school and community habilitation agencies must coordinate and interact using the Individual Transition Plan (ITP) on an annual basis to ensure that upon graduation a student does not return home to lifelong nonproductivity and isolation. Many investigators agree that transitional planning should not simply involve the last two years of school but should be directed toward the entire life span of the student, starting with early school years and continuing through adulthood (Ianacone & Stodden, 1987).

Systematic training procedures must be used (Bellamy et al., 1982; Lynch & Singer, 1980). Under this broad procedural category, the use of applied behavioral analysis, applied in a respectful and humanistic way, would be the most important tool of the trainer.

Early and sustained *generalization training* in less restrictive settings with different vocational trainers and on many different tasks and jobs is also essential for effective programming with students with severe handicaps. An indirect effect of generalization training is refinement of staff expectations and student potential in regard to actual vocational settings.

Parental involvement is crucial to the success of a vocational program. Many parents have extremely low vocational expectations for their children, which may have been instilled early by well-meaning professionals. Parents also have strong concerns regarding cessation of public assistance payments for their child if he or she is shown to have vocational potential. Although funds could not be denied based on the mere demonstration of vocational potential, often parents are confused and fearful about this issue. This is understandable considering the financial expense involved in maintaining a person with severe or profound handicaps in the home (Hill, Hill, & Wehman, in press). Because of these and other factors, parents, if not involved, can actually thwart a vocational program and inhibit the vocational transition of their child (Hill, Hill, Wehman, & Goodall, 1986). Continuous parental involvement and education is, therefore, very important.

Advocates of vocational training accept the fact that individuals with more severe disabilities have vast and diverse training needs and that only one of these needs is vocational skill development. However, vocational advocates contend that *more complex program models* could be developed and interfaced with work training. In other words, language training does not have to occur during a language period, hygiene training during a self-help period, etc. Instead, appropriate objectives in other curricular areas could be formulated and addressed based on the functional needs identified during the vocational training period in integrated community settings. For instance, personal hygiene could be approached before the student leaves the school building for community crew work, language objectives could be approached in appropriate community settings, etc.

A vocational program, perhaps more than any other training area, should be as *chronological age appropriate* as possible, regardless of the developmental level of the student. Even with students who have profound handicaps at the middle school level, their vocational training program area should look and feel like a place where young people are learning how to work. Particular attention should be given to the establishment of an age-appropriate physical environment. Staff visits to more advanced vocational settings such as entry level community jobs, crews, and enclaves should demonstrate what the atmosphere should look like. The vocational training should be in an area separate from the other training activity areas. A separate work training area, preferably off-campus in the community, will provide environmental cues that prompt work behavior. The area itself should be free of toys, gadgets, and bulletin board decorations. The reason for such austerity is to demonstrate clearly to all who enter that the training area reflects a serious commitment to a program goal involving true employment outcomes in the futures of these students. It also helps teachers, aides, and students develop an appropriate perspective regarding vocational training.

Instead of spending funds on expensive vocational kits or gathering up as many developmental materials as possible, attempts should be made to secure real materials pertaining to jobs or tasks that exist in the local community. Whenever possible, one should obtain real work or jobs the students can perform according to their individual productivity level. Commitment to real work is critically important to the program because it exposes students and staff to work expectations that are considerably different from those of make-work or simulated work. To ensure greater exposure and refinement of student objectives, efforts to perform the work in a host company in an enclave or in a competitive employment setting should be a prime goal of the vocational training effort.

Staff and students should take the training seriously even if initial efforts appear less than hopeful as can often be the case with students who have had little work and/or community exposure. In the work setting, the relationship should no longer be teacher/student but rather supervisor/worker. Teachers obviously are largely responsible for shaping their own behavior toward students first. If student hand holding, coddling, or hugging is exhibited toward adolescent or adult students, the teacher may first need to modify his or her own behavior.

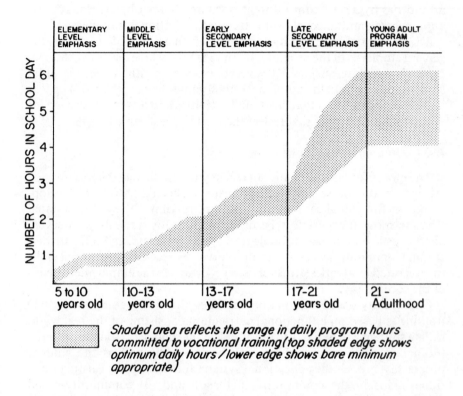

Figure 13-1 Time Commitment: Vocational Training for Students with Severe or Profound Handicaps throughout School Years.

The appropriate amount of time committed to daily vocational training can vary greatly according to student age and other program require-ments. Increasing time commitments are needed as a student progresses into the secondary level and toward graduation. Figure 13-1 illustrates increases in vocational training time in a school system from elementary school levels, through middle and secondary, and finally to adult programs. The figure shows that when one begins in the secondary level program, vocational training should optimally consist of two hours, advancing to three hours per day; or, on the lower end, at least one full hour, advancing to two hours per day by the time the student reaches 17 years of age. It is important to note that this model of increasing voca-tional emphasis supports the contention that other curricular areas, such as motor, hygiene, communications, or social objectives, can be approached simultaneously with structured vocational training.

The amount of time committed to any given activity often reflects the general emphasis of the program. If, for example, whole days of vocational programming are suspended several times a month to permit older students to attend field trips or basketball games, the program will appear to be quite committed to recreational activities and less so to the need for vocational experiences that reflect the world of real work.

Use Community-Based Instruction

The most pronounced change in recent years in the way schools provide services to students with severe handicaps has been to shift from developmental to functional community-based instruction. Falvey (1986) stated that the most appropriate type of curriculum for students with severe handicaps is functional, chronological age appropriate, and reflects transition. Community-based instruction involves teaching vocational skills in integrated real work settings chosen according to the employment needs of the community.

Community-based instruction includes three key components: (1) training is based on a functional curriculum consisting of the real world skills a student will be likely to use after leaving school; (2) training is longitudinal in that vocational training begins early, and as the student progresses through the educational system, the time spent learning functional skills in the community increases; and (3) community-based training provides for the integration of students with handicaps with individuals without handicaps in the community.

The caveat regarding community-based instruction is that it must include *training*. It is not enough to take large groups of students with severe or profound handicaps and put them through activities just for the sake of being in the community. Educators and administrators must resolve scheduling and staffing problems so that teachers can take small groups of students (two or three) into community settings and actually *teach* skills that will increase students' ability to function independently in the community. Many students with severe handicaps have never been given the opportunity to learn functional skills in the real world as have students without handicaps.

A variety of implementation issues need to be resolved before community-based training can be realized. Exhibit 13-2 lists a sampling of questions dealing with these issues.

Exhibit 13-2 Crucial Questions Regarding Community-Based Training

Target group	Which groups of students will receive community-based instruction? What ages will they be, and what percentage of their day will be taught in the community? Will students with similar (homogeneous) or differing (heterogeneous) skill levels be grouped for community instruction? Will students with severe multiple handicaps at least partially participate in community-based instruction?
Staffing	Which teachers will be responsible for community-based training? Will staff be responsible for community-based training only, or will they have classroom responsibilities as well? Will volunteers or peer tutors be used for additional coverage? Can team teaching be used to resolve staffing issues?
Transportation	How will transportation be provided to community-based training settings? Can the type of transportation chosen accommodate wheelchairs and other adaptive equipment?
Scheduling	What is the most efficient way to schedule community-based training so that students receive the maximum amount of time in meaningful instruction both in the community and in the classroom? Will support service staff provide services in the community, the classroom, or in both settings?
Cost	Are there any additional costs such as transportation, staff, or materials incurred due to community-based instruction? Can funds be transferred to cover any additional costs?
Liability	Will the regular school insurance cover training that will occur in the community? What are the liability issues if teachers transport students using their own cars?
Parents	How will parents be informed of and included in the program? How can we help alleviate parents' concerns about the change to community-based instruction?
Staff	What staff are enthusiastic and interested in community-based training? What staff will be chosen to implement training in the community?
Medical/Health	How will medical needs be dealt with in community training settings? How will time spent receiving instruction in the community be arranged to coincide with medication schedules? What adaptive equipment or medication will need to be taken with the student into the community?

Evaluate Student Progress and Vocational Outcomes

Planning for evaluation is a necessary step in program development and should include evaluation not only of students' progress but of the effectiveness of the program, especially in the eyes of the community and community vocational habilitators. Evaluation of students' progress should include assessment of student acquisition and production rates on work tasks. Other less obvious areas of student evaluation are degree of work endurance, appropriateness of behavior and attitudes while working, work quality, speed of applying skills, and generalization of critical nonvocational skills. Ultimately, the success of a transition program culminates in employment options for students upon leaving school. Periodic follow-up of students can provide schools with information on the number of students employed, work retention rates, and other measures that can be used to evaluate the effectiveness of the school's vocational training program. Community acceptance of a program is also an indicator of effectiveness. Therefore, one should survey community consumers and community vocational habilitators for data related to social validation of the content and direction of the program (Rusch, 1979).

Modify Program Based on Evaluation Data

The final step in program development involves the maintenance of program flexibility that will allow modifications when necessary. Modifications may be needed based on evaluative data or when a new vocational resource becomes available. As a program's reputation and the degree of community acceptance grow, many changes in the program will and must occur.

Innovative Vocational Programming Models

Vocational options for people with severe handicaps have evolved through a variety of supported employment models. Supported employment is defined as follows: ". . . paid employment that: (1) is for persons with developmental disabilities for whom competitive employment at or above minimum wage is unlikely and who, because of their disabilities, need intensive ongoing support to perform in a work setting; (2) is conducted in a variety of settings, particularly worksites in which persons without disabilities are employed; and (3) is supported by any activity needed to sustain paid work by persons with disabilities including supervision, training, and transportation." (Bellamy, Rhodes, & Albin, 1986, p.

133). Supported employment is different from traditional habilitation models because it is not a preparatory model and does not require individuals to be "job ready." Therefore, it is designed to provide paid employment opportunities in integrated work settings to all individuals regardless of the severity of their handicaps.

It is also not a time-limited service but provides the long-term assistance needed for people with severe handicaps to maintain employment. The supported employment model has four characteristics: (1) paid employment; (2) employment in an integrated setting; (3) subsidized ongoing support throughout the person's employment; and (4) the presence of a severe disability that requires this type of support for the person to gain and maintain employment (Bellamy, Rhodes, & Albin, 1986).

Recently, creative supported employment alternatives have emerged in an attempt to meet the employment needs of people with more severe handicaps. The Federal Rehabilitation Services Administration is currently funding states to develop statewide systems of supported employment. The focus of these programs is to change the predominant nature of day support and vocational services toward the provision of paid employment opportunities in integrated work settings. These opportunities should be established at the onset of services, *not* as an eventual result of pre-employment preparation.

Currently, the Commonwealth of Virginia is funded to develop a state system of implementation to facilitate a variety of supported employment options throughout the state. These options create an array of supported employment services intended to change the predominant nature of day support and vocational services toward the provision of paid employment opportunities in integrated work settings. These options include the individual placement, enclave, work crew, and entrepreneurial models (Britt, Griffin, Hill, Hincker, Ruth, & Proseus, in preparation). The characteristics of each are depicted as follows.

Individual Placement Model

Definition. The *Job Coach Model of Supported Employment* (or Supported Competitive Employment) refers to the placement of an individual with a severe disability into integrated competitive employment with job coach support. This support is initially one-to-one for the entire work day and gradually decreases as the worker becomes more proficient. Support is ongoing, as needed, for as long as the worker is employed. Each employee is hired directly by the employer, works equal to or greater than 20 hours per week, and is paid minimum wage or greater. The benefit package provided to all eligible employees should be available to the individual with a severe disability as well.

Major Service Components. Each of the following is a necessary component in the development and maintenance of an individual placement:

- *Job Development/Job Analysis:* This involves structured efforts at finding jobs for individuals. A job bank is developed. Each available position is analyzed in great detail to ascertain suitability for an individual with a severe disability and to obtain information to choose the best worker for the position.
- *Individual Assessment:* This includes a review of the individual's records, observations, interviews, active involvement with parents and family, planning for transportation arrangements, and social changes in order to identify the individual's strengths and needs.
- *Client/Job Match:* This refers to the process of choosing the best job for the individual with a severe disability. This process involves carefully matching the job features to the individual's strengths and needs. Key matching factors include accessibility to the job, physical ability, family support, social skills, motivation, and daily living skills. The individual whose strengths and needs are best suited to the requirements of the position is offered the job. Individuals are not placed based on position on a waiting list.
- *Job Site Training and Advocacy:* Beginning on the first day of employment, a trained job coach provides the individual with intensive on-site training aimed at specific job skills and ancillary training needed to assist the individual to keep the job (i.e., transportation and budget training). The job coach also works extensively with employers and co-workers in the development of a supportive work environment through feedback, advocacy, and education.
- *Ongoing Assessment and Support:* The job coach provides regular written feedback to the employer on the employee's progress. Staff use behavioral data related to work speed, proficiency, need for staff assistance, etc. to identify ongoing support needs. These reports are shared with the local vocational rehabilitation counselor and case managers who authorize continued funding. Staff implement planned efforts at reducing intervention, but provide ongoing support to the employee through telephone calls and visits to the employee and supervisor as needed. The job coach also communicates to the employer that staff are always accessible when needed. Regular periodic on-site follow-up is maintained.

Quality Considerations.

- *Wages:* The employee with a severe disability is to be paid at least minimum wage, and the wages should go directly to the employee, not to the provider agency and then to the employee. The job benefits should include all fringe benefits available to other eligible company employees.
- *Hours:* The job must offer at least 20 hours of employment per week according to minimal supported employment standards outlined by the federal government. Preferably, the work is not temporary or seasonal, due to the problems associated with social security benefits when there are continual changes in earnings and the need for intensive training at each new job.
- *Integration:* The job should offer the employee with a severe disability the same opportunities for social integration it would offer any other employee occupying that position (i.e., lunch, breaks, work station with other company employees).

Advantages of the Job Coach Model. Wages, benefits, and a chance for upward mobility are the obvious advantages over the traditional day support services available to individuals with severe disabilities. In addition, the individual is working in an integrated work environment with continual exposure and contact with workers without handicaps. The individual placement model naturally supports community participation and other opportunities that enhance the image of the employee with a severe disability.

The Enclave Model of Supported Employment

Definition. The *Enclave Model of Supported Employment* refers to the employment of a full-time supervisor and a small group (three to eight) of individuals with severe disabilities at an industry where they will work together (Cho, 1981; McGee, 1975; Mank, Rhodes, & Bellamy, 1987; Rhodes & Valenta, 1985). The individuals may be employed by the industry itself or by an employment services program (human services provider). Each enclave employee works 20 or more hours per week and is paid on the same basis as his or her co-workers who are not disabled. The benefit package provided to all eligible employees should be available to individuals with severe disabilities.

Major Service Components. Each of the following is a necessary component in the development and maintenance of an enclave:

- *Enclave Site Development:* Establishing an enclave requires a lengthy planning and negotiation process including conducting a community feasibility study, contacting and approaching industries, analyzing operations, establishing a contract agreement with preferred industry, and *planning* for a systematic start-up including hiring the supervisor and persons with severe disabilities.

- *Individual Assessment and Consumer Job Match:* The approach to this component is similar to or identical with that described for the individual placement model.

- *Job Site Training and Advocacy:* Training is initiated differently among programs and individual supervisors based on the needs of the individuals with severe disabilities. A systematic approach to training, complete with an individualized program plan, is necessary. Calculating individual salaries in accordance with Department of Labor (DOL) guidelines is necessary if a set wage rate has not previously been established or unless the individuals are paid at least minimum wage.

- *Ongoing Assessment and Support:* Continuous ongoing supervision is provided to the employee of an enclave. Training and supervision continue based on individual need. The reassessment of salary and ability to work with less supervision is accomplished by the supervisor who remains on the job site. Assessment includes careful screening of production rate as well as behavioral observation regarding each individual's adjustment in the integrated work setting. Employers should be surveyed in a brief written format periodically to ascertain their level of satisfaction.

Quality Considerations

- *Wages:* Payment based on the prevailing hourly wage, for the particular type of work performed, is the most desirable situation. Payment of anything less than minimum wage must be based on the individual's productivity and must be a percentage of minimum wage (according to DOL guidelines).

- *Hours:* The job must offer at least 20 hours of employment per week. Preferably, the work is not temporary, due to the problems associated with social security benefits when there are continual changes in earnings and retraining requirements.

- *Transportation:* For employees who cannot get to work on their own, it is most desirable that they arrive in carpools with co-workers or by public transportation. Segregated transportation systems are less desirable.

- *Number of Enclave Employees:* There must be a small group (three to eight) of employees with severe disabilities working with a supervisor. Four to five seems to be the most desirable number. However, this must depend on the individual needs of the employees with severe disabilities and group make-up.
- *Integration:* Most enclave employees follow the same routines as the other employees in their work area. This encourages social integration during breaks, lunch, and after hours. At the very least, the group is physically integrated, and the employees with severe disabilities are working alongside co-workers without disabilities.

Advantages of the Enclave Model. Wages, benefits, and integration opportunities leading to image enhancement are the primary advantages over the traditional day support services available to persons with severe disabilities. In addition, enclaves may be an appropriate option for individuals who need ongoing support that would not be available from co-workers or other staff who are not trained to respond to the particular needs of the individual. Enclaves are appropriate for persons with severe disabilities who have multiple needs and may require supervision and intervention on a daily and ongoing basis. Individuals whose production rates preclude them from competitive employment may also be good candidates for an enclave.

The following questions illustrate possible misconceptions and clarification of the enclave model:

- *Isn't an enclave the same concept as a mobile crew, only the employees work inside an industry instead of outside?* Employees of an enclave may work inside or outside a building. The real difference is that an enclave works for one industry at one work site as opposed to moving about the community from contract to contract as a mobile crew does.
- *Shouldn't employees of an enclave earn equal to or greater than minimum wage; otherwise, it's not really supported employment?* Ideally, employees of an enclave would earn at least minimum wage. However, they are frequently paid a piece rate or a salary based on their individual rate of production. This is still a form of supported employment as long as they work at least 20 hours per week, have opportunities for integration, and need intensive training along with ongoing support to obtain and retain their employment.

The Mobile Crew Model of Supported Employment

Definition. The *Mobile Crew Model of Supported Employment* refers to the employment of a full-time supervisor and a small group (three to eight) of individuals with severe disabilities who travel together to two or more work sites in the community where they engage in contracted work (Bourbeau, 1985; Wald & Rhodes, 1984). Each mobile crew employee works 20 or more hours per week and is paid on the same basis as their co-workers without disabilities. The benefit package provided to all eligible employees should be available to the individuals with severe disabilities.

Major Service Components. Each of the following is a necessary component in the development and maintenance of a mobile crew:

- *Contract Development:* More complicated than job development, contract development includes searching for work, figuring and submitting bids, writing contracts, and planning for an orderly start-up in which the work will get done.
- *Job Analysis:* The contracted work must be broken down into jobs for the crew members. For each of the jobs, an analysis must be done to serve as the basis of the client/job matching and training.
- *Individual Assessment and Client/Job Match:* This process is similar to or identical with the one described for the individual placement process.
- *Job Site Training and Advocacy:* Initial training for crew work will vary with the program and with supervisors. Some programs may have a job coach come in and work one-on-one with a new crew member. Others may give the initial training responsibility to the supervisor, who will bring in an employee with a severe disability when the rest of the crew is functioning more smoothly. All programs, unless they pay at least minimum wage, are responsible for determining a fair wage for the employee from the very start in accordance with DOL guidelines, and for redetermining the wage as the employee's productivity improves.
- *Ongoing Assessment and Support:* The mobile crew model provides continuous ongoing support by program staff. The crew supervisor is always available to provide training and supervision, and to assess, periodically, the employee's wages and ability to move into a less restrictive form of employment. Assessment includes security of production rates as well as behavioral observations of an individual's

adjustment to the crew and the integrated work setting. The host company's satisfaction must also be evaluated.

Quality Considerations.

- *Wages:* Some programs will pay their mobile crew employees minimum wage. Others will pay wages commensurate with the employee's productivity. DOL guidelines allow for much subjectivity in determining wages; therefore, care must be taken to assure employees are paid on the same basis as their co-workers who are not disabled. The job should include all fringe benefits available to other eligible employees of the program.

- *Hours:* The job must offer at least 20 hours of employment per week. Because of the nature of contract work, some programs may experience some "down time," i.e., when they cannot offer substantial work to the employee. Consideration must be given to how often and for how long such periods occur and what the current prospects are for a more stable work schedule.

- *Transportation:* Most often, it is provided by the human services provider employing the mobile crew. Members frequently travel to individual contract sites in a company or agency van.

- *Number of Mobile Crew Employees:* There is usually a small group of employees (three to eight) with severe disabilities working with one supervisor. Some proponents argue for crews that consist of a homogeneous group of individuals with the same disability who need supported employment services. This line of thinking argues that the supervisor is thus forced to provide appropriate training and a variety of interesting work opportunities to all employees. Others argue for the inclusion of crew members who are not disabled or who have varying disabilities, from mild to severe, and insist that the supervisor has extra time to train the employee with more intensive needs while individuals who are more independent work with less supervision. Experimentation with individual groups is warranted.

- *Integration:* Unless the crew itself contains co-workers without disabilities, integration is often problematic for crews, especially if they work in the evenings when the buildings they work in are closed to its employees and the public. In such cases, there must be a plan for integration, such as having dinner and breaks in public places, away from the work site.

Advantages of the Mobile Crew Model. Crews may be the most appropriate form of supported employment for individuals who exhibit challenging behaviors that would not be tolerated in a community work setting. Mobile crews can also be the only possible employment opportunity for individuals with transportation problems if the crew's van can be used to pick them up and take them home. Individuals who cannot approximate competitive speed required in competitive employment may also be appropriate for crew work.

The following questions illustrate possible misconceptions and clarification of the mobile crew model:

- *Doesn't a crew consist entirely of people who need supported employment services?* There is a debate among proponents of mobile crews about whether or not it is better for the supported worker to be in a homogeneous or heterogeneous crew, but there is nothing in the definition that requires that a crew contain more than one person who needs supported employment services. More natural integration may occur when co-workers without disabilities are on a crew.

- *Aren't crews just another form of low paying, segregated day care, except they happen at night?* Some crews undoubtedly are low paying and very segregated, even if they do not happen at night. Care must be taken to ensure that fair wages are paid and that there is integration of employees into settings where they can interact with individuals who are not disabled. Most individuals with severe disabilities find that their wages go up when they join a crew, but there is certainly no guarantee that wages or integration will improve unless the crew is well run and integration is planned.

The Entrepreneurial Model of Supported Employment

Definition. The *Entrepreneurial Model of Supported Employment* refers to a private business that produces goods or services either on a subcontract basis or as a prime manufacturer. The business employs a small group of individuals (three to eight) with severe disabilities as well as co-workers who are not disabled (Boles, Bellamy, Horner, & Mank, 1984; O'Bryan, 1985). Each employee works 20 or more hours per week and is paid on the same basis as their co-workers who are not disabled. The benefit package provided should be available to all eligible employees.

Major Service Components. Each of the following is a necessary component in the development and maintenance of an entrepreneurial business model:

- *Management:* Like all established businesses, this model includes well-defined procedures for planning agency goals and activities. Proper organization and staffing are essential for accomplishing these goals.

- *Contract Development:* This model may require acquisition of a building with adequate floor space to accommodate a production area and a storage/supply area. Also involved are procurement of contracts, job design, production and quality control, and assurance that deadlines are met.

- *Individual Assessment and Client Job Match:* Ideally, employees with severe disabilities are gradually phased into the business to allow for adequate training of each individual. Employees are paid either minimum wage, piece rate (as in a benchwork model), or hourly wages based on the individual's productivity. Pay scales must be based on the prevailing industry wage.

- *Job Site Training and Advocacy:* Implementation of initial training varies with each business and with different supervisors. Some businesses may have a job coach come in and work one-on-one with a new employee. Others may give the initial training responsibility to the supervisor who will bring in an employee with a severe disability when the rest of the business is functioning smoothly. All programs (unless they pay at least minimum wage) are responsible for determining a fair wage for the employee from the very start in accordance with DOL guidelines, and for redetermining the wage as the employee's productivity improves.

- *Ongoing Assessment and Support:* Continuous, ongoing support is provided for each employee. Training continues based on individual employee need and the reassessment of salary and ability to work with less supervision. Assessment must be completed on a fixed schedule.

Quality Considerations

- *Wages:* It is most desirable for the employee to be paid at least minimum wage. However, employees may be paid either piece rate or hourly wages that result in subminimum wages. This must be based on the individual's productivity and DOL guidelines.

- *Hours:* The job must offer at least 20 hours of employment per week. Many employees will work up to 40 hours, depending on individual stamina. Preferably, the work is not temporary or seasonal, due to the problems associated with social security benefits when there are continual changes in earnings.

- *Number of Employees:* The number of employees may vary greatly depending on the make-up of the business. If employees work in a group, no more than eight employees with disabilities may work together. However, the number of employees in a group will vary depending on the skill level of the employees and interaction with co-workers who are not disabled.
- *Integration:* This model provides integration opportunities with co-workers who are not disabled. Generally, the employees with severe disabilities interact with the nondisabled employees while working, during breaks, and at lunch.

Advantages of the Entrepreneurial Model. The Entrepreneurial Model of Supported Employment may be advantageous to individuals with severe disabilities who need integration opportunities at work and more intensive training and supervision. Due to the variety of business opportunities, a variety of interests can be served. Also, due to the flexibility of a privately owned and operated work site, challenging behaviors may be more easily tolerated and managed. The following questions illustrate possible misconceptions and clarification of the entrepreneurial model:

- *Is the entrepreneurial model just another form of a sheltered workshop?* No. These are small businesses set up to provide employment opportunities but also structured to support social integration of the employee with a severe disability. They are privately owned and operated as either a profit making or a not-for-profit business.
- *Is it limited to benchwork?* No. The benchwork model is but one of a variety of possibilities for the entrepreneurial model. The possible goods or services produced are varied and virtually limitless.

CONCLUSION

Massive advancements in the area of employment support for persons with severe disabilities have occurred, especially over the last six years. The advancements are being brought about as a result of the rapidly expanding body of research and demonstrations showing that persons with severe disabilities can successfully, and therefore should, enter the mainstream of the community work world. Tremendous movement toward expanding integrated employment opportunities for persons with severe handicaps has also been made possible by various federal initia- tives in priorities and policies (Elder, 1984; Will, 1984).

Over the last 10 to 15 years, many positive changes have occurred in our system of vocational services delivery. For too long, however, we have funded and developed programs aimed only at the "readiness" of individuals for community employment. Instead of getting people "ready" for work, our system must provide individuals with ample and varied opportunities *to work* in their own communities with the appropriate and necessary level of support. These efforts must involve the provision of ongoing service in the context of paid community employment rather than in unending preparation for work readiness. Supported employment is the logical extension of the tremendous strides that have been made in the area of vocational training in recent decades, and it is a realistic means of establishing a comprehensive system of employment opportunities for all persons regardless of the severity of their disabilities.

REFERENCES

Bellamy, G.T., Horner, R., & Inman, D. (1979). *Vocational habilitation of severely retarded adults: A direct service technology.* Baltimore: University Park Press.

Bellamy, G.T., Peterson, L., & Close, D. (1975). Habilitation of the severely and profoundly retarded: Illustrations of competence. *Education and Training of the Mentally Retarded, 10,* 174-186.

Bellamy, G.T., Rhodes, L.E., & Albin, J.E. (1986). Supported employment. In W.E. Kiernan, & J.A. Stark (Eds.), *Pathways to employment for adults with developmental disabilities* (pp. 129-138). Baltimore: Paul H. Brookes.

Bellamy, G.T., Rhodes, L.E., Bourbeau, P.E., & Mank, D.M. (1982). *Mental retardation services in sheltered workshops and day activity programs: Consumer outcomes and policy alternatives.* Paper presented at the National Working Conference on Vocational Services and Employment Opportunities. Madison, WI.

Bellamy, G.T., Rhodes, L.E., Bourbeau, P.E., & Mank, D.M. (1986). Mental retardation services in sheltered workshops and day activity programs. In F.R. Rusch (Ed.), *Competitive employment issues and strategies* (pp. 257-271). Baltimore: Paul H. Brookes.

Belmore, K.J., & Brown, L.A. (1978). A job skill inventory strategy designed for severely handicapped potential workers. In N. Haring & D. Bricker (Eds.), *Teaching the severely handicapped* (Vol. III) (pp. 223-262). Columbus, OH: Special Press.

Boles, S.M., Bellamy, G.T., Horner, R.H., & Mank, D.M. (1984). Specialized training program: The structured employment model. In S.C. Paine, G.T. Bellamy, & B. Wilcox (Eds.), *Human services that work: From innovation to standard practice* (pp. 181-208). Baltimore: Paul H. Brookes.

Bourbeau, P.E. (1985). Mobile work crews: An approach to achieve long-term supported employment. In P. McCarthy, J. Everson, S. Moon, & M. Barcus (Eds.), *School to work transition for youth with severe disabilities.* (Monograph) (pp. 151-166). Richmond: Virginia Commonwealth University, Project Transition into Employment.

Brooke, V., Hill, J.W., & Ponder, C. (1985). A demonstration of the acceptability of applied behavior analysis in a natural job environment. In P. Wehman & J.W. Hill (Eds.), *Competitive employment for persons with mental retardation: From research to practice* (pp. 398-415). Richmond: Virginia Commonwealth University, Rehabilitation Research and Training Center.

Britt, C., Griffin, S., Hill, J., Hincker, A., Ruth, D., & Proseus, T. (in preparation). *Virginia state system of supported employment: A resource manual.* Richmond, VA: Department of Mental Health/Mental Retardation/Substance Abuse Services.

Cho, D.W. (1981). Japanese model factory employment of handicapped persons. *Evaluation Review, 5*(4), 427-450.

Elder, J. (1984). Job opportunities for developmentally disabled people. *American Rehabilitation, 10*(2), 26-30.

Falvey, M., Brown, L., Lyon, S., Baumgart, D., & Schroeder, J. (1980). Strategies for using cues and correction procedures. In W. Sailor, B. Wilcox, & L. Brown (Eds.), *Methods of instruction for severely handicapped students* (pp. 109-133). Baltimore: Paul H. Brookes.

Falvey, M. (1986). *Community-based curriculum integration strategies for students with severe handicaps.* Baltimore: Paul H. Brookes.

Flexer, R., & Martin, A. (1978). Sheltered workshops and vocational training settings. In M.E. Snell (Ed.), *Systematic instruction of the moderately and severely handicapped* (pp. 414-430). Columbus, OH: Charles E. Merrill.

Flippo, K., & McDaniel, R. (1986). *Telesis supported employment resource manuals.* University of San Francisco, Department of Rehabilitation Administration.

Gersten, R., Crowell, F., & Bellamy, T. (1986). Spillover effects: Impact of vocational training on the lives of severely mentally retarded clients. *American Journal of Mental Deficiency, 90*(5), 501-506.

Gold, M., & Pomerantz, D. (1978). Issues in prevocational training. In M.E. Snell (Ed.), *Systematic instruction of the moderately and severely handicapped* (pp. 431-440). Columbus OH: Charles E. Merrill.

Gold, M. (1973). Research on the vocational habilitation of the retarded: The present, the future. In N. Ellis (Ed.), *International review of research in mental retardation* (Vol. 6) (pp. 97-147). New York: Academic Press.

Gold, M. (1976). Task analysis of a complex assembly task by the retarded blind. *Exceptional Children, 42,* 78-84.

Hagner, D., Nisbet, J., Callahan, M., & Moseley, C. (1987). Payment mechanisms for community employment: Realities and recommendations. *Journal of the Association for Persons with Severe Handicaps, 12*(1), 45-52.

Hansen, C.L. (1980). *History of vocational habilitation of the handicapped.* Washington, DC: United States Department of Education, Office of Special Education and Rehabilitation Services.

Hasazi, S., Gordon, L., & Roe, C. (1985). Factors associated with the employment status of handicapped youth exiting high school from 1979–1983. *Exceptional Children, 5,* 455-469.

Hill, J.W., Banks, P.D., Wehman, P., & Hill, M. (in press). Effects of individuals' characteristics and environmental experiences on competitive employment success of persons with mental retardation. *Mental Retardation.*

Hill, J., Hill, M., Wehman, P., Banks, D., Pendleton, P., & Britt, C. (1985). Demographic analyses related to successful job retention for competitive employed persons who are mentally retarded. In P. Wehman & J. W. Hill (Eds.), *Competitive employment for persons with mental retardation: From research to practice*(Vol. 1)(pp. 65-93). Richmond: Virginia Commonwealth University, Rehabilitation Research and Training Center.

Hill, J., Hill, M., Wehman, P., & Goodall, P. (1986). Differential reasons for job separation of previously employed mentally retarded persons across measured intelligence levels. *Mental Retardation, 24*(6), 347-351.

Hill, J., Seyfarth, J., Banks, P.D., Wehman, P., & Orelove, F. (1985). Parent/guardian attitudes toward the working conditions of their mentally retarded children. In P. Wehman & J.W. Hill (Eds.) *Competitive employment for persons with mental retardation: From research to practice* (Vol. 1). Richmond : Virginia Commonwealth University, Rehabilitation Research and Training Center.

Hill, J., Wehman, P., & Pietruski, W. (1982). *Vocational skill instructional guide for severely handicapped youth.* Richmond: Virginia Commonwealth University, Rehabilitation Research and Training Center.

Hill, M., Banks, P.P., Handrich, R., Wehman, P., Hill, J.W., & Shafer, M. (1987). Benefit-cost analysis of supported competitive employment for persons with mental retardation. *Research in Developmental Disabilities, 8,* 71-89.

Hill, M., Hill, J., & Wehman, P. (in press). An analysis of monetary and nonmonetary outcomes associated with competitive employment of mentally retarded persons. *Applied Research in Mental Retardation.*

Hill, M., & Wehman, P. (1983). Cost benefit analysis associated with the competitive employment of moderately and severely handicapped persons. *Journal of the Association for the Severely Handicapped, 8*(1), 30-38.

Ianacone, R.N., & Stodden, R.A. (1987). Transition issues and directions for individuals who are mentally retarded. In R.N. Ianacone & R.A. Stodden (Eds.) *Transition issues and directions* (pp. 1-7). Reston, VA: The Council for Exceptional Children, Division on Mental Retardation.

Karan, O., Wehman, P., Renzaglia, A., & Schultz, R., (Eds.). (1976). *Habilitation practices with the severely and developmentally disabled*(Vol. 1). Madison: University of Wisconsin, Waisman Center on Mental Retardation.

Larson, K., & Edwards, J. (1980). Community based vocational training and placement for the severely handicapped. In C.L. Hansen & N.G. Haring (Eds.), *Expanding opportunities: Vocational education for the handicapped* (pp. 93-120). Washington, DC: United States Department of Education, Office of Special Education and Rehabilitation Services.

Laski, F.J. (1979). Legal strategies to secure entitlement of services for severely handicapped persons. In G.T. Bellamy, G. O'Connor, & O.C. Karan (Eds.), *Vocational rehabilitation of the severely handicapped: Contemporary service strategies* (pp. 1-32). Baltimore: University Park Press.

Lynch, A., & Singer, T. (1980). Vocational programming for the severe and profound in the public schools. In C.L. Hansen & N.G. Haring (Eds.), *Expanding opportunities: Vocational education for the handicapped* (pp. 45-71). Washington, DC: United States Department of Education, Office of Special Education and Rehabilitation Services.

Mank, D., Rhodes, L., & Bellamy, G.T. (1986). Four supported employment alternatives. In W.E. Kiernan & J.A. Stark (Eds.), *Pathways to employment for adults with developmental disabilities* (pp. 139-154). Baltimore, MD: Paul H. Brookes.

McAlees, D. (1984). The need for trained personnel in rehabilitation facilities by 1990. *The RTC Connection, 5,* 1-5.

McGee, J. (1975). *Work stations in industry.* Omaha: University of Nebraska.

Moon, S., Goodall, P., Barcus, M., & Brooke, V. (Eds.). (1986). *The supported work model of competitive employment for citizens with severe handicaps: A guide for job trainers.* Richmond: Virginia Commonwealth University, Rehabilitation Research and Training Center.

Moss, J., Dineen, J., & Ford, L. (1986). University of Washington employment training program. In F. Rusch (Ed.), *Competitive employment issues and strategies* (pp. 77-85). Baltimore: Paul H. Brookes.

O'Bryan, A. (1985). The STP benchwork model. In P. McCarthy, J. Everson, S. Moon, & M. Barcus (Eds.), *School to work transition for youth with severe disabilities.* (Monograph) (pp. 183-194). Richmond: Virginia Commonwealth University, Project Transition into Employment.

Pietruski, W., Everson, J., Goodwyn, R., & Wehman, P. (1985). *Vocational training and curriculum for multihandicapped youth with cerebral palsy.* Richmond: Virginia Commonwealth University, Rehabilitation Research and Training Center.

Renzaglia, A. (1986). Preparing personnel to support and guide emerging contemporary service alternatives. In F.R. Rusch (Ed.), *Competitive employment issues and strategies* (pp. 303-316). Baltimore: Paul H. Brookes.

Rhodes, L., & Valenta, L. (1985). Industry-based supported employment: An enclave approach. *Journal of the Association for Persons with Severe Handicaps, 10*(1), 12-20.

Rusch, F., & Mithaug, D. (1980). *Vocational training for mentally retarded adults: A behavior analytic approach.* Champaign, IL: Research Press.

Rusch, F. (1979). Toward the validation of social vocational survival skills. *Mental Retardation, 17*(3), 143-145.

Rusch, F.R. (Ed.). (1986). *Competitive employment issues and strategies.* Baltimore: Paul H. Brookes.

Schalock, R.L. (1984). *Services for developmentally disabled adults.* Baltimore: Paul H. Brookes.

Shafer, M., Brooke, V., & Wehman, P. (1985). Developing appropriate social-interperson skills in a mentally retarded worker. In P. Wehman & J.W. Hills (Eds.), *Competitive employment for persons with mental retardation: From research to practice* (pp. 358-375). Richmond: Virginia Commonwealth University, Rehabilitation Research and Training Center.

Snell, M. (1987). *Systematic instruction of persons with severe handicaps.* Columbus, OH: Charles E. Merrill.

Stark, J.A., Kiernan, W.E., Goldsburg, T.L., & McGee, J.J. (1986). Not entering employment: A system dilemma. In W.E. Kiernan & J.A. Stark (Eds.), *Pathways to employment for adults with developmental disabilities* (pp. 199-204). Baltimore: Paul H. Brookes.

Umbreit, J., Karlan, G., York, R., & Haring, N. (1980). Preparing teachers of the severely handicapped: Responsibilities and competencies of the teacher trainer. *Teacher Education and Special Education, 3,* 57-72.

Vogelsburg, R.T., Ashe, W., & Williams, W. (1986). Community based service delivery in rural Vermont. In R. Horner, L.M. Voeltz, & B. Fredericks (Eds.), *Education of learners with severe handicaps: Exemplary service strategies* (pp. 29-59). Baltimore: Paul H. Brookes.

Wald, B.A., & Rhodes, L.E. (1984). Developing model vocational programs for severely retarded adults in a rural setting: Mobile crew model. *Proceedings of the International Conference on Rural Rehabilitation Technologies* (pp. 10-18). Grand Forks, ND.

Wehman, P. (1981). *Competitive employment: New horizons for severely disabled individuals.* Baltimore: Paul H. Brookes.

Wehman, P., & Hill, J. (1980). *Vocational training and placement of severely disabled persons* (Vol. 11). Richmond: Virginia Commonwealth University, Rehabilitation Research and Training Center.

Wehman, P., & Hill, J.W. (Eds.). (1985). *Competitive employment for persons with mental retardation: From research to practice* (Vol. I). Richmond: Virginia Commonwealth University, Rehabilitation Research and Training Center.

Wehman, P., Hill, J.W., Wood, W., & Parent, W. (1987). A report on competitive employment histories of persons labeled severely mentally retarded. *Journal of the Association for Persons with Severe Handicaps, 12*(1), 11-17.

Wehman, P., Kregel, J., & Barcus, J.M. (1985). From school to work: A vocational transition model for handicapped students. *Exceptional Children, 52*(1), 25-37.

Wehman, P., Kregel, J., Barcus, M., & Schalock, R. (1986). Vocational transition for students with developmental disabilities. In W. Kiernan & J. Stark (Eds.), *Pathways to employment for developmentally disabled adults* (pp. 113-127). Baltimore: Paul H. Brookes.

Wehman, P., Kregel, J., & Seyfarth, J. (1985). Employment outlook for young adults with mental retardation. *Rehabilitation Counseling Bulletin, 29*(2), 91-99.

Wehman, P., Moon, M.S., & McCarthy, P. (1986). Transition from school to adulthood for youth with severe handicaps. *Focus on Exceptional Children, 18*(5), 1-12.

Whitehead, C. (1979). Sheltered workshops in the decade ahead: Work and wages or welfare. In G.T. Bellamy, G. O'Connor, & O.C. Karan (Eds.), *Vocational rehabilitation for developmentally disabled persons: Contemporary service strategies* (pp. 71-84). Baltimore: University Park Press.

Will, M. (1984). *OSERS programming for the transition of youth with disabilities: Bridges from school to work life.* Position paper. Washington, DC: Office of Special Education and Rehabilitation Services.

Wolfensberger, W. (Ed.). (1972). *The principle of normalization in human services.* Toronto, Canada: National Institute on Mental Retardation, York University Campus.

Wolfensberger, W. (1983). Social role valorization: A proposed new term for the principle of normalization. *Mental Retardation, 21*(6), 234-239.

Part VI

Summary

Chapter 14

Future Educational Concerns: Crucial Questions

Les Sternberg

Most of the information presented in this text examined the currently considered best practice interventions for students with severe or profound handicaps. Past and present efforts have been based on initiatives established by those who are most keenly interested in the provision of appropriate educational services and the realization of positive educational outcomes for this population. The future for these students will be based, in large part, on not only whether the field generates continued initiatives but on how the field and society in general react toward those initiatives. As is typically the case, generation of and reaction toward initiatives will be considerably influenced by a myriad of personologic, sociologic, economic, and political variables. Perhaps what will prove most influential, however, is how we begin and continue to address crucial questions of today. These questions concern educability, the right to an existence and control over one's life, and the meaning and relevance of education itself. Answers to these questions will create the foundation for what future education will or will not be for students with severe or profound handicaps.

QUESTIONS OF EDUCABILITY

When students with extremely severe debilitating types of handicaps are exposed to the educational arena, an overriding question often surfaces: Can what we do really have any *dramatic* effect on the individual's future quality of life? Can these individuals really benefit from educational interventions?

Noonan, Brown, Mulligan, and Rettig (1982) summarized the legal issues concerning educability for individuals with severe or profound handicaps. Whether one is entitled to the right to an education has become a somewhat loaded issue, with strong support both for and against the assumption that all individuals are educable (Noonan & Reese, 1984). The problem may be in how one defines "educability." Usually, the definition includes the potential or probability of benefit from exposure to educational services. If one could benefit from the exposure, the individual would be considered educable. However, how *benefit* is judged may be the key.

Some individuals think benefit can only be assumed if the individual attains some predetermined *end* (Bailey, 1981; Ellis, Balla, Estes, Hollis, Isaacson, Orlando, Polk, Warren, & Seigel, 1978; Kauffman & Krouse, 1981). This example can be clearly seen in a New Jersey Supreme Court decision (*Levine v. New Jersey Department of Institutions,* 1980) where the court found that institutionalized children with profound mental retardation did not have the right to a free public education because they could not be expected to acquire normalized types of behaviors (e.g., work skills). However, if one views "benefit" as synonymous with displaying change as a result of exposure to educational services (a more *process-based* approach to determining benefit), then one would be hard pressed to find any individual noneducable. Baer (1981) pointed out that proving that one is uneducable must be considered an impossibility if one sees educational progress depending on the implementation of *all* educational intervention options that are possible.

Others view uneducability as a function of the unavailability of best practice interventions rather than anything inherent in the individual (Favell, Risley, Wolfe, Riddle, & Rasmussen, 1981; Ulicny, Thompson, Favell, & Thompson, 1985). And as Noonan and Reese (1984) stated: "educational benefit [should be used as the] criterion for judging the appropriateness of individualized education *not* as a criterion for deciding which children are entitled to an education" (p. 11).

It appears as if expectations are the foundation for determining educability. Even if one wishes to draw a distinction between children with profound handicaps and those with lesser degrees of disability, one would still be hard-pressed to assume that members of the former group might not benefit from educational interventions. The fact is that only recently have students with profound handicaps been exposed to educational interventions designed, in part, to improve their quality of life. It is indeed much too early to posit or accept *any* expectations about their future life, for the information is simply not there. Given the infinite quality of educational interventions, the question of educability should become moot: ". . . there is no way to affirm at the level of fact that some children cannot be taught effectively; and there is no way to affirm at the level of fact that all children can be taught effectively" (Baer, 1981, p. 97).

QUESTIONS OF ETHICS

Some individuals take the educability issue to an even more basic level. It is not an uncommon occurrence for many of us involved with students with profound handicaps to begin to raise questions regarding ethics. It seems that over the last few years the professional literature and lay press have repeatedly exposed us to issues regarding the conditions and anticipated quality of life of individuals born with extremely debilitating types and degrees of handicap. By merely walking into classroom programs for many of these students and observing the day-to-day attempts at providing not only education but the means for their survival, we are often confronted with questions and issues that will undeniably affect and circumscribe everything we propose to do.

Given first impressions and human nature, initial questions surface that, in essence, define or redefine concepts of life itself (Bostrom, 1983). Why are these children alive? What "master plan" could anyone come up with that could justify existence of this type? These, indeed, are difficult questions to deal with, let alone answer. The questions have significantly influenced issues regarding *euthanasia,* the withdrawal of treatment to allow an individual to die.

In response to some of these questions, Cohen (1981) presented an overview of the moral, ethical, and legal concerns involved with euthanasia. These concerns are especially crucial to one who is born with a significant degree of handicap. As she pointed out, those in favor of euthanasia seem to have a much more united front than those who oppose it.

Lusthaus (1985) took the issue a step further. She outlined the various rationalizations used to justify euthanasia, and concluded that only one seems to have noteworthy support: that euthanasia would be justified if it were considered to be for the good of the disabled individual. In many respects, this has to do with whether the individual would be considered "human" if left alive, and if his or her present and future quality of life would be classified as meaningful. Those who support euthanasia for the good of the individual have attempted to classify some types of individuals with profound handicaps as nonhuman and as persons who lack the necessary quality of life to exist meaningfully. Those who reject euthanasia find fault with attempting to classify anyone as nonhuman, and contend that quality of life is, at best, an elusive concept to define or predict.

Hardman (1984) viewed legislative initiatives as a key to addressing the problems of euthanasia. Using the Baby Doe case as a key point of discussion (in which an infant with Down syndrome born with an incomplete esophagus was denied medical treatment based upon parental request), the litany of legal points and counterpoints is chronicled. Emphases in the initiatives typically focused on issues regarding discrimination against seriously ill newborn infants, especially decision-making policies that might be necessary to counter discriminatory or capricious practices. Although others might disagree, Hardman insisted that continued and sustained Congressional involvement is crucial to efficacious systems change regarding right-to-life issues.

Perhaps the answer to many of these concerns, however, lies once again in the realm of expectations. Advances in medical technology have indeed been responsible, in major part, for initial and sustained existence of many children with profound handicaps. Expectations for the future quality of life for these individuals are often generated by the medical field itself (Weir, 1984). These often pessimistic expectations are then used in decision making concerning termination of life. It would be enlightening, however, to review many of the past quality-of-life prognoses generated by the medical establishment for students with only a severe degree of handicap. The success of these individuals at improving their quality of life would contradict many of the initial prognoses (Rynders, 1982). As Lusthaus (1985) stated: "The quality of life experienced by people with disabilities may depend more on how others relate to them than on their problems at birth" (p. 92).

QUESTIONS OF CHOICE

Freedom of choice is a cherished right of most individuals. For those with handicaps, the right to choose what one wishes to do is often superceded by what others *think* the individual ought to do. This situation is especially apparent for individuals with severe handicaps (Guess, Benson, & Siegel-Causey, 1985; Guess & Siegel-Causey, 1985; Shevin & Klein, 1984; Zeph, 1984). The typical nonchoice scenario is based on the assumptions that (1) individuals with severe handicaps cannot make choices for themselves; and (2) even if they were capable of choice behavior, their choices would most probably not be correct (Guess & Siegel, 1985). Even though there are findings that indicate that encouraging choice making by students with severe handicaps will lead to an increase in their participation in certain activities (Dattilo & Rusch, 1985) and more vertical (student-to-adult) social interactions (Peck, 1985), it seems as if current classroom interaction patterns do not lend themselves to optimal student choice development (Houghton, Bronicki, & Guess, 1987).

Guess et al. (1985) rather concisely delineated the major philosophical and methodological issues surrounding the choice making of individuals with severe handicaps. They view choice making as being composed of three interrelated concepts. The first is whether one has a liking or *preference* for something. The second is whether the individual actually has a *choice* in obtaining what he or she likes. The third is whether the individual realizes that *options* concerning choice are available.

Regarding preferences, these authors presented methodological suggestions that would be difficult for anyone to deny as best practice. By viewing early prelinguistic communicative efforts of individuals, including those with extremely limited behavioral repertoires (see Chapter 10), preferences can be assumed and later confirmed by caregivers or teachers. For example, if a child continues to cry or exhibit a particular primitive reflex pattern when positioned in a certain manner, one might *assume* the position is not preferred by the child. Subsequently, a caregiver would likely change the position of the child. If the same behavioral indices were consistently forthcoming, one would be hard pressed not to consider them indices of a preference. Once this preference was confirmed, it could be used to develop further communicative exchanges. For example, if the child were placed in situations where a predetermined preference were available, one might expect that some type of communication for that preference could be exhibited. And if these communicative behaviors are followed consistently by the provision of the preferred object, person, activity, etc., gaining preferences is indeed being encouraged and developed.

The area of intentional choice making, however, does involve more than merely making a preference known. Communicating that one prefers something is a preamble to choice. Actual choice making involves choosing the preferred alternative (e.g., object, person, or activity) when other alternatives are apparent and available (Shevin & Klein, 1984). As Guess et al. (1985) pointed out, for most persons with severe handicaps choice making has been limited to selecting which reinforcer one prefers. However, interactions that would be completed by use of that reinforcer are typically chosen by a significant other rather than by the individual.

Although there is no extensive research base supporting or rejecting the expansion of choice making to other situations with persons with severe handicaps (e.g., choosing the task one is to complete; Guess et al., 1985), more active and longitudinal attempts at incorporating choice making into curricula for students with severe or profound handicaps seem not only proper but mandatory. Indeed, others have taken initial steps in this direction (Dattilo & Rusch, 1985; Shevin & Klein, 1984; Wuerch & Voeltz, 1982).

The last concept related to choice making is an individual's options and control. As previously described, it is certainly not unexpected that other individuals, in effect, will *totally* control the lives of persons with severe or profound handicaps. Although many might consider this "outer" or "other" control as in the best interests of the person with severe or profound handicaps, in many respects it may simply serve as a barrier to more meaningful and functional progress. As Guess et al. (1985) pointed out repeatedly, unless an individual realizes that he or she has some semblance of control over his or her life, should significant and sustained progress be expected from that individual? In many cases, such feelings of noncontrol result in a reverse trend, as in *learned helplessness* (Seligman, 1975). It would, therefore, seem very appropriate to imbed choice making into *all* curricular efforts with students with severe or profound handicaps, especially in the framework of an integrated approach leading to increased personal autonomy (Shevin & Klein, 1984). The comments of Guess et al. (1985) concerning this point are noteworthy.

> Our position is that the ability and opportunity to express preferences, make decisions, and exercise choices are, in themselves, invaluable contributions to adaptive behavior and should be an integral component of the education of persons with severe handicaps. Moreover, it is our position that consistent opportunities to choose and express preferences might well have a positive impact on the learning process (as a means) as well as on the more long term personal development of persons with severe handicaps (as an end result) (Guess et al., 1985, p. 84).

QUESTIONS OF VALIDITY

Anything we propose to do for students with severe or profound handicaps will finally be judged by whether or not significant positive outcomes were achieved as a result of our efforts. Voeltz and Evans (1983) indicated that procedures for determining educational validity must be carefully scrutinized. It appears as if problems have arisen due to the apparent separation of the concept of "significant positive outcomes" from the reality within which those outcomes should be viewed. In the past, developmentally based assessments often were used on a pre-/post-test/post-test basis to assess program gains. Voeltz and Evans, as well as others, questioned the relevance of such gains to actual meaningful skill development; and very few attempts have ever been made to assess developmental gains in terms of functional skill acquisition.

The use of single-subject validation designs to measure program outcomes (even with replication across individuals and environments) has also received criticism. Such critiques usually focus on the often "unnatural" aspects of the intervention itself (e.g., the artificial, highly controlled types of interventions that may not be reasonable in typical instructional environments) and the apparent lack of concern for the interrelated nature of behavior itself (how one behavior may positively or negatively affect the occurrence of another).

Voeltz and Evans proposed that future efforts to determine educational validity must include procedures for measuring three aspects of intervention: whether what we do as practitioners actually accounts for the changes made with students with severe or profound handicaps (*internal validity*); whether practitioners are doing what they actually proposed to do in relation to those interventions (*educational integrity*); and whether the behaviors acquired as a function of our interventions are truly beneficial to the student (*empirical validity*) and valued by significant others (*social validity*).

They also recommend that consideration be given to the implementation of a number of procedures. First, to establish internal validity, it should be sufficient for a teacher only to verify that progress was made while an intervention was conducted. The acceptability of this procedure is based on the assumption that, with students with severe or profound handicaps, baselining is frequently unnecessary (students often show either extremely low rates of behavioral deficits or high rates of behavioral excesses during measured baselines). Also, because communication among caregivers and teachers can be scheduled on a regular basis, and sufficient and represented data can be collected using a consistent time frame, it would seem unreasonable to assume that some other unnoticed intervention was responsible for skills change. Second, educational integrity can only be assessed through a careful and thorough functional analysis of the antecedents of educational change. Included in this analysis should be systematic observations of teacher behaviors, environmental arrangements, and duration of instructional episodes. Third, empirical validity must be judged by not only how functional a targeted skill might be but how that behavior might impact other skills development. If, by teaching specific behaviors, other behavioral excesses are decreased and behavioral deficits increased, the actual benefit of that instruction is greatly magnified. Fourth, to assess social validity, consideration must be given to targeting behaviors that have both immediate *and* longer term impact. These targets must be judged as socially valid by individuals in the environments in which the skills will be displayed. Therefore, exemplars of social validity cannot be determined without input from all present and potential caregivers and significant others.

Perhaps what is most noteworthy about these recommendations is their intent. Although positive outcomes can be and have been demonstrated through the use of developmental assessment and formal single-subject experimental designs, the utility of the method and the real meaning of the outcomes have sometimes been suspect. However, it is not that developmental concepts should be ignored or that the use of more formal evaluation and validation designs should be discontinued. If we view outcomes from the standpoint of what is realistic and meaningful for both the student and his or her interactions with the environment, much of what we *have* done to determine validity can be used to design and implement more accountable systems.

CONCLUDING REMARKS

Education of students with severe or profound handicaps is still in its infancy stage. In other related educational areas of concern, this level of development is often construed as operating from a trial-and-error basis, with accurate and effective direction only coming as a result of "accidental" knowing. But in the education of students with severe or profound handicaps, this has apparently not been the case.

Educators and researchers have continued to operate from a historical viewpoint of instructional best practices. They investigated past efforts with students with milder degrees of handicaps, and used the results and methods as foundations for present best practice attempts with students with more pronounced handicaps. This commitment to understanding the historical foundation of methods has certainly provided ample impetus to furthering our knowledge of what may or may not work for students with severe or profound handicaps. And what is perhaps even more important, researchers and practitioners seem to have followed the appropriate adage that it is all right to look at the past as long as one does not continue to stare.

Seymour Sarason, in a keynote address made before a group of special educators (1986), indicated that we must all be cognizant of certain crucial barriers to educational progress for all students with handicaps. One of these occurs when individuals either cannot or do not possess the "virtue of ignorance." Using personnel in medical research as exemplars of individuals possessing this virtue, Sarason pointed out that support for medical research will most assuredly continue, with very few questions asked concerning the relevance or meaning of such research. This is due to the fact that medical researchers have and continue to admit that problems exist and that *they do not have all of the solutions.* However, given adequate support, they certainly will continue to try to discover the answers. Many within the professional educational community, on the other hand, have apparently never possessed this virtue. More often than not, these individuals insist that the answers are here now; that best practices of today can meet every student's needs. Unfortunately, when failures or breakdowns occur, the educational community is left somewhat defenseless, and support begins to erode.

We who are involved with students with severe or profound handicaps actually find ourselves in a very enviable position. Due to the infancy of our field, we can hopefully avoid the errors of the past and commit ourselves to the "virtue of ignorance." As Sarason pointed out, it might be uncomfortable, but we must admit that educational problems are not finite and simple; and that their perplexity can only lead us to a commitment to continue to try.

REFERENCES

Baer, D.M. (1981). A hung jury and a Scottish verdict: "Not proven." *Analysis and Intervention in Developmental Disabilities, 1,* 91-98.

Bailey, J.S. (1981). Wanted: A rational search for the limiting conditions of habilitation in the retarded. *Analysis and Intervention in Developmental Disabilities, 1,* 45-52.

Bostrom, S. (1983). Jennifer. *Journal of the Association for the Severely Handicapped, 8,* (1), 58-62.

Cohen, L. (1981). Ethical issues in withholding care from severely handicapped infants. *Journal of the Association for the Severely Handicapped, 6* (3), 65-67.

Dattilo, J., & Rusch, F.R. (1985). Effects of choice on leisure participation for persons with severe handicaps. *Journal of the Association for Persons with Severe Handicaps, 10*(4), 194-199.

Ellis, N.R., Balla, D., Estes, O., Hollis, J., Isaacson, R., Orlando, R., Polk, E.E., Warren, S.A., & Seigel, P.S. (1978). Memorandum in *Wyatt v. Hardin,* C.A. 3195-N. U.S. District Court, Middle District of Alabama.

Favell, J.E., Risley, T.R., Wolfe, A.F., Riddle, J.I., & Rasmussen, P.R. (1981). The limits of habilitation: How can we identify them and how can we change them? *Analysis and Intervention in Developmental Disabilities, 1,* 37-43.

Guess, D., Benson, H.A., & Siegel-Causey, E. (1985). Concepts and issues related to choice-making and autonomy among persons with severe disabilities. *Journal of the Association for Persons with Severe Handicaps, 10*(2), pp. 79-86.

Guess, D., & Siegel-Causey, E. (1985). Behavioral control and education of severely handicapped students: Who's doing what to whom? And why? In D. Bricker & J. Filler (Eds.), *Severe mental retardation: From theory to practice* (pp. 230-244). Reston, VA: The Council for Exceptional Children.

Hardman, M.L. (1984). The role of Congress in decisions relating to the withholding of medical treatment from seriously ill newborns. *Journal of the Association for Persons with Severe Handicaps, 9*(1), 3-7.

Houghton, J., Bronicki, G.J.B., & Guess, D. (1987). Opportunities to express preferences and make choices among students with severe disabilities in classroom settings. *Journal of the Association for Persons with Severe Handicaps, 12*(1), 18-27.

Kauffman, J.M., & Krouse, J. (1981). The cult of educability: Searching for the substance of things hoped for; the evidence of things not seen. *Analysis and Intervention in Developmental Disabilities, 1*, 53-60.

Levine v. New Jersey Department of Institutions (1980). 3 EHLR 552:163.

Lusthaus, E. (1985). "Euthanasia" of persons with severe handicaps: Refuting the rationalizations. *Journal of the Association for Persons with Severe Handicaps, 10*(2), 87-94.

Noonan, M.J., Brown, F., Mulligan, M., & Rettig, M.A. (1982). Educability of severely handicapped persons: Both sides of the issue. *Journal of the Association for the Severely Handicapped, 7*(1), 3-12.

Noonan, M.J., & Reese, M. (1984). Educability: Public policy and the role of research. *Journal of the Association for Persons with Severe Handicaps, 9*(1), 8-15.

Peck, C.A. (1985). Increasing opportunities for social control by children with autism and severe handicaps: Effects on student behavior and perceived classroom climate. *Journal of the Association for Persons with Severe Handicaps, 10*(4), 183-193.

Rynders, J. (1982). Research on promoting learning in children with Down's syndrome. In S. Pueschel & J. Rynders (Eds.), *Down's syndrome: Advances in biomedicine and the behavioral sciences* (pp. 389-451). Cambridge, MA: Ware Press.

Sarason, S. (1986). *You are looking forward, I am looking back.* Keynote address. Storrs, CT: Special Education Center Reunion and Dedication, University of Connecticut.

Seligman, M. (1975). *Helplessness: On depression, development, and death.* San Francisco: W.H. Freeman.

Shevin, M., & Klein, N.K. (1984). The importance of choice-making skills for students with severe disabilities. *Journal of the Association for Persons with Severe Handicaps, 9*(3), 159-166.

Ulicny, G.R., Thompson, S.K., Favell, J.E., & Thompson, M.S. (1985). The active assessment of educability: A case study. *Journal of the Association for Persons with Severe Handicaps, 10*(2), 111-114.

Voeltz, L.M., & Evans, I.M. (1983). Educational validity: Procedures to evaluate outcomes in programs for severely handicapped learners. *Journal of the Association for the Severely Handicapped, 8*(1), 3-15.

Weir, R. (1984). *Selective nontreatment of handicapped newborns: Moral dilemmas in neonatal medicine.* Ontario, Canada: Oxford University Press.

Wuerch, B.B., & Voeltz, L.M. (1982). *Longitudinal leisure skills for severely handicapped learners: The Ho'onanea curriculum component.* Baltimore: Paul H. Brookes.

Zeph, L. (1984). *The model of CHOICE: A curriculum framework for incorporating choice-making into programs serving students with severe handicaps.* Paper presented at the Eleventh Annual Conference of the Association for Persons with Severe Handicaps, Chicago, IL.

Author Index

485

Subject Index